New Directions for Applying Astrological Measurements

The science of astrology rests on measurement of the heavens in relation to the Earth. But the *art* of astrology relies on human interpretation of those scientific measurements for understanding.

Due to computer technology, today's astrologers' ability to make sophisticated measurements has been greatly enhanced. Yet, while measurement is important, the quantity, diversity, and precision of measurement is not the ultimate goal of astrology. The astrologer's *true* goal is to adapt celestial measurement to the human condition in a meaningful way.

Interpreting specialized measurements in a meaningful way is what *Astrology's Special Measurements* is all about. The sheer number of options and perspectives generated by trying to work with too many measurements can confuse and overwhelm astrologers. And not all measurements work in every horoscope or for every astrologer. You, as an astrologer, need to decide what measurements are important to you, which ones fit your individual standards and interpretive style.

This book will help you decide which measurements are meaningful for you. It will introduce you to exciting new measurement techniques that will greatly expand your interpretive horizons. It will guide you in interpreting special measurements and applying them to deepen your and your clients' understanding of life. *Astrology's Special Measurements* is a tremendous resource for astrologers open to adding new measurement techniques to their diagnostic repertoires.

To Write to the Authors

If you wish to contact the authors or would like more information about this book, please write to the authors in care of Llewellyn Worldwide, and we will forward your request. Both the authors and publisher appreciate hearing from you and learning of your enjoyment of this book and how it has helped you. Llewellyn Worldwide cannot guarantee that every letter written to the authors can be answered, but all will be forwarded. Please write to:

Llewellyn's New Worlds of Mind and Spirit
P.O. Box 64383-864, St. Paul, MN 55164-0383, U.S.A.
Please enclose a self-addressed, stamped envelope for reply, or $1.00 to cover costs. If outside U.S.A., enclose international postal reply coupon.

Free Catalog from Llewellyn

For more than ninety years Llewellyn has brought its readers knowledge in the fields of metaphysics and human potential. Learn about the newest books in spiritual guidance, natural healing, astrology, occult philosophy, and more. Enjoy book reviews, New Age articles, a calendar of events, plus current advertised products and services. To get your free copy of *Llewellyn's New Worlds*, send your name and address to:

Llewellyn's New Worlds of Mind and Spirit
P.O. Box 64383-864, St. Paul, MN 55164-0383, U.S.A.

Llewellyn's New World Astrology Series
Book 13

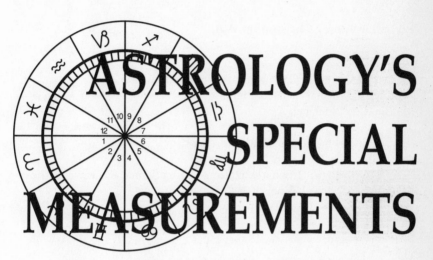

ASTROLOGY'S SPECIAL MEASUREMENTS

How to Expand the Meaning of the Horoscope

edited by
Noel Tyl

1994
Llewellyn Publications
St. Paul, Minnesota, 55164-0383, U.S.A.

FIRST EDITION, 1993

Cover Design by Christopher Wells

Library of Congress Cataloging-in-Publication Data
Astrology's special measurements /
   edited by Noel Tyl.
      p.   cm. — (Llewellyn's new world astrology series ; bk. 13)
   Includes bibliographical references.
   ISBN 0-56718-864-8
      1. Astrology. 2. Self-realization—Miscellanea. 3. Consciousness—
Miscellanea.   I. Tyl, Noel, 1936–. II. Series.
   BF1729.S38E868   1993   93-34544
   133.5—dc20   CIP

♻ Printed on recycled paper.

Llewellyn Publications
A Division of Llewellyn Worldwide, Ltd.
St. Paul, Minnesota 55164-0383, U.S.A.

The New World Astrology Series

This series is designed to give all people who are interested and involved in astrology the latest information on a variety of subjects. Llewellyn has given much thought to the prevailing trends and to the topics that would be most important to our readers.

Future books will include such topics as astrology and sexuality, astrology and counseling, and many other subjects of interest to a wide range of people. This project has evolved because of the lack of information on these subjects and because we wanted to offer our readers the viewpoints of the best experts in each field in one volume.

We anticipate publishing approximately four books per year on varying topics and updating previous editions when new material becomes available. We know this series will fill a gap in your astrological library. Our editor chooses only the best writers and article topics when planning the new books, and we appreciate any feedback from our readers on subjects you would like to see covered.

Llewellyn's New World Astrology Series will be a welcome addition to the novice, student, and professional alike. It will provide introductory as well as advanced information on all the topics listed above—and more.

Enjoy, and feel free to write to Llewellyn with your suggestions or comments.

Other Books in this Series

Forthcoming

Contents

Noel Tyl

For over 20 years, Noel Tyl has been one of the most prominent astrologers in the Western world. His 17 textbooks, built around the 12-volume *Principles and Practice of Astrology*, were extraordinaily popular throughout the 1970s, teaching astrology with a new and practical sensitivity to modern psychotherapeutic methodology. At the same time, Noel presented lectures and seminars throughout the United States, appearing in practically every metropolitan area and on well over 100 radio and television shows. He also founded and edited *Astrology Now* magazine.

His book *Holistic Astrology: The Analysis of Inner and Outer Environments*, distributed by Llewellyn Publications, has been translated into German and Italian. He is one of astrology's most sought-after lecturers throughout the United States, and his international lectures are very popular throughout Denmark, Norway, South Africa, Germany, and Switzerland, where for the first three World Congresses of Astrology he was a keynote speaker.

Most recently, Noel wrote *Prediction in Astrology* (Llewellyn Publications), a master volume of technique and practice, and edited Books 9 through 12 of the Llewellyn New World Astrology Series, *How to Use Vocational Astrology, How to Personalize the Outer Planets, How to Manage the Astrology of Crisis,* and *Exploring Consciousness in the Horoscope.* In the spring of 1994, his master opus, *Synthesis and Counseling in Astrology—The Professional Manual* (almost 1,000 pages of analytical technique in practice), was published. Noel is a graduate of Harvard University in psychology and lives in Alexandria, Virginia.

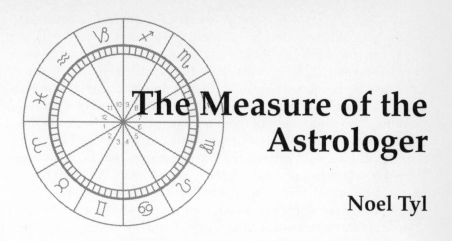

The Measure of the Astrologer

Noel Tyl

E very new student of astrology looks with bewilderment at that first horoscope and asks, "What's it mean when there's *nothing* in a house? It's my 7th! Won't I ever get married?" The student feels *the strong need to measure*. Something must define the space in the house; something must give meaning to the picture.

Putting furniture into a room establishes the size of the room. The furniture tells us what kind of room it is and how it will be used. On a floor plan, we don't know that a room has a vaulted ceiling unless an elevation drawing—a different kind of measurement—shows us this extra dimension. Gradually, measurements build up dimension and define perspective.

The royal architect of the Khufu (Cheops) pyramid speaks to us over millennia about the solar system measurement codes built into the pyramid's units of construction. At this level, the explanation of measurements leads us beyond routine significance to quite other dimensions.

It's obvious that we do need to measure in order to know, and that there are all kinds of measurements. Their meanings lead us to many different levels. This is the process of analysis, of course, and, in that sense, in astrology particularly, *measurements become diagnosis*.

As proficient as we are at measuring, there is always so much more to do. On the grand scale, for example, we still have the symmetrical but incomplete gamut of zodiac sign-rulers; perhaps life on earth is not yet ready for fully confirmed and "operative" new bodies to rule Virgo and Libra (or Gemini and Taurus), just as humanity waited a long, long time to discover Uranus, Neptune, and Pluto and put them into their proper places. On the small scale, we have yet to measure the relationship between planets and genes. Perhaps the measurements we do seek are related to when and to what degree we need them. We don't need to read a blueprint, for example, until we are building a house. We notice advertisements only when we need to, when the offers are relevant to our condition. While we celebrate life through astrology, when will we be able to measure death? *Should* we have that capacity someday? The need to know varies in intensity, in direction, and in fulfillment individually and generationally.

Everywhere, not just in astrology, the computer has given scope, variety, accuracy, and speed to measurement as hardly ever imagined before. Today, the new astrologer is still initially bewildered by an empty house in the horoscope, but that astrologer quickly learns to press some buttons and make measurements that move the furniture in, define purpose and potential, and project that house and its meanings into time and space.

But how many measurements do we need now in our astrology? How many should fortify us for a meaningful conversation with our client, give us a good start in our everyday work? Ten, twelve years ago, I saw horoscopes that were practically obliterated by myriad measurements, those made by hand and calculator by astrologers who pursued the scientific grail, but left the human being behind in the process. And today I often see horoscope "files" that are megabyte masterpieces but humanistically lifeless. These extremes are real. Where *should* we be? These are important questions if we are to appreciate where we are in our development as astrologers and how we measure up ourselves.

Often I recall a telling insight attributed to Paracelsus, the great man-of-every-talent, seer, doctor, and astrologer of the early sixteenth century in Switzerland: he said or wrote so simply, *the planets are within.* That has always struck me as the absolutely essential balance to the astrological (Hermetic) doctrine of what is above and what is below.[1] With the planets within, then life expression, behavior, and events are without. A grand-cross of philosophical measurement is formed; axes interact to suggest wholeness, and the mind of man is off to the spaces!

How simple some measurements are, and how grand are their significances. Here's a down-to-earth example: in early March 1991, as the world was coming out from under Desert Storm, I was preparing for publication an article of world predictions. The chart for the USSR Revolution (November 8, 1917 at 02:12 A.M. GMT for Petrograd; the time frozen on a clock face, perhaps by a stray bullet, when Bolshevik Red Guards under the direction of Lenin arrested the Provisional Government) had held up well under scrutiny for some time. Before me, two new measurements emerged: Solar Arc Pluto had advanced to a position 2-1/2 degrees above the Ascendant and exactly square the Midheaven; and, at the same time, SA Saturn had advanced to square the Moon (seventy-five years)! The explanation of these measurements in terms of potential is simple indeed: the country would undergo a tremendous change of perspective to challenge its very identity. Reinforcing measurements in this chart (and in Gorbachev's horoscope) supported the once-in-a-lifetime prediction I made and published about the ouster of a leader and the total reorganization of the largest country on the planet.

Another example is the change of the party-in-power in the Israeli elections in Spring 1992: transiting Pluto opposed the national Sun as transiting Saturn opposed the national Pluto. Loss, change, and new perspective were clearly indicated, as were the ramifications of many world issues anchored in Israel.

While making the measurements was very easy, the time had to be right to see their potential fit with reality, with what actually was going on in world events, i.e., neither of these eventuations would be a surprise; and the human dimension had to be there, the skill and confidence to say with conviction and grace what *could* be.

Measurement and meaning, analysis and diagnosis—no matter how precise—*rely on the human being for perspective.* This is the art of astrology, the adaptation of celestial measurement to the

---

1 In occult texts, this teaching of Hermes, the legendary Egyptian god of learning, is translated as "what is below is because of what is above, and what is above is because of what is below," a most interesting primal relationship of cause and effect.

human condition. Without astrologers, *there is no astrology*. And this leads me to know that the quantity of measurement, the precision of measurement, or the diversity of measurements does not crown our quest. Too many measurements can present too much data, too many perspectives; the room in the house can lose its function, a stellium can blur significance, astrologers can lose confidence within the multiplicity of options; glut defies digestion. While the computer is fulfilled, we astrologers must hold our position as its (and astrology's) link with relevance.

Some Brass Tacks

I too am caught up in the groundswell of computer power and measurement strength. All those colors on the monitor, all that speed, all that accuracy . . . but is it actually helping me with my clients? Is all of this taking me further along than the set of measurements I have been using routinely for some twenty years? The question quickly becomes, "How long has it been since I've been open to change?" I have always had the do-you-really-think-that-measurement-will-make-a-difference attitude. I have made changes in my tightly choreographed style, but only after being sledgehammered into it by reality: there *are* new measurements and new meanings that *do* help. Each of them comes when we need to know.

For example, while editing Lynn Koiner's fine chapter on Transpluto in this volume, one sentence in particular jumped forward: "In the charts of [the] lottery winners [I have studied], I found that *all* were experiencing a conjunction or square from transiting Transpluto to the ruler of the 2nd House cusp, a planet in the 2nd House or Venus, the natural ruler of the 2nd House." Now, *that's* a zinger!

A client of mine had just recently received a great deal of money unexpectedly; it was changing his life. We had seen the big change well ahead-of-time in his horoscope, but that such money would be involved was not clearly suggested in the measurements I could bring into the situation. I have now gone back to his horoscope and found that, when his financial situation had changed, transiting Transpluto had indeed made a transit station only 37 minutes of arc away from opposition with his natal Venus. The far-flung, the improbable had happened!

Now this new measurement has been around a long time(!): Transpluto (or Vulcan) has been theorized for almost 50 years, plotted carefully for quite some time, and explored by European astrologers for years. Apparently, it is making its way into the consciousness of astrology. Perhaps we are all almost ready to take Transpluto into our pantheon of planet-gods. A "special" measurement is settling in. This is how change happens, and it is exciting.

Let's look at an example that is a corollary to the simple, successful Transpluto measurement: here are long-established measurements building a valid analysis, *which may be completely wrong*.

David Koresh (born Vernon Wayne Howell), the self-proclaimed "sinful reincarnation of Jesus" at the center of the Waco, Texas inferno, was born August 17, 1959 in Houston, TX (Chart 1, page 6), according to newspaper and magazine accounts of his life. It was easy to see in the ephemeris how tried and true astrological measurements fit the accounts of Koresh's character: the Moon would be in Aquarius, a perfect springboard of humanitarian needs to channel his Leo-leadership energies, the theatricality of it all; Saturn in Capricorn as the final dispositor of the horoscope (on a powerful degree) would be trine the Sun and trine Pluto, a kind of ministerial, leadership power, for sure; the Sun-Uranus conjunction turns on the brightest stage lights, introduces the potential for eccentricity, even genius, and this conjunction is tightly square Jupiter in Scorpio, always a suggestion of intense religious involvement or intense rejection of such involvement; and perhaps that Jupiter could be in the 3rd House channeling all that tension into the thinking process and communication skills, reinforced splendidly by the Leo Mercury that probably opposed his Moon; and finally in that first look, there would be a Venus-Mars conjunction in Virgo, a kind of passionate chastity, an adrenal conflict of values, etc.

A little more preparation led to a trial rectification, instinctively working with a 12th House Sun, beginning at 7:30 A.M. Testing media reports of developments in Koresh's life with Solar Arc movements and transits altered the time to 7:55 A.M.: Mars to the Ascendant (Koresh was sent to his grandmother's to live); Venus to the Ascendant at five years of age (Koresh returned to his mother); SA Sun to the Ascendant at 29-30 measured the time he changed his name and announced himself as Jesus reincarnated. SA Uranus squared the Midheaven of this chart and conjoined the

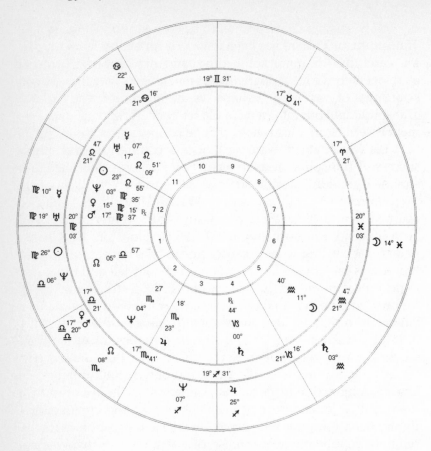

Chart 1
David Koresh
Houston TX
August 17, 1959, 7:55 A.M. CST
95W21   29N45

Ascendant, with transiting Saturn opposed his natal Sun, exact in April 1993 when Koresh died in his own light.

All of this is sound astrology, using well-tested measurement techniques and deeply established sign symbolisms. There are also the Saturn retrograde and Venus retrograde phenomena natally, relating to his father problems and to his contrapuntal sociosexual ethics, respectively. The corroborating list is long. *But,* his maternal grandmother, who raised him on and off in her own home for some fifteen years, has stated to an astrologer that Koresh was born on *September 15*, 1959, the mother having arrived at the hospital around 8 in the morning. Understandably, the grandmother may have forgotten the actual date or confused the dates of two children born into that extended family group, or, indeed, she may be correct.

Chart 2 is for the grandmother's September date, trial-corrected to 9:48 A.M., again with Solar Arcs (and transits) to the angles. What a dilemma: here we have a weaker Moon, if you will, in Pisces but extraordinarily empowered by the opposition with Pluto, which is conjunct Venus in Virgo (!); there's another dose of Virgo with the Sun-Mercury conjunction, reinforcing the orator skills, perhaps to pedantry. The arcs work out pretty well, with Neptune coming to the Ascendant (a time of befuddlement and identity breakdown) and the Midheaven to Uranus, around the time when Koresh reportedly returned to his mother's home to live for a while at age five; and the blazing arc of Mars conjunct Ascendant exact April 19, 1993, the day of the end.

Which birthdate is correct? What time on which date? It is amazing that, not knowing this dilemma, either set of measurements cursorily studied here *would be persuasive* as David Koresh's actual horoscope. What's going on?

Maybe Transpluto plays a role here. Koresh had had no windfall of dollars, to be sure. But Koiner shares with us much more about Transpluto than the good-fortune zinger we have already demonstrated. She animates Transpluto with psychodynamic concepts concerning perfectionism and self-sufficiency; she suggests the "Reformer Complex," alienation factors, and much more.

For the September 15 Koresh (grandmother's date, Chart 2, page 8), natal Transpluto was at 10 Leo 06, possibly square our test-rectification Ascendant. This would channel some of the Transpluto measurement meaning into the Koresh image, but the angles (the birthtime) are still very conjectural. (Transpluto would be conjunct the Midheaven at a 10 A.M. birth, but arcs and transits would lose applicability within the overview of this test chart.) In April 1993, transiting Transpluto at 22 Leo 23 made no contact with the natal horoscope within the tight orb required for such a slow moving measurement.

But for the August 17, 1959 Koresh (the date of public media record, Chart 1, page 6), natal Transpluto at 10 Leo 06 was opposed the Moon, which of course is so dependent upon the

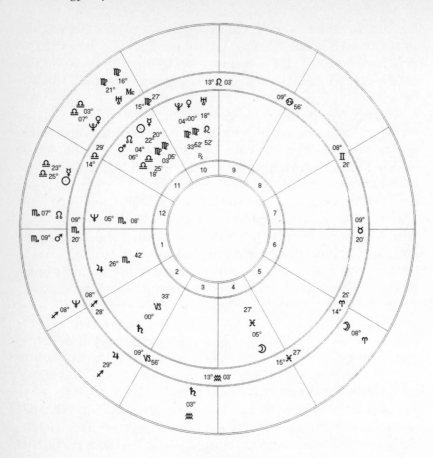

Chart 2
David Koresh
Houston TX
September 15, 1959, 9:48 A.M. CST
95W21   29N45

birthtime as well, let alone the date itself. For this Moon contact (and certainly tied into the mental process with the Moon's opposition to natal Mercury, ruler of both the Ascendant and the Midheaven in the trial horoscope), Koiner submits in part, "The fear of emotional closeness is pronounced . . . [one feels] that there is something wrong with being different because the mother [or grandmother?] was very critical of non-conformity. Being self-sufficient is a means of being free from the disapproval of others."

Now, *that's* something we can get a grip on; it fits snugly into the Koresh profile: his being shunted back and forth between two female-dominated households; his lifelong non-conformity; his rebellion against society; his self-exile with his cult of non-critical supporters. In April 1993, transiting Transpluto at 22 Leo 23 was conjoining Koresh's Sun in the August 17 chart, with transiting Saturn at 28 Aquarius 14 opposing that Sun (exact just five weeks earlier!). Koiner says, "Transpluto triggers changes in the nature of separation, alienation, or even a loss in order to reestablish self-sufficiency in the life." If there is a threat to that psychodynami-cally distanced social position, that defensive enclave where one rules one's own lot, "it seems that Transpluto accompanies a cri-sis to reestablish self-sufficiency in life." There certainly is nothing more self-distancing or self-sufficient than engineering one's own death. Even the prophecy of it adds to its allure and power; for some, it can indeed be the ultimate approval.

Again, for the September date, Chart 2, page 8, the Sec-ondary Progressed Moon (a measurement that's been around since the first decade of the 1600s through the work of Antonius Maginus with Kepler's ephemeris) in April 1993 was at 23 Taurus, trine the Sun and opposed Jupiter. We could muse that Koresh was pleased to fulfill his prophecy and leave this plane.

For the August date, Chart 1, page 5, the Progressed Moon was at 3 Taurus opposed natal Neptune. We could suggest a time of ecstasy, especially with the Progressed (and Solar Arc) Mid-heaven exactly trine natal Jupiter, or we could suggest a time of ultimate self-delusion.

There were no lunation phenomena involved here, not even the eclipse preceding either birthdate.

The North Lunar Node brings this exercise to a strong close: in Chart 1, there is no telling contact between the Nodal axis and any natal planet. But in Chart 2, grandmother's date, page 8, the North Lunar Node is conjoined with Mars (just within the tradi-tional two-degree orb range). In this volume about "special mea-surements," Dennis Flaherty suggests, "When the Dragon's Head conjoins Mars, there is an intensification of desire. This can lead to great ambition, inspiration, passion, and accomplishment. This person can be a powerful proponent of personal conviction. There is often worldly recognition from Mars being linked with the materialization process. But when blocked in fulfilling worldly desires, these individuals can easily experience anger and express violence."

Now, what *is* going on here? Have "special" measurements rescued us in our date/time dilemma? There are more we could try, but it is becoming obvious to me that the public media date of record, August 17, gains stature throughout this process of conjecture. But how can the two dates be so commensurately compelling?

The problem here has nothing to do with the computer or with the quantity or selection of measurements. It has to do with the *interpretation* of the measurements that we have. I remember the great theologian Paul Tillich telling a story about a cloud formation that was dramatically conspicuous in the summer sky, and how a friend of his as a young man was deeply moved by it. He saw the letters "GP" in the clouds and interpreted them as meaning "Go Preach!", and this vision changed his life. Tillich then wryly added that the real meaning behind those two letters, much to the dismay of his friend, was "Go Plough!" *Interpretation is all.*

Dane Rudhyar, in his *Astrology and Personality*, written just over 50 years ago, linked the vagueness in astrology, especially in foretelling the future, with man's free will: "the coefficient of inaccuracy is the coefficient of freedom." He called the birth-chart "nothing but a set of potentialities . . . entirely abstract . . . purely symbolical . . . There is not one single precise event of a man's life to be found as such in his birth-chart. What can be traced are more or less definite types of potential eventualities, with varying degrees of 'actualizability' at certain more or less accurately determinable times of his life." So, from this point of view, we can ask who needs a computer? And what measurements do what kind of job?

Rudhyar strongly suggested that astrology should help us understand life, illuminate the past, and not seek the future. In that frame, he stated clearly that all systems (of prediction) in astrology work because they are all symbolic, i.e., *they all come to life through what we human interpreters read into them.*

It bears repetition here that there is no astrology without astrologers. The measurements guide us as human interpreters to some understanding of life. And here in the Koresh example, no one could quibble with either quick astro-sketch I have presented. *Either* date works! In this case, when we find out the correct birth date—let alone the time—*will it be more convincing than what we have read from our test data?*

So we have a reminder that, no matter how many measurements we have, no matter how sophisticated they are, we still have to know that it is our interpretation of them that gives them meaning. Without greater significance, Khufu is just another pyramid. Without astrologers, measurements are nothing.

Our Measurement Responsibilities

How we measure is closely tied to how we see the world. Our measurements are like lenses placed before our eyes to improve our vision, to see nearer, farther, with greater contrast and clarity. A new measurement comes into experimental fashion, or an updated interpretation of a standard measurement commands notice, and our evaluation of it is in terms of *whether or not it works FOR ME.* We are our lens. We see the world through our experiences, through our value systems.

As professional astrologers, we build our clientele through our style of doing horoscopes, i.e., how we see the world, how we talk about other people's worlds. For example, I never meet with a client interested in finance. The reason is that I am totally unsophisticated about finance, Wall Street, investments, etc. Indeed, I have clients who are bank presidents, but we never talk about financial strategies; we talk about other areas of life development, areas in which I have much experience. Astrologers gain specializations through their personal lens, through the measurements that support that view of the world. Our brain is patterned that way through repetition, and this patterning advertises itself and our expertise. *We become our astrology.*

We must observe again that not all measurements work in every horoscope or for every astrologer. "New" ones, "special" ones must go through our personal lens and measure up to individual standards and styles. Our field of vision expands as we ourselves grow. With care, we measure up to what is possible and to what we can do.

I remind us of the observation made by Paracelsus, that the planets *are* within, and I add, please, *so are the magic measurements we seek.*

Lynn Koiner

Lynn Koiner has been a professional astrologer since 1969. Her studies in economics and international relations at American University in Washington, DC belie her sensitive understanding of psychology, especially within relationships.

In 1981, Lynn helped organize Amethyst, a public service astrological organization, headquartered in Silver Spring, Maryland. In its early years, the organization emphasized its study work in esoteric astrology and esoteric psychology, guided by the work of Alice A. Bailey and H. P. Blavatsky. After six years, Amethyst took its spiritual orientation back to traditional astrology to effect enriched, practical applications.

Since 1984, Lynn has been editor of *The Amethyst*, the organization's quarterly astrological newsletter.

For the last three years, Lynn has taken on "serious" travel programs twice a year to Germany and Czechoslovakia, extending her research through astrologers in these countries to their mundane astrological data. Her network of contacts includes astrologers centered in Berlin, Prague, Poland, and Romania.

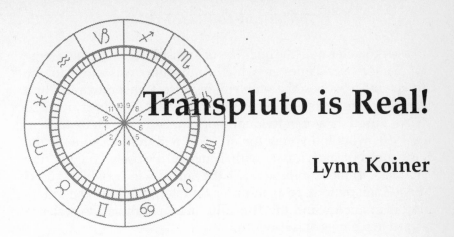

Transpluto is Real!

Lynn Koiner

I n 1972, I obtained the first Transpluto ephemeris, which was published in Germany by the highly respected astrologer/scientist, Theodor Landscheidt. Relying upon my respect for this man and his work, I presumed that there was validity to this hypothetical "planet."

Since the discovery of Pluto, scientists have agreed that Pluto was too small to induce the irregular orbits of Uranus and Neptune. Yet, it was a similar type of calculation that identified the approximate position of Pluto before *it* was discovered. Because Transpluto moves so slowly—from 1938 to 1993, it has moved only 23 degrees—the verification of this planet through photography will be a tedious and prolonged task. All of this notwithstanding, something *is* there.

When I first obtained the Transpluto ephemeris, I hypothesized that this planet would rule either Taurus or Virgo. Both of these signs share a dual rulership—both Taurus and Libra are presently ruled by Venus, and both Gemini and Virgo are presently ruled by Mercury. In the past, both Capricorn and Aquarius were ruled by Saturn until the discovery of Uranus; both Sagittarius and Pisces were ruled by Jupiter until the discovery of Neptune; and both Aries and Scorpio were ruled by Mars until the discovery of Pluto. Later astronomical discoveries will resolve the pairing of Gemini/Virgo and Taurus/Libra.

Technique for Research

In order to determine the qualities of Transpluto, I selected a large number of horoscopes in which Transpluto was close to the Ascendant. This posed a problem, because Transpluto and Pluto were in conjunction in the 1930s and 1940s. For most of these charts, I used data of individuals born in the 1950s. Those born in the 1960s were too young for my 1972 research. I also used the horoscopes of individuals with Transpluto closely conjunct the natal Sun. In most of these cases, the Sun was in Leo. I later used Moon-Transpluto aspects in order to determine how the Transplutonian energy and the Transplutonian childhood experience related to feelings of self-worth.

In order to determine the personality traits associated with Transpluto, I did not interview the individual with Transpluto rising; rather, I interviewed that individual's closest friends, who I felt would be more objective. *In every case*, the friend described their Transplutonian friend as "critical, analytical, fastidious, and very much a perfectionist." Other descriptions were "an eye for detail and very self-critical and introspective." These descriptions seemed to identify Virgo as the sign ruled by Transpluto.

In order to verify the Virgo rulership, I worked with the progressed Moon and its progressed aspects to Transpluto. The nature of the event would give further clues as to the nature of Transpluto or how this planet operates in the horoscope. Furthermore, when Transpluto is aspected by the progressed Moon, the house ruled by Transpluto (the house with Virgo on the cusp) should be correspondingly activated. Indeed, *this appeared to be the case!*

Because Transpluto is a hypothetical planet, the accuracy of the Landscheidt ephemeris had to be determined. In this case, I selected horoscopes with Transpluto in the 4th or 10th Houses. Using Solar Arc directions, generalizing one degree to equal one year of life, I discovered that this ephemeris was as accurate as any ephemeris for the known planets.

In some rare cases, I was able to examine the event effects of the transiting Transpluto. This is rare because of the very slow movement of this planet. In 1973, I was observing the horoscope of an assistant researcher. This chart had Virgo rising, Transpluto in the 11th House sextiling her Gemini Sun in the 9th House. On August 15, Transpluto would transit an exact sextile to the natal

Sun. On that date, she received a notice stating that her application had been accepted to teach and conduct research at a local college.

Another example shows the effect of transiting Transpluto upon the Virgo House cusp. In this chart, Transpluto was transiting an exact conjunction with a Leo Ascendant, and Virgo was on the 2nd House cusp. At the time of the exact conjunction, a very materialistic woman became introspective, reevaluated her life situation, and "changed her ways" with regard to her materialism.

In researching the influence of transits and progressions involving Transpluto, I gave a group of individuals a list of dates on which Transpluto was active. I requested a description of the event, and, in retrospect, what they felt was the psychological effect of the event. I asked them to look at all of the events and describe a psychological theme accompanying these occurrences.

There are other well-known astrologers who ascribe different sign rulerships to Transpluto. These rulerships have not been given without some facts to back them up. I have often found much validity to their findings. I ask my readers to keep an open mind and test all theories with their own charts.

Transpluto (Vulcan) Ephemeris
Prepared by Michael Munkasey

Date	Longit.	Latit.	Rt. Asc.	Decln.	H. Long.	Dist.
01/1/1900	11Cn37R	0N00	6:50:31	22N57	11Cn35	75.28
07/1/1900	11Cn49	0S00	6:51:22	22N56	11Cn51	75.38
01/1/1901	12Cn10	0S00	6:52:55	22N54	12Cn08	75.49
07/1/1901	12Cn21	0N00	6:53:41	22N53	12Cn24	75.60
01/1/1902	12Cn43	0S00	6:55:19	22N51	12Cn41	75.71
07/1/1902	12Cn53	0N00	6:55:58	22N50	12Cn57	75.82
01/1/1903	13Cn16	0N00	6:57:41	22N47	13Cn13	75.93
07/1/1903	13Cn24	0N00	6:58:15	22N47	13Cn29	76.04
01/1/1904	13Cn49	0S00	7:00:02	22N44	13Cn45	76.15
07/1/1904	13Cn57	0N00	7:00:34	22N43	14Cn01	76.26
01/1/1905	14Cn21	0N00	7:02:19	22N41	14Cn17	76.37
07/1/1905	14Cn28	0S00	7:02:49	22N40	14Cn33	76.48
01/1/1906	14Cn53	0N00	7:04:39	22N37	14Cn49	76.58
07/1/1906	14Cn59	0N00	7:05:03	22N37	15Cn05	76.69
01/1/1907	15Cn26	0N00	7:06:58	22N34	15Cn21	76.80
07/1/1907	15Cn30	0S00	7:07:17	22N33	15Cn37	76.91
01/1/1908	15Cn58	0N00	7:09:16	22N30	15Cn52	77.02
07/1/1908	16Cn02	0N00	7:09:33	22N29	16Cn08	77.12
01/1/1909	16Cn29R	0S00	7:11:30	22N26	16Cn24	77.23

Transpluto Ephemeris (con't)						
Date	**Longit.**	**Latit.**	**Rt. Asc.**	**Decln.**	**H. Long.**	**Dist.**
07/1/1909	16Cn32	0N00	7:11:45	22N26	16Cn39	77.34
01/1/1910	17Cn01	0N00	7:13:46	22N22	16Cn55	77.45
07/1/1910	17Cn03	0S00	7:13:56	22N22	17Cn11	77.55
01/1/1911	17Cn32	0S00	7:16:02	22N18	17Cn26	77.66
07/1/1911	17Cn33	0N00	7:16:07	22N18	17Cn41	77.77
01/1/1912	18Cn04	0N00	7:18:17	22N14	17Cn57	77.87
07/1/1912	18Cn05	0S00	7:18:20	22N14	18Cn12	77.98
01/1/1913	18Cn34	0S00	7:20:28	22N10	18Cn28	78.09
07/1/1913	18Cn35	0N00	7:20:29	22N10	18Cn43	78.19
01/1/1914	19Cn06	0S00	7:22:42	22N05	18Cn58	78.30
07/1/1914	19Cn05	0S00	7:22:38	22N06	19Cn13	78.41
01/1/1915	19Cn37	0N00	7:24:54	22N01	19Cn29	78.51
07/1/1915	19Cn35	0N00	7:24:45	22N01	19Cn44	78.62
01/1/1916	20Cn07	0S00	7:27:06	21N56	19Cn59	78.72
07/1/1916	20Cn05	0N00	7:26:55	21N57	20Cn14	78.83
01/1/1917	20Cn37	0N00	7:29:13	21N52	20Cn29	78.93
07/1/1917	20Cn35	0S00	7:29:01	21N52	20Cn44	79.04
01/1/1918	21Cn08R	0S00	7:31:23	21N47	20Cn59	79.14
07/1/1918	21Cn04	0N00	7:31:06	21N48	21Cn14	79.25
01/1/1919	21Cn38	0N00	7:33:32	21N43	21Cn29	79.35
07/1/1919	21Cn33	0S00	7:33:10	21N43	21Cn43	79.46
01/1/1920	22Cn08	0N00	7:35:39	21N38	21Cn58	79.56
07/1/1920	22Cn03	0N00	7:35:16	21N39	22Cn13	79.67
01/1/1921	22Cn37	0S00	7:37:44	21N33	22Cn28	79.77
07/1/1921	22Cn32	0S00	7:37:18	21N34	22Cn42	79.87
01/1/1922	23Cn07	0N00	7:39:49	21N28	22Cn57	79.98
07/1/1922	23Cn00	0S00	7:39:20	21N29	23Cn12	80.08
01/1/1923	23Cn37	0S00	7:41:55	21N23	23Cn26	80.18
07/1/1923	23Cn29	0N00	7:41:21	21N24	23Cn41	80.29
01/1/1924	24Cn06	0N00	7:43:59	21N18	23Cn55	80.39
07/1/1924	23Cn58	0S00	7:43:24	21N19	24Cn10	80.49
01/1/1925	24Cn35	0S00	7:46:00	21N13	24Cn24	80.60
07/1/1925	24Cn26	0N00	7:45:23	21N14	24Cn38	80.70
01/1/1926	25Cn04	0S00	7:48:03	21N08	24Cn53	80.80
07/1/1926	24Cn54	0S00	7:47:22	21N09	25Cn07	80.90
01/1/1927	25Cn33R	0N00	7:50:05	21N02	25Cn21	81.00
07/1/1927	25Cn22	0N00	7:49:20	21N04	25Cn36	81.10
01/1/1928	26Cn02	0S00	7:52:07	20N57	25Cn50	81.21
07/1/1928	25Cn51	0S00	7:51:21	20N59	26Cn04	81.31
01/1/1929	26Cn30	0N00	7:54:06	20N52	26Cn18	81.41
07/1/1929	26Cn19	0S00	7:53:18	20N54	26Cn32	81.51
01/1/1930	26Cn59	0S00	7:56:06	20N46	26Cn46	81.61
07/1/1930	26Cn46	0N00	7:55:14	20N49	27Cn00	81.71
01/1/1931	27Cn27	0N00	7:58:06	20N41	27Cn14	81.81
07/1/1931	27Cn14	0S00	7:57:10	20N43	27Cn28	81.91

Transpluto Ephemeris (con't)

Date	Longit.	Latit.	Rt. Asc.	Decln.	H. Long.	Dist.
01/1/1932	27Cn56	0S00	8:00:05	20N35	27Cn42	82.01
07/1/1932	27Cn42	0N00	7:59:08	20N38	27Cn56	82.11
01/1/1933	28Cn23	0S00	8:02:01	20N29	28Cn10	82.21
07/1/1933	28Cn10	0S00	8:01:03	20N32	28Cn24	82.31
01/1/1934	28Cn52	0N00	8:03:59	20N24	28Cn38	82.41
07/1/1934	28Cn37	0N00	8:02:57	20N27	28Cn52	82.50
01/1/1935	29Cn20	0S00	8:05:56	20N18	29Cn05	82.60
07/1/1935	29Cn04	0N00	8:04:50	20N21	29Cn19	82.70
01/1/1936	29Cn48R	0N00	8:07:52	20N12	29Cn33	82.80
07/1/1936	29Le32	0S00	8:06:45	20N15	29Cn46	82.90
01/1/1937	00Le15	0S00	8:09:45	20N06	0Le00	83.00
07/1/1937	29Le58	0N00	8:08:37	20N10	0Le14	83.09
01/1/1938	00Le42	0N00	8:11:39	20N00	0Le27	83.19
07/1/1938	00Le25	0S00	8:10:27	20N04	0Le41	83.29
01/1/1939	01Le10	0N00	8:13:33	19N54	0Le54	83.38
07/1/1939	00Le51	0N00	8:12:17	19N58	1Le08	83.48
01/1/1940	01Le37	0S00	8:15:26	19N48	1Le21	83.58
07/1/1940	01Le18	0S00	8:14:10	19N52	1Le34	83.67
01/1/1941	02Le03	0N00	8:17:16	19N43	1Le48	83.77
07/1/1941	01Le45	0S00	8:15:58	19N47	2Le01	83.86
01/1/1942	02Le30	0S00	8:19:08	19N36	2Le15	83.96
07/1/1942	02Le11	0N00	8:17:46	19N41	2Le28	84.05
01/1/1943	02Le57	0N00	8:20:59	19N30	2Le41	84.15
07/1/1943	02Le37	0S00	8:19:34	19N35	2Le54	84.24
01/1/1944	03Le24	0S00	8:22:49	19N24	3Le08	84.34
07/1/1944	03Le03	0N00	8:21:24	19N29	3Le21	84.43
01/1/1945	03Le50R	0N00	8:24:36	19N18	3Le34	84.53
07/1/1945	03Le29	0S00	8:23:10	19N23	3Le47	84.62
01/1/1946	04Le17	0N00	8:26:26	19N12	4Le00	84.72
07/1/1946	03Le55	0N00	8:24:56	19N17	4Le13	84.81
01/1/1947	04Le43	0S00	8:28:15	19N05	4Le26	84.90
07/1/1947	04Le21	0S00	8:26:42	19N11	4Le39	85.00
01/1/1948	05Le09	0N00	8:30:03	18N59	4Le52	85.09
07/1/1948	04Le47	0S00	8:28:30	19N04	5Le05	85.18
01/1/1949	05Le35	0S00	8:31:49	18N53	5Le18	85.27
07/1/1949	05Le12	0N00	8:30:15	18N58	5Le31	85.37
01/1/1950	06Le01	0S00	8:33:36	18N46	5Le44	85.46
07/1/1950	05Le38	0S00	8:31:59	18N52	5Le57	85.55
01/1/1951	06Le28	0S00	8:35:23	18N40	6Le10	85.64
07/1/1951	06Le03	0N00	8:33:43	18N46	6Le22	85.73
01/1/1952	06Le54	0N00	8:37:09	18N33	6Le35	85.82
07/1/1952	06Le29	0S00	8:35:29	18N39	6Le48	85.91
01/1/1953	07Le19	0N00	8:38:53	18N27	7Le01	86.00
07/1/1953	06Le54	0S00	8:37:11	18N33	7Le13	86.09
01/1/1954	07Le45R	0S00	8:40:38	18N20	7Le26	86.18
07/1/1954	07Le19	0S00	8:38:53	18N27	7Le38	86.27

Transpluto Ephemeris (con't)

Date	Longit.	Latit.	Rt. Asc.	Decln.	H. Long.	Dist.
01/1/1955	08Le10	0N00	8:42:22	18N14	7Le51	86.36
07/1/1955	07Le44	0S00	8:40:34	18N20	8Le04	86.45
01/1/1956	08Le36	0S00	8:44:06	18N07	8Le16	86.54
07/1/1956	08Le09	0N00	8:42:17	18N14	8Le29	86.63
01/1/1957	09Le01	0N00	8:45:46	18N01	8Le41	86.72
07/1/1957	08Le34	0S00	8:43:57	18N08	8Le54	86.81
01/1/1958	09Le26	0S00	8:47:29	17N54	9Le06	86.90
07/1/1958	08Le58	0N00	8:45:37	18N01	9Le19	86.98
01/1/1959	09Le51	0S00	8:49:10	17N47	9Le31	87.07
07/1/1959	09Le23	0S00	8:47:15	17N55	9Le43	87.16
01/1/1960	10Le16	0N00	8:50:51	17N40	9Le56	87.25
07/1/1960	09Le47	0N00	8:48:56	17N48	10Le08	87.33
01/1/1961	10Le40	0S00	8:52:30	17N34	10Le21	87.42
07/1/1961	10Le12	0N00	8:50:34	17N42	10Le33	87.51
01/1/1962	11Le05	0N00	8:54:10	17N27	10Le45	87.59
07/1/1962	10Le36	0S00	8:52:11	17N35	10Le57	87.68
01/1/1963	11Le30R	0S00	8:55:50	17N20	11Le10	87.76
07/1/1963	11Le00	0N00	8:53:48	17N28	11Le22	87.85
01/1/1964	11Le54	0N00	8:57:29	17N13	11Le34	87.93
07/1/1964	11Le24	0S00	8:55:27	17N22	11Le46	88.02
01/1/1965	12Le19	0N00	8:59:06	17N07	11Le58	88.10
07/1/1965	11Le48	0N00	8:57:04	17N15	12Le10	88.19
01/1/1966	12Le43	0S00	9:00:44	17N00	12Le22	88.27
07/1/1966	12Le12	0S00	8:58:40	17N08	12Le34	88.36
01/1/1967	13Le08	0N00	9:02:22	16N53	12Le47	88.44
07/1/1967	12Le36	0N00	9:00:15	17N02	12Le58	88.52
01/1/1968	13Le32	0S00	9:04:00	16N46	13Le11	88.61
07/1/1968	13Le00	0N00	9:01:53	16N55	13Le23	88.69
01/1/1969	13Le56	0N00	9:05:35	16N39	13Le35	88.77
07/1/1969	13Le24	0S00	9:03:28	16N48	13Le46	88.85
01/1/1970	14Le20	0S00	9:07:12	16N32	13Le58	88.94
07/1/1970	13Le47	0N00	9:05:02	16N41	14Le10	89.02
01/1/1971	14Le44	0N00	9:08:49	16N25	14Le22	89.10
07/1/1971	14Le11	0S00	9:06:36	16N35	14Le34	89.18
01/1/1972	15Le08R	0N00	9:10:24	16N18	14Le46	89.26
07/1/1972	14Le35	0N00	9:08:12	16N28	14Le58	89.34
01/1/1973	15Le32	0S00	9:11:58	16N11	15Le09	89.42
07/1/1973	14Le58	0N00	9:09:44	16N21	15Le21	89.50
01/1/1974	15Le56	0N00	9:13:33	16N04	15Le33	89.58
07/1/1974	15Le21	0N00	9:11:17	16N14	15Le45	89.66
01/1/1975	16Le19	0S00	9:15:07	15N57	15Le56	89.74
07/1/1975	15Le44	0N00	9:12:48	16N07	16Le08	89.82
01/1/1976	16Le43	0N00	9:16:40	15N50	16Le20	89.90
07/1/1976	16Le08	0S00	9:14:22	16N00	16Le31	89.98
01/1/1977	17Le06	0S00	9:18:11	15N43	16Le43	90.06
07/1/1977	16Le31	0N00	9:15:52	15N53	16Le55	90.14

Transpluto Ephemeris (con't)

Date	Longit.	Latit.	Rt. Asc.	Decln.	H. Long.	Dist.
01/1/1978	17Le29	0N00	9:19:44	15N36	17Le06	90.22
07/1/1978	16Le54	0S00	9:17:23	15N47	17Le18	90.29
01/1/1979	17Le53	0N00	9:21:16	15N29	17Le29	90.37
07/1/1979	17Le16	0N00	9:18:53	15N40	17Le41	90.45
01/1/1980	18Le16	0S00	9:22:48	15N21	17Le52	90.53
07/1/1980	17Le39	0N00	9:20:24	15N33	18Le04	90.60
01/1/1981	18Le38R	0N00	9:24:17	15N14	18Le15	90.68
07/1/1981	18Le02	0S00	9:21:53	15N26	18Le27	90.75
01/1/1982	19Le02	0S00	9:25:48	15N07	18Le38	90.83
07/1/1982	18Le25	0N00	9:23:22	15N19	18Le50	90.91
01/1/1983	19Le25	0N00	9:27:19	15N00	19Le01	90.98
07/1/1983	18Le47	0S00	9:24:51	15N12	19Le12	91.06
01/1/1984	19Le48	0N00	9:28:50	14N53	19Le24	91.13
07/1/1984	19Le10	0N00	9:26:22	15N05	19Le35	91.21
01/1/1985	20Le10	0S00	9:30:18	14N46	19Le47	91.28
07/1/1985	19Le32	0S00	9:27:50	14N58	19Le58	91.35
01/1/1986	20Le33	0N00	9:31:48	14N38	20Le09	91.43
07/1/1986	19Le55	0N00	9:29:18	14N51	20Le20	91.50
01/1/1987	20Le56	0S00	9:33:18	14N31	20Le32	91.58
07/1/1987	20Le17	0N00	9:30:45	14N44	20Le43	91.65
01/1/1988	21Le19	0N00	9:34:47	14N24	20Le54	91.72
07/1/1988	20Le40	0S00	9:32:15	14N36	21Le05	91.79
01/1/1989	21Le41	0S00	9:36:14	14N17	21Le17	91.87
07/1/1989	21Le02	0N00	9:33:42	14N29	21Le28	91.94

Date	Longit.	Latit..	Dist.	Rt. Asc.	Decln.	H. Long	H. Lat.
01/1/1990	22Le04R	0S00	91.27	9:37:43	14N09	21Le39	0N00
07/1/1990	21Le24	0S00	92.83	9:35:08	14N22	21Le50	0N00
01/1/1991	22Le26	0S00	91.42	9:39:11	14N02	22Le01	0N00
07/1/1991	21Le46	0N00	92.96	9:36:34	14N15	22Le12	0N00
01/1/1992	22Le49	0S00	91.57	9:40:38	13N55	22Le23	0N00
07/1/1992	22Le09	0S00	93.11	9:38:02	14N08	22Le34	0N00
01/1/1993	23Le11	0N00	91.71	9:42:04	13N48	22Le45	0N00
07/1/1993	22Le31	0S00	93.24	9:39:27	14N01	22Le56	0N00
01/1/1994	23Le33	0S00	91.85	9:43:30	13N40	23Le08	0N00
07/1/1994	22Le52	0N00	93.37	9:40:52	13N54	23Le18	0N00
01/1/1995	23Le55	0N00	92.00	9:44:56	13N33	23Le30	0N00
07/1/1995	23Le14	0S00	93.50	9:42:16	13N46	23Le40	0N00
01/1/1996	24Le17	0S00	92.14	9:46:22	13N26	23Le51	0N00
07/1/1996	23Le36	0N00	93.64	9:43:42	13N39	24Le02	0N00
01/1/1997	24Le39	0S00	92.27	9:47:46	13N18	24Le13	0N00
07/1/1997	23Le57	0S00	93.77	9:45:05	13N32	24Le24	0N00
01/1/1998	25Le01	0S00	93.12	9:49:11	13N11	24Le35	0N00
07/1/1998	24Le19	0N00	93.90	9:46:29	13N25	24Le46	0N00
01/1/1999	25Le23R	0S00	92.56	9:50:36	13N04	24Le57	0N00
07/1/1999	24Le40	0N00	94.02	9:47:52	13N18	25Le08	0N00
01/1/2000	25Le45	0N00	92.70	9:52:00	12N56	25Le19	0N00
07/1/2000	25Le02	0S00	94.16	9:49:16	13N11	25Le29	0N00

Transpluto and Its Effect Upon
the Developing Personality

In my earliest research, I observed a very specific personality type unfolding with a strongly placed natal Transpluto. Indeed, when Transpluto closely conjuncts the natal Sun, the perfectionist Virgo qualities can frequently dominate the influence of the Sun sign, itself. For example, the sign of Gemini, particularly expressive with the Moon in Gemini, is the most acute conductor of the Transpluto influence. I observed this through the critical, perfectionist parental experiences manifested during childhood development, when Transpluto was sextile to Gemini placements.

In surveying the effect of Transpluto upon ego development, I examined only the hard aspects of Transpluto to the Sun, and Transpluto conjunct the 1st, 4th, and 10th House cusps. In these cases, the Transplutonian parent had been subjected to much criticism as a child, and this, in turn, was projected onto the individual offspring whose chart I was examining. Specifically with the Sun-Transpluto aspect, the father was experienced as a critical, perfectionist man who punished the child with exacting demands. As the individual matured, the same exacting standards continued to be used in evaluating self and others.

Used constructively, self-criticism and the perpetual alert for imperfections can motivate the individual continually to strive to do better, to achieve a standard of excellence and to make improvements where needed for the betterment of all. If a child has but one experience of approval from a perfectionist parent, this will be carried over into adulthood as a pattern for finding contentment. The more experiences of approval from the perfectionist parent, the more contentment the individual will find in life.

Used destructively, perfectionism never allows the individual to be content. Always dissatisfied and troubled by self-recriminations, the ego is diminished by low self-esteem, an image unfairly projected by the parent. In anticipating failure, the individual painfully procrastinates or gives up before efforts see fruition. To dodge failure (often found when there are many Mutable placements in the horoscope), the individual may take on an irresponsible attitude, drift from one job or relationship to another, and never really try anything. Such an attitude reinforces the belief that the perfectionist parent is correct:"I am a failure." It is common to find such extreme cases when the individual never experienced any approval from the perfectionist parent.

The Personality Keywords for Transpluto are *The Perfectionist/Perfectionism, Self-sufficiency, The Reformer Complex*, and *Alienation*.

The house position of Transpluto shows in what area of experience perfectionist demands were placed upon us as a child, and where we then place perfectionist demands upon ourselves as adults. According to the celebrated psychologist, Karen Horney, a perfectionist is one who fears criticism. If the person is perfect and always right, there will be no vulnerable areas for criticism to find a foothold.[1] Perfectionism and its resulting fear of failure and disapproval invariably lead to the next Transpluto quality, self-sufficiency.

Self-sufficiency is the Transplutonian ideal. Perfection is not a practical ideal since it is impossible to achieve, but self-sufficiency is always possible. The house position of Transpluto shows where we psychologically need to be self-sufficient.

Self-sufficiency is a self-protecting mechanism whereby others can never get so close that they can criticize, try to change us, or tell us what to do. If the individual experiences a personal failure, others are never close enough to discover the shortcoming and make recriminations. As a client told me, "If I do it myself, if it is mine, then no one can criticize me, tell me what to do, or how to do it!" When self-sufficiency is being lost or undermined, the individual can become quite critical, which drives the undermining person away and, thus, re-establishes self-sufficiency.

The Reformer Complex is an expressive mode of creativity for Transpluto because it involves maintaining high standards and continually making improvements.

In Transpluto, there is a Virgo-type idealism in its quest for perfection. However, it is an idealism that is seen through the eyes of a critic. This idealism cannot be satisfied because the individual is always aware of the flaws, yet continually seeking perfection. The concern is that the Transplutonian individual will desire to change, reform, or reconstruct people and the world in a highly subjective style, rather than as would be best for those concerned.

---

1 *The Neurotic Personality of Our Time*, Karen Horney, M.D., pages 242 and 243.

Alienation is an anxiety-avoidance reaction that serves to remove the individual from any painful reminder of a personal image of failure, something that brought about a psychologically painful critical reaction from the Transplutonian parent. Consequently, the individual may avoid working closely with others in order not to be subjected to criticism. Close relationships may be difficult to establish.

I found the Alienation Factor very apparent in my observations of transits and progressions involving Transpluto. When dependency became a problem in that it allowed others to get close enough to criticize, to try to change or tell the individual what to do, alienation occurred. Often a critical exchange of words served to effect the alienation.

Through my observations of Transpluto in Leo, I was able to ascertain the Dignity and Exaltation of this planet.

Since the rulership dignity of Transpluto is Virgo, its detriment would be in Pisces. Pisces is a very idealistic sign; the critical tendencies of Transpluto can destroy Piscean dreams and illusions. The Reformer Complex of Transpluto can be used in a positive and supportive manner when directed toward broad social requirements. For this reason, Transpluto is exalted in Aquarius. When the critical, perfectionist demands of Transpluto are aimed at the individual, it can severely punish and undermine the ego. Therefore, Transpluto is in its Fall in Leo.

Transpluto and Its Effect upon the Development of the Emotions

In researching the effect of Transpluto upon the development of the emotions, I observed horoscopes with hard aspects from Transpluto to the Moon and Venus. The emotional development is traditionally attributed to the mother. It is through her role that we should be taught to feel good about ourselves, to feel secure and loved. Ideally, the mother should convey the concept that we are loved no matter what happens, that we are accepted just as we are, and that we are loved unconditionally. For most of us, this is an ideal and not a reality!

With hard Transpluto aspects to the Moon, mother becomes the perfectionist parent who drew critical attention to shortcomings and constantly monitored the child with reprimands and orders. Because of these tendencies in the mother, the individual often creates a form of emotional alienation and self-sufficiency as a subconscious anxiety-avoidance reaction to the pain of her criticizing remarks or demands.

The fear of emotional closeness is pronounced. This can be frustrating for Moon signs that require closeness in order to feel loved and secure. It is a fear that, when others are allowed to get too close, they will criticize, try to change or express disapproval. Always on the alert for such a threat, the individual with a strong Moon-Transpluto placement will criticize first in order to drive others away, or at least keep them at a safe distance.

Relationships become stressed when the individual over-reacts to anything that sounds like a criticism or an attempt to effect any type of change. In my couple counseling, the Moon-Transpluto individual frequently complains that the partner is "always criticizing." The use of absolutes such as "always" and "never" is a common Moon-Transpluto habit. A simple comment such as, "Did you take out the trash today?" is seen as a harsh reprimand. Coming to terms with this hypersensitivity is important to establishing positive relating patterns, finding emotional satisfaction with a partner, and cultivating a capacity to share one's self with others. Self-sufficiency can be very lonely!

Maternal Jealousy in the Female Horoscope:
Over the years, in working with my clients, I discovered a correlation between the Moon-Transpluto aspect and maternal jealousy. Previously, I associated this pattern of parent-child relating with Moon-Mars (maternal competitiveness) or Moon-Pluto (the projection of maternal resentments and feeling out of control onto the child). Most of my work on this subject has been with females and their relationship with the mother.

While the behavior of the critical, perfectionist mother is usually the projection of the mother's own fears, failures, and shortcomings *onto* the Moon-Transpluto child, this behavior can also be symptomatic of the mother's own frustrations and lack of emotional fulfillment. This includes sexual frustration.

As the young female child begins to develop some autonomy, often observed at the time the child enters grade school, the mother resents the freedom and the talents expressed by the child.[2] The mother subsequently uses criticisms and putdowns to sabotage the child's efforts to be successful in any undertaking deemed threatening to the mother.

In some way, the Transpluto mother sees herself as a failure. Her own perfectionist attitudes hold her down and keep her from trying to succeed, i.e., a fear of failure and rejection. As her Moon-Transpluto child begins to achieve personal successes and popularity, it is a painful reminder to the mother of these personal failures and lack of achievement in her own life. If the child is successful, the mother can become both critical and angry. The child does not understand what is happening.

Mothers are supposed to be proud of the achievements of their children. She may even encourage the success of the child but, out of jealousy, then attack the child at every turn. This gives rise to a fear of success in the child. In this case, it is not a fear of failure but a fear of rejection, recrimination and psychological retaliation from the mother that success would engender.

I have a female client of many years whose rising Moon in Taurus aspects the difficult stellium of Mars, Saturn, Pluto, and Transpluto in Leo. Transpluto is close to the I.C. The learned pattern of gaining approval through being of service to others produced a desire to pursue a career in nursing. My client's mother herself had once longed for such a career but gave up this notion for marriage. Resenting this sacrifice because of a lack of emotional satisfaction in family life, she then resented the daughter attempting to succeed where she had failed. The mother sabotaged the daughter's attempts to be a nurse by telling her that she was not smart enough and she would not help her financially. The daughter never became a nurse, but she did marry a much older man whom she "nursed" for many years.

Moon Signs in Transpluto Aspects

I have discovered that the quality of aspect between the Moon and Transpluto did not necessarily determine whether the perfectionist relationship had a positive or negative influence. Rather, it is the *sign* in which the Moon is found that more often

---

2   *The Drama of the Gifted Child* by Alice Miller is suggested reading for anyone interested in this aspect of mother-child relationships.

than not describes how the individual reacts to the Transplutonian energy.

Moon in Aries: There can be a rash or impulsive reaction to criticism. This can often lead to crises in the life, sharpening the intellect but sacrificing emotional development. In extreme cases, sensitivity to criticism can keep this defensive individual on edge.

Moon in Taurus: The fear of criticism and disapproval causes the individual to internalize feelings and to "swallow one's words," blocking both personal creativity and communications. In order not to provoke recrimination, the individual may appear to go along with what another says, but go his or her own way in the end. The combination of Taurus and Transpluto can make the individual quietly willful.

Moon in Gemini: Because Gemini absorbs Transpluto readily, the individual can criticize thoughtlessly. Criticism can be expressed indirectly through humor or pranks, which often drives others away. All too easily this mercurial sign substitutes the intellect for the emotions. The need to feel bright and chipper divorces the individual from sensitive feelings.

Moon in Cancer: This is an overly sensitive sign that becomes secretive about feelings and quietly retreats into a protective shell. A conjunction with Transpluto can be quite harsh for this sensitive Moon sign that feels a strong emotional bond with people who criticize and reject.

Moon in Leo: The pride and respect needs of this sign are not compatible with a critical, demanding parent. Much showiness is a manifestation of a need for approval and reassurance. A conjunction with Transpluto often indicates a mother who criticized because her own emotional needs were being neglected. The mother may have been very competitive with the child.

Moon in Virgo: This sign emphasizes the Virgoan need for approval through being of service to others. Fussy habits are developed to establish self-sufficiency in the daily life. The individual becomes difficult to please emotionally. In a male horoscope, the mother could have been a perfectionistic "Super Mom," and other women never seem to measure up to her standards.

Moon in Libra: Transpluto can add discrimination to this sign, allowing the individual to weigh and assess details better. Yet, the fear of criticism can make this Moon even more indecisive. The individual is highly critical of anything that seems unjust and unfair.

Moon in Scorpio: This Moon can harbor deep resentment toward parental demands that make the individual feel powerless. The individual can become highly critical and disapproving of others and control through poor cooperation. A strong element of competitiveness colors the maternal relationship.

Moon in Sagittarius: This Moon can cultivate very high standards, codes and ethics when combined with Transpluto. The liability here is self-righteousness. Criticizing and finding fault with others can be a defensive means by which an insecure individual can appear better than others. A religious upbringing can be a problem.

Moon in Capricorn: This Moon describes a "favorite child" upon whom high expectations were placed, yet the individual always feels like a failure who did not measure up to the parental expectations. Trust on an emotional level is difficult to achieve. The need to achieve is a manifestation of the need to be self-sufficient.

Moon in Aquarius: Mother was perceived as unusual in some way. As a child, she felt different, not like other children her age and not accepted as is. As a result, the individual with this Moon opposing or inconjunct Transpluto will feel that there is something wrong with being different because mother was very critical of non-conformity. Being self-sufficient is a means of being free from the disapproval of others.

Moon in Pisces: At times, the individual feels criticized by others for any sensitivity to the downtrodden. If unable to establish emotional self-sufficiency, the tendency to whine and complain about personal dissatisfactions can be emphasized. There can be a vague discontent with life's imperfections.

A trine from Transpluto can provide the discrimination needed by this empathetic Moon sign to separate the desires of self from others. It is a positive influence for those in the "helping" professions.

Transpluto and the Development of Sexuality

In 1974, I placed a notice in the American Federation of Astrologer's monthly bulletin, requesting research subjects for medical aspects of Transpluto. With the incoming letters, my research was suddenly side-tracked into a new area of investigation.

One of my research subjects wrote in detail about her Venus-Transpluto conjunction in the 5th House. Shortly before the birth of her baby brother, when her Solar Arc Transpluto conjoined her 5th House Venus, her mother decided to tell her all about pregnancy. Shocked by this information, she never realized that men had anything to do with it. "I figured that 'father' was just an honorary term for the man who married your mother." When the transiting Transpluto crossed the 5th House Jupiter (conjunct Venus), the mother "tactlessly and bluntly" informed her about the specifics of sex. Feeling that this was "the most disgusting thing I'd ever heard," she lost all respect for her mother. (This was not an isolated incident. I received many letters describing similar occurrences, especially when there were strong aspects involving Venus-Transpluto.)

Confirming my observations of Transpluto, my research subject who had the Moon in Gemini sextiling Venus-Transpluto then described her mother, who had no Virgo planets, as "the most critical person I have ever known. I could not even strike a match correctly. I grew up thinking that, whatever I did, it would be wrong." Her mother further reproached her by saying that "You will never have any friends, especially if they knew you like I do." Out of this fear, this subject "was afraid to invite anybody to my house or to let them really get to know me." The fear of closeness was instilled by a mother who warned that, if others got close enough to know her, they would disapprove and reject her. This is clearly negative Transpluto indoctrination.

In evaluating the responses to my inquiries, I determined that the Venus-Transpluto individual experiences conflict in sexuality and relating *due to a sense of unlovability,* a fear that they are not good enough, and a strong guilt about sexuality.

Frequently, there was a strong religious focus in the childhood that instilled a perfectionist moral code that created blocks, inhibitions and frustrations about sexuality. If the Venus-Transpluto aspect has any connection with the 3rd House, the individual may have attended a religious school. I have also found that Saturn connected with the 3rd House rules parochial schooling.

In my own chart, I have Venus at 29 Cancer conjunct Saturn at 20 Cancer and Transpluto at 4 Leo. Libra (ruled by Venus) is on my 3rd House cusp. I attended Catholic schools for nine years.

Not feeling loved or accepted for one's self during the formative years, the individual can project the inner unworthiness by attracting people who are underdogs, people who are not performing up to their potential, or people who are socially or economically inferior, i.e., people who will make the Transplutonian individual feel superior.

Rather than remaining hard to please and rather than expecting perfection from others, it is essential that the individual concentrate on what is right about a relationship and not the numerous flaws and inadequacies. Discrimination is a healthier ideal for Transpluto.

With a strong Venus-Transpluto connection, the individual grows up with an emphasis upon being a good boy or a good girl, with the concept of "good" being prudish and unrealistic. This can create an inner battle with sexuality. A man with Venus conjunction Transpluto in Leo can frequently become a "male chauvinist prude," having sexual relationships while dating, but, in the end, wanting to marry a virgin!

I observed another version of sexual conflict when the 8th and 11th Houses were involved with Venus and Transpluto. When a boy is told, "Nice boys don't sleep with girls!" he can be programmed that he can only sleep with other boys. Sexual ambivalence was not uncommon. This occurs when the individual is confused about his or her sexuality. The confusion can make the individual asexual or seemingly disinterested in sex. Transpluto in the 5th, 8th, or 9th House with strong aspect to Venus can cause periods of celibacy in the life, wherein the individual withdraws in order to sort out the conflicting sexual urges.

A Venus-Transpluto aspect in the horoscope does not necessarily indicate that there will always be sexual blocks and frustrations. The early blocks and feelings of guilt can be overcome with positive sexual experiences that give reassurance and fulfillment.

I tell my clients that they should use guilt as an indicator as to whether or not they are doing something right! If you do something that makes you feel guilty, then you know that you did the *correct* thing. Guilt means that you did something for yourself and not for others. If you go along for months without feeling guilty, find a good therapist because you are living your life according to the expectations of others. This is a very simplistic approach but it has been very helpful to many of my guilt-ridden clients.

Transpluto, Pregnancy, and the 5th House

Over the years, I have observed that the 5th House rules our early "play" experiences, how we played as a child, how we entertained ourselves and how we had fun. Spontaneity in childhood playtime usually produces a highly creative adult.

The 5th House colors our attitude toward children and child-rearing in general. How we are parented determines how we parent our own children. Transpluto in the 5th House describes a critical, perfectionist parent, usually the mother, who feels that, if she is not constantly monitoring the child, the child is being neglected.

One research subject with Transpluto in the 5th House stated that her "judgment of people in general is pretty critical, especially children. I figure, if I could not get away with it, why the #*&# should I have to be tolerant of them (children)!"

The phrase "tearing apart" relates to the alienation factor in the Transpluto experience by which the perfectionist behavior serves to drive away or alienate the child emotionally. This, in turn, relates to the self-sufficiency ideal of Transpluto. With Transpluto in the 5th House, independence and self-sufficiency in children is essential. The parent does not want a child to be needy, dependent or vulnerable. The child is urged to "do it for yourself" and not rely upon the parent.

The "tearing apart" can produce a miscarriage or abortion. I found miscarriages which were influenced by Transpluto to be psychogenic, i.e., there was a strong psychological motivation for the miscarriage. For example, the woman did not really love the man and she did not want to be tied down with his child. Although she may have wanted a child, she did not want his. In rejecting the child through miscarriage, she was rejecting the husband's love. In the horoscopes of women who never had children, they described not wanting to give up their own self-sufficiency. These women felt that they had always taken care of themselves, and they did not want to devote the next twenty-one years to taking care of a child.

In 1973, I conducted a small research study on miscarriages. I did find that, if natal Transpluto was heavily afflicted at conception, a miscarriage was likely to occur.

Transpluto Burn-Out and the Perfectionist, the Self-Sufficient, Other-Directed Personality

When Transpluto is strong in the horoscope by house position or aspects to the personal planets, it can create a condition whereby the perfectionist, self-sufficient person cares too much what other people think. This personality type tends to be a "giver" who feels uncomfortable receiving. In Transactional Analysis, this trait is called "Heavy Parenting." It describes a person who was only rewarded for perfect conformity, obedience, compliance, doing exactly what he or she was told, blocking out personal nurturing needs.[3] These people become so fearful of receiving (nurturing) that they cut off others when they try to give, and they set themselves up with a bevy of "receivers," or people who enjoy taking and enjoy dependency. This "giving" service provides the perfectionist, self-sufficient personality type with a considerable amount of control over others (the receivers) and a valid purpose in the receiver's life.

This fear of receiving stems from childhood experiences wherein the early environment stressed obedience, compliance and a critical emphasis upon detail so that the individual came to be molded by the parental ideal without regard for the true inner self.[4]

---

3 *I'm OK You're OK*, Thomas A. Harris
4 In *Your Inner Child of the Past*, Dr. Hugh Missildine states on page 77 that the second most common pathogenic parental attitude in our culture is the perfectionist parent, frequently combined with the most common pathogenic parental attitude, over-coercion.

Such individuals possess a subconscious childhood memory of being quite vulnerable in the position of "receiver" (from the parents, as all children are), a position in which they were subjected to criticism, the parents trying to change them and cast them in a parental mold. As adults, when in the position of receiving, the Transpluto-afflicted individual does not feel worthy. In receiving, the individual fears that he or she will once again be placed in that position wherein the person giving will try to change them and tell them what to do.

When raised in an environment of conditional love—I love you if . . . if you do your homework, if you get good grades, if you clean your room, if you choose acceptable friends, if you do this or if you do that—such individuals learn that they can only gain approval though service and that they are only deserving of love and approval when they do something for it. The Moon's house position and sign will show where approval and acceptance is sought. It is this aspect of Transpluto that directs the individual to employment in the "helping" professions, including astrological counseling, which is an outreach of the core feeling that the individual is only worthy when doing something for others.

Being sensitive to criticism as a result of the perfectionist childhood environment, the goal and ideal of the Transplutonian individual is to strive for self-sufficiency. Self-sufficiency is a psychological, protective mechanism whereby others are not allowed to get so close that they could criticize, reject, try to change, or make demands. The life-direction of service is actually a means of being in control. That is, those on the receiving end of the service are dependent upon the activity of the server.

The Burn-Out dilemma of the perfectionist, self-sufficient, other-directed personality type arises from a pattern of many years of giving energy to others and not allowing reciprocation. Usually at the time of strong transiting Saturn aspects, the Transplutonian individual comes to feel depleted and burned out. Feelings of anger begin to surface under the pressure of fatigue. The "receivers" in the life are resented because it is felt that they have used without returning. While blaming others, the fault actually lies within the Transplutonian individual. These individuals control their relationships through their giving and doing for others, becoming frustrated when the giving starts to control them!

The Transpluto Burn-Out symptoms are physical and emotional exhaustion, feeling unloved and unappreciated by the "receivers" in their life, having no sense of purpose or drive, since most of the activities are geared toward the needs of others. Caught in this pattern for many years, they have no idea how to change this situation. As perfectionists who fear criticism, they are driven by the projection that people will not love them if they do not continue to give their time and energy. They come to resent the people to whom they give.

Yet, the thought of allowing others to do things for them stimulates shudders of horror, since the primary memory of receiving is from the critical parents. These perfectionists see nurturing as dependency and vulnerability. If one can not get nurturing from others by allowing them to do things for you, at least nurture yourself. This means getting in touch with what you want, what you need, and what you feel. The action of Transpluto upon the developing psyche is to detach and intellectualize the emotions. Getting in touch with real feelings becomes very difficult. Shop-a-holic compulsions and the Sara Lee Surrogate Mother Syndrome are merely emotional substitutes!

There are entire generations of individuals who are highly susceptible to the perfectionist burn-out of Transpluto. Those born during 1946-48 when Saturn in Leo was conjunct Transpluto, and during 1953-55 when Saturn in Scorpio squared Transpluto. For such individuals I developed the following suggestions for dealing with Burn-Out:

1. Learn to ask for what *you* need and want. When others offer, do not cut them off, SAY YES! Sounds easy? If you wince at this thought, you are a prime candidate for Transpluto Burn-Out.

2. Do not give unless the other person asks. This will eliminate compulsive doing and giving. Put an end to volunteerism!

3. Make yourself less available to others. Wean off the receivers and seek other types of relating. Find activities that are for your pure pleasure alone. If employed in a "helping" profession, decide when you are working. Simply because "problem solving" is easy, you may not consider it work, but it *is!*

4. Do not do what you do not want to do! You cannot eliminate everything that is unpleasant, but you *can* eliminate those things over which you have control.

Transpluto in Transits and Progressions

As I described earlier in "Research Techniques," my research subjects were given a list of transits and progressions involving Transpluto in their life. They were asked to describe the nature of the event, as well as the psychological theme. From the responses, I developed key phrases to describe the effects of Transpluto in terms of events.

In the personal horoscope, Transpluto triggers changes in the nature of a separation, alienation, or even a loss, *in order to re-establish self-sufficiency in the life.* Where dependency upon some form of security has undermined self-sufficiency, being one's own person and doing things for one's self, an alienation or loss has occurred. Changes to remove a dependency situation were often emotionally traumatic, but the individual recovered, emotionally stronger and more self-reliant.

A client with a 6th House Transpluto had become very dependent upon a relative to run her business. The relative was a very well-organized perfectionist. (Where Transpluto falls in the horoscope shows where you must be self-sufficient and not reliant upon others. If you give up your self-sufficiency, it seems that Transpluto accompanies a crisis to re-establish that self-sufficiency in your life.) When transiting Pluto squared and the progressed Moon crossed her natal Transpluto, there was a relationship crisis and this relative quit the job and moved away. This was traumatic to my client, who had become very dependent upon this relative. This separation forced my client to take charge and run the business herself.

I firmly believe that we can "appease the planets" so that negative effects are greatly diminished. If a choice for self-sufficiency is made in order to eliminate a dependency situation, it will not be forced upon the individual. One such person, experiencing a progressed Sun-Mercury aspect to her natal 9th House Transpluto, decided that she had become too dependent upon her current friendships at work and transferred to the west coast. She never said what circumstances led up to this decision, but it was a very satisfying move.

I often find that a criticizing exchange of words often leads to the removal, the relocation, "getting out of Dodge." Criticism is used by Transpluto to push people away. A woman who had worked for a small organization had always felt that, when someone criticized how she ran the organization, she would know that it was "time to leave" and start her own business. When her progressed Moon in the 3rd House sextiled her 11th House Transpluto and transiting Pluto squared it, a new administrator came into the organization and found her way of doing things too "non-traditional." She diplomatically submitted her resignation and successfully started her own business.

The progressed Moon aspecting Transpluto frequently triggers minor self-sufficiency changes. One woman had a brother who continually called her for advice and to complain about family matters. When her progressed Moon in the 3rd House squared her 11th House Transpluto, she criticized him bluntly, telling him to make his own decisions and to discuss his problems with his wife and not her. For months, the brother never spoke to her, but it ended his dependency upon her for "a shoulder to cry on."

In this regard, we found a strong association between Transpluto and small pets. Transpluto rules a pet upon whom there is a strong emotional dependence, one's "baby" so to speak. Venus-Transpluto and Moon-Transpluto can trigger the loss of such a pet.

I have studied horoscopes in which the pet became a substitute for emotional companionship. Transpluto can serve a harsh blow when it removes the animal from the life. In the 1970s, I acquired cats as substitutes for people. When Transpluto periodically took one of the cats away, while emotionally traumatic, I felt a sense of relief and freedom from the mutual dependency. I no longer have such a relationship with my pets, and Transpluto no longer affects their well-being.

One research subject gave a particularly insightful overview of the effects of Transpluto in his life. With the Sun conjunct Saturn in Cancer and the Moon conjunct Neptune in the 1st House, he described himself as a very dependent man with a strong Mother Complex. With Transpluto conjunct Mercury, the ruler of his Ascendant, in the 11th House, he felt that he was continually attracted to meddlesome Transplutonian individuals, upon whom he became dependent for advice and direction.

During progressed and transiting aspects of Transpluto, these meddlesome security figures were removed from his life. This separation was always followed by feelings of loneliness, isolation, and alienation, but these events always compelled him to cultivate self-sufficiency and a self-determined direction in his life. Since most of the aspects were favorable, he made the decision himself to remove these individuals from his life. However, the decision was made only after the meddlesome associations exerted "unbearable" pressure in trying to change him.

Transpluto can bring positive changes, often in the career or finances, that liberate the individual into self-sufficiency. Career changes can establish the individual in a position of self-sufficiency, a position wherein others are not so close that they can criticize, try to change, or tell the individual what to do, and wherein the individual can conduct work routines "their way."

An actress whose natal 9th House Transpluto trined her 5th House Sun (ruling the 10th House cusp) and Mars (ruling the Ascendant and 6th House cusp) had been out of work for over a year. When the progressed Moon in Sagittarius (1st House) trined the 9th House Transpluto, she received her first leading role.

Financial gains occurring under a Transpluto event also liberated the individual into a position of self-sufficiency, a position wherein others were no longer needed financially. I collected data of lottery winners: Transpluto was active *in all of these cases.*

Transpluto and the Lottery

A few years ago, I heard astrologer Joyce Wehrman state that she had found Transpluto prominent in major lottery wins. I began to examine the horoscopes of lottery winners. I have two friends, each of whom won over $1 million in the Maryland lottery. In the charts of lottery winners, I found that *all* were experiencing a conjunction or square from transiting Transpluto to the ruler of the 2nd House cusp, a planet in the 2nd House, or Venus, the natural ruler of the 2nd House.

The psychology involved in this transit was to liberate the individual into a state of financial self-sufficiency. One of my winning friends was a taxi driver supporting seven children. He had used creative visualization to manifest the winning numbers. I did not have his exact birth data, but the major win was clearly shown in his wife's chart: transiting Transpluto squared her natal Venus in Scorpio.

One of my students, who also used creative visualization to manifest the winning numbers, won the lottery when transiting Transpluto crossed her natal Venus and Mercury, Mercury ruling the 2nd House cusp. Her family had been abandoned by the husband and her personal finances were running out. Her yearly income from the lottery was exactly the amount of her ex-husband's salary. Now self-sufficient, she no longer needs her husband or his money.

I personally found Transpluto to be active in small wins. In 1991, when transiting Venus was conjunct the transiting Midheaven and both were exactly square my natal Transpluto, I won a door prize, an eyeglass case. Of course, I was not liberated into self-sufficiency but I did need the eyeglass case!

The Medical Influences of Transpluto

In reviewing the events produced by Transpluto, I found a strong connection with psychosomatic blood sugar disorders (diabetes and hypoglycemia), female problems, and herpes. All of these ailments had a psychological association with love and rejection.

A friend in New York collected many charts of hypoglycemics and diabetics. She found similar patterns through which we developed a hypoglycemia personality profile. Because my friend was not an astrologer, she was not influenced by astrological factors.

First, I found a psychological factor in which the individuals were subjected to "little blows" psychologically from a critical, perfectionist parent. In turn, they became very self-critical, putting themselves down in the same manner as the critical parent. The self-criticizing trait seems to create a vulnerable point in the psychological make-up or stress on the system through the function of the liver. Any shock or trauma that upsets some source of security then triggers a pancreas dysfunction found in hypoglycemia or diabetes.

I found a physiological weak link created by the use of stimulants: smoking, caffeine from smoking, drinking coffee, tea, and sodas, diet pills, drugs, and alcohol, etc. The alloplastic factor was an event in the nature of a separation, alienation, or loss of some source of love or security in the life. The event may have been a divorce, a broken relationship, a change of residence, or a change of schools. The emotional disruption to the sense of security triggered the psychogenic reaction.

The body, in its attempt to compensate for the loss of love, would shoot a little sugar to itself in the form of glycogen from the stressed liver. The onset of the blood sugar dysfunction—diabetes or hypoglycemia—usually occurred within 6 months of the loss or change.

An example: a young man experienced the perfectionist standards we have been discussing from his Scorpio mother. He felt closely tied to her. My assistant researcher stated that, "He is a very insecure young man who puts others down so that they are not as good as he is, making himself seem superior." He had indulged in all forms of stimulants: amphetamines, LSD, and a heavy coffee habit. At eighteen years of age, exactly when Solar Arc IC conjuncted his 4th House Transpluto, his mother left his home with another man. Transiting Mars was crossing Transpluto on the day that she left. Within six months, he developed diabetes.

In 1975, I corresponded with one of the leading hypoglycemia research physicians, Harry M. Salzer, in Ohio. While he was very open-minded about consulting with an astrologer, he did not feel that there was a psychological basis for disease. He did, however, concur with the physiological weak link.

I developed a planetary picture or formula for these blood sugar disorders. For diabetes, I used Transpluto + Jupiter – Venus. For hypoglycemia, I used Transpluto + Jupiter – Mars. Charles Emerson, in his early research, preferred Saturn rather than Jupiter. [These formulae should be managed just as one computes the Part of Fortune, i.e., Ascendant position + Moon position – Sun position.—Ed.]

It was not until the early 1980s, when I studied esoteric astrology and the Alice A. Bailey material, that I felt I had discovered the significance of Jupiter and Saturn. In esoteric psychology, Bailey discussed the transfer of energy from the sacral chakra to the throat chakra, and from the solar plexus chakra to the heart chakra. When the Jupiter formula (the derived point) had a strong position in the horoscope, the individual was learning detachment in relationships as energy was being transferred from the solar plexus to the heart chakra. When the Saturn formula had a strong position in the horoscope, the individual was trying to cultivate creativity as energy was being transferred from the sacral to the throat chakra. Bailey referred to blood sugar disorders as one of the diseases of discipleship, an imbalance that occurs while one is developing spiritually.

My research with female problems, dysfunction with the uterus and ovaries, is limited. One subject made the decision to have a hysterectomy when her progressed Mercury conjuncted her natal Transpluto. The progressed Moon in the 12th House squared Transpluto. Tumors were found in the uterus wall. The psychological factor related to these surgeries was described as a way of rejecting or removing the "critical, rejecting" mother.

Over the years, I have obtained many charts for herpes in women. I associate it with the sign of Leo, but I noticed that the onset occurred at the time of a major Transpluto progression or transit. The women interviewed described a psychological factor in which they rejected love in their lives. One subject was in a relationship with a married man. She could not break away from this emotional tie. Under a progressed Mercury-Transpluto conjunction, she developed herpes. This condition abruptly ended the relationship.

I interviewed several women who described finding real love for the first time in their lives and suddenly developed herpes. They felt that this was a psychological projection of unworthiness and an attempt to drive this type of love away because they did not deserve it. If they could resolve the issue of unworthiness, the herpes outbreak did not reoccur.

Transpluto as a Beginning and Ending Planet

A Beginning Planet is one that is the earliest by degree in the horoscope. This does not involve the sign, only the degree number. However, the planet must be between 0 and 5 degrees of a sign. With a Beginning Planet, the individual is young in the experience of the energy of the planet and, therefore, it is not used effectively. This can cause a block or distortion of which the individual is not aware.

An Ending Planet is one that is the latest by degree in the horoscope, and must occur between 25 and 29 degrees of a sign. This is an energy that has been over-developed, and the individual must learn to release or let go of the qualities ruled by the planet.

During the mid to late 1930s, Transpluto was the Ending Planet in almost every chart. At this time, Transpluto was transiting the late degrees of Cancer. By 1938, Transpluto was the Beginning Planet for most people because it entered the sign of Leo and it stayed in 0 to 1 degree Leo for about four years.

Beginning Transpluto is very insecure in new situations. This makes the individual very critical, especially self-critical, wanting to be perfect in the project or endeavor. In order to feel safe, these individuals repeatedly told me, "If it is going to be done right, I must do it myself!" There is a lack of tolerance with ineffectiveness, ineptness, incompetence, and poor work habits in others. The fear of failure in a new situation and a sensitivity to any criticism creates a high degree of tension for the individual. This can cause poor cooperation in a work situation.

Ending Transpluto is in the process of releasing these critical, perfectionist tendencies. Individuals are learning to be *more tolerant of self and others*, less inclined to analyze every situation critically. As one student stated, "I have come to realize that I cannot do it all myself and that somebody else might be able to do it a lot better than I can!"

Conclusion

In all my studies, Transpluto does not appear to be a charitable planet. It makes harsh demands upon us but, when used constructively, it strengthens us with a fortification that allows us to be our own person. It is the "Tough Love" planet. We cannot be influenced by trends, peer pressure, or the wave of mass consciousness. We must be steadfastly loyal to our true inner nature.

Transpluto is a loner planet. Through its energy and lessons, we must walk the path toward Self-Mastery. This mastery must not make us feel arrogant or superior to our fellow man. Transpluto rules the act of striving for perfection in an imperfect world. The virtue of Transpluto is tolerance. In seeing the flaws, we must know that the flaws are in all of us. "I am human, therefore, nothing human is alien to me," is the spiritual philosophy of this planet.

Mary E. Shea

Mary Shea has her Master's Degree in Counseling Psychology. The technique of Solar Return analysis in astrology is one of her specialties. Mary has written a definitive presentation of the technique: *Planets in Solar Returns: A Yearly Guide for Transformation and Growth* (1992 ACS).

Mary is also writer/co-editor of a yearly electional astrology datebook called *Good Days Action Planning Guide*, a book that can be understood by the general public yet has the technical information professional astrologers want and need for day-to-day time evaluation.

Central to her counseling work, Mary uses psycho-spiritual approaches, chiefly Flower Essence therapy, in which discipline she is certified. From her office in Glenelg, Maryland, Mary's work with astrological and energy counseling reaches out across the nation through telephone and tape consultations. She is a lecturer at many astrological conventions and is on the faculty of the Princeton Astrological Society.

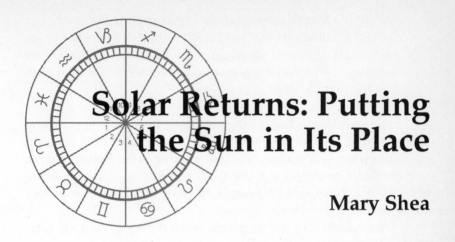

Solar Returns: Putting the Sun in Its Place

Mary Shea

A wealth of information can be gained from Solar Return charts. They are easy to interpret and give valuable clues regarding major cycles of growth and transformation. Why then aren't they a more popular astrological tool? Why aren't they at least as popular as Secondary Progressions and Transits?

I believe that the Solar Return's lack of astrological prominence is linked to the misunderstandings and controversies surrounding their calculation and interpretation. I want to dispel this confusion. Let's address these specific points head on:

- **Tropical versus Sidereal**
  Should you calculate a *tropical* Solar Return chart or a *sidereal* one? What is the difference between the two and how would you interpret each kind?

- **Precession**
  What is precession and should you precess a Solar Return chart?

- **Location**
  Which location do you use for calculating the chart? Place of birth? Residence? Present location? And what happens if you are traveling when the Sun returns to its birth position?

- **Single chart or double chart interpretation techniques**
  Should we interpret the Solar Return chart in reference to the natal chart or does it stand on its own? In using a two-chart technique, which chart goes into the center and which goes into the outside ring?

Once we tackle these long-standing questions concerning Solar Returns, we will have a clearer understanding of the choices available when calculating and interpreting Solar Return charts, and the purpose of each option. Clarity breeds insight and, eventually, Solar Returns will assume their rightful place as a very valuable astrological tool.

After addressing the issues mentioned above, I will demonstrate how I interpret Solar Returns and integrate their information with insights provided by transits and progressions. I will not be giving broad interpretations outside of the charts that I am interpreting, since space is limited. For further information, I refer the reader to my *Planets in Solar Returns: A Yearly Guide for Transformation and Growth* (ACS Publications, 1992). In this book, there are many detailed interpretations of the various planetary house positions in the Solar Return, and further information on how to interpret these charts.

Definition of a Solar Return Chart

A Solar Return chart is a chart set for the exact time of the Sun's return to its natal position. At the moment of birth, the transiting Sun has a very specific zodiacal position that is defined in terms of degrees, minutes, and seconds of arc. Each year, the Sun returns to this exact natal position, and the time of the return can be determined. This time is then used to calculate the Solar Return chart itself, and this chart forecasts the year ahead in life. (Calculations are difficult and, for this reason, computer printouts are highly recommended. Age regression charts and logarithmic calculations *do not work*.) The time of the Sun's return is hardly ever the birth time, and sometimes does not even occur on the birthday. The Sun may return the day before the birthday, the day of, or the day after. The yearly transit of the Sun through the zodiac is different from the 365 daily rotations (days) experienced on Earth during a year. There is approximately a six-hour difference between the two. In other words, a true solar year (Sun's yearly transiting time) is about 365.25 days long. That is, of course, the reason for February 29, a leap day occurring every four years. The extra day corrects for this known discrepancy. Because of the difference between the true solar year (Sun's transit) and the number of days in a year, the time of the Sun's return advances approximately six hours each year, while dropping back a whole day during leap years.

Tropical or Sidereal

When calculating Solar Returns, everything becomes a lot clearer if you remember not to mix apples and oranges. Astrology has been divided between the tropical and sidereal systems for a long time. The points of reference for these two systems are very different. Solar Returns are subject to the confusion associated with these two systems since we have the option of either calculating a tropical or a sidereal Solar Return chart. But regardless of the method of calculation chosen, each Solar Return chart needs to be handled and interpreted in a manner that is consistent with the originating system and its customary interpretation techniques.

Tropical astrology is based on the relationship between the Sun and the Earth, and the Sun's apparent path projected on the Earth's surface (ecliptic). Twice a year, the Sun's declination becomes zero as it crosses the equator. The northward crossing is viewed as the rite of spring called the Vernal Equinox, and is defined as the beginning of the zodiac or "0 degrees Aries." The southward passage marks the Autumnal Equinox and defines "0 degrees Libra." The maximum northern declination of the Sun is the Summer Solstice and "0 degrees Cancer," while the maximum southern declination of the Sun is the Winter Solstice and "0 degrees Capricorn." Tropical systems are very Earth-oriented, consistent with the change of seasons we experience. They have little to do with stellar placements and alignments, or the Precession of the Equinox (primarily a sidereal concern).

Sidereal astrology is-star based. "0 degrees Aries" is always associated with the beginning of the Aries constellation formed by stars. Whenever the Sun is in this part of the stellar sky, in this constellation, it is in Aries, *regardless of where the Sun falls in relation to the equator or what time of year or season it is here on earth.* Because of the wobbling of the earth on its axis and the resulting Precession of the Equinox (which is some 26,000 years in cyclical duration), sidereal timing shifts slightly every year and the discrepancy between tropical "0 degrees Aries" and sidereal "0 degrees Aries" grows. Presently, the timing of the tropical Aries point differs from the timing of the sidereal Aries point by almost one month!

Because these two systems have such different points of reference, it seems logical to assume that tropical Solar Returns should be handled differently from sidereal ones. The Solar Return chart is basically like a temporary natal chart and can be treated as such. Therefore tropical Solar Returns could be interpreted like any other tropical chart, and all tropical techniques such as Sabian symbols, fixed stars, asteroids, house placements, and aspects should apply. On the other hand, sidereal Solar Returns could be interpreted like any other sidereal chart, and all sidereal techniques would apply to *them*. The Universe is internally consistent, and it makes sense that what works for one chart in its system will probably work for other charts within their systems, i.e., calculated in the same manner, and intended for a similar purpose.

Unfortunately in the history of Solar Returns, this is not what happened. Until recently, there has been very little information available on Solar Return charts, and the few books that have been published were written almost exclusively by siderealists. However, the majority of astrologers in this country are tropical astrologers. It was easy to make the mistake of applying sidereal techniques to tropical charts.

The emphasis placed on foreground and background planets with sidereal orientation proposed in these books is not totally foreign to tropical astrology, but its use is primarily emphasized in horary astrology, or in regard to planetary strength based on whether a planet is angular, succeedent, or cadent. For the most part, though, popular tropical astrology has traditionally dealt with the *whole* chart, *all* the planets, houses, signs, and aspects, so it seems logical to look at the whole chart when interpreting a tropical Solar Return. We do not need to stand on our heads to interpret these charts or deviate from what we already know. Within this approach, the background 12th House planets would be every bit as important as the foreground 1st House planets. Equal weight and interpretation would be given to each of the planets in each of these houses.

The same is true of *sidereal* Solar Returns. They should be interpreted with sidereal techniques which may include, but are not limited to foreground-background interpretations and demi-Solar Returns. Please keep in mind that these sidereal techniques may not work as well with tropical Solar Return charts, and tropical techniques may not suit sidereal Solar Returns.

I am a tropical astrologer, not familiar with sidereal techniques. I am a tropical astrologer. When I first started studying Solar Returns back in the 1970s, I ran into the problems facing many astrologers today. It was at that time that I tested with both tropical and sidereal charts. I ultimately "connected" with the tropical Solar Return and saw many correlations between what my clients were telling me and what I was seeing in the Solar Return chart itself. Some interpretations were so blatantly obvious, they could not be denied!

Donna

For example, here is the Solar Return chart for a newly divorced woman named Donna. She had been married for at least ten years. During most of her marriage, she was very overweight and appeared unattractive since she did not care how she looked. She spent her time raising her children and rarely went out. Finances changed, and the family needed more money. Donna was forced to go out and get a part-time job at a local supermarket. She had felt very restricted by her husband for most of her marriage, and, once she was out working, she made friends quickly. Slowly, her weight began to come down. As Donna began to care for her appearance, a beautiful woman emerged.

Donna's husband felt very threatened by these changes in his wife and sought to control her even more. By then, though, she would have none of it and resisted any and all limitations. Fighting broke out and this areaDonna eventually asked her husband to leave the house, then filed for a divorce. This Solar Return starts just as the divorce is finalized. Donna is on her own and raising two children. Being alone and independent is a new experience, since she married right out of high school, and went from her parents' home into her marriage.

As we look at the chart, key planetary placements are loud and clear: note the emphasis on the 1st House and the need to do something "on your own, for yourself, and by yourself." Both the

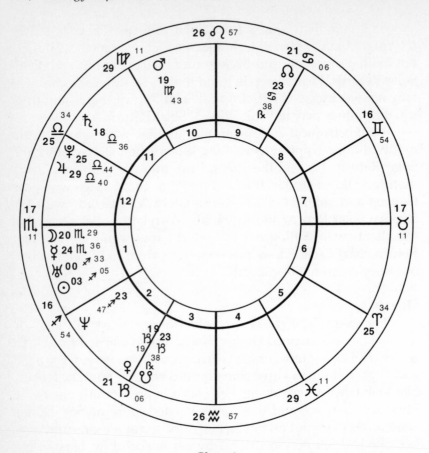

Chart 1
Donna
Solar Return, 1981
Placidus Houses

Sun and the Moon are in the 1st House, lending great importance to this area of self-projection. When both of the lights are in the same house in a Solar Return chart, this indicates that *a new beginning is taking place according to that house position.* In this case, there was a new beginning for Donna. When the Sun and the Moon are in the same house, but in *different* signs, this indicates that the conscious urges and needs are different from the unconscious urges and needs. The individual may experience *two very different sides of his or her personality.*

On one level, Donna loved her freedom and wanted no limitations whatsoever. She was enjoying herself and frequently went out with friends from work. Her personality bloomed as she learned to have fun, and her appearance continued to improve throughout the year until she became quite striking.

But on another level, Donna's needs and urges were different. Her Moon was in Scorpio conjunct Mercury in the 1st House and she had just discovered sex. For the first time in her life, she was orgasmic. She said, "I never knew it could be like this!" She loved sex and she already had a steady lover named Joe. The security and stability of this affair comforted her. But her steady lover wanted to marry Donna and tie her down again. Joe had also recently left a marriage and was looking seriously for a new mate. Donna was torn. She knew if she did not settle down Joe would move on. She loved Joe and she loved sex with him, but she also loved her freedom and would not compromise. For most of the year, she was able to juggle both.

Other placements in the chart continue the drama: finances, normally associated with the 2nd House, were very "iffy" (see Neptune in the 2nd squared by Mars; Venus there, squared by Saturn). Donna only had a part-time job, and though she was trying to move to full-time employment at the supermarket, she was placed on a waiting list for this change. To compensate for the delay and reduced hours, she worked extra hard (Mars in the 10th House) and applied for all the extra hours she could get. Her employers saw her as a very energetic and willing worker. She did her best to please the management even when decisions seemed arbitrary to her.

Goals had to be completely redefined (Saturn in the 11th House). In light of her circumstances, Donna had to be very practical and plan for the future. The move to full-time employment might not come during the year. This is especially true with Saturn in the 11th House of promotions. In fact, it did not, but Donna was able to manage by picking up extra hours her co-workers did not need or want.

And what about the only two planets in cadent houses? Jupiter in the 12th House indicates that an inner enthusiasm for life keeps you going. For those who are religious, it is like having a Guardian Angel watching over you. Donna radiated hope and enthusiasm. Pluto in the 12th House indicates the possibility of psychological deception. With this placement, one's personal problems can easily be attributed to others. Personal responsibility is dismissed and your problems are not your own. It was easy for Donna to see the psychological problems her husband and lover had, but she was blind to her own idiosyncrasies. When Pluto is in the 12th House of the Solar Return chart, it marks a time when it is more difficult to see yourself and be introspective, but also when it is very important to do so.

Planets in Signs

An important distinction needs to be made here regarding the interpretation of tropical Solar Return charts. You cannot treat them totally like a temporal natal chart since the house positions of a Solar Return planet are much more important than the signs. This greatly simplifies Solar Return interpretation, making these charts even easier to interpret than natal charts. There are logical reasons why signs are not particularly important.

- The Sun is always the same and never changes sign or longitude position.

- Mercury can only be plus or minus one sign from the Sun and therefore has limited movement.

- Venus, because of its closeness to the Sun, routinely has eight different Solar Return placements. After eight years, the placements begin to repeat as a new cycle begins. Ascertaining these eight positions can tell a lot about your love life.

- Jupiter changes sign each year and consistently goes from one sign to the next.

- Saturn, Uranus, Neptune, and Pluto will probably stay in the same sign for everyone during the year and it is unlikely that the sign will greatly influence the interpretation.

- And finally, the Moon also has a limited number of placements since it is involved in a nineteen-year eclipse cycle with the Sun. Once the cycle is completed, the nineteen positions are repeated.

Mars is the only planet which is erratic and changes signs regularly and freely; therefore this might be the only planet for which sign is important. So when interpreting a Solar Return chart, it is more important to emphasize the house position than to focus on a planet's sign.

Precession

Earlier, we discussed that precession is a sidereal concept that has little to do with the tropical system. Some astrologers feel that a Solar Return chart should be precessed or advanced to make allowances for the gradual shift in the Precession of the Equinox. This may be very true for sidereal Solar Return charts, but there is no theoretical basis for precessing a tropical Solar Return. Precession, by its very nature indicates stellar influences. There are *no* stellar, sidereal, or precessional influences innately important to the tropical system.

In all things astrological, we must look at the theoretical basis for what we are doing and stay within the theoretical system. If the theory cannot hold water, then we must be very careful about what we research.

In my studies of Solar Return charts, I originally looked at precessed and non-precessed tropical and sidereal Solar Returns. I eventually settled on a tropical non-precessed chart. My interpretations are very psychologically oriented and the tropical chart seemed to fit what I was seeing in my clients. Ultimately, I studied tropical non-precessed Solar Returns for ten years, carefully noting the comments and situations of others in regard to their Solar Return placements.

Patty

For me, precessed tropical charts do not work and make no theoretical sense. They did not work for me back in the 1970s and they do not work for me now. While writing this article, I reviewed my opinion on tropical precessed Solar Return charts by looking at some new charts. My opinion is unchanged. A classic example of the differences between a non-precessed tropical Solar Return (chart 2, on page 50) and a precessed one (chart 3, page 51) is given.

This is the tropical non-precessed Solar Return chart for Patty as she begins a hot new romance. She falls head over heels

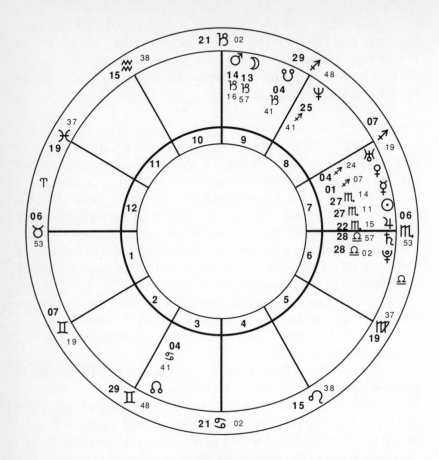

Chart 2
Patty
Non-Precessed Solar Return, 1982
Placidus Houses

in love and gives everything she has for this relationship. She sells the family farm and moves to another state to be with her lover. She leaves her old job and old life behind. Any time there are four or more planets in a Solar Return house, the focus there in life tends to be overwhelming. Other areas of life may be neglected since the attention is so narrow. This was particularly true in Patty's case, and there was no doubt what it was that interested her.

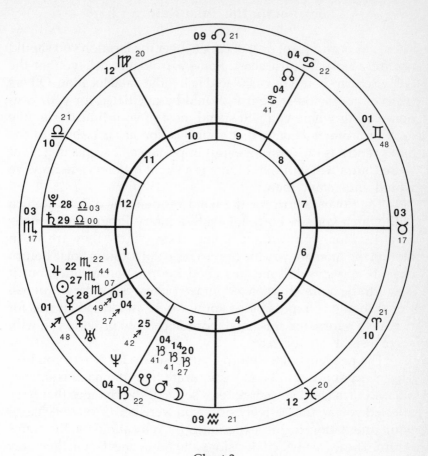

Chart 3
Patty
Precessed Solar Return, 1982
Placidus Houses

Now look at the precessed tropical Solar Return (chart 3). The emphasis is very much on the 1st House. The interpretation is more likely to indicate that Patty was living alone and on her own. Instead, she was in the process of moving in with someone and having one of the most significant relationships in her life.

If there are astrologers out there who believe in or use precessed tropical Solar Return charts, your findings could show us how you would interpret these two charts differently.

Location for the Solar Return Chart

There has been a great deal of debate over the location you should use for a Solar Return chart. Some astrologers believe that the Solar Return should be calculated using the natal location. Others believe that the Solar Return should be calculated for your residence or for where you will spend most of your time during the year. Still others believe that your location *at the moment* of the Sun's return is the one of greatest importance. It seems that all of these charts will work, but there is a slight difference in how we would understand them.

The Solar Return for the natal residence is a Solar Return with which you are born. Like a Secondary Progression for the natal location, you can not change these charts; they are set in motion the moment you are born. This natal location Solar Return chart is *always* valid and has good information to offer, but it seems to be more internalized, indeed like a Secondary Progression. When it is impossible to know where an individual was for the Sun's return, use this natal location chart to provide you with some insight into the year.

The resident Solar Return chart is set up for where you live. This chart appears to be more accurate than the natal residence Solar Return chart since it reflects some of the changes that have affected you accumulatively since you were born. You *can* change your orientation in life experience by relocating for the Sun's return. These free-willed decisions and adjustments will then only appear in the Solar Return calculated for your exact location at the time of the Sun's return.

I believe that the Solar Return chart *set for your location at the exact time of the Sun's return is the most accurate*. The other charts are valid and readable, but this one seems to be the most true. Of course, the aspects are the same no matter where you go, since we are dealing with one moment in time viewed from different locations. Configurations (T-squares, Grand Trines, and Grand Crosses) remain. The degrees and minutes of the planets' positions will not change if you travel. This is because the GMT time of the Sun's return stays the same no matter where you go, *but the Ascendent, Midheaven, and the orientation of the planets in the Solar Return wheel will slowly rotate as you move east or west*. By relocating or traveling for your Solar Return, you can adjust your focus of attention and the house placements for the planets.

For example, say you have a difficult T-square in your residential Solar Return which falls in the cadent houses. You might be concerned about your health if the opposition falls from the 12th to the 6th House. Perhaps you are planning to move across the country during the year and you decide that, since you are already anticipating major career and home changes, you might as well place this opposition in the 10th and 4th Houses and deal with problems this way. You adjust the orientation of the T-square by traveling to another part of the country for your Sun's return.

To make adjustments, you must pick your location carefully and make sure your destination has the qualities you are looking for. Through Solar Return relocation, an individual can make a conscious choice for growth and face issues in a certain way or from a particular geographic venue. Since energy follows thought, this commitment to a new orientation will occur. You can not avoid issues by changing your location, you can only decide how you wish to handle things. This is extremely important to understand the strategies linked to Solar Return location choices and interpretations.

There are certain things traveling for your Solar Return can not do. You can not negate influences seen in Transits, Progressions, and Solar Arcs. Problems or challenges seen in all of these charts will need to be faced and handled, even if you have sought to negate them from the Solar Return chart through relocation. Traveling will not change this. Solar return relocation is only a channeling process. You channel or direct your attention to handle matters in a certain way by making a conscious choice. You decide how you would like to experience the changes in consciousness that need to occur and in which area of your life you wish to experience them. You can not decide to hide or avoid completely. Keep in mind that although we are free-willed beings, there is only so much latitude we can experience. Some events or experiences *are* necessary for the soul growth.

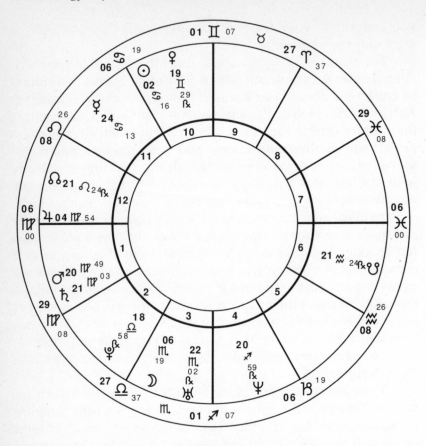

Chart 4
Joann
Natal Location Solar Return, 1980
Placidus Houses

Joann

On the following pages are examples of these three types of Solar Return charts. Chart 4 is the natal location Solar Return for Joann. She wants to quit her job, but is afraid to do so. Notice the Sun and Venus in the 10th House of career and the possibility of her doing really well on her own. It is common for an individual to become self-employed while the Sun is in the 10th. The 10th House is also the house of destiny path-changes, and important decisions are made while the Sun is here.

The Sun is sextiled by Jupiter which is poised to cross the Ascendent. Because it is within two degrees of the house cusp, Jupiter can be interpreted and read for both the 1st *and* the 12th Houses. Be aware that Jupiter will eventually cross into the 1st House by transit. Transits to Solar Return chart angles, i.e., within the Solar Return year, are significant and can be used for timing. Jupiter in the 1st House indicates a self-made opportunity or a position of great benefit that you create for yourself, but you must be the one to create it, since it will not be handed to you ready made. For example, you might start your own business or invent a new product.

With Saturn and Mars conjunct in the 1st House, much discipline and effort will be required if Joann is to get what she wants. Since natal Saturn is in the 1st House of Joann's birth chart, she is equal to the task. Pluto in the 2nd House shows a dramatic change in income. Salaries either go way up or way down. Since Mercury in the 11th House of long-term goals squares Pluto, Joann can expect money to decrease as she initiates long-term changes while still handling bills with short-term finances. Security is a little uncertain since Neptune opposes Venus from the 4th House.

There is a major problem within this chart. Joann has been thinking of quitting her job for years and has always been unable to do so. The Moon and Uranus are intercepted in Scorpio in the 3rd House. Interceptions suggest limitations (a Horary concept that seems to apply to Solar Return) and for this reason it will again be difficult for Joann to make the decision and to say the words, "I quit."

Joann does not live in her birth town anymore. She has moved south only 4 degrees of latitude and 2 degrees of longitude, but there is very little change in the residential Solar Return (chart 5, page 56). Notice that it has the same planetary placements and the 3rd House interception. This residential Solar Return is essentially the same as the natal location Solar Return.

To illustrate further, look at the *exact-location* Solar Return (chart 6, page 57). Joann was not at home for her Sun's return that year. She had decided to travel to Boston to free up the interception in the 3rd House (almost 1 degree north and 7 degrees east of her birthplace). This was a conscious and willful decision on her part. With this act, she was stating her intention to quit her job. Notice the 3rd House cusp in the exact location Solar Return

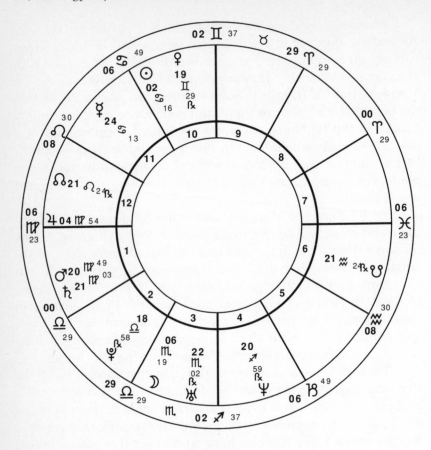

Chart 5
Joann
Residential Location Solar Return, 1980
Placidus Houses

chart. It is now in Scorpio and Joann's house of decision and communication is no longer intercepted.

As it turned out, Joann did not have to quit. She was fired. The afternoon she was to depart for Boston, she had a run-in with the boss. When Joann returned to her office, she began to bad-mouth the executive loudly, sounding off and using strong words. One of her coworkers activated the public address system and sent her conversation all through the building. Her boss heard everything she said and immediately terminated her

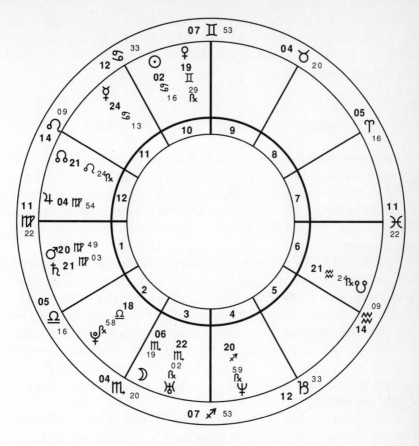

Chart 6
Joann
Exact-Location Solar Return, 1980
Placidus Houses

employment. This turned out to be very fortuitous for Joann: she was able to collect unemployment while setting up her own business. Though money was tight, she managed. Within a year, she became a successful businesswoman, running her own one-person show.

I know from my lectures that many astrologers have very strong opinions about which location is the most important one to use for Solar Returns. To me, all of them are valid and I do not discount any of them, though I prefer the exact location. You, yourself may use whichever one you please to calculate your Solar Returns. I suggest you test the three and form your own opinion. There are no wrongs in this matter, only preferences. See which one works for you.

Single and Double Chart Techniques

Astrologers read Solar Returns as a single chart and/or in relationship to the natal. Many believe that the Solar Return chart can only be read in reference to the natal and can not stand alone. In fact, in the study guidelines for the NCGR examination for professional astrologers, this is stated very clearly: "Solar and lunar returns are meaningless unless compared to the natal chart."

I do not know about lunar returns, but it is my considered opinion and experience that Solar Return charts *can* stand alone and be read as single charts. Some ninety percent of the necessary information can come from the Solar Return chart itself. The information gleaned from the relationship between the Solar Return chart and the natal is generally a reiteration *of what is already seen in the Solar Return chart itself alone.* Although the added information is nice and provides further insight, it is generally not necessary.

If you intend to look at the Solar Return chart in relationship to the natal chart, use a two-chart technique and *place the Solar Return on the INSIDE wheel.* This preserves the integrity of the Solar Return houses and the placement and orientation of the planets. When the Solar Return chart is placed outside the natal chart, I think it becomes very difficult to get an overall view of year and the interpretation can suffer. You can not treat a Solar Return like a Secondary Progressed chart. It is a birth chart for the new cycle of growth and should be respected in its entire presentation.

Let us look at some charts which demonstrate these ideas. The visual element brings ideas into focus, making them more understandable.

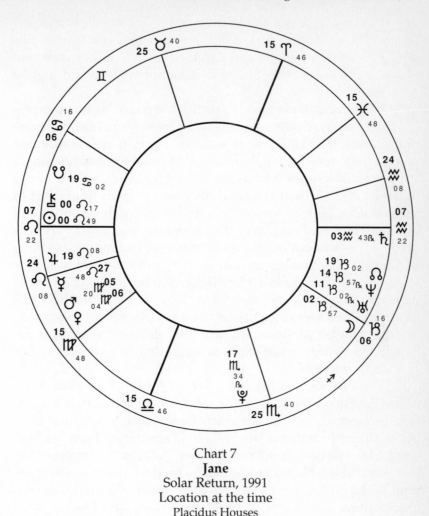

Chart 7
Jane
Solar Return, 1991
Location at the time
Placidus Houses

Jane

Jane is a middle-aged woman who is dissatisfied with her present occupation and is looking to switch careers. She wishes to study massage and open a small healing practice. Money is not a problem for her. She is married, and her husband earns a good salary. She can easily pursue her studies.

But Jane is a very intuitive person and is very troubled by the messages she is getting. She thinks she is being told to leave her husband to pursue a spiritual path. She likes her husband

and does not understand the meaning of the symbols she perceives. The confusion makes her very anxious and fearful. She
does not know how she can support herself on her own and
study at the same time. She also does not wish to end a good
relationship.

It is very common for a spiritual aspirant to misinterpret
symbols and overestimate the level of sacrifice needed for spiritual growth. The Universe is actually a very gentle and loving
place. Upon questioning, Jane revealed more information about
her relationship with her husband. They had always done things
together, and she had followed his lead for many years, but as
she got older, Jane hungered more and more for the intuitive and
spiritual. Her husband, ever the rationalist, remained very left-
brained. He was not interested in massage, healing, or anything
esoteric. Jane felt uneasy breaking away mentally and was slow
to get on with her studies. Her Higher Self began to send her the
message "to go off on her own" and "leave her husband behind."
Jane took these messages to heart and understood them to mean
she must physically leave. In actuality, she needed to think for
herself, and study what she was interested in *regardless* of her
husband's interests.

When we look at her Solar Return for this time period, we
notice the Sun in the 12th House. This can be both a sign of spiritual development and a sign of emotional anxiety. Saturn so close
to the 7th cusp confirms Jane's sense of separation from her husband. She will need to follow her own path. Saturn opposes the
Sun from the 6th House indicating the need to work from the spiritual realm to the physical. The three outer planets in the 6th
House show an interest in health, nutrition, and healing techniques. Dietary changes and improving health habits are likely
during the year. Jane may lose weight or cut back on certain foods
(Saturn in the 6th). Chronic health problems (Saturn), physical sensitivities or allergies to certain foods may arise (Neptune in the
6th). Meditation and quiet times will help her relax and alleviate
nervous tension (Uranus in the 6th). Mars is in the 2nd, indicating
that the more Jane hustles, the more she will earn. If she decides to
cut back or quit, her salary will be cut. And if she finishes school
and takes on many clients, her salary will increase. She will have
many money-making ideas with Mercury in the 2nd and will
always be comfortable with the amount of money she has to spend

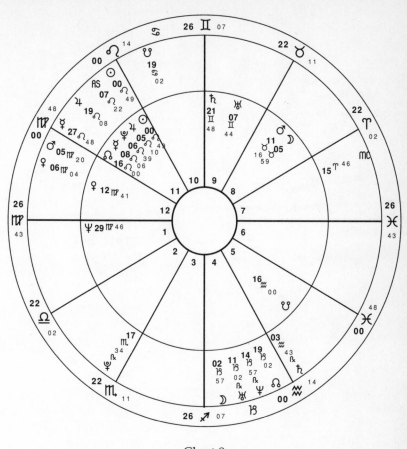

Chart 8
Jane
Solar Return Outside Ring, Natal Inside Ring, 1991
Placidus Houses

(Venus). The 2nd House Virgo planets are trine to the Capricorn planets showing a positive connection between Jane's personal health studies or healing and her ability to make money. What she does for herself, she can use to help others.

During the year, Jane and her husband sold their second home. Notice Pluto in the 4th. Since the summer cottage was in England, the sale was complicated. Jupiter in the 1st again indicates that self-made opportunity. This is a wonderful time for Jane to do her own thing.

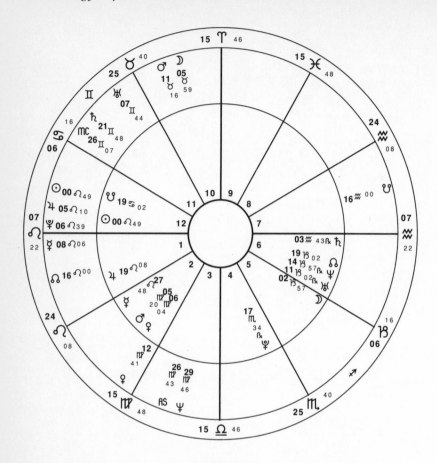

Chart 9
Jane
Solar Return Inside Ring, Natal Outside Ring, 1991
Placidus Houses

Chart 8 shows the natal chart with the Solar Return chart around the outside. Notice that the Solar Return chart has lost all visual definition. Though there is an emphasis on goals (11th House), we are not sure what these goals will be about. We have no sense of working with the body and the physical. We do know there will be a financial change since the SR Pluto falls in the 2nd natal House, squaring SR Jupiter and the natal 11th House planets. The sale of the small cottage is reflected in the Capricorn Solar Return planets falling into the 4th House.

Now look at the Solar Return chart *with the natal planets in the OUTSIDE ring* (chart 9). This double chart is the reverse of the one you have just seen. Within *this* setup, Jane's fear becomes obvious. Natal Pluto with Jupiter and Mercury conjunct the SR Ascendant. A natal planet that conjuncts a Solar Return angle has a special significance. When the natal planet conjuncts the Ascendant, it generally relates to an underlying motivation that fuels the activity of the coming year. Jane was afraid to go off on her own, and natal Pluto conjunct the SR Ascendant confirms this fear. But Pluto is also the planet associated with aloneness and isolation. The motivational desire for Jane was to be free to study whatever interested her, and to walk her own path. This freedom was easily given. Jane's husband had no intention of limiting her interest. He actually encouraged it, but did not wish to come along. Natal Mars and Moon square the SR Ascendant from the 10th House of destiny-path and career choices. Stepping out on her own intellectually was a very big step for Jane.

The Unique Characteristics of Solar Return Charts

Solar returns are very different from other trend techniques such as Transits, Solar Arcs, and Secondary Progressions for the following two reasons.

- **You are looking at an integrated whole,** not isolated aspects occurring one after another or for only a short span of time. A Solar Return chart presents a complete picture that will be in effect for most of the year and all of the planets will mean something. There is a wholeness and staying power to this technique that is not so readily apparent with other astrological methods. You have time to live with the chart and come to know the symbolic meaning of each of the planets and houses. Lessons are well-defined and you have plenty of time to work on them.

- **Solar Returns have a natural and understandable cycle** from one year to the next. Because the time of the Sun's return changes approximately six hours each year (see earlier discussion), the Sun rotates in a predictable pattern from year to year for those individuals who remain in the same location. The Sun moves clockwise three houses each year. This movement introduces *a knowable cycle* to guide understanding and growth. For example, an angular Solar Return Sun will tend to rotate from one angular house to another. The movement might be from the 4th House to the 1st House to the 10th to the 7th. After spending approximately ten years rotating through the angular houses, the Sun will begin to rotate through the succeedent houses. After approximately ten more years, the Sun will begin to rotate through the cadent houses. In thirty-three years, the SR Sun will return to the natal Sun's house placement, and the SR angles will return to the natal angles for those living in their birthplace.

Where your Sun is now in your Solar Return is dependent on what house it is in in your natal horoscope, how old you are, and where you are for the Sun's return. When the Sun is in the process of flipping from one type of house (angular, succeedent, or cadent) to another, crossovers will occur. Extreme northern and southern latitudes and signs of long and short ascension can also cause distortions.

Let's look at a series of four Solar Returns for "Gloria." We will start with her 1989 Solar Return, and finish with the 1992 chart. I do not use Solar Returns as a technique isolated from other astrological methods, but in conjunction with them. So while interpreting these Solar Return charts, I will also discuss Transits, Secondary Progressions and Solar Arcs, integrating all the information with the Solar Return. For this reason, both the natal and the Solar Return chart will sometimes be presented. The reader will be asked to visualize transits, and secondary progression and solar arc placements since those charts will be discussed, but not presented here. Timing will be given when important.

One of the first things we notice about Gloria's Solar Return (chart 11, page 66) is the number of planets in the 6th House. Gloria did not have any health problems this year though she was concerned with her diet and exercise routine. She worked as an executive assistant to the owner of a software company and was beginning to do some private new-age work on the side. During the Solar Return year, she became very interested in buying a

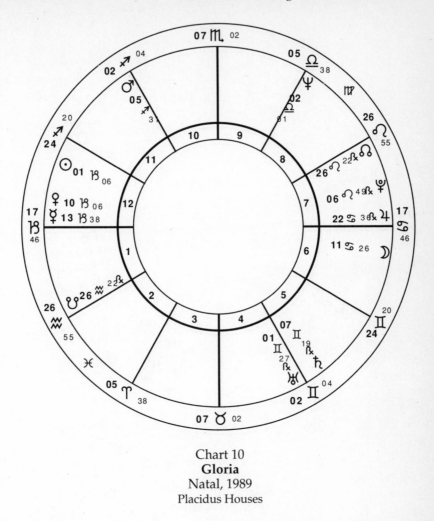

Chart 10
Gloria
Natal, 1989
Placidus Houses

seafood restaurant and owning her own business. The possibility of her taking on such a large endeavor came about through her personal and professional relationship with Larry. As we investigate the predictive astrology further, we will see how important relationships would be in the events of the year.

Gloria had been living with George for fifteen years. During this time, George had had numerous affairs. While Neptune transited conjunct Gloria's natal Venus and opposite her natal Moon, George became heavily involved with a woman he refused to give up. Gloria was not happy. From her Solar Return (page 66),

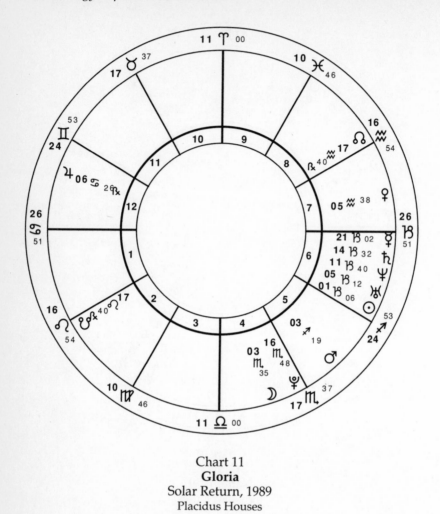

Chart 11
Gloria
Solar Return, 1989
Placidus Houses

we can see that Venus in the 7th House of relationships is squared
by the Moon in the 4th. There is a conflict between Gloria's intimacy needs and her homelife. She felt that she and George did
not have a real relationship. He did not treat her well, and she
wanted to leave. But Gloria lived with George rent free and this
gave her natal Cancer Moon a great deal of emotional and financial security. She was deeply in debt and feared having to fend for
herself. The likelihood of a difficult or protracted move is shown
by SR Pluto in the 4th. Financial repercussions might be suggested by this Pluto square to the node in the Solar Return 8th.

Transits	2nd Progressions	Solar Arcs
Pluto sex Asc	MC trine p-node	Venus opp node
Neptune stat conj Asc	Venus sex p-Mars	
Neptune conj Mercury	Venus sex Venus	
Uranus stat conj Venus		
Uranus sex MC		
Saturn conj Asc		

The transits, secondary progressions, and solar arcs Gloria had in the spring, summer, and fall of 1990 fill in the rest of the picture. Relationships would be in total fluctuation during this time. All four of the outer planets contacted either Venus or the Ascendant, and there were progressions and solar arcs involving Venus too. With Neptune transiting Mercury also, Gloria's thinking might not be clear either.

Gloria met Larry as transiting Jupiter crossed her natal Ascendant in mid-June 1990. She married him as Jupiter crossed her SR Ascendant in early August. It was a whirlwind romance. The sexual relationship was wonderful (Mars in the SR 5th House sextile to Venus), and Larry claimed to have a lot of money which would wipe out Gloria's debt. They planned to borrow money to purchase a restaurant. They also put money down on two houses under construction, one to live in and the other to rent out. Gloria had always hoped to live in the small town of Lambertville, New Jersey, and now her dream was coming true.

But all was not well as you can imagine from Gloria's transits, progressions, and arcs. As Gloria's SA Moon entered Virgo in mid-September and transiting Mercury turned direct while aspecting her natal Moon and Venus, Gloria started to wake up from the Neptunian dream. Checks were bouncing everywhere. Larry did not have any of the money he claimed to have. Not only was he broke, but he was using an alias. Gloria confronted Larry with her realizations in early October. Larry admitted everything. By the beginning of November, Larry had moved out, and Gloria had filed for an annulment, which was granted in December 1990.

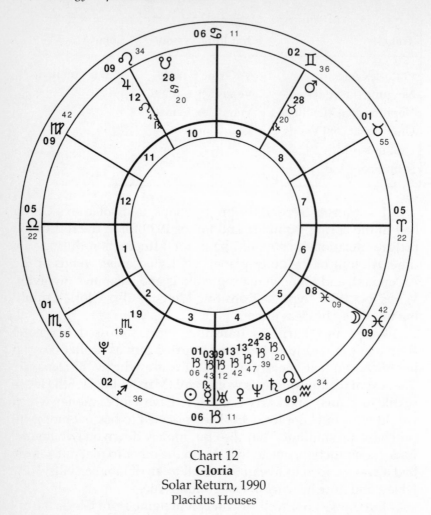

Chart 12
Gloria
Solar Return, 1990
Placidus Houses

Notice that the Sun has rotated to the next cadent house in the 1990 Solar Return (chart 12, page 68). Notice also that it is very close to the 4th House cusp and Gloria may be crossing over into angular houses soon. From this chart we can see problems with the homelife: Saturn, Uranus, and Neptune in the SR 4th House indicate numerous and sometimes difficult domestic changes. Gloria had left George, asked Larry to leave, and was presently living alone in a new house she could not afford and did not own. The builders were very kind, but since Larry's deposit check had

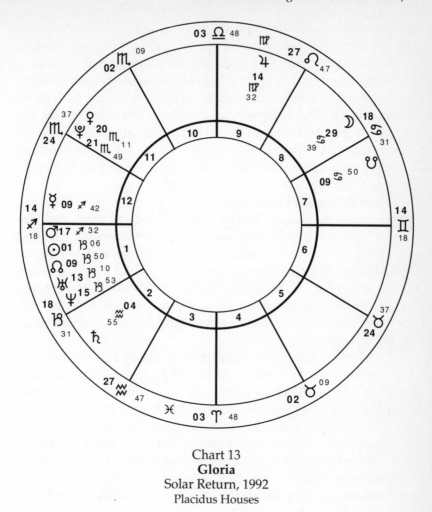

Chart 13
Gloria
Solar Return, 1992
Placidus Houses

bounced, they could not settle on the house and Gloria was forced to move as quickly as possible. She had always feared living on her own and being financially responsible for herself. Now she had no choice. She had to look for an apartment.

Unfortunately, Gloria was carrying an even greater debt. Larry had borrowed thousands of dollars from her until his "ship came in." In the Solar Return, Pluto is in the 2nd House of money showing a dramatic financial change. Gloria had to totally re-establish herself. She charged everything on credit cards in order to survive. She went to estate sales and purchased a lot of furniture at cut-rate prices. She had none of her own furniture since she had lived at George's for so long. She found an apartment in a senior citizens complex where she felt very safe since her neighbors were home most of the day and watched out for each other. This was her first year living alone, and she felt very uneasy. She always ate out and was seldom home. The discomfort she felt with the home environment is evident in the SR 4th House. Saturn, Uranus, and Neptune in the 4th House tend to indicate restlessness. One does not feel at home when at home.

Mars in the 8th House shows the possibility of conflict over shared resources. Gloria had to write all the creditors and disavow all her husband's bills and charges. Fortunately, she had never let Larry near any charge cards that were in her own name. Gloria eventually recovered the money she had given to Larry, and the major bank loan was approved, difficult to believe, given Larry's credit record, but true. The restaurant deal fell through, however, because the owner refused to sell to someone with Larry's reputation.

In Gloria's next Solar Return chart (page 69), the Sun has now crossed over into the angular 1st House. Gloria has only herself to rely on. Although she is dating, there is no one special in her life. She finds that she has the ability to handle life on her own. She received a substantial raise from her employer which lifted her above the financial restrictions she has been living with. Notice the Pluto-Venus conjunction in the SR 11th House of promotions and pay raises. She also was beginning to restructure her finances and save money to return to Lambertville and purchase a home. Saturn in the SR 2nd indicates the ability to live on less. Many times the individual does not have to live on a budget, but chooses to do so to save money for a major purchase. This was Gloria's case.

Gloria has been dating Tom off and on when she discovers he is mentally unstable. The Moon in the SR 8th House can indicate emotional involvement with someone who needs counseling. Tom has a very dark side which he keeps hidden most, but not all, of the time. As this year begins, Gloria becomes aware that "all is not well" and ends the relationship immediately.

Next she begins to date John, someone possessive and smothering. Gloria finds this difficult to deal with. Remember all those SR 1st House planets? She decides to tell her new friend that she must travel a lot for work and cannot see him all the time. John jumps to the conclusion that Gloria works for the CIA. Since this gives Gloria a perfect out, she continues the deception most of the year (one of the less evolved interpretations for Neptune in the SR 1st House). Talk about intrigue! Notice Gloria's transits (captured in the Solar Return) with both Neptune and Uranus conjunct her natal Ascendent and her SA Venus square natal Uranus! There is a strong desire for freedom coupled with identity confusion.

Transits	2nd Progressions	Solar Arcs
Neptune conj Asc Uranus conj Asc	MC trine node	Venus sex Sun Uranus conj Jupiter Venus sq Uranus

The Moon in the SR 8th House can also indicate a strong connection to a woman. In this case, the woman is the deceased wife of the man, John, who Gloria began to date. Although Laura had died before Gloria met her widowed husband, Laura was the same size as Gloria and John passes on a lot of Laura's clothes to her. Gloria hears many stories about Laura and has much respect for her, and Gloria attributes a monetary windfall she received from John to Laura's earlier money management. After Gloria and John stopped dating, they remained friends. One day John gave Gloria $35,000 in a paper bag. This is a very small portion of the money Laura had saved. It was her money-managing ability which made her family well off and gave John the option of helping Gloria financially when she wished to buy a house late in the Solar Return year.

Gloria wanted to be independent (four planets in the Solar Return 1st House), and she wanted to live in her own house. John and Laura helped to make this possible. Project the SA Venus square Uranus and the SA Uranus conjunct Jupiter in the natal 7th House (chart 10, page 65; arc 51 degrees): surprise benefits from others. Gloria returned to Lambertville and moved into her new home. The cash was received and the house purchased very late in the Solar Return year. For this reason, it is important and advisable to look at the next Solar Return, since its significance is already beginning even though the old return is still in effect. A new Solar Return can be significant as soon as three months before your birthday and an old Solar Return can last as long as three months after your birthday.

The financial support Gloria received from John and Laura is shown by Pluto in the 8th House of shared finances and Jupiter in the 7th House. Jupiter in the 7th indicates, "Ask and you shall receive." This is a time when you can benefit either directly or indirectly through another person. Gloria benefitted through another's generosity. She could not have purchased the house without the extra capital.

Jupiter in the 7th House also indicates that relationships were improving. After Gloria's trial with George, disaster with Larry, difficulty with Tom, and smothering by John, she met someone new who was very nice to her. After a period of time, she asked him to move into her new home and live with her. This relationship had a wonderful effect on Gloria. She stopped eating out, became a homebody, and started to cook and entertain again.

The SR Sun is now conjunct the Midheaven and Gloria has the option of choosing a new destiny path for herself. She is starting a new life with a new home and man. She also wants to change jobs during the year and it is likely that she will do so with Uranus and Neptune in the SR 10th House. Her present employer is erratic and moody.

The SR Moon is the 9th House indicates that Gloria is reassessing her beliefs concerning relationships. Practical down-to-earth techniques are needed if she is to make this relationship work. Beliefs cannot be too pie-in-the-sky, but must work on a practical, everyday level. Consistency and stability in relationships are important since the Moon sextiles Venus conjunct Saturn.

Conclusion

A Solar Return chart is just like a "temporary natal chart" and can be very easy to read. The placements should be interpreted in a straightforward manner which is consistent with common astrological methods. With charts as easy to understand as the ones I have presented here, it does make one wonder why Solar Return charts aren't more in the mainstream of astrological usage.

Joan McEvers

Author of *12 Times 12*, and co-author with Marion March of the highly acclaimed teaching series, *The Only Way to . . . Learn Astrology*, Joan McEvers is a busy practicing astrologer in Coeur d'Alene, Idaho. She grew up in Chicago where she majored in art and worked as a model and illustrator, later moving to Los Angeles where she met her husband and raised their children.

Joan began studying astrology on her own in 1965, later studied with Ruth Hale Oliver, and has established an international reputation as a teacher and lecturer, speaking to many groups in the U.S. and Canada. Her articles have been published in several national and international astrological magazines.

In 1975 Joan and Marion March founded Aquarius Workshops, Inc. and began publishing *Aspects*, a quarterly magazine. They also collaborated on computer programming for vocational guidance and won the Regulus Award for contributions to astrological education.

Joan edited the first eight volumes of the New World Astrology Series, the anthology series published by Llewellyn Publications, continues to work with Marion March on their series of books, and writes for various astrological publications.

A double Aquarius with Moon in Leo, when she isn't preoccupied with astrological activities, Joan enjoys spending time with her husband, four children, and five grandchildren.

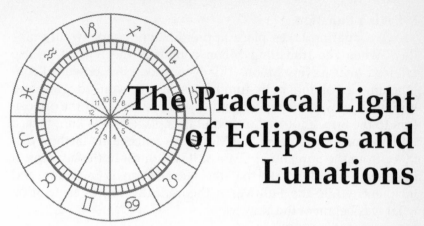

The Practical Light of Eclipses and Lunations

Joan McEvers

A s a novice astrologer many years ago, the concept of Solar and Lunar Eclipses fascinated me, but there was little information available about how they worked in the horoscope. The early books I read, written by either Alan Leo or Charles Carter, mentioned them in passing as a great way to time events, but it was only much later that I began to understand the practical application of Eclipses as a timing device, particularly in connection with Secondary Progressions and Solar Arc Directions. Since many years of practice have shown me how helpful these phenomena can be in marking the month when progressed aspects may be triggered off, I would like to share some of this information with you.

This is not an article on the why and how of Eclipses and Lunations, nor an explanation of the fascinating "Saros Cycle." This information has already been effectively presented by Robert Carl Jansky in his landmark book *Interpreting the Eclipses*, which is available at all astrological book stores. As my title states, I will present a practical way to use both Eclipses and Lunations to time events possible in the life of the individual.

What is a Lunation?

A Lunation takes place approximately every twenty-nine days when the transiting Moon conjuncts the Sun. It is also referred to as a New Moon. This New Moon is a powerful conjunction, involving both luminaries at the same degree and minute. Two weeks later, when the Moon has reached the opposition to the Sun, another Lunation takes place and is known as a Full Moon. At this point, the Moon has reached its farthest distance from the Sun and appears at its brightest in the heavens. It is generally understood that the New Moon is initiating and incipient, while the Full Moon theoretically brings to fruition what was begun at the New Moon.

What is an Eclipse?

An Eclipse is the partial or total obscuring of one of the luminaries by the shadow of the other. At the same time, either or both luminaries are within orb of an aspect to the Lunar Nodes. The Eclipse is considered a Solar Eclipse when the Sun and Moon are conjunct (a New Moon); it is considered a Lunar Eclipse when the Sun and Moon are in opposition (a Full Moon).

In the case of a Solar Eclipse, the Moon comes between the Earth and the Sun, cutting off the light of the Sun from our view on Earth. This only occurs at the time of the New Moon, when both the Sun and Moon are conjunct one of the Nodes at which the orbits of the Sun and Moon intersect.

The Lunar Eclipse occurs only at the time of the Full Moon when the Sun and Moon oppose each other close to the Moon's Nodes. The Earth comes between the Sun and Moon and casts a shadow on the Moon. From the Earth, it looks very dark and shadowed. An Eclipse of the Sun comes from the west; that of the Moon from the east.

The Solar Eclipse is listed in the Ephemeris at the degree of the Sun; a Lunar Eclipse is listed at the degree of the Moon. Both Solar and Lunar Eclipses can occur at either Node. The ancient rule was that the effect of a Solar Eclipse lasts as long in years as the eclipse lasts in hours, and that of the Lunar Eclipse lasts a month for every hour. Perhaps in Mundane Astrology this is an applicable rule, but I have not found it effective when applied to Natal Astrology.

As I pursued my investigation of Eclipses, I came to the conclusion that Lunations are just as significant timing devices as

Eclipses. Eclipses differ from ordinary Lunations because of their extraordinary appearance in the heavens. Though they frightened primitive man by obscuring the light of the Sun or Moon for a short time, modern people realize that they are merely natural phenomena. Ancient superstition portrayed Eclipses as evil, most likely through ignorance and fear of darkness, but modern astrologers tend to view them as neither favorable nor unfavorable, preferring to assess their effect through the planets they contact. From a psychological viewpoint, it depends on how the person is using the energy of the planet aspected by the Lunation or Eclipse that determines what the result will be.

Obviously, as with all transits, those that *conjunct* natal planets seem to be the most powerful. When the force of both luminaries conjuncts another planet, there is great potential for action. If the Lunation or Eclipse squares or opposes a planet, setting up resistance factors, again some action seems likely. My guidelines for using these phenomena are relatively simple and at most times are quite effective when applied to timing. However, I do not just rely on Eclipses and Lunations but use them in context with or as a confirmation of other forecasting methods.

When an astrologer sets up a natal chart and subsequently adds Progressions (Secondary) and Directions (Solar Arc), the prevailing way to look into the future is to relate the progressed or directed planets back to the natal positions. For instance, if the natal Sun is at 6 degrees Aries and secondary Venus has progressed to that position, you, in discussing this aspect with the client, explain that the planet of pleasure, love, partnership, and money is conjunct the Sun and it is possible to fall in love (depending of course, on house and sign position of both planets), or that a financial windfall could occur, a partnership be initiated, and so on. You might engage in a lively discussion with your client about these wonderful possibilities. Then comes the comment, "All that sounds delightful, but when will it happen?" or something similar. Whenever the astrologer suggests some kind of event or gives a list of potentials to the client, the timing element invariably arises.

Naturally, you the astrologer, have looked at transits as well as the Secondary Progressed Moon, which I feel acts much like the second hand on a clock and can be used well as a timer, but the client usually wants specifics. At least, this has been my experience. And it was this that eventually led me to explore some kind of *additional* monthly timing device.

I had watched Eclipses for years, based on the works of early astrologers. I recall reading (unfortunately I cannot remember where) that the Eclipse pattern with its repetitious emphasis on certain degrees of the zodiac acted as a timing device to help judge when certain events would occur. The author used the chart of a foreign ruler to illustrate his point. However, I was not able to see this work out in the charts of family, friends, or clients.

There was a series of Solar and Lunar Eclipses in the early 70s which contacted a friend's Sun/Moon/Mars T-Square, and his wife (a fellow astrologer) and I watched with baited breath as these three key points in his chart were triggered. Since Mars was the fulcrum planet and was in the 10th House, it seemed likely that he would make a career, or at least a job, change. *He didn't.* We also considered the possible loss of a parent. *His parents are still alive.* Maybe he and his wife would separate or divorce (Sun in the 7th, Moon in the 1st). *They are still together.* Thank goodness, none of these things happened. The potential of Eclipse patterns continued to elude me.

As my clientele grew, I persevered in seeking timing methods *that worked.* Solar Returns provided a lot of information and progressing them was an effective timing concept, but this worked best *after the fact.* I have always watched transits to the natal and progressed planets, but the outer planets move so slowly that it can take months for an aspect to become exact. And what happens when Jupiter, Saturn and the transcendentals contact a planet three times in a one- or two-year period? Which will be the trigger for an event to take place? I was still having trouble with timing.

I wish I could tell you the exact moment when it occurred to me that perhaps I was overlooking something. But as all astrologers eat, sleep, and dream astrology, sometimes you have trouble remembering just when some great concept pops into your head. I started listing the monthly New Moon along with transits and how they affected the client's chart. When clients returned the following year for an update, they often commented on how timely my forecasting of events was. After this happened several times, I realized that *the New Moon each month activates the house it falls into.* Now when clients ask when an event may take place, I have a useful tool that works most of the time.

There are two ways to use Lunations and Eclipses for timing. The first is to track when they conjunct (square or oppose) a natal planet. If you consider the concept of a Lunation as the beginning of a cycle of light, it becomes simple to consider that if a New Moon contacts a planet in the natal chart, it may coincide with the inauguration of an action or event connected with that planet, the sign and house it is in and its natal aspects. For instance, if the Aries New Moon in March conjuncts Jupiter in the 5th House, ruler of the 2nd, you might suggest to your client that there may be an opportunity to invest money in some new venture. If Jupiter has challenging aspects natally, it may be wise for her/him to check into whatever investment carefully as to what future opportunities it will provide. Naturally, you know whether investing is a likely activity for 5th House emphasis in your client's life. The Full Moon may connote fulfillment to some notable degree, but *my experience puts New Moons much above Full Moons in importance as transit timers.*

The second way to use the New Moon each month is to consider into which house it falls in the natal horoscope; if you can conceive of it as the beginning of light, it illuminates that house for the time it is there. To paraphrase Jung, *the Solar Eclipse or New Moon kindles a light in the darkness.* And that light shines in and activates the affairs of the house. For example, if you have pointed out to your client that a potential job change is on the horizon and you need to know when this will occur, one possibility will be when the New Moon is in either the client's 6th or 10th House. This phenomenon in either the 2nd or 8th may be a harbinger of financial activity of some kind; in the 3rd or 9th, it may confirm travel opportunity. The list is endless.

An example comes to mind: a young man's chart indicated a change in how he performed his work, as well as a possible raise in pay. He was somewhat skeptical. My assumption of change was predicated upon an active 2nd House (income potential) in his Solar Return; Solar Arc Uranus square his Midheaven; also SR Moon quincunx Uranus in his 6th (how he performs his work), as well as SR Pluto sextile Uranus. I explained that it looked quite positive, but that while the type of work could remain the same, perhaps he would do it differently or in another place. Also, it seemed he had the potential for a pay raise. He was a special education teacher and was in full charge of that division in a small town school system. He liked his job, but was feeling a bit burned out.

Our appointment was in early February, and he had no concept of where to seek a new job; in fact, he was even reluctant to consider it. He asked when this could possibly happen; I replied that it could be quite soon. The March and April lunations were both in his 2nd House and transiting Jupiter, ruler of his natal Midheaven was opposing Mars in his 2nd house in March and squaring his MC in April. As I have learned, and you will too, Eclipses and Lunations overlap and you should always give a little extra time for their effect to be felt.

He phoned the first week in March and told me a friend had called and suggested he apply for the position of Head of Special Education for a town about sixty miles north. The pay was almost double, and he would be in full charge of Adult Special Education; both a change in the way he performed his work and potential for increased income. He applied and got the job, however he will not start until July or August to prepare for the beginning of the new school year in September. In June, the Lunar Eclipse at 14 Sagittarius will conjunct his MC and the July Lunation is in his 6th house. Nothing like more confirmation!

Often timing is visible because of the aspects of the progressed Moon. In his case, however, the Moon was not applying to any aspects until December; perhaps the signal for followup adjustment after the change.

I suggest keeping very tight orbs when aspecting the natal planets, one to two degrees at the most with both Lunations and Eclipses. You may use wider orbs if you wish, but accuracy in forecasting has proven that the tighter the orb, the more likely an event will coincide with the aspect. You may also choose to use trine, sextile, and quincunx aspects from lunations; in fact, quite often a quincunx does trigger some kind of action. In my experience, soft or flowing (trine and sextile) aspects do not bring enough discomfort to motivate activity.

I do not record Full Moons in my transit register as I have not found very much coincidental action. However, I find that Lunar Eclipses (which is, of course, a Full Moon) often do correspond with some kind of finishing action: a relationship may end if it falls into the 7th or 5th House; a job may be lost if the Eclipse is in the 6th; a partnership may break up if in the 7th, and so on. Of course, other indications—and preconditions—must be present. The mere fact of a Lunar Eclipse falling into the 11th House, does not of itself augur the end of a friendship or departure from group activity. I would like to reiterate that though Lunations and Eclipses are excellent timing devices, they *do not* work of themselves, *but must be considered in the light of Progressions, Directions, and Transits.*

A few more thoughts on Eclipses: many astrologers advocate the pre-natal Eclipse as a very significant factor in chart interpretation; some even go so far as to say that you can recognize your client's spiritual path from the placement of this point. I would certainly like to tell you that this is true and expound for pages on how well I have seen it work. However, *such is not the case.* Even when this Eclipse point is strongly aspected and angular, I, to my chagrin, do not find that it has much significance, and it certainly has not given me added insight into a person's spiritual or philosophical path. I investigated this pre-natal Eclipse in all the charts I interpreted for a period of more than ten years and only once or twice did I find it to be significant for day-to-day activities. If you are into esoteric analysis of a client chart, you may wish to use it. Just look in any Eclipse table and mark the Eclipse before birth, whether Solar or Lunar.

Some astrologers refer to the pre-natal Eclipse degree before birth as a sensitive point, to be carefully observed, especially in relationship to subsequent Eclipses by conjunction, square or opposition, but also when aspected by Progressions, Directions and Transits. To my way of thinking, this is just another of those extraneous points or placements that astrologers fall back on, when they are not well-versed in interpreting the signs, planets, houses, and aspects, and how these all come together to show the whole person in the framework of the horoscope.

Using Lunations and Eclipses

Let's use the charts of the British Royal Family for the years 1991, 1992 and 1993. Queen Elizabeth II called 1992 *annus horribilis,* which the tabloids freely translated as "The Year from Hell," and, when you view the progressed and directed aspects as well, as the timing factors of the Lunations, you can easily see how she came to refer to it this way.

When forecasting for a client I usually take into consideration a three-year period: the current year, the preceding one, and the succeeding. So in the following analysis of the charts of the Queen, Prince Charles and Princess Diana, Prince Andrew and the Duchess of York, as well as Princess Anne, I will refer to their Progressions, Directions, and Solar Returns for 1992, but will also assess aspects and transits that occurred in 1991 in some instances, and in 1993 in others.

Although this presentation covers the use and understanding of Lunations and Eclipses, it is necessary that you, the reader, understand that it is necessary to regard and include in your analysis, as mentioned earlier, *other* factors as well (Progressions, Directions and Transits) to get the complete picture. Therefore, in examining the charts of the royal family, all telling factors will be taken into consideration.

Eclipse Table for 1991 Through 1994

Year	Eclipse	Date	Kind of Eclipse
1991	25 Capricorn 20	Jan 15	Solar
	5 Capricorn 08	Jun 27	Lunar
	18 Cancer 59	July 11	Solar
	3 Aquarius 09	Jul 26	Lunar
	29 Gemini 09	Dec 21	Lunar
1992	13 Capricorn 51	Jan 4	Solar
	24 Sagittarius 24	June 15	Lunar
	8 Cancer 57	June 30	Solar
	18 Gemini 13	Dec 9	Lunar
	2 Capricorn 27	Dec 24	Solar
1993	0 Gemini 32	May 21	Solar
	13 Sagittarius 54	June 4	Lunar
	21 Scorpio 46	Nov 13	Solar
	7 Gemini 01	Nov 29	Lunar
1994	19 Taurus 49	May 10	Solar
	3 Sagittarius 38	May 25	Lunar
	10 Scorpio 55	Nov 3	Solar
	25 Taurus 36	Nov 18	Lunar

As you can see from the table above, during this period the Eclipse pattern moves backward through the zodiac, starting in January of 1991 in Capricorn/Cancer, and proceeding through Sagittarius/Gemini into Scorpio/Taurus over the four-year period. In observing the chart of the family, I will refer to this table. It is very helpful for a quick review of which areas in their charts will be triggered during these years.

Review of Events in the Lives of the British Royal Family   1992

January 1992 Queen Elizabeth has discussion with the Duchess of York about her public behavior.

March 1992 Publication of the first very revealing book about Princess Diana by Andrew Morton.
Fergie and Andrew separated for the first time.

April 1992 Diana's father dies. Princess Anne is divorced.

May 1992 Prince Charles and his friend Camilla Bowes-Parker rendezvous in Italy.
Prince Andrew and Sarah, the Duchess of York, separate permanently.
"Fergie," the Duchess of York, moves into her own home.

September 1992 Fergie photographed cavorting with Texas millionaire.

October 1992 Fergie breaks down in public.

November 1992 Prince Charles and Princess Diana have disastrous trip to Korea.
It is announced that Queen Elizabeth is considering paying taxes for the first time.
Newspapers disclose that Charles talks of handing the throne to William.
Fire at Windsor Castle.
Princess Diana moves out.

December 1992 Princess Anne marries for the second time.
Announcement of the end of the marriage of Prince Charles and Princess Diana.

Obviously the British Royal Family is living through challenging times. Both Princes' marriages have broken up publicly, the Queen endured the loss of many precious artifacts in the

Windsor Castle fire; she was also advised to pay income taxes, unheard of until this year. Both Princess Diana and Fergie, the Duchess of York, were caught in soap opera-like liaisons; so was Prince Charles. Prince Philip hasn't exactly escaped either (celebrity-bashing author Kitty Kelley is planning a book about him; hardly good news, as she is known for her ability to ferret out secrets and tar-brush her subjects). The only pleasant thing that happened to any family member was the marriage of Princess Anne to Cmdr. Timothy Laurence.

Is it possible to see this pattern of upheaval in the horoscopes of this beleaguered family? Let's look.

Queen Elizabeth II

Queen Elizabeth was born April 21, 1926 at 2:40 A.M. GMD in London, England 51N30 0W10, according to official palace bulletins and the corroboration of many researchers (see her chart on page 79).

The Queen has a 0 degree Taurus Sun, Capricorn rising, and the Moon in Leo. She has a formidable T-Square from her Saturn/Midheaven conjunction square Neptune in the 7th opposed by the Mars/Jupiter conjunction in Aquarius in the 1st House. With Saturn, her Ascendant ruler, conjunct the Midheaven, she is very focused on her image as a reigning monarch and can, at times, according to most accounts, be obsessively business oriented. Serious and distant, she tends to treat others, including her family, with royal protocol, which does not allow much room for warmth and closeness. True to her elevated Saturn, presenting the proper image seems imperative. Even in private, it would be rare for her to relax the rules, especially since Jupiter, the ruler of her 12th, squares Saturn.

The Sun in Taurus can be quite rigid and unbending. Since her Sun makes no planetary aspects, she may find it difficult to relax and be herself. While the Moon in Leo is often known for gregariousness and a fine sense of drama, Elizabeth has only one significant aspect to her Moon, a quincunx to Venus, ruler of her Sun's sign. The limitation presented by the lack of challenges to the luminaries in her chart easily describes her very circumscribed existence. She was raised to be careful of the image she presents; the peccadilloes engaged in by her two oldest sons must be difficult for her to understand or forgive. But the trine from

Saturn to Uranus in and ruling her 2nd house of values would seem to ease some of the anxieties and distress. She is, after all, the Queen of England, and she probably realizes that scandals are soon forgotten, if not forgiven.

In spite of her somewhat austere attitude in public, she forgives her children a lot. With her Sun conjunct Charles' Moon and her Moon in Leo in his 1st House, she certainly understands where he is coming from. A Sun/Moon conjunction between any

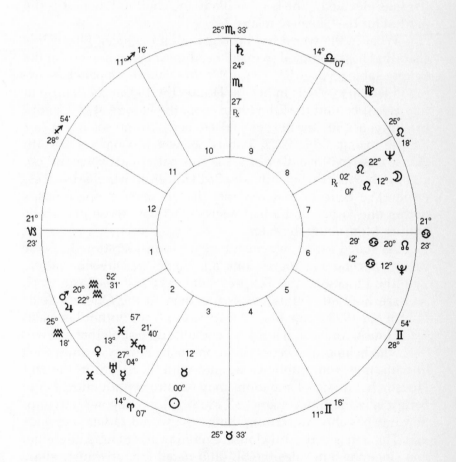

Queen Elizabeth II
April 21, 1926, London, England
2:40 A.M. GMD
51N30   0W10
Koch Houses

two people can be an aspect of unconditional love and it works invariably in this way between parent and child. Prince Andrew's Moon conjuncts his mother's MC/Saturn and indicates that she feels great responsibility for him. His Sun is exactly sextile hers and is another strong bond of understanding.

The child Elizabeth doesn't always see clearly is Princess Anne, whose Sun at 22 Leo conjuncts the Queen's Neptune and squares her Saturn, involving her T-Square. Anne is quite headstrong with Pluto conjunct her Sun and, at times, is rebellious (Uranus elevated). She is most likely the child to whom it is the hardest for the Queen to relate.

What in the world has been going on in Queen Elizabeth's chart that has prompted so many headlines? When we look at the Eclipse Table on page 82, we can see that the Eclipse pattern starting in January 1991 is in her 1st House, the 19 Cancer Eclipse in July is just behind the 7th House cusp, the Eclipse at 29 Gemini conjuncts her 6th, the next one falls in her 12th and so on. The last Eclipse in our Table is 25 Taurus 36, which conjuncts her 4th House cusp in November of 1994. This pattern activates the 1st, 12th, 11th, 9th, 6th, 5th, 4th, and 3rd Houses in her chart successively. The Eclipses that conjunct planets and/or house cusps within one to one-and-a-half degrees, activate those planets or houses. More about this later.

As stated earlier, we must take into consideration the Solar Return, Secondary Progressions, and Solar Arc Directions along with the Lunations and Eclipses. Let's take just one year, 1992, and see how all of this works together. In the Queen's Solar Return for 1992 (page 87), 10 Capricorn, from within her natal 12th House, comes to her SR Ascendant, suggesting that she will deal with behind-the-scenes situations, that she may at times wish to withdraw from public view, and, with SR Saturn in the 2nd House, that financial situations may require her attention. Natal Saturn is in the 10th conjunct SR Pluto, catapulting her into public view, possibly concerning things she would rather keep hidden. The Sun is in the 3rd House: everyday affairs need attention, and since the Sun rules the SR (and natal) 8th, obviously some debts may have to be discharged.

As you can see in the Solar Return chart, SR Saturn conjuncts natal Mars/Jupiter and SR Pluto conjuncts both the natal MC and Saturn, activating her natal T-Square. The SR Uranus/Neptune

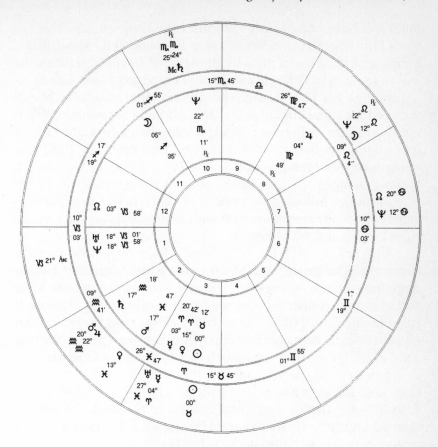

Queen Elizabeth II
Solar Return, 1992, London, England
Natal Chart, Outer Ring
000W10   51N30
Koch Houses

conjunction reaches her natal Ascendant and opposes natal Pluto
while SR Venus squares the whole thing, creating another T-
Square that sets up for the year ahead. Though natal Pluto does
not actually oppose her natal Ascendant, *SR Venus ties the configuration together*. These T-Squares challenge the chart for the whole
year and the Lunations and Eclipses help time the action.

In studying the Progressions and Directions for 1992 and
1993 (not shown here), we note that Secondary Progressed Mercury trines her natal Midheaven, ensuring that any action she

takes will be respected by her constituents; Venus sextiles Uranus. Since both Mercury and Venus are in her natal 2nd House, this is hardly an indication of the new, unexpected financial realities she was beset with in 1992. However, her Progressed Moon was moving through her 12th House, a progression that invariably brings the need for some kind of self-examination. In September 1992, it opposed Pluto in her natal 6th (pressure being brought to bear that may affect her position, because Pluto rules her 10th) and quincunxed its own position in the 7th (emotional reasons for making changes or adjustments, quite likely in public; the Moon is in an angle), followed by a sextile to Venus in October (perhaps some enjoyable event connected with family or travel since Venus rules her 4th and 9th Houses).

In April of 1993, the progressed Moon *conjuncted her natal Ascendant*. The progressed Moon crosses the Ascendant two or three times in the average lifetime and invariably forecasts some sort of change connected with the house it is in, and/or the one it rules. In Elizabeth's chart, this is the 7th House, and the indications seem to be concerning her 2nd child, Princess Anne, who is the first child of a reigning British monarch ever to divorce and remarry.

Solar Arc Mars quincunxed Saturn. Since natal Mars comes from her 1st House and rules the 3rd and the 10th (I use Mars as a co-ruler of Scorpio) and natal Saturn is conjunct the MC, it seemed highly likely there would be some kind of change in her image, or in the way she conducts her business.

In January 1992, the Solar Eclipse at 13 Capricorn fell in Queen Elizabeth's natal 12th House and opposed natal Pluto, in her 6th, ruler of her MC. This was the month she talked with Sarah (Fergie), Duchess of York, about her behavior. This was not an easy chore for the Queen; communicating on a personal level is a challenge and, with natal Jupiter, ruler of her 11th House of in-law children conjunct Mars, square Saturn, and opposed to Neptune natally, it is obvious that it was an effort for her. In October and November, the Lunations were at 2 Scorpio and 2 Sagittarius, respectively, in the Queen's 9th and 10th Houses, catapulting her into the international limelight quite dramatically. This was the disastrous month when part of Windsor Castle was destroyed by fire, and when she volunteered to pay taxes on her private fortune, as well as take all members of the royal family off the public payroll except for herself, her husband, and her mother. Charles discussed giving up the monarchy and Princess Diana moved into a place of her own.

If you wish to stretch the orbs on Lunations to two degrees, the one in October (2 Scorpio) opposed her Sun, ruler of her 8th House of taxes, and the one in November (2 Sagittarius) quincunxed the Sun in her 3rd. The Lunar Eclipse in December of 1992 fell in her 5th House and this was the month that Anne married. At least there was one event to be happy about!.

Prince Charles

Prince Charles was born November 14, 1948 at 9:14 P.M. GMT in London, England according to public record (see chart, page 90).

Charles expresses his intense 4th House Scorpio Sun through an aristocratic Leo Ascendant. His Taurus Moon is exactly conjunct his mother's Sun, a very strong bond. Since his Moon is in his 10th House of career, it is very likely he will carry on his mother's duties when the time comes. At least this was foreordained until recently. In spite of his rather austere demeanor, the Prince is not without charm, as attested by Venus in Libra, conjunct Neptune and sextile Mars and Pluto. A rather introspective person (eight planets below the horizon), he really enjoys sports, especially anything involving horsemanship as you can readily see with Mars and Jupiter in Sagittarius in the 5th House. Pluto rising is usually the sign of the autocrat, and though this planet is generally well-aspected, it does square the Sun which it rules, suggesting a double dose of "We'll do it *my* way." This aspect plus the ruler of his 7th House, Uranus, opposed by Jupiter does not bode well for conjugal compatibility.

Though his relationship with Princess Diana has been distressful for several years, in 1992, for all intents and purposes, it ended. In December of 1991, the Lunar Eclipse at 29 Gemini 09 (see table, page 82) conjuncted Uranus, the ruler of his 7th, suggesting that partnerships needed attention; this was followed by the 13 Capricorn Eclipse in January 1992, which squared his Midheaven. Apart from the usual business, recognition, and prestige matters, the 10th House is the 4th of the 7th and also shows how a marriage may end. Quite possibly, at this time, Charles recognized that the relationship was not salvageable.

In his Solar Return for 1991 (see chart, page 91) Charles' 4th House (the entire sign of Scorpio intercepted natally) comes to the

Ascendant, and the Sun is conjunct it within little more than a degree, suggesting a core emphasis on family matters. The Sun rules the SR 9th: some activity concerning in-laws (sibling's spouse), travel, and possible legal matters. SR Mars and Pluto are "attacking" the Ascendant and are conjunct his Sun from the 12th House, an indication of possible hidden situations coming to light, with a vengeance. In March 1992, the first book about his wife's possible dalliances was published; in April his father-in-law died; in May his vacation with his "friend" Camilla was

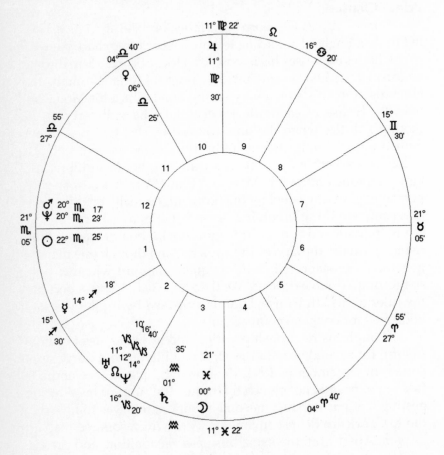

Charles, Prince of Wales
November 14, 1948, London, England
9:14 P.M. GMT
51N30 0W10
Koch Houses

widely covered in the tabloids; and in November, he and his consort made the unfortunate trip to South Korea where the grim-faced couple refused to speak to or even look at each other during the welcoming ceremonies.

By Secondary Progression, Prince Charles' Ascendant was conjunct Saturn in and ruling his 3rd House (in the Progressed chart); how he expresses himself. Obviously, it was easy for him to keep his own counsel, be stoically saturnine, and quite "uncharming," even though his Sun sextiled Mercury. Since Mercury and the Sun are natally both in the 4th House, he probably was

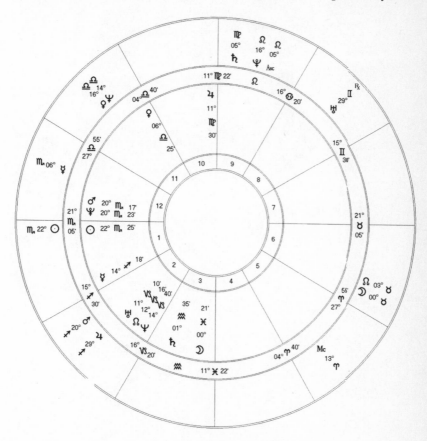

Charles, Prince of Wales
Solar Return 1991, London, England
51N30 0W10
Koch Houses

more relaxed within his own four walls than in public. His progressed Moon in Sagittarius was moving through his 4th and 5th
houses in 1991/92, so most of the time he was focusing his mental and emotional energy on home (4th) and romance (5th).

The Moon trined Neptune by Solar Arc and both SA Pluto
and SA Neptune (in sextile natally) quincunxed the natal Moon,
forming a Yod involving his 10th (Moon's natal position), 1st and
4th Houses (Pluto and Neptune's natal positions). This indicated
a change of direction connected with his public image (Moon/
10th), his persona (Pluto/1st), and his home situation (Nep-

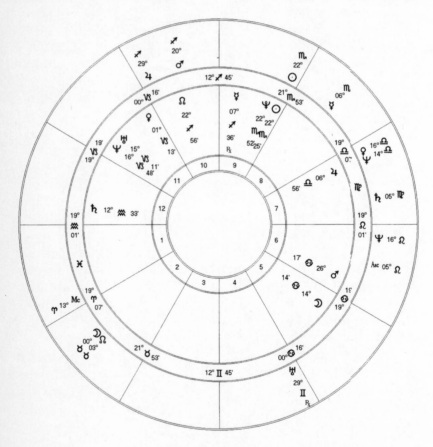

Charles, Prince of Wales
Solar Return 1992, London, England
51N30 0W10
Koch Houses

tune/4th). And of course, it shows a lack of accord with mother (Moon), and possibly other family members as well. SA Jupiter and Uranus, however, aspect his Midheaven, by sextile and trine respectively, suggesting that although people in some quarters disapproved of his actions, there were still some supporters out there. SA Mercury conjunct Mars is probably what gave rise to his petulant announcement, shortly after his 44th birthday in 1992, that he was "thinking about pulling out of the whole sticky mess and handing over his place in line to his son William."

His 1992 Solar Return certainly put marital affairs front and center (see chart opposite). His natal 7th House was rising; the Sun was in the 9th of legal matters and ruled the SR 7th. During both 1991 and 1992, Charles' progressed Jupiter (ruling his natal 5th House) was opposing Diana's natal Sun, showing a lack of rapport and amplifying their differences.

On December 9 of 1992 (see table, page 82), the Lunar Eclipse at almost 19 Gemini/Sagittarius was conjunct/opposed the Prince's natal Mars in the 5th House. His relationship with Camilla was reported to be heating up at this time; almost certainly it was more obvious to outsiders. On December 9, 1992, there was an official announcement that the marriage of Prince Charles and Princess Diana was at an end. The general assumption at that time, despite official denials, was that a quiet, no-fault divorce would follow in two or three years, leaving both parties free to remarry. In 1993, just prior to his birthday in November, there is a Solar Eclipse conjunct his Sun in the 4th, ruler of his 1st. It seems quite likely that around this time he will take some kind of affirmative action. In December of 1993 the Lunation at 21 Sagittarius will be conjunct Mars, ruler of his Midheaven. It is possible at this time that he could get back into the good graces of the public.

As far as resigning the throne, it is feasible that, if he does, it will be in April or May of 1994, when the Lunation is at 21 Aries quincunx his Sun, followed by the Eclipse at 19 Taurus 36 opposed his Sun, both from the 10th House of his public image and standing. [McEvers wrote this presentation in March 1993. —Ed.]

Princess Diana

Princess Diana was born July 1, 1961 at 7:45 P.M. GMD in San-dringham, England, 52N30 0E30, according to British astrologer, Charles Harvey, who quotes her mother (see chart, page 95).

Diana's Cancer Sun marks her as sensitive and emotional; its placement in the 7th House describes one who requires an equal partnership but who also enjoys a challenge and seeks confronta-tion. Since her Sun rules her 9th House, ceremony and rites intrigue her, and she did appear to relish the pomp and splendor of her world-ranging role as the Princess of Wales. Her Moon in Aquarius in the 3rd House opposes Uranus and squares Venus, ruler of the 10th, suggesting challenges in handling her public image, and it also characterizes a certain emotional vulnerability. Even though the Moon here can be quite detached, and at times even cold, the Cancer Sun/Mercury conjunction confirms her fragile disposition. As a Cancer Sun, Diana has a knack for maneuvering or manipulating to get what she wants, especially from her partner (Sun in the 7th House). Her Sagittarian Ascen-dant marks a need for independent action, and this is also revealed by the fact that Jupiter, the Ascendant ruler, is in Aquar-ius. It is true that Diana can march to the beat of a different band, let alone drummer.

The Yod from Jupiter in her 2nd House to Mercury in the 7th and Pluto in Virgo in the 9th, suggests that shifts, changes, and reorganization are normal for her. She endured the divorce of her parents, the ignominy of being shuttled off to various boarding schools, and a difficult relationship with her stepmother. She undoubtedly viewed her marriage to Prince Charles through rose-colored glasses (Mercury, ruler of the 7th House trine Nep-tune), expecting to live happily every after, but finding instead the cold, hard reality of a husband who was not very romantic and who had an ongoing "friendship" with another lady.

In March of 1992 when the book *Diana, Her True Story*, was published revealing the fractured fairy tale of the royal marriage, the Lunation was at 14 Pisces in her 3rd House. Her 1991 Solar Return (July 1991–July 1992) clearly highlighted her 5th House of romantic encounters. This book was the first disclosure of her relationship with James Gilbey, several suicide attempts, and her total lack of interest in her husband's polo playing, hunting, fish-ing, and love of classical music.

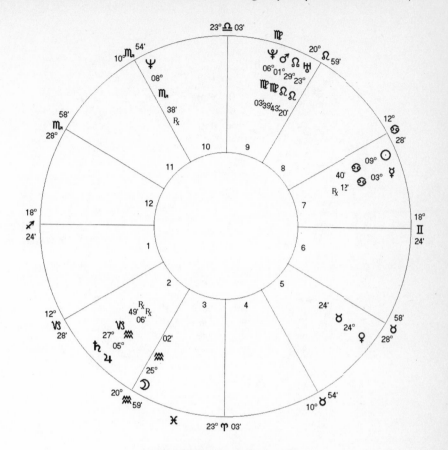

Diana, Princess of Wales
July 1, 1961, Sandringham, England
7:45 P.M. GMD
52N30 0E30
Koch Houses

Whether Diana's suicide attempts were serious or merely attention-getting cries for help, they were only the tip of an iceberg of unhappiness and dissatisfaction with a loveless marriage gone awry. When this information was made public, though it was devastating for her, she "toughed it out" and, in so doing, has endeared herself to a large part of the British public.

In her 1991 Solar Return chart (page 96), Taurus was rising in the SR chart with natal Venus in the 1st House and SR Venus in the 5th, square its natal position and conjunct natal Uranus and

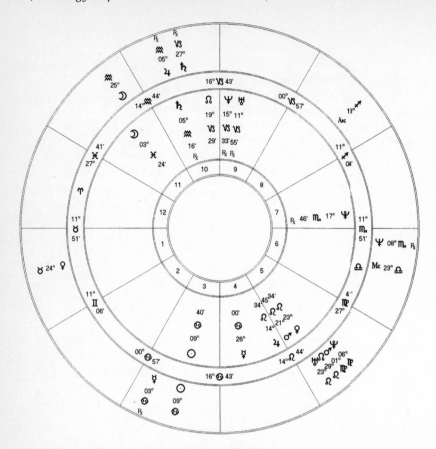

Diana, Princess of Wales
Solar Return 1991, Sandringham, England
52N30 0E30
Koch Houses

SR Mars, definitely indicators of the revelation of a love affair, as well as personal confusion and vulnerability. Though Diana seems to hold up well in public (natal Sun in the 7th House, well-aspected), the natal lunar aspects are intense and complex; she most likely learned at an early age that her emotional desires would seldom be met.

SR Saturn in and ruling the 10th is conjunct natal Jupiter ruler of her SR 8th, a sign of having to cope with a loss, even a possible death. Her Sun, representative of male relatives (father/ husband), is opposed by SR Uranus, portending unexpected events around a man in her life. Her father died suddenly early in April when she and Charles were in Austria with their two sons. In the month of April, her progressed Moon was at 13 Aries and *the Lunation that month was at 14 Aries conjuncting it!*

Diana's relationship with her father was especially tender and loving in spite of his old-style, aristocratic method of child-rearing. Her mother had run off with another man and left Diana and her siblings with her father when she was six years old. The highly charged aspects to the natal Moon as well as the Yod reflects the difficult relationship with her mother. Her father adored her and was very proud of the way she carried off her role of Princess with charm and poise. Natally, Venus rules her 10th House relating to the male parent and though Venus has some formidable aspects, it trines natal Saturn, the natural ruler of the 10th and reflects a strong bond with her 10th House parent. When her Ascendant, by Solar Arc direction quincunxed natal Venus, her parents divorced. Mars, ruler of her 4th House (mother) is in the Yod and conjuncted natal Pluto when her mother left.

Her 1992 Solar Return (see chart on page 98) finds the Sun in her 11th SR House, ruling the Ascendant which comes from her natal 8th, foretelling unexpected events (11th) and endings (8th). Natal Uranus is rising (highlighting her rebellious streak) and rules the 7th House of the Solar Return. It is opposed by transiting (SR) Saturn, which is in the 7th and widely squares her natal Venus, which is in the SR 10th. There is a Grand Cross for her to contend with: SR Pluto opposes natal Venus, triggering her natal T-Square involving Moon-Uranus and Venus. A T-Square is a very resistant aspect and it generates activity, the focal point of which is often focused in the empty house. The Grand Cross, on the other hand, is a frustrating configuration because it has no empty area for the energy to flow.

In Princess Diana's 1992 Solar Return chart, the Grand Cross formed (Moon-Venus and Venus-SR Pluto) involving her angular houses, suggesting that her quandary encompasses taking personal action (1st), home reorientation (4th), partnership issues (7th), and her public reputation and standing (10th). In her natal chart this Cross energizes her 3rd, 5th, 9th and 11th houses, totally different, but none-the-less challenging circumstances. Her social status could change (11th), legal and in-law matters could

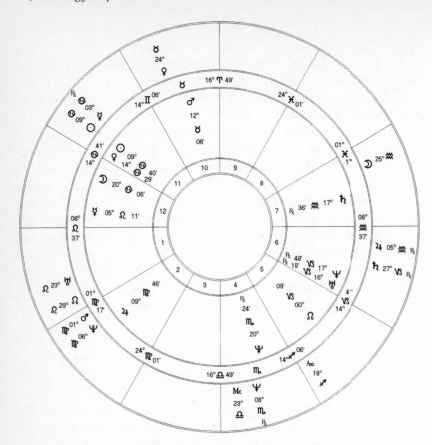

Diana, Princess of Wales
Solar Return 1992, Sandringham, England
52N30 0E30
Koch Houses

come into play (9th), love relationships and possibly children may cause concern (5th), while everyday or sibling relationships may need attention (3rd).

How has this all worked out for Diana? During the fall, two more books were published reporting her so-called romantic escapades (5th House) and, in August, the transcript of a 23-minute phone conversation between her and her close friend James Gilbey was aired in *The Sun*, revealing to the world that she answers to the nickname Squidgy; she describes life with Prince Charles as "real torture" and she sometimes catches the 92-year-old Queen Mum watching her "with a strange look in her eyes." Additionally, an ex-army lance corporal said he had witnessed decidedly indiscreet action between the Princess and her riding instructor, Major James Hewitt. The media hounds smelled blood and, by September 1, Diana's relationship with Hewitt had been feverishly dissected. Much of this is reflected in the 1992 Solar Return with the disconcerting configurations. In August, the Lunation at 5 Virgo was in her 9th natal House conjunct natal Pluto, ruler of her natal 11th and 12th Houses. Contacts to Pluto often reveal hidden events and situations as they did here. The 4 Libra Lunation in September was also in her 9th House, possibly prompting the comment about her in-law grand-mum.

Secondary Progressed Mercury, which natally is in and rules her 7th House, quincunxed the Moon in the 3rd, ruler of the natal 8th, clearly an indication of a change of partnership attitudes (7th), if not actual partners, and adjustments in her sexual feelings (8th) as well as her emotional disposition (Moon). Secondary Venus, which is in her 5th House natally and rules her 5th and 10th Houses, quincunxed natal Saturn in and ruling her 2nd. Besides the previously mentioned adjustments, she was faced with a need to reorganize her feelings of self-worth (2nd) and her romantic outlook (5th). Faced with the fact that the public certainly viewed her in a different light (10th), she undoubtedly did a lot of soul-searching in connection with her marriage to Charles, as well as with her place in the royal family.

With the Lunar Eclipse on December 9, 1992 at 18 Gemini/ Sagittarius, falling exactly across her natal Ascendant/Descendant, an announcement was made at 3:30 P.M., on that very day, of a royal separation between Princess Diana and Prince Charles. British Prime Minister John Major announced, "This decision has been reached amicably" and added that Princes William and Harry would "retain their position in the line of succession," and that "there is no reason why the Princess of Wales should not be crowned Queen in due course." It was announced that Diana would remain with the boys at Kensington Palace, while Charles will continue to spend time at Highgrove, his Gloustershire estate and while in London, he would stay at Clarence House, the Queen's residence. Clearly, all these events reflect what was going on in her horoscope and the timing is confirmed by the monthly lunations.

Her biographer, Andrew Morton, commented that he, for one, is betting on Diana's political instincts serving her well in the future. "She's building up an international platform for herself . . . A phoenix Princess will arise from the ashes of this whole crumbling mess of a monarchy." Solar Arc Moon sextiled Venus and Pluto trined Jupiter. These aspects surely helped Diana achieve a *coup de maitre* in the game of royal manipulation. Only time will tell how it will all work out.

Prince Andrew

Prince Andrew was born February 19, 1960 at 3:30 P.M. GMT in London, England 51N30 0W10, according to public records.

With a 0 degree Pisces Sun, Leo rising and the Moon in Scorpio, you can see the ties with both his mother's and brother Charles' charts. His Sun sextiles his mother's exactly; he shares a Leo Ascendant with the Prince of Wales, and his Scorpio Moon is in the 4th House like his brother's Sun. Furthermore, his Moon conjuncts his mother's Midheaven and Saturn. Although capable of arrogance (Leo rising), Andrew with his sensitive Pisces Sun seems more compassionate than either his brother or his mother. With the Sun in the 7th House, he is concerned for what other people think and feel; Uranus rising, however, shows a rebellious nature at times, and its wide square to the Moon, as well as the quincunx to Mercury, suggests a lack of tact and a proclivity for saying what he thinks, often without thinking. For much of his high-spirited life, Prince Andrew was known as Britain's playboy prince, the fun-loving escort of starlets and models and one of the world's most eligible bachelors, until he married childhood playmate, Sarah Ferguson, on July 23, 1986.

Jupiter, ruler of the free-wheeling, fun-loving 5th House is in it and trines Pluto, conjunct his 2nd House cusp and ruler of his 4th (Scorpio intercepted). Uranus in the 1st often indicates the person who struggles against tradition, and Andrew cut a wide swath in his pre-marriage years. When we consider all her children, the Queen is probably closer to and more indulgent of Andrew than she is of either Anne or Charles. His contacts with her chart are easier than those of his siblings. The 4th House Scorpio Moon though it activates his mother's T-Square, trines his Mercury, suggesting good lines of communication with her, as well as with women in general. Venus and Mars, rulers of his parental houses, are conjunct each other and sextile his Moon, reinforcing not only a close rapport with both parents, but also an ongoing accord with the public.

Always willing to play the role of the clown (Pisces Sun), Andrew captained the cricket team at prep school, but is probably best remembered for shinnying up the school flagpole and tying a shirt to it. When he was 13, like his father and brother before him, he enrolled at Gordonstoum School, known for its rugged education. He learned to fly a glider at age fifteen (Ascendant trine

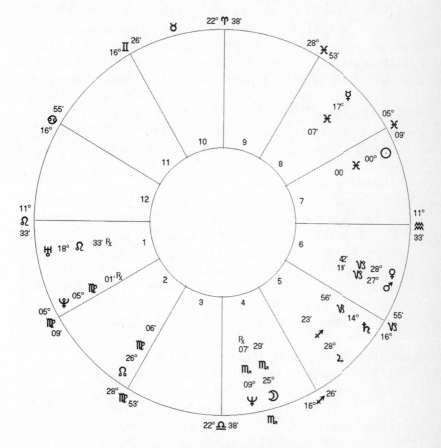

Prince Andrew, Duke of York
February 19, 1960, London, England
3:30 P.M. GMT
51N30 0W10
Koch Houses

Jupiter by Solar Arc), and engaged in sailing, rugby, canoeing, and shooting. He completed his education in Canada before joining the navy at age 19 when his progressed MC squared his Ascendant. It was around this time that he was said to have accumulated a circle of girlfriends who became known as "Andrew's Harem." During his naval career he was stationed in the Falkland Islands, where he acquitted himself well in the line of duty when he flew helicopters on dangerous missions against Argentine forces.

In a 1983 interview with David Frost, he referred to himself as a recluse and said "I try and keep out of people's way. I try and avoid the press." Spoken like a true Pisces Sun with Moon in Scorpio in the 4th House. But the 7th House placement of his Sun opposed to Pluto, as well as the rising Uranus square the Moon has fractured that concept. As a dashing bachelor, Andrew, when he wasn't indulging in romantic liaisons, learned photography and is also a talented landscape painter, parachutist, and wind-surfer. All of this is reflected in his natal chart: Pisces often has an interest in the arts; Jupiter in and ruling the 5th House in Sagit-tarius and Uranus in the 1st reinforce the love of outdoors and adventure.

With Uranus ruling his 7th House, Andrew needed a partner who was unique and unusual in some way, yet someone with whom he felt a strong rapport and whose needs were similar to his (Uranus in the 1st). With the Sun in the 7th, partnership seems necessary, but it is often difficult for him to realize that his part-ner's wishes are as important as his own. The opposition from Pluto can indicate willfulness and, at times, arrogance which is confirmed by the Leo Ascendant. With the Sun here, even with non-challenging aspects, it is necessary to learn to compromise.

Sarah (Fergie) Ferguson, Duchess of York

In many ways "Fergie" filled the bill for Andrew. She shared his sense of fun, and their relationship was strongly based on being good friends and enjoying life together. Her Aries Moon in the 5th House complements his Leo Ascendant and her Sun in Libra is a good match for his 7th House Sun. His Moon is in Scor-pio and she has a Scorpio Ascendant, so on a personal level (Ascendant) and emotional level (Moon) they could, and did, con-nect. These are astrological affinities that boded well for a good, long-lasting marriage. What happened?

The natal Moon decribes where we seek change. In Sarah's chart the Moon is in Aries in her 5th House of love and romance, and is the focal point of a Yod to Venus/Pluto and Mercury/Neptune. With a Libra Sun and a very active 12th House, she needs constant confirmation of love and affection, as well as affirmations of concern and tender reassurances of her appeal. Mars conjunct the Sun can be very sexual and in her chart Mars rules the 5th House of love affairs. Perhaps romantic/sexual affairs were

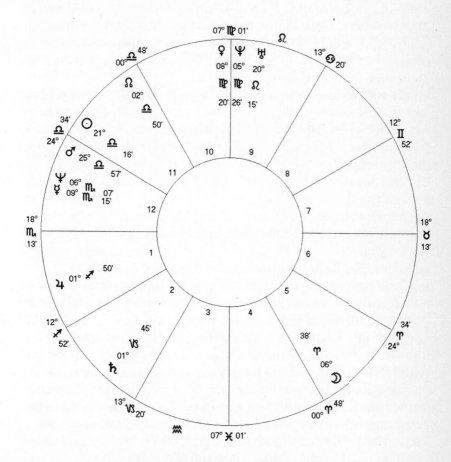

Sarah Ferguson, Duchess of York
October 15, 1959, London, England
9:03 A.M. GMT
51N30 0W10
Koch Houses

ways for her to assuage her self-doubts about her own self-worth (Saturn in the 2nd House).

Despite his reputation, Andrew has often described himself as a lonely recluse who enjoys his own company. His assignment as a naval officer keeps him away from home for long periods of time, and during one of these periods, Fergie, who was no doubt feeling neglected, became friendly with Texan Steve Wyatt. In March of 1991, when Andrew was at sea, she invited Wyatt to Buckingham Palace to a joint birthday party for the Queen Mother, Princess Margaret, Princess Anne, and Prince Andrew in March of 1991. She had met him when she was five months pregnant with Eugenie, when she accepted his mother's invitation to stay in her Houston home. When the Queen took her to task about her friendship with Wyatt, she complained that she was lonely for Andrew. She was already on the royal "list" after her trip to Australia after Bea's birth, when she prolonged her stay to six weeks when the baby was only a few weeks old. The public's enchantment with the Duchess of York took a dramatic turn for the worse in 1992.

In January when Queen Elizabeth discussed her public behavior with her, the Progressed Moon was at 9 degrees Aries in her 5th House (affairs) quincunx natal Mercury in the 12th House of clandesine relationships, although Fergie's relationships were not very covert.

Her 1991 Solar Return chart (on page 105) has 13 Virgo 31 rising, bringing strong attention to her natal 10th House. When this house is prominent in the yearly return, reputation and public behavior are highlighted. This year marked the end of the Duchess' affair with the British public. She had endeared herself to them in the early years of her marriage to Prince Andrew, but as the children arrived and the separations continued between the pair, she found ways to amuse herself which did not please her former partisans. Her SR Sun was in the 2nd House and rules the 12th, suggesting that she needed to reevaluate (2nd) on an inner level (12th). Her natal Yod was triggered by SR Venus/Jupiter conjunct natal Venus/Pluto. The natal Moon is in the SR 7th and the quincunxed planets are in the 12th and 2nd/3rd suggesting that reorganization of her private life (12th), public life and partnership (7th), as well as her values and comportment (2nd/3rd) needed some overhauling.

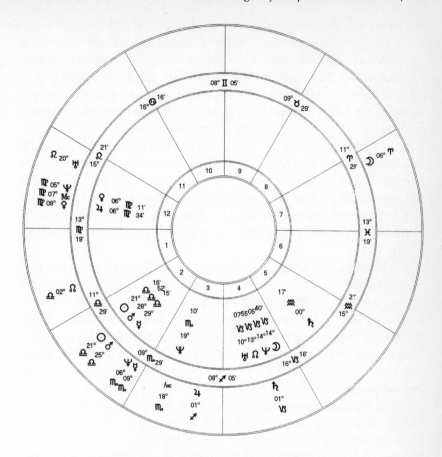

Sarah Ferguson, Duchess of York
Solar Return 1991, London, England
51N30 0W10
Koch Houses

Secondary Progressed Mars conjuncted her natal Ascendant, almost always an aspect that precipitates action, often ill-advised. With the square from natal Uranus to natal Ascendant, some unexpected events could occur. By Secondary Progression her natal Jupiter square Venus had become exact from the natal 1st House to the natal 10th. Quite obviously, her public was not necessarily viewing her with adoration and love as they have in the past. The progressed Moon was moving through her 7th and 8th Houses, focusing her emotional and mental energy in the partnership area and then into the house of sharing and sex. In March of 1992, when she and Andrew separated for the first time, the Lunation was at 14 Pisces in her 4th House, heralding a change in home situations. In May, when they separated permanently, the New Moon was at 12 Taurus close to the 7th cusp but in her 6th House. It seems obvious that her habit pattern (6th) would change, considering that she moved from a palace to a normal, everyday house.

In October, when the Duchess of York, buffetted by scandal and scorn, broke down in public, the Lunation was at 2 Scorpio in her 12th House. With the New Moon here it is usually advisable to keep a low profile, recharge your batteries, take time by yourself to be quiet and reflective. This was when Fergie began treatment for depression at a well-known London psychology clinic (12th House).

How has this affected Prince Andrew? When they separated for the first time in March, the New Moon in Pisces was in his 8th House, an indicator that the backing and support he receives from others as well as his financial affairs and sex life would be highlighted. The final separation in May found the New Moon in his 10th House focusing on status, reputation, and possibly the end of the marriage (4th of the 7th). This Lunation opposed his 4th House Neptune at 9 Scorpio, a very obvious change on the home scene. Neptune rules his natal 8th, again emphasizing all 8th House situations. Andrew has kept a low profile through all the acrimonious reports about his wife's liaisons with her various amours. It has been reported lately that the couple is seeing each other socially. Is a reconciliation in the offing? Perhaps, in view of the basic harmony and accord in their natal charts.

Princess Anne

Princess Anne of England was born August 15, 1950 at 11:50 A.M. GMD in London, England, according to public records.

A Leo, Anne expresses her sports and fun-loving Sun through her social Libra Ascendant. With three planets in Virgo, including her Moon, she is known for her attention to detail and her commitment to causes. The most willful and self-motivated (seven planets east of the horizon) of all the Queen's children, it is not surprising that she would be the first to divorce and remarry. It is interesting that while her brothers, Charles and Andrew, have Sun square and opposed Pluto, respectively, she is the royal with the Sun conjunct

Pluto, an aspect of great tenacity as well as a certain arrogance and resolution. With Neptune rising sextile Sun and Pluto, what you see is not always what you get with the Princess. She has an ability to dissemble and play whatever role is required of her.

Her love of horses is visible with Jupiter in Pisces in her 5th House. As the handle of her Fan Pattern chart, Jupiter is highlighted (all the energy of the other nine planets is focused into Jupiter) and is in a Grand Trine with Uranus and Mars, revealing an easy emotional attitude and ability for physical action (the

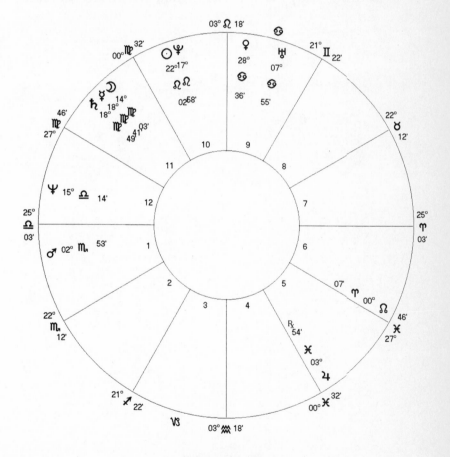

Princess Anne
August 15, 1950, London, England
11:50 A.M. GMD
51N30 0W10
Koch Houses

trine is in the houses held by Fire signs in the natural distribution of signs). Anne is an accomplished equestrienne and is the only member of the family to ride competitively, another reflection of the Sun/Pluto conjunction.

Mars rules her 7th House of partnership and is in the 1st, suggesting that she may at times try to dominate any one-on-one relationship. Mars square Venus in the 10th can imply rather stormy going in partnership areas, in spite of its placement in the Grand Trine which, according to astrological lore, suggests a long, enduring, happy relationship. Anne's marriage to Mark

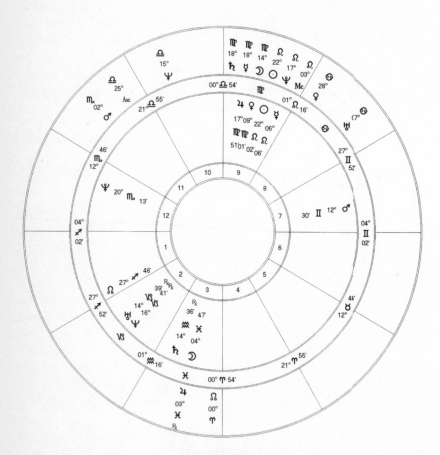

Princess Anne
Solar Return 1992, London, England
51N30   0W10
Koch Houses

Phillips in 1973 produced two children and, for the first few years, they seemed quite happy. By 1980, however, each apparently had decided to cultivate separate friendships. They parted in August of 1989 and divorced in April, 1992 after a proper two-year waiting period. On December 12, 1992, Anne married a second time. Her current spouse is Cmdr. "Tiger" Tim Laurence, a dashingly handsome officer commander of the frigate HMS Boxer.

How appropriate that in April of 1992, the Lunation at 14 Aries was conjunct Anne's 7th cusp when she received her divorce decree. At the time of Anne's second marriage, the Lunar Eclipse at 18 Gemini 13 on December 9, 1992 fell across her 9th/3rd axis, an apt time for a second legal commitment. But the Eclipse alone is certainly not enough to promote a marriage. In her SR for 1992 (see page 108) the Sun is in the 9th House in a T-Square with SR Pluto square her natal Sun/Pluto and SR Saturn opposing it. SR Jupiter is conjunct her Virgo stellium and the SR Moon on her birthday conjuncted natal Jupiter, activating her Grand Trine, which includes the ruler of the partnership 7th, Mars. Quite an auspicious array for a royal wedding!

Secondary Progressed Venus was conjunct natal Saturn, possibly a portent of a long and loyal relationship; her Ascendant sextiled the natal Moon, implying happy emotional expression. Her progressed Moon in Pisces was moving through her 6th House, and, though it did not make an aspect in December, it trined Venus in February of 1993.

The Solar Arc aspects were many and varied: I hope the foregoing look at a year in the life of a famous, but troubled, family was a learning experience in regard to using Lunations and Eclipses as astrological timing factors. This is the easiest and quickest way I have found to time events, and it works well with transits and the Secondary Progressed Moon to pinpoint possible months when certain actions may take place. However, I am not the kind of astrologer who tries for specific timing. Hitting a month seems accurate enough to me. And I always explain to my clients that if I say something could happen in August, they had better start watching in late July and certainly be aware that it could take place in early September.

Michael Erlewine

Michael Erlewine is a computer programmer and the Director of Matrix Software, the largest center for astrological programming and research in the Western hemisphere. Michael has been a practicing astrologer for 30 years, with an international reputation in the field. His original contributions to astrology include the Local Space astrolocality technique and Interface Nodes, and he is a modern pioneer in heliocentric astrology. His books include *Astrophysical Directions*, *Manual of Computer Programming for Astrologers*, and *Interface Nodes*. He is the editor of the *Matrix Journal*, a technical research journal for astrologers, and of the ongoing *Astro Index Encyclopedia* project. He has won the PAI Award from Professional Astrologers, Inc.

Michael Erlewine is active in Tibetan Buddhism and serves as the director of Heart Center Karma Thegsum Chîling, a main center in North America for the translation, transcription, and publication of texts and teachings of the Karma Kagyu lineage of Tibetan Buddhism. Michael is also a music buff and has edited and published the *All-Music Guide*, a 1200-page reference of 23,000 rated recordings of over 6,000 musicians in 26 categories of music, with definitive commentary from over 80 of today's most respected music reviewers. The *All-Music Guide* is more than a book—it is an ongoing database project, which will soon be available as an on-line service in record stores, and as a CD-ROM.

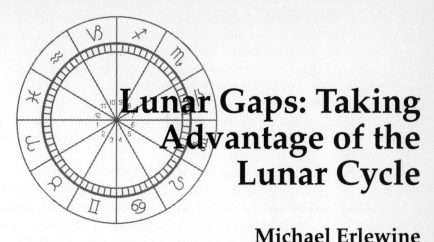

Lunar Gaps: Taking Advantage of the Lunar Cycle

Michael Erlewine

The phases of the Moon have been observed for ages. The "Moon," from a Sanskrit term for "measure," is the primary means by which the majority of the people in the world (even in the 20th century!) measure time and events in their own lives. This article takes a look at what astrologers (and ordinary people) have come to understand about the lunation cycle—the phases of the Moon. In particular, we will contrast methods of using the lunar cycle in the East and in the West.

Lunation Cycle in Western Astrology

Eastern and Western astrologies use the lunar cycle in both the same and different ways. In the West, the lunar cycle is most often seen as a key to the personality and the birth chart. While books such as Rudhyar's *The Lunation Cycle* and many others describe the cycle as a dynamic process that unfolds each month, the practical orientation of their focus is not so much with this day-to-day process as it is with individual snapshots (the various lunar types) extracted from the overall process. And then there are also books along the lines of William Butler Yeats' *A Vision*. This extremely involved intellectual study attempts to deal with concepts of anima and animus, the endless process of psychological self-projection and its resolution. Although somewhat a mental challenge, analogous to a tongue-twister in speech, the practical benefit to this kind of writing is questionable. In this article we will not deal with these highly intellectual approaches to the Moon. First, let's take a quick look at how the Moon has been considered in Western astrology. Here is a summary, as any competent astrologer might present it to us:

The phases of the Moon are known to all. From the dark of the New Moon, the cycle builds through 1st Quarter and on to the brightness of the Full Moon (start of 3rd Quarter), after which the lunar light begins to diminish. After the Full Moon, as the Moon's light starts to fail, comes the quarter Moon phase, which rapidly darkens until the New Moon. The lunar cycle is perhaps the easiest to grasp of all astrological cycles. It is longer than the cycle of a day and shorter than the cycle of a year—both of which are hard to keep in mind.

As mentioned, the lunar cycle extends from the New Moon (Moon and Sun conjunct the same point in the zodiac) through the Full Moon (Moon and Sun on opposite sides of the Earth), and back to another New Moon. The New Moon point is considered a time of conception and beginning, the Full Moon a time of fruition and fullness. It is often stated in the astrological literature that a seed idea, impulse, or insight present at the New Moon is externalized through the first two quarters (waxing Moon) and reaches completion or fullness at the Full Moon. After the Full Moon, the implications or "meaning" of what was achieved through the externalization process of the waxing Moon is realized, the lesson is learned, and preparation takes place for a new and perhaps perfected idea to form at the next New Moon.

Keep in mind that the cycle of the Moon resembles *all* cycles (the heartbeat, the breath, the day, the year, etc.); the cycle has a point of greatest inwardness or conception (New Moon, inhalation-point), and a point of greatest externalization or fullness (Full Moon, exhalation-point). Projects begun at the New Moon are said to reach fulfillment at the Full Moon. The first two quarters (when the Moon is waxing and growing with light) represent a period of striving and building into reality a project that was conceived around the time of the New Moon. This is the time to project outward and to make real something we have visualized in our minds. We all have projects—a new effort, a new lawn, a new start, a new anything.

In the Western tradition, the time period from the New Moon through the 1st Quarter is good for making this push from an insight outward, making our dreams into reality. The New Moon point is a time for vision and a new seed impulse. The 2nd quarter (end of the 1st) represents a crisis in action when we must carry our new impulse or idea beyond the planning stage and into the sphere of action, a time when the idea breaks into reality and is launched. The 1st Quarter is a time to get underway and to figure out how to make our dreams (ideas) come true.

The end of the 1st Quarter and beginning of the 2nd Quarter marks that point in the lunar cycle when we are able to bring across some portion of an insight or idea into reality. The 2nd Quarter through the Full Moon (beginning 3rd Quarter) represents the time when we achieve outward realization or actualization of what we saw or felt at the New Moon impulse. It is a time for physical work and externalization. It is during the 2nd Quarter that we put into our project the energy and material that give it substance and form.

The Full Moon marks outward extension and completion of the project. For better or worse, this is it! If we have tuned into the insight available at the New Moon—and if we have worked to that end—the Full Moon can represent a time of fruition and completion. What we have dreamed or seen in the mind is now real and can be experienced in the flesh. If we have worked at cross purposes to the New Moon message, then the Full Moon might bring home that fact as well. We can reap the reward of our misguided effort. Above all, the Full Moon represents an experience—a fullness, if you will.

The 3rd Quarter is a time during which we can appreciate, enjoy, and begin to reflect on the experience that peaked at the time of the Full Moon. This quarter is traditionally a time for learning and assimilation. The Full Moon impact and experience begin to pass, and we find ourselves having thoughts about that experience. If nothing more, we sense that the experience is over and is passing. Reflection occurs. We begin to grasp and appreciate the Full Moon experience, for better or for worse. As the lunar light begins to diminish, we start drawing conclusions of one sort or another.

The start of the 4th Quarter marks a crisis in consciousness. The experience of the Full Moon is over, and we are left to draw whatever conclusions we can from it. It is during the 4th Quarter that we prune and weed out from our lives what we have seen to be of no value or use in this experience. It is a time for constructive elimination and release. It is often referred to as a "seed time," and it is here that we keep or take to heart the seed or kernel of the experience we had at the full of the Moon. We are drawing that experience to a close, along with the entire month's cycle. We are approaching another New Moon and the start of a new cycle and impulse.

Since we are dealing with a cycle or circle, there is no real beginning or end. All circles or cycles are endless or eternal (eternally repeating). The lunar cycle (phases of the Moon) is something that we can learn to use. After we read about and become aware of the different parts of this cycle, we can begin to observe the cycle happening around us. The lunar cycle described above in theory is seldom experienced in such clarity in everyday life. Over time, we recognize parts of the cycle and learn to use them. For example, we might find it hard to push or begin projects during the 4th quarter (in particular the three days or so just before a New Moon). But this time is a good time to finish up a project, or to clean up loose odds and ends of business, draw things to a close. We could find that get-togethers, parties, and social events seem to come off well around or just before the Full Moon.

We learn to take advantage of the qualities and opportunites of each section of the Moon cycle. And we don't have to wait to begin, since we are already—right now—somewhere in that cycle. What we develop then is an awareness of the Moon cycle.

Seed Impulse: Lunar Themes

An important concept to grasp is that the lunar cycle is experienced by all. The seed insight or impulse available at the New Moon is open to each of us. It is a global experience belonging to the entire planet. Although we may take it personally and in our own way, it is, above all, a common experience. Each passing month or lunar cycle modifies this experience and presents a new or slightly altered theme or impulse at New Moon for us to consider. Endless variations on the theme, this seed-thought or impulse, somehow set the tone for succeeding lunar cycles. The moments of New and Full Moon are considered special. This is particularly true at the time of an eclipse.

Eclipses

Eclipses are simply New or Full Moons with extraordinary alignment or focus. For centuries, they have been considered to be astrological events of the first magnitude. If we consider New and Full Moons to be important, then eclipses represent the keys to the lunar cycle for any year.

We mentioned earlier about the New Moon containing an impulse or insight that grows to fruition at the Full Moon. Eclipses, then, provide moments when extraordinary insight or vision is available to us. It is possible for some of us, at least at certain times in our lives, to experience what has been called the vision of the eclipse, and to remember or keep that vision in mind. There appears to be a theme or principle insight connected with major eclipses.

Let me make clear just what we mean here by the word vision. "Vision" does not mean the fairytale dream picture we might conjure up, but it is related: a vision is a moment of extreme clarity or understanding when, "in a flash," we know or experience something in its entirety. We take it in.

There are times in each of our lives when we "have vision," or become aware of some intrinsic truth about our lives, about life in general. As mentioned earlier, there appears to be a common or communal vision that occurs around the time of major eclipses. While each of us interprets the insight or vision in a personal way, the theme or essence of the vision is a common (global, if you will) experience. And it is possible to share that vision. Although we all experience it at once, only some of us are capable of remembering the experience in a conscious fashion. It seems that we are privileged to be consciously aware of the vision of an eclipse at special or crucial moments in our lifetimes, times when we are particularly aware.

The message or vision of any given eclipse will tend to dominate our deeper or subconscious minds for months surrounding that eclipse. It is a peculiarity of these eclipse moments that they can happen days or even weeks before or after the actual moment of an eclipse. That is, the eclipse theme pervades the time prior to and after the actual physical event.

Often, eclipses happen in pairs, two weeks apart. These are particularly powerful, and the whole time between these events can be a kind of waking vision. Learning to recognize a moment of vision and taking advantage of these enhanced moments of vision surrounding an eclipse can be important. If the point in the zodiac where an eclipse occurs is in high focus in your natal chart, then the particular eclipse may have special importance for you.

In general, eclipses of the Sun (New Moons) represent vision into the nature of our life (ideas about life), while eclipses of the Moon (Full Moons) represent a waking experience or sensational event (life in our own dream).

Lunar Astrology from an Eastern Perspective

There is general agreement (East and West) about the nature of the lunation cycle, its archetype, in that it proceeds from some sort of seed time at the New Moon to a fruition at the Full Moon, as we have just reviewed. The lunar cycle endlessly expands and contracts, bearing forth and taking back, creating and destroying. Given this fact and the tradition that has built up around it, those in the East who study the lunar cycle seek to take advantage of this regular cycle and its very regular opportunities. In the West, this very practical knowledge has either been lost or never really accumulated. It is hard to tell. My guess is that it has never been studied here in as much detail as in the East.

The East seldom mentions the individual birth chart. The primary interest in the East is in the dynamics of the lunation cycle itself, which is divided up and analyzed in great detail in order to make use of the opportunities it offers for day-to-day decision-making. In other words, in the East, the lunar cycle is used as a means to determine the kind of activity appropriate for each successive lunar day. *This amounts to a form of electional astrology.*

In the West, electional astrology is thought of as a means of picking an appropriate time in the future for a particular ceremony or happening. Eastern astrology also uses electional astrology in this manner, but more often it uses electional astrology as a guide to day-to-day personal living and practice. Rather than concern itself with what lunar type a given phase of the Moon might produce (birth chart), oriental astrology asks *"What is the current lunar phase good for?* What kind of action is auspicious (or not) today?" In India and Tibet, it is the lunation cycle rather than the yearly Sun or solar cycle that is the primary reference used to plan activities and guide personal decisions. In the East, people live by and follow the cycle of the Moon on a day-to-day basis.

A very clear illustration of this idea is the fact that, in most Eastern countries, birthdays are observed according to the particular day of the Moon cycle (lunar phase angle) during which a person was born, rather than according to the solar return, as here in the West. If we celebrate your birthday in Nepal, we celebrate that phase of the Moon (the lunar day) you were born in. Moreover, due to the fact that lunar months do not fit nicely within the solar year, a birthday in the East for any given individual can be up to a month away (during some years) from the solar return, our Western-style birthday. This simple fact makes it clear how important the Moon and the lunar cycle are in these countries. A study of the existing literature on the meaning and use of the Moon in astrology (East and West) shows much similarity, but also considerable difference.

The Moon receives more attention in Eastern astrology. And it is not just a matter of increased emphasis: there are major qualitative differences in approach. The emphasis is seldom on the type of individual that typifies a given lunar phase. Instead, it is on analyzing the entire lunar cycle in order to take advantage of its ongoing opportunities, to use the Moon cycle for living. This Eastern approach is *very* practical.

Eastern astrologers use the lunar cycle to gauge and measure their lives. They have learned how to take advantage of the opportunities they have discovered within the lunation cycle. This is an important concept to grasp. They conceive of these opportunities as *gaps,* as articulation points, much like an elbow where the arm is articulated. These gaps are natural joints in time/space upon which time and space turn, and through which it is sometimes possible to gain access to information about the larger, dynamic life process that already envelops us.

Eastern literature on this subject perceives life as being filled with the noise of our problems (obscurations), often making clear insight difficult. These obscurations can be many and their accumulation amounts to the sum total of our ignorance, i.e., that which we ignore. Therefore, in Eastern astrology, these articulation points or windows in time/space, these gaps are very much to be valued. In fact, Eastern astrologers analyze the lunar cycle, in minute detail, in order to isolate these moments, the gaps in time/space where insight into our larger situation can be gained. Much of so-called Eastern religion amounts to a scheduling of precise times for personal practice or activity built around the natural series of gaps that can be found in the continuous lunar cycle. In its own way, it is a very scientific approach. In the East, they have been astute observers for many centuries.

Tithis and Lunar Gaps

In India and Tibet, the 29.5-day lunar synodic cycle is divided into 30 parts, called tithis. A tithi or lunar day is the time it takes for the aspect between the Sun and Moon (elongation, angular separation) to reach a multiple of 12 degrees. Thus each tithi is 12 degrees of solunar angular separation.

It might interest readers to know that each tithi is further subdivided into two parts, called karanas, and that this additional subdivision finds wide use in India, Tibet, and other Eastern countries. However, for the purposes of this article, the division of the lunar cycle into 30 parts or lunar days will suffice.

Tithis are measured as follows: the moment of the New Moon (0 degrees angular solunar separation) marks the end of the 30th lunar day and the start of the first. The first lunar day, or tithi ends at 12 degrees of solunar separation, and the 2nd lunar day begins. And so it goes, on and around.

What is interesting about how the lamas (and most Hindus too) view this 30-day cycle is *that the 30 lunar days are not considered of equal importance.* The monthly cycle has very definite points in it of increased importance, and these points are the lunar gaps. It is at these lunar gaps or openings that it is possible to get special insight into different areas of one's own life. In fact, the Tibetans take full advantage of these lunar gaps to perform very specific practices. That is, certain of the lunar days have proven themselves to be auspicious for particular kinds of activities.

In the East, they speak of mental obscurations that tend to cloud our minds, but that can sometimes clear up, just as the Sun can reappear from behind the clouds. Therefore, in Eastern countries, these lunar gaps are very much valued. In fact, the Eastern approach is to analyze the lunar cycle in minute detail in order to isolate these moments where insight into our larger situation can be gained.

Here in the West, we are no stranger to clear days in our mind. We have those too! The only difference is that we tend to believe that these so-called clear days appear *randomly,* every now and then. The more sophisticated (and ancient) psychological analysis of the East has found that these clear days are (for the most part) *anything but random events.* They have their own internal ordering, and oftentimes this ordering can be associated with the phases of the Moon.

There are times each month when it is more auspicious or appropriate to perform or be involved in one kind or another of activity. These are the gaps in the general obscuration or cloudiness of our mind when we can see through the clouds, when penetrating insight is possible. Knowing when and where to look for these insight gaps has been the subject of study and research in Tibet for centuries.

And this is not just academic research, reserved for the pundits. *Everyone* uses the lunar calendar on a regular basis. Lunar gaps are used to plan a wide variety of events in the Tibetan calendar, everything from finding a time to perform a simple healing ceremony to full-scale empowerments.

Aside from knowing when these lunar gaps can be experienced, the other major thing to know about this subject is what to do *when* the gaps occur. As you might imagine, there are a wide range of practices, depending on the particular lunar gap (phase) and the personal needs of the practitioner. However, in general, these lunar gap times are set aside for special observation. Tibetans observe these days with great attention and care. In fact, in many Eastern countries, Saturday and Sunday are not holidays; instead, New and Full Moon days are considered holy days (holidays), and normal routines are suspended at these times.

This word "observation" is worth our pause here. In the West, we might use the word meditation. In Tibet, there are many words that come under the general concept of meditation. The

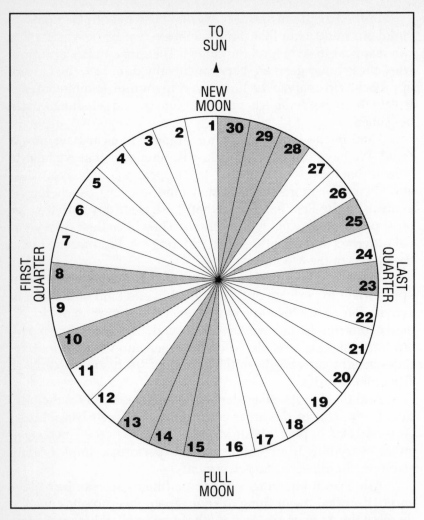

TO
SUN
▲
NEW
MOON

FULL
MOON

word "observe" is a lot closer to what happens during these lunar gaps. OBSERVE the nature of the day. OBSERVE your mind at that time. Be alert, be present, and set that time aside for just examining yourself, your mind, the time . . . what-have-you? It is while being present—observing these seed times—that the so-called lunar gap can show itself.

And lest we get too far afield sitting there waiting for a gap in time or space to occur, let me restate: the gap that appears is a gap *in our particular set of obscurations,* our own cloudiness. When such a gap takes place, there can be an intense insight into some aspect of our situation, the effects of which stay with us for a long time. One moment of real insight or vision can take weeks or months to examine in retrospect. Each time we bring it to mind, its richness is such that it continues to be a source of inspiration. This is what lunar gaps are all about.

Although measuring time and life by the Moon is ancient, it is more than just some primitive sort of clock. The very sophisticated concept of lunar gaps springs from centuries of painstaking psychological observation by the Tibetan lamas and the Hindu sages. They practice it today with the same vigor and intensity as they did a thousand years ago. Unlike many other traditions, where the line of successors (lineage) has been broken due to various events, the dharma tradition of Tibet remains pure and unbroken to this day.

Although much of the Tibetan dharma tradition requires dedication and intense practice, learning to use the Moon's phases and the concept of lunar gaps is easy to get into. The theory is simple. It involves the ongoing relationship between the Sun, the Moon, and the Earth, the monthly cycle of the phases of the Moon. We already know about the Moon cycle, and can even walk outside at night and see which lunar phase we are in.

This is not the place (and I am not the expert) to describe to you either the very complicated astronomical motions these three heavenly bodies produce, or the profound theories of what all of this motion means in a philosophical sense. However, what is quite accessible to us is this concept of lunar gaps.

Quarter Moons and Specific Lunar Days

It seems that, although East and West agree on the importance of New and Full Moons, there is less congruence when it comes to the Quarter Moons. Here in the West, the lunar Quarters are next in importance after the New and Full Moon times. However, in the East there are other days that are considered of greater importance, such as the 10th and 25th lunar days.

In both traditions, there is agreement that the two or three days preceding the moment of the New Moon are difficult ones that require special observation. In the West, these days have been called the dark of the Moon, or devil's days, days when the darker forces have power. Both traditions affirm that we sort of survive these final days each month. Check it out for yourself. The three days before the New Moon can be a hard time. The

East is in total agreement on this point, and the days prior to the New Moon are set aside for invoking the fierce dharma protectors, those energies that ward off harm and protect us during the worst of times.

In particular, the 29th day (the day before New Moon) is called dharma protector day. It is a time given over to purification and preparation for the moment of New Moon. Ritual fasting, confession of errors, and the like are common practices. In a similar vein, the days just prior to the Full Moon (the 13th and 14th) are also days of purification, days in which the various guardian and protector deities are again invoked, but in a somewhat more restrained way. For example, the 14th day is often given over to fire *puja*, a ritual purification. During the days prior to Full and New Moon, there is some attempt at purification, both physical and mental, in preparation for the auspicious events soon to come.

The times of the New and Full Moon are considered of great importance, days set aside for special rituals and worship. The Full and New Moons (Full more than New) are times of collective worship and public confession. In many traditions, the monks and priests assemble for a day of special observance. In the East, the Full Moon celebration and the entire waxing lunar fortnight are oriented to the masculine element in consciousness, what are called the father-line deities. The New Moon and the waning fortnight are given over to the mother-line deities and the feminine element. The Full Moon completes the masculine, or active, waxing phase of the cycle, and the New Moon completes the feminine, waning phase of the month. To my knowledge, this kind of analysis does not exist in the West.

In addition to the New and Full Moon, the two most auspicious lunar days in the East are the 10th and the 25th. The 10th day (108 degrees to 120 degrees), called Daka Day, is considered auspicious for invoking the father-line deities, the masculine. The 25th day (288 degrees to 300 degrees), called Dakini Day, is given over to the feminine principle and the mother line deities. These two days, the 10th and the 25th, are formal feast days, days of observation when extra offerings are made and increased attention is given to what is happening. There is some sense of celebration at these points in the month. In many respects, these two days even rival the New and Full Moon days in importance. The fact is that these four days (New, Full, 10th, 25th) are the primary auspicious days as practiced in many Eastern rituals.

There are many other days of lesser importance, which might also interest Western astrologers. Health and healing are important in Eastern ritual, and the 8th and 23rd days of the lunar month are auspicious for this purpose. It is these days that straddle the first and last lunar quarters. The 8th day (84 degrees to 96 degrees) is often called Medicine Buddha Day. Again this occurs in the male, or father-line, half of the month. The 23rd day (264 degrees to 276 degrees), occurring in the feminine half of the month, is dedicated to Tara practice. Tara is the female deity connected to health, long life, and healing in general.

Earlier, we mentioned the days given over to purification, most prominently the 13th and the 29th. In addition, on a lesser scale, the 9th and the 19th days are also noted as days when the protector deities should be invoked and kept in mind. These, too, are days of purification. And there are more, still finer subdivisions that are made.

In this brief chapter, these major observance days are enough to give us the idea of how Eastern astrologers approach the lunar cycle. It should be kept in mind that, in the East, astrology is practiced by the general public. So it is not just astrologers who are using the lunar days; *everyone* observes these days.

The Value to Us—Mind Practice

We might ask ourselves how this Eastern approach to the lunation cycle might be of value in the West. As mentioned earlier, a major fact is that the lunar cycle is perceived as having a variety of gaps, joints, or points of articulation that can be used. These gaps can be seen as chinks in the armor of our particular obscurations. Many Western mystery traditions also observe the times of the Full (and sometimes the New) Moon. Full Moon meditations are common. The Quarter Moons are given less attention, and few Western rituals exist (to my knowledge) for these events.

It is an intuitive fact that moments of clarity, these gaps for insight, do come in the course of living. What Eastern astrology suggests to us is that many of these gaps are not just random events that occur in our life, haphazardly. They are *regular oppor-*

tunities, joints in the nick of time, when insights are somehow *more possible* than at other times. Therefore, it is common practice to set aside some portion of these special days for observance, for meditation.

The lunar cycle and its gaps are available to everyone, all the time. If we don't observe these special times, it is because we have set no time aside to observe, to check it out for ourselves. In the East, most people are introduced to basic observation techniques or mind practice at a very early age. It is unfortunate that mind practice is not much known of here in the West. I mean, how many people do you know who practice observing or using their mind anyway? Most of us assume that the mind is perfectly usable just as we find it, and doesn't require any practice!

In Tibet, mind practice is not only acceptable, it is pretty much obligatory. This is true for countries such as Tibet, Nepal, much of India, and even parts of China and Japan. Over there, the mind is considered by nature to be unruly and hard to manage. No one would think of trying to do much with it without considerable practice. Mind practice or mind preparation or training, as it is sometimes called, is standard fare in the orient.

We might wonder why this style of mind practice has never caught on in North America. In part, this is due to our whole take on meditation and what we think that is. Meditation in the West has come to mean something almost like relaxation therapy, a way to relax and get away from it all, to escape the worries of the world in the contemplation of some inner landscape. Somewhere, perhaps early in this century, the word meditation lost any semblance to its Eastern counterpart and became what most understand as meditation today: a way to relax and get rid of tension.

Of course, this is nothing like the Tibetan concept of mind practice or mind preparation, which involves the intense use of the mind. Let me clarify what it is that the Tibetan Buddhists (and other groups too) do when they sit down on their cushions. In general, if you ask *them* what they are doing, the answer will not be that they are "practicing" or that they are "sitting." But, indeed, *that* is what takes place. They sit, and they observe.

There are many Tibetan words for the different kinds of mind practice that are possible, while in the West we have just the one word: meditation. The most important difference between sitting practice (mind practice), and meditation as it is understood in this country, is that mind practice is anything but relaxing or passive. It is very active.

The actual technique is quite simple, taking only a few minutes to learn. And it is worth getting this instruction from someone authorized to give it. Most Buddhist and some Hindu groups offer this type of mind practice. When looking for training in mind practice, be sure to ask for a technique that emphasizes concentration on the present moment—being present—and not some of the more dreamy relaxation techniques. What you need in order to use lunar gaps is to become very alert and observant. The technique is called Shamata training in Tibetan Buddhism, and Zazen in Zen Buddhism. I would be happy to send a list of well-respected centers to anyone who writes to me at 315 Marion Avenue, Big Rapids, MI 49307. It is important that you receive instruction from someone trained in the technique, and get an authentic connection with a tradition.

When the Eastern mind meditates on special lunar days, it sets aside a time to observe with great care *the nature of that particular day*. Meditation, as taught in Tibet and Japan, is a technique that increases our abilities to observe. The meditator is not lost in deep inner space; that is our Western take on the concept of meditation. In the East, the meditator is right here, now, observing the mind and life. This is why it is said that these special days are days set aside for observation.

Here in the West, we are beginning to learn these techniques of observation. By setting aside a time on these special lunar days for observation, we can be open and aware to the possibilities of insight. This kind of awareness appears to be what is required to pick up on these natural events. If we have an insight at one of these times, we might be more willing to give it credence, knowing that it is happening on such-and-such a lunar day. And so on.

It is quite clear from the Eastern teachings that the moments of Full and New Moon are times when the various channels in the psychophysical body are somehow aligned. This is not to say that the New or Full Moon days are days of peace and quiet. It is taught in the East that, although a New or Full Moon day may tend to be wild or hectic, any patience or forbearance we can muster at that time will be much rewarded. In other words, there can be deep insights available to us at these times. According to these same teachings, an eclipse at the Full or New Moon is even more auspicious. In the teachings it is said that, during these very special events, both male and female energies (channels) are in simultaneous alignment, the ultimate opportunity.

In Eastern astrology, any lunar theory is put to the test. It exists as a guide to practice. In other words, in the East they practice what they preach. Here in the West, it would appear that we are somewhat more theoretical. We read about and discuss ideas on the lunar cycle, but very few astrologers I have met make use of the lunar-phase cycle as a guide to day-to-day practice. As a society, we don't even observe the Full or New Moon, much less the quarters or any of the other possible lunar days.

It is true, of course, that most astrologers are aware of the zodiac sign the Moon is in, but here we are not examining that part of the tradition; we are looking at the *cycle of the lunar phases*. Here in the West, we may know that it is New or Full Moon, but we do nothing out of the ordinary in response to that information. And, of course, the general public rarely even takes note of lunar events.

The Eastern approach to the lunar cycle is quite ancient and very detailed. East or West, I assume that both astrological traditions have been engaged in recording something rather than nothing all of these centuries. In other words, I assume that the existing lunar tradition, East and West, is a reflection of reality rather than something we have made up. After all, that is what astrology is all about and why we practice it.

On a personal note, my study of the lunation cycle has led me from Western to Eastern texts in an attempt to obtain more practical information for day-to-day living. When I ran out of new texts to study, I sought out some of the living Eastern meditators who observe the lunar cycle on a regular basis. For example, we have had a wide variety of Eastern astrologers living and working at our center in Big Rapids in recent years. One individual skilled in Sanskrit and Tibetan astrology spent almost two years here, translating various Buddhist texts on the subject.

From my experience with these sources, the primary piece of information that stays with me is that reading about or listening to someone with experience in this area is, by definition, preliminary. Both text and teachers (however fine they may be) can but point beyond themselves to the lunar cycle itself. Through any differences that exist, all sources seem united in this one maxim: go and see for yourself. Check it out. *The purpose of the teachings is the experience itself that waits to be known.* They are telling us: Observe these days. Call it meditation or observation (whatever), but reach with care and attention for the insight gaps that are there.

Science and the Lunation Cycle

We have presented thoughts from both sides of the world on lunar astrology. Is there any scientific evidence to back all this up?

Scientific research into the lunation cycle over the last fifteen to twenty years is fascinating from an astrologer's perspective. It was not very many years ago that science gave little or no credence to the possibility of a lunar effect on life here on Earth. Today, it is no longer a question of "is there an effect?" but rather one of "let me count the ways." In fact, the research at this point is so extensive that in this brief article we can only mention some of the high points in the existing literature.

It should go without saying, but I will repeat it here, that science still has little or nothing to say about psychological or personal events connected with lunar activity. Instead, it has been discussed how the Moon relates to such things as rainfall, weather, and atmosphere. More important to astrologers, and a step closer to the psychological, is the growing evidence for a hard connection between lunar activity and geomagnetic activity. It is this connection that we will detail here.

Geomagnetic activity coming from beyond the Earth's aura or atmosphere has been linked to all kinds of mundane activities ranging from radio reception to the aurora borealis type displays and so on. The picture that emerges from modern research is one where each body (the Earth, the Sun, and perhaps even each of us) is surrounded by some sort of magnetic field. We radiate, and this radiation surrounds us and even keeps some things out. This is our aura or mandala.

The *Earth's* aura (or magnetosphere, as it is called) keeps at bay enormous amounts of radiation coming from the Sun and from the galaxy of which our solar system is a part. Very energetic particles can penetrate our magnetosphere and find their way through the atmosphere to the surface of the Earth itself. For the most part, these particles funnel in from the north and south polar caps via field lines of high geomagnetic declination. During times of increased solar activity such as solar flares, or during the peak of the sunspot cycle (like 1993), very much more solar radiation reaches the Earth than at other times. The weaker cosmic radiation must wait for the years of sunspot minimum to reach their maximum penetration. Please inspect the diagrams of the magnetosphere shown on page 59 as we examine some of the scientific evidence that relates to the lunation cycle, to lunar power.

Auroras

Although we have long studied oceanic tides, we know now that there are atmospheric tides as well that move in response to the position of the Moon. For example, auroras are caused by the excitation of atmospheric molecules by energetic, charged particles penetrating the atmosphere along geomagnetic field lines. Although the mechanism of this phenomenon is still being examined, it is generally understood that auroras are associated with the arrival of solar corpuscular radiation in the magnetosphere, one to three days after a solar flare. These particles (depending on their intrinsic energy and the current density of the atmosphere) penetrate the atmosphere.

These auroral peaks and valleys are modulated by the position of the Moon. This lunar auroral tidal effect in the upper atmosphere can be correlated with flood and ebb tides on earth.

Rainfall

It has been well-documented that rainfall is correlated with the Moon's position in its monthly cycle. According to many studies, rainfall maximizes midway through the 1st and 3rd quarters of the lunar synodic month. In other words, about a half week after New and Full Moon, rainfall reaches a peak. Correspondingly, a low point in rainfall occurs during the 2nd and 4th quarters, with the lowest point of all occurring some three days before New or Full Moon.

In addition, it was found that increased rainfall at these two peak times in the month was greater at solar minimum than at solar maximum. The lunar cycle accounts for 65 percent of the variance during years of solar minimum, but only 14 percent during the year surrounding solar maximum. It has been suggested that cosmic radiation may be a factor, since this form of radiation penetrates more deeply into the solar system during years of low solar activity. During the years of high solar activity, a more powerful solar wind helps to keep out cosmic radiation.

Thunderstorms and Cosmic Radiation

It has been shown that the maximum in thunderstorms coincides with the maximum in galactic cosmic radiation and vice versa, that minimum thunderstorm activity coincides with the minimum in galactic cosmic ray radiation. There have been many studies on the relationship of cosmic radiation to lunar activity. Cosmic radiation consists of energetic particles entering our solar system from beyond its aura, or magnetosphere. As already mentioned, there is an inverse relationship between cosmic radiation and solar activity. In other words, the increased solar wind at sunspot maximum keeps cosmic radiation out of the solar system and away from the earth. During the years of sunspot minimum, cosmic radiation is strong enough to penetrate the solar aura and reach the Earth's atmosphere.

Thunderstorms and the Moon

It has been shown that the maximum in thunderstorms coincides with maximum geomagnetic activity. In addition, it has been shown that thunderstorm activity is modulated by lunar position. The greatest number of thunderstorms occurs after either New or Full Moon. Thunderstorm frequency reaches a maximum two days after Full Moon and remains high for most of the third quarter.

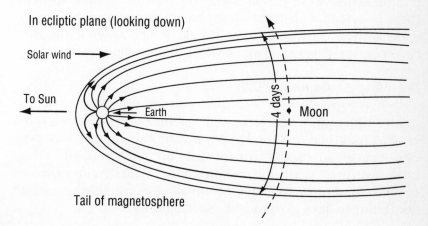

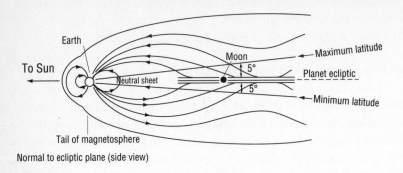

Normal to ecliptic plane (side view)

The Moon and Geomagnetic Activity

The Kp-geomagnetic index varies with the lunar phases. When the Moon is less than 3.5 degrees from the plane of the ecliptic, geomagnetic activity reaches a minimum during the 2nd lunar quarter and a maximum during 3rd lunar quarter. Lunar modulation while near the ecliptic suggests that the Moon is influencing the solar corpuscular flux which, guided by the solar magnetic field, approaches the earth generally from close to the plane of the ecliptic. Some of these particles become trapped in the magnetosphere.

There is a thin, neutral-sheet region close to the ecliptic plane in the tail of the earth's magnetosphere that the Moon might be modulating when it is traveling near the plane of the ecliptic. The high density of field lines near the ecliptic would make this region particularly sensitive to a magnetic perturbation, which could modulate the flux of particles reaching our atmosphere. In short, there is evidence that the Moon has a magnetohydrodynamic wake with an enhanced magnetic field, which, when in the magnetospheric tail, causes magnetic disturbances on the earth.

Polar Cap Absorption (PCA)

PCA happens when solar protons from solar flares enter the earth's upper atmosphere in high geomagnetic latitudes, often causing radio blackouts and increased auroral activity. These periods of severe ionospheric disturbance are often marked by Forbush decreases, when the counting rate of background galactic cosmic radiation has a sudden anomalous decrease which might take hours to days to recover to normal levels.

In effect, it is as if there were a magnetic screening of galactic cosmic radiation by the enhanced solar plasma. It has been noted, but unexplained, that PCA events and Forbush decreases seem to be ordered with the lunar synodic period (29.5 days). When this research was begun, it was expected that a 27.3-day period would be found, indicating a link with solar rotation. It was a surprise to scientists when, instead, results fingered the lunar synodic period (29.5 days). Therefore, it is possible that the Moon somehow controls solar corpuscular radiation streaming toward the earth. The mechanism is still undetermined at this time.

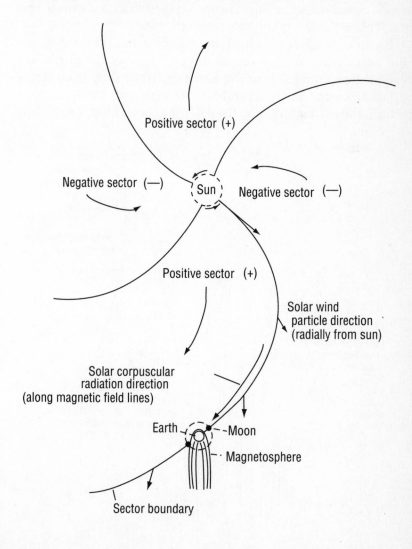

Solar Sectors

Solar sectors and the geometry of the solar magnetic field represent important areas for research. The solar wind is a plasma of charged particles being ejected endlessly from the surface of the Sun. These particles tend to concentrate in the plane of the ecliptic. All of the planets are within the aura or atmosphere of the Sun, the solar wind. Each charged particle moves away from the Sun in a straight line; however, since the Sun itself is rotating, these particle streams get bent into a spiral of the type made famous by Archimedes. In addition, this plasma contains a frozen-in magnetic region constituting the Sun's magnetic field that conforms to this spiral. This is the interplanetary magnetic field.

Because of this spiral effect, the magnetic field at the distance of the Earth is oriented about 45 degrees west of the Earth-Sun line, on the morning side of the Earth. Both the slow (four days) and fast (10 minutes to several hours), charged, solar particles approach the earth guided by the solar magnetic field. They come

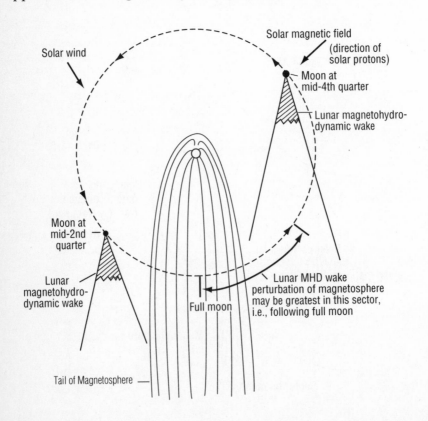

in from the western side of the Sun (morning side of earth) at about a 45-degree angle to the earth, although this angle fluctuates from moment to moment, based on the changes in the solar plasma. The fact is that each of us is exposed to this general direction around 9 A.M. each morning. We are most shielded from this direction around 9 P.M. each night.

The great rotating disk of the solar magnetic field itself is divided into four primary sectors, each with an alternating polarity. The magnetic field direction is either positive (away from the Sun) or negative (toward the Sun). These sectors are tied into definite regions on the surface of the Sun, which are of corresponding magnetic signs. It has been suggested that this may be thought of as a rigid disk in the plane of the ecliptic with four quadrants connected to the Sun and rotating with it in its 27-day rotation cycle—the co-rotating sector structure.

It has been found that geomagnetic and cosmic ray activity, as well as the velocity and number density of the solar wind flux, vary as a function of position within the solar sectors; thus there is a weekly fluctuation in the Kp-geomagnetic index. Studies show a maximum in thunderstorm activity when the earth passes from a positive sector into a negative sector. These four great sectors like a great pinwheel rotate past the earth exposing our planet to alternating positive and negative solar phases.

A study of the lunar position in relation to the Kp-geomagnetic index, PCA, and Forbush decreases shows that PCA and Forbush decreases reach a minimum during the middle of the 4th lunar quarter when the Moon is near the 45° axis and thus between the Earth and the spot where the charged particles arrive from the Sun. A maximum for these values is reached when the Moon is in the 2nd quarter, unable to block the particle advance. It has been shown that the Moon has an electrical charge of at least 100 V/m, which means that the Moon has a positive electrical charge that can deflect solar protons.

There is also a minimum in the Kp-geomagnetic index during 2nd quarters when PCA and Forbush decreases are at a maximum. It has been suggested that at 2nd quarter the Moon may least disturb the geomagnetic field, which is, at that time, most active.

There is a sharp rise in the Kp index just prior to Full Moon and continuing into third quarter. It has been suggested that this might be due to the magnetohydrodynamic wake of the Moon

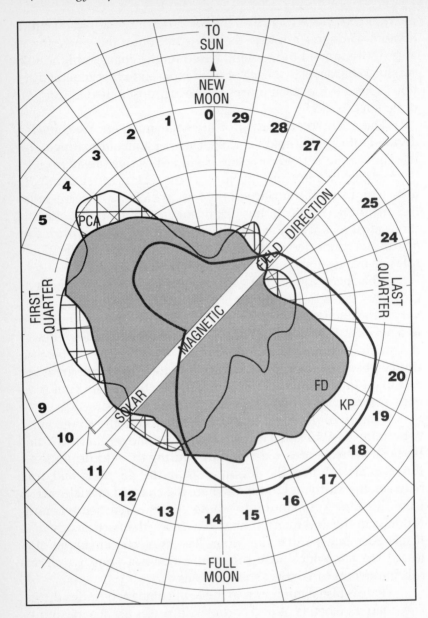

interacting with the tail of the magnetosphere or modulating the flow of solar particles to the tail.

It is interesting to note that around the 2nd quarter, the 10th/11th day, there is maximum PCP activity. This is when *the father-line deities are observed in Eastern astrology.* The 25th/26th days are when the Moon somehow blocks or inhibits the solar magnetic field. This is when *the mother-line deities are celebrated in that tradition.* Thus the time of greatest activity (male) has some scientific backup, and the same for least activity and greatest calm (female).

Tidal and Electrical Influence

The western portion of the Sun is strongly magnetically linked to the Earth, while the eastern portion of the Sun is not. This is due to the fact that solar corpuscular radiation approaches the Earth from the west, guided by the solar magnetic field. As pointed out, these particles come in from the Western side of the Sun at about a 45° angle to the morning side of earth. Statistical studies show that solar flares occurring on the eastern portion of the Sun are much less frequently associated with geomagnetic storms than those occurring near the central or western portion.

Flares occur during periods of solar activity, which typically last a few days. These regions of activity (near sunspots) travel from east to west across the face of the Sun, with a sunspot taking about seven days to travel from the central meridian to the western limb. Thus active solar regions (generating particles capable of reaching the Earth) move into and through the western section of the Sun, which is magnetically linked to the Earth. During this period, recurrent particle streams from an active sunspot region can reach the Earth. Some periods, when solar protons have bombarded the upper atmosphere, over ten days.

This has been a very brief description of some of the geophysical research that has been performed in the last 20 years and that might be of interest to astrologers. It seems that all bodies have a field or aura around them. The Earth and the Sun radiate, and that radiation is swept along behind whatever trajectory the object travels. It is fascinating to see scientific evidence emerging that seems to conform with the astrological tradition.

As pointed out in the previous section on the lunation cycle, the 10th and 25th lunar days have been found (for ages) to be significant periods within the month, where some kind of change or transition takes place. It is interesting to note that these points are more or less in line with the 45-degree vector along which solar corpuscular radiation reaches the earth.

The Moon in its monthly cycle appears to modulate this stream of radiation when it reaches the area surrounding a solunar phase angle of some 315 degrees. At this point the Moon (perhaps due to its magnetic field) effectively blocks and cuts off some of the radiation stemming from the Sun. At the opposite point in its orbit (around 135 degrees), the Moon reaches a point of least blockage, where the most solar radiation can penetrate and reach the Earth.

It is this point in the lunar 2nd quarter, during which the greatest amount of radiation is available to the Earth, that the Eastern astrologers have set aside as a time for the masculine (active) element. The fourth quarter, where the Moon effectively blocks the solar radiation, is the point when the feminine energies are most observed.

It is interesting that, on the surface at any rate, ancient tradition and modern science appear to have some general agreement. Personal observation fills in the gaps.

Exoteric References

Bell, B., and R. J. Defouw. "Dependence of the lunar modulation of geomagnetic activity on the celestial latitude of the Moon," *J. Geophys. Res. 71* (1966), 951-957.

Bradley, D. A., M. A. Woodbury and G. W. Brier. "Lunar synodical period and widespread precipitation," *Science 137* (1962), 748-749.

Brier, G. W., and D. A. Bradle. "Lunar synodical period and precipitation in the United States," *J. Atmos. Sci. 21* (1964), 386-395.

Dodson, H. W., and E. R. Hedeman. "1964: An unexpected effect in solar cosmic ray data related to 29.5 days," *J. Geophys. Res. 69*, 3965-3972.

Harang, L. *The Aurorae.* New York: John Wiley & Sons, 1951, 44.

Haurwitz, B. "Atmospheric Tides," *Science 144* (1964), 1415-1422.

Herman, J. R., and R. A. Goldberg. *Sun, Weather and Climate*, National Aeronautics and Space Administration (1978).

Lethbridge, M. "Solar-Lunar variables, thunderstorms and tornadoes," *Dept. of Meteor. Report,* College of Earth and Mineral Sciences, Penn. State Univ., University Park (1969), 58 pp.

Linlo, W. I. "Electric fields in space and on the lunar surface," in S. Coroniti and J. Hughes (eds), *Planetary Electrodynamics*, Vol. 2 (Gordone & Breach, New York 1969), 369.

Markson, R. "Considerations regarding solar and lunar modulation of geophysical parameters, atmospheric electricity and thunderstorms," *Pure and Applied Physics 84* (1971), 161-200.

Ness, F. F. "The magnetohydrodynamic wake of the Moon," *J. Geophys. Res. 70* (1965), 517-534.

Stolov, H. L "Further investigations of a variation of geomagnetic activity with lunar phase," *J. Geophys. Res. 70* (1965), 77-82.

Wilcox, J. M., and N. F. Ness. "The interplanetary magnetic field, solar origin and terrestrial effects," *Space Sci. Rev. 8* (1968), 258-328.

Esoteric References

Iyer, N. P. Subramania. *Kalaprakasika*, Ranjan Publications, 1982.

Karthar, Ven. Khenpo. Rinpoche. From a teaching on Buddhist Festivals, given at Big Rapids, MI

Pillai, D. Bahadur L. D. Swamikannuu. *Panchang and Horoscope*, Asian Educational Services, 1985.

_____. *Indian Chronology*, Asian Educational Services, 1982.

Prakashananda, Swami, personal communication.

Sundar Das, Shyam, personal communication.

Wangchug, Sange, personal communication, and translation of Tibetan texts.

Dennis Flaherty

Dennis Flaherty has been an astrologer since 1972, and a full time professional since 1986. He practices both Western and Vedic Astrology, and holds degress in English and Sociology from the University of Massachusetts. Dennis has served two terms as the President of the Washington State Astrological Association and serves as a Coordinator for AFAN.

Dennis is a popular lecturer at national and international conferences and has appeared on radio and televison across North America and Australia. In 1992, he was a recipient of the United Astrology Congress Regulus Award for "Most Promising Newcomer in Astrology." He co-writes a monthly Astrology column, *Celestial Cycles,* in Seattle.

Dennis is co-founder of the Greenlake Metaphysical Center in Seattle, where he maintains a busy clientele and teaching schedule. He is deeply involved in Eastern philosophy, from meditation to the martial arts, holding a 3rd degree Black Belt in Shotokan Karate.

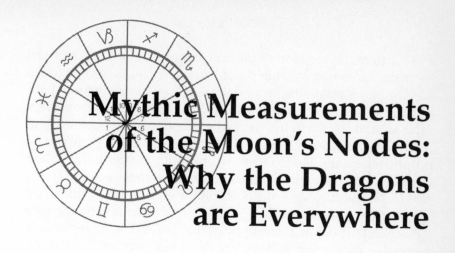

Mythic Measurements of the Moon's Nodes: Why the Dragons are Everywhere

Dennis Flaherty

There is much mystery surrounding the Moon's nodes in chart interpretation. They are not planets, so how are we to consider them in our interpretation? Why are they associated with dragons and serpents?

The Moon's nodes are called the Dragon's Head and Tail in tropical western astrology, and Rahu and Ketu in sidereal Hindu astrology. Rahu and Ketu are recognized as serpent powers in the Hindu system. The etymological roots of our word "dragon" derive from the Greek word *drakon*, meaning "large serpent." So, it seems we have a kinship in name between the dragons of the west and the serpents of the east.

Let's examine the Moon's Nodes using cross-cultural mythologies of both eastern and western dragon/serpent legends, their meanings and usage in both western and Hindu astrology, integrating common themes toward a principle thesis. And let's test this thesis by examining planetary combinations involving close contact with the Moon's Nodes.

The Nodal Axis

The Earth revolving around the Sun enscribes a large circle in the heavens. From our vantage point here on earth, though, it looks like the Sun is revolving around the earth, and this apparent path of the Sun across the sky is called the ecliptic. The Moon in its orbit around the Earth intersects the ecliptic at two points. These points are the Moon's Nodes. The North Node is the point on the ecliptic where the Moon crosses from south to north. It is called the ascending node, since the Moon rises above the ecliptic at this point. The South Node is the point on the ecliptic where the Moon crosses from north to south. It is called the descending node, since the Moon falls below the ecliptic at this point. The nodes have a regressive movement as they are displaced westerly along the ecliptic, much the same as the precessional movement of the equinoxes. The nodes move in retrograde fashion precessionally through the signs, stopping and stationing, then moving forward briefly, only to stop and station resuming their regressive movement. This regressive movement of the Nodes has *an 18.6 year cycle of return.*

The Nodes were considered very important by ancient astrologers as these points of contact on the ecliptic between the orbits of the Moon and Sun. Philosophically, this represented where the personal (the Moon) touched the divine (the Sun). They symbolically represented where the divine could enter into our personal lives. If the divine could enter our lives, then these points on the ecliptic were where that entrance would take place. Such an entrance of solar light-energy into our lives must represent an act of Grace, or an act of Karma, depending on our philosophical vantage point of reference.

Further, the ancient astrologers/astronomers noticed that eclipses took place at least twice a year on or very close to these Nodal contact points at the ecliptic. In fact, the very definition of a Solar or Lunar eclipse is that the New Moon or Full Moon must conjoin the Moon's Nodes within a specified number of degrees. The closer the eclipse takes place to the Nodes the closer to total it will be.

The phenomenon of eclipses deepened the meaning of the Nodes even further in the minds of the ancient astrologers: the Nodes were places where omens ushered forth from the heavens;

they were places where darkness overcame the Luminaries. This led to a development of a powerful mythos surrounding these contact points on the ecliptic. They seemed to be two points in the sky where the Sun and the Moon were temporarily swallowed by some large demonic force. And so, among ancient cultures, we have the development of complementary mythologies involving dragons, serpents, and demons, and the struggle with the forces of light. It was an eternal battle between the gods and demons, with the existence of humanity hanging in the balance.

Cross Cultural Mythologies of Creation

In the creation myths of both western and eastern cultures from the earliest of times, there is the lore of an immense dragon or serpent encircling the earth with its many coils. The gods of the particular culture almost always do battle with this demon in a primordial struggle between the forces of light and darkness. In examing these various myths, we find startling similarities that enrich our understanding of the serpentine energy.

The Babylonian Creation Epic is a long poem that tells a tale of how humanity came into existence. In the beginning, there were only two primordial energies in the universe, called Apsu and Tiamat. Apsu was male primeval energy and Tiamat was female primeval energy. Tiamet is described as a fearsome serpentine being with horns. Their union produced the first gods, and in a short time these new gods turned on the old. They murdered Apsu, and Tiamat, in vengeance, had a second group of offspring that resembled dragons, demons, centaurs, and monsters. This led to an inevitable battle, and to the victor went control of the universe.

Marduk was selected from the first Gods to fight with Tiamat. Tiamat was slain by Marduk, and so was her monstrous offspring. From the body of one of Tiamat's monstrous offspring, Marduk removed the Tablets of Destiny and accordingly established order, assigning functions to all the gods, including the Moon as keeper of the time. Lastly, from the blood of one of the murdered gods he created man, who was to serve the gods.

This epic lore was sacred in Babylonian culture and was recited regularly after the New Year's celebration to ensure heavenly order would continue. It is one of the earliest creation myths and depicts *the struggle of the gods of order over the demons of chaos with the ensuing emergence of man.*

Similar myths of a god slaying a serpent were also shared by the Assyrians, who later conquered the Babylonians, and the Egyptians. In Egyptian mythology, the serpent Apep threatens the Sun god Ra in his daily sojourn across the sky. Apep attempts daily to engulf the boat of Ra with the greatest threat being the falling of night. He occasionally seems to succeed during eclipses. The protector of Ra is the Egyptian god Seth, who rides in the bow of Ra's boat. Seth nightly slays Apep and decapitates him, cutting him into pieces, so that Ra's boat may arise at dawn and sail across the sky once more.

Here we see the serpent's head cut off and the forces of light and order winning over the forces of darkness and chaos.

The first chapters of the Book of Genesis contain the Hebrew account of the creation of the world. In one account, God breaks the heads of the dragons inhabiting the waters of the universe. God also shatters the heads of Leviathan, who is a monster characterized with burning eyes and fiery breath. God then gives the remains of this dragon-like creature to the inhabitants of the wilderness for their sustenance. Leviathan, like many dragons in the myths, circles the globe with his coils and holds his tail between his teeth. Leviathan is destined to slay and be slain by Behemoth on the Day of Judgment. On that day his flesh will be given as food to the righteous and his brilliant scales will cover the walls of Jerusalem, making the city visible to the whole world. Once again, a battle is fought that ends with the slaying of the dragon for the benefit of humanity.

In the ancient Grecian creation myths, we encounter the serpent. In the beginning was Chaos who gave birth to Night; the darkness, and Erebus; death in the dark void. Together, they conceived a wind-borne egg called Love. Gaia, Mother Earth, gives birth to Ouranus; Father Heaven, who with Gaia creates Chronos and Rhea. They give birth to Zeus, supreme among the gods. But Rhea also mated with Tatarus of the Underworld to produce a race of monsters and demons. One of these was the fearsome Typhon, a serpent-god who expressed himself as a whirlwind. He had a hundred dragon's heads, eyes that flashed fire, wings and serpentine coils that embraced all he came across. In his presence, all the gods of Olympus but Zeus fled. In his battle with Typhon,

Zeus besieged him with thunderbolts and, as they fought across the sky, they ravaged the earth. Typhon at first subdues Zeus, but, regaining his strength, Zeus rides a winged chariot across the sky eventually defeating Typhon and imprisoning him in the Underworld beneath Mount Aetna. Here again, the serpent is vanquished by the most supreme of the gods and heavenly order is restored over the demonic forces of the earth. It is after this epic battle that the first golden race of men were brought forth.

In the Nordic myths of creation, a limitless abyss pervades all of space. From this abyss emerges land and water and the creation of the first being, the giant Ymir. Ymir's son gives birth to Odin. Odin and his brother kill Ymir, and from his remains they create the earth, the sky, and the seas. Sparks from the land of fire, Muspelheim, were used to create the Sun, Moon, and stars. A great wall was fashioned from Ymir's eyebrows, and within this wall the first man and woman were created from an ash and elm tree. The universe, in Nordic mythology, is supported by an ash tree called the Yggdrasil Tree. This tree supports nine levels of life and has three roots that are anchored in the three worlds of existence. These worlds are: Asgard, the fortress city of the gods; Midgard, the world of humanity; and Niflheim, the underworld. It is in the underworld of Niflheim that the dragons, called Nidhoggr, bite at the roots of the tree Yggdrasil, threatening to destroy the world. The great tree is guarded by the three Norns. The three are Urda, the past; Verdandi, the present; and Skuld, the future. But, the tree is doomed and the eventual battle between the gods and demons arrives. The most infamous of the Nidhoggr is the fire-god, dragon Loki. He gives birth to a brood of monsters comprised of a demon called Hel, a wolf named Fenrir, and the Serpent of Midgard, inhabiting the world of men. Hel was cast into the underworld of Niflheim and the Serpent of Midgard was cast into the ocean where it grew in darkness to a size where it girdled the earth, full-circle, grasping its tail in mouth.

The gods of Asgard will confront the monsters of Niflheim in the battle of Ragnarok at the end of the world. There will be three winters in which the world is consumed in war; the Sun and the Moon will be swallowed, and the Earth will quake. The Serpent of Midgard will lash out with its tail, flooding the earth with tidal waves and causing terrifying storms. The gods of Asgard will rally, led by Odin. Many of the gods die in this final battle;

Odin is slain by Fenrir, and Thor succumbs after killing the Serpent of Midgard. At this time, *the Sun turns black*, the stars fall from the heavens, and Earth sinks in the sea. The world is destroyed, but several gods and a man and woman survive, to give rise in time to a new world with a reign of one that is more powerful than Odin. This slaying of the serpent in the Nordic myths comes at the end of creation, not at the beginning. It shares this trait with the Chistian myths.

The Christian myth of creation says that, in the beginning, God created the heaven and earth. He called the darkness Night and the light Day. God created the lower life forms first, and then created Man in the image and likeness of God. Genesis states that the serpent was more subtle than any other creature God created. Eve, the first woman, asks the serpent if she and Adam, the first man, may eat the fruit of the tree in the forbidden garden. The serpent tells her they will be like gods, immortal and having the knowledge of good and evil. Eve's consumption of the forbidden fruit precipitates a fall from Eden; the place of God's bounty. They lose paradise and immortality forever. After the fall, they bring forth the first of the human children with their sons, Cain and Abel. The serpent in this myth serves to bring chaos and destruction to the world that the first humans knew. Later, in Revelations, the Christian myth of The Apocalypse foretells the end of the world. Here is seen a return of the serpent-dragons struggling with the angelic forces of light. According to St. John the Divine, in the Book of Revelations, a horde of dragons and monsters descends on humanity consuming all sinners on the Day of Judgment. First there appears a seven-headed dragon that the Archangel Michael, with a host of other angels, battles. This serpent-dragon is directly named the Devil and Satan. He is cast out, with his kind, into the realm of the earth where, like the serpent of Eden, he will deceive humanity. It is then that the Beast of the Apocalypse appears and is defeated by a similar angel. The beast is bound and cast into a bottomless pit with a seal set upon it for a thousand years. The Christian cataclysm of the Apocalypse, like the Nordic cataclysm of Ragnarok, promises that *the world will start anew*. This theme will later be of special importance in the rich allegorical symbolism of the serpent-dragons.

In the ancient Aryan myths of creation, there is much in common with western myths. Churning the cosmic waters of the abyss creates the higher and lower worlds with the earth, a total of three worlds like the Nordic myths. The gods are created by Varuna, the sky god and the Earth. They give rise to Manu, the first man. The god Vishnu, most supreme of Hindu gods, reclines on the cosmic ocean, resting on a couch made of the seven coils of the giant serpent Ananta, "the infinite one." Ananta is a symbol of the all-pervasive cosmic energy. He is a beneficial serpent and is never slain. While supported on this serpent, Vishnu dreams the dream that is the world we experience. The end of the world will come when Vishnu awakes, only to begin again, when he dreams the dream of existence. In another myth, a malevolent serpent of the Abyss carries the Earth off to the depths of the cosmic ocean, where Vishnu must intervene and slay the serpent to save the Earth.

Like the Greek myth in which Zeus battles Typhon, the Aryan god Indra battles the serpent demon Vritra. Vritra is a serpent of the atmosphere, and he obstructs the waters so that the Earth becomes barren. *The Sun is blocked out by an ensuing darkness.* Vritra grows immensely until he encompasses and obstructs the Earth. The gods grow fearful that Vritra will one day encompass their world also. Of all the gods, only Indra will face the serpent. In some versions of the myth, Indra is at first swallowed by Vritra and then regurgitated. Indra finally rides his chariot across the sky, and, with the help of Vishnu, hurls a thunderbolt at Vritra, slaying him. The serpent's death releases water for the world, and Indra puts the Sun back in the sky.

The most profound Hindu myth, for our purposes, tells of how the serpent king of the nether world was employed by the gods in churning the waters of the cosmic oceans in search of the nectar of immortality. In the continuing battle with the demons, the gods fear for their mortality. They consult Vishnu, and he instructs them to churn the cosmic ocean where the nectar of immortality, Amrita, will arise, along with a poison that, when drunk, turns one blue. The demons steal the Amrita and Vishnu wins it back. Upon receiving the Amrita, Vishnu distributes it among the gods, planets, and luminaries. However, a serpent hides among the gods and partakes of this nectar of immortality. He is soon discovered by the Sun and the Moon. Vishnu then hurls his discus at the demon and cuts him in half. The demon's name is *Rahu*, and he is already immortal from drinking the nectar. He becomes a head, without a body, and a serpent's body without a head. His body falls to earth and from its scattering over the Earth, the jewel kingdom is created. Thus, in one of the oldest myths, we have a direct reference to one of the names of the Moon's Nodes.

Summary

These cross-cultural mythologies of creation have several themes in common: serpent-dragons and gods are natural parts of creation; the universe is created by gods and serpent-dragons alike; gods battle the serpent-dragons for supremacy over the world. Often the world is destroyed, only to arise again in a new form. Often the Sun and Moon are threatened by the serpent-dragons. Often the serpent-dragons are decapitated or cut into many pieces when slain. Lastly, there is a similarity of serpent-dragons encircling the globe and grasping their tail in their mouth. This symbol was called the *Uroboros* by the Greeks, meaning "tail biter." It represented the cycle of death, fertilization, and rebirth. The serpent-dragon in the form of a circle biting its tail was to become a symbol of eternity with a promise of life forever in the never-ending cycle of life, death, and rebirth. The serpent-dragon, unfurled in the form of a snake, was to become a symbol of the linear line of time; a representation of life, which had a beginning, a middle, and an end. Remarkably, the serpent-dragon became a symbol of both death *and* immortality: its recurrence in the creation myths promise the end of the world in a battle with the gods, but the world will arise again. This theme of life, death, and rebirth is linked with the serpent-dragons throughout the creation myths. We will latter see these *same* themes applied to the Moon's Nodes

The Serpent-Dragon Legends of the West

Western mythology is steeped in lore depicting heroic struggles with serpent-dragons. These struggles are often to rescue some fair maiden, to prove valor or strength, or to claim some treasure or prize.

The legends surrounding the Greek hero, Herakles, tell of several serpent-dragons encounters. Because Herakles was Zeus' son, the jealous goddess Hera was determined to kill him. To this end, she sent two snakes to kill him while he was yet a baby in his crib. But his strength was so enormous that he strangled them both, one in each hand. The slaying of the serpent here depicts humanity's conquest over the lower forces of nature. Even as a baby, the hero Herakles knows these serpents are evil.

Another myth involving the serpent-dragon image is called the "Twelve Labors of Herakles." The king of Mycenae, Eurystheus, gave Herakles twelve humanly impossible labors to perform as a penance to purify him for the murder of his family. One of his labors was to kill the serpent-dragon beast the Hydra. Like the serpents of the Apocalypse, this creature had several heads. With the help of his nephew, Iolaos, Herakles slays the beast. Another labor was to bring back the Golden Apples of Hesperides, which were guarded by one of Typhons' brood of serpent-dragons, Ladon. Ladon was a serpent-dragon with a hundred heads that each spoke in a different voice. Herakles either fooled Ladon into falling asleep, or slew him for his immortality. In compensation for his defeat by Herakles, Ladon was placed in the heavens by the gods. He became the constellation Draco. There is lore that says when the head of the constellation Draco is in certain positions in the night sky, one's wishes will be granted.

The epic Greek poem, "The Quest of the Golden Fleece," involves the Greek hero, Jason, in his search for a prize guarded by a fierce serpent-dragon. The fleece is protected by a serpent-dragon that never sleeps. The enchantress Medea accompanies Jason on this quest, for she is to lull the beast to sleep so Jason can snatch the fleece. Before this can happen, Jason is swallowed by the beast and later regurgitated. He is revived by Medea, and only after she charms the serpent-dragon with a magical song can Jason acquire the golden fleece and continue his journey. Here we see the theme of the hero being swallowed, yet "reborn" after being regurgitated by the serpent-dragon, much like the themes in the earlier creation myths.

Our last of the Greek myths concerns a mortal named Melampus. Feeling pity, he saves and rears two baby snakes after his servant kills their mother. One night while asleep, they lick inside his ears. Startled, he awakens to find he can suddenly understand the language of all flying and crawling creatures. He learned the art of divination as a result of this experience and became a famous soothsayer.

Likewise, in the Arthurian legends there are many tales of Knights slaying dragons. One of the most famous is Sir Lancelot's bout with a dragon to save the Lady Elaine. After conquering the dragon, Lancelot proceeds to sleep with the fair maiden. The result of their union produces a child, who later becomes the most chivalrous of all of King Arthur's knights, Sir Galahad. In this case, the treasure is the maiden and the slaying of the dragon becomes part of a ritual to bring into the world a virtuous, noble being in the form of the Galahad.

Similarly, in the Nordic myths of mortal encounters with dragons, we have the Saga of the Volsungs. The hero, Sigurd, lies in wait for the dragon, Fafnir, that guards a treasure. He slays the dragon and cuts out the dragon's heart. While roasting the heart some blood spurts on his finger. He tastes it and finds that he, like Melampus of the earlier Greek myth, can understands the language of the birds. In some versions of this myth, he rescues a lady as well, and bathes in the blood of the dragon to become invincible. Here is the repeated theme of the protected treasure and the rescued maiden. The dragon, in death, also offers wisdom, protection, and invincibility.

Lastly, the Christian myths offer numerous dragon slayers. Of these the myth of "St. George and the Dragon" is by far the most well-known. Like many Christian saints, he was martyred and April 23 is commemorated as St. George's Day. His many myths extend from Egypt to Europe, where he is continually showing up to save the local populace from a dragon that is besieging their fair city. Part of the dragon's tribute is usually children, or a maiden to be sacrificed. St. George usually comes along when the tribute happens to be the local King's daughter and goes about rescuing both the maiden and the community by slaying the dragon. There are many versions of this popular myth. He usually marries the fair lady as reward. We see here a sanctified hero doing battle with an evil dragon who threatens humanity. The slaying of the serpent restores order for humanity, the hero proves his valor and gets the fair lady as well.

These few western myths (of many, many more) correlate serpent-dragons with several important themes: first, the hero proves his valor by conquering these fearsome beasts; the serpent-dragons often guard over some treasure or kingdom; the hero receives this material treasure or other reward in conquering or slaying the dragon. There is a theme of rebirth or immortality associated with the heroic serpent-dragon struggle. The Greek dragon, Ladon, placed by the gods in the heavens as a constellation, has the power to grant wishes when the positioning of the "dragon's head" in the sky is auspicious by omens. Lastly, the serpent-dragons can bestow magical powers and wisdom. This last theme is strongly supported by eastern serpent-dragon lore.

The Serpent-Dragon Legends of the East

Eastern legends of the serpent-dragons comprise two general bodies of lore: the Indian and Chinese. The images of the serpent-dragons in these legends are distinctly different from the lore of the west. The serpent-dragons are generally looked upon as *benevolent* beings. They are seen as protectors of the people and also as semi-divine beings. They too, like the western serpent-dragons guard treasures, but they also guard the rivers and oceans and even the heavenly realms. They guard knowledge and even dispense it to those they deem worthy of it.

In Hindu mythology, there is a group of serpentine beings called "Nagas." One of them, Rahu, whom we have already encountered, drank the nectar of immortality before he was cut in half by the god Vishnu. In Indian lore, these beings are considered semi-divine. They have the ability to change shape, and even assume human form. They are distinguished from snakes; being upright beings they do not crawl. Many Indian family trace their ancestry back to the Nagas. Sages and astrologers Brigu and Jaimani and many princely families trace their lineage directly back to the Nagas. Gatama Buddha, himself, is said, in some myths, to have been born as the Naga King Bhuridatta, in the jeweled kingdom beneath the sacred river Jumna.

In Indian mythology, there are eight Great Naga Kings. They live in palaces adorned with jewels and splendor. The myths divide the Nagas into four categories, much like the four levels of Varna, or castes of Indian society. First are the Celestial Nagas, who guard and maintain the heavenly sphere itself. Second are the Divine Nagas, who maintain the weather and earthly sphere. Third are the Early Nagas, who guard over streams and rivers, and help them to flow in times of need. Fourth, and last, are the

Hiding Nagas, who guard earthly treasures and bestow blessings on humanity. Thus, as in the creation myths, the serpent-dragon Nagas pervade all levels of existence. In Indian mythology they occupy important places in both heaven and earth.

One popular Hindu myth involves Gatama Buddha with the Naga King of Lake Mucilinda. In the fifth week, after attaining Perfect Enlightenment, Buddha arrived at the shores of Lake Mucilinda. There he meditated under the branches of a great tree. At that time a great storm arose on the earth and the Naga King, Mucilinda, arose from beneath the lake, wrapping his serpent coils seven times around Buddha. He protected Buddha for seven days, until the rains ceased; then transformed himself into the shape of a young man to pay homage to the great sage. Here the theme is seen of the Nagas as protectors of humanity and spiritual seekers of enlightenment.

The serpent-dragon myths of China share a similar body of lore with the Indian myths. There is perhaps no greater body of lore, even rivaling the myths of India, than the serpent-dragon legends of the ancient Chinese dragons. Unlike the previous myths, China's dragons do not appear in their creation mythology. Like the Indian myths, they are generally benevolent and helpful to humanity, rarely confronting heroes or gods. Much of the Indian mythology and religion, particularly Buddhism, took root in China and flourished. Like the Indian Naga Kings, the Chinese developed the "Lung Wang," or Dragon Kings. The similarities between the two are remarkable because of the shared cultural influences of Buddhism. Where the Nagas carried jewels, often in their foreheads, the Dragon Kings carried precious pearls, enclosed in their claws or in their throats. They lived under lakes, and, like the Nagas, were divided into four categories. The "Tien Lung" were dragons that supported the mansions of the gods. The "Shen Lung" were dragons that worked the weather. The "Ti Lung" were the controllers of the rivers and streams, and lastly, the "Fu-Tsang Lung" guarded the treasures of the earth.

The Dragon Kings, like the Nagas, could take human form to help or hinder humanity. There is a lore of the curative powers of dragon's bones, scales, teeth, etc. According to other legends, several Chinese emperors were so knowledgeable of dragons that they were employed to shuttle them across their empires. As in India's mythology, China regards the serpent-dragons as benevolent beings, so much in fact that the Emperor adorned his robes with the Five-Dragon Emblem. They are found in all levels of existence and are guardians and givers of knowledge and treasure.

These various eastern myths share several themes in common. The serpent-dragons live on all planes of existence and help support the universe. They are mostly highly evolved and they benefit humanity with spiritual knowledge, wisdom and treasure. They control the weather, and flow of the rivers, as part of a universal plan. There are few, if any, myths that depict heroic valor by slaying the serpent-dragons. They generally protect and at large serve the localities in which we find them.

Toward an East/West Mythological Synthesis

Serpent-dragon lore from the creation myths and legends of both east and west reveals a similar symbolic continuity: the creation myths associate the serpent-dragons with the creation and destruction of the world; the serpent-dragons swallow the Sun and Moon, and at times the sky and the earth; they exist on all planes of the universe; and the slaying of the demon restores order to the Universe. The death of the serpent-dragons gives rise to and often benefits humanity.

The serpent-dragons of western legends also share several common themes. The dragons threaten humanity. They guard lakes and localities. They also hoard and guard earthly treasures. The hero proves his valor and is rewarded for slaying the serpent-dragon. There are themes of death and rebirth, invincibility, immortality associated with them. The serpent-dragons touch or blood gives magical powers. The dragons head, in the constellation Draco, has the power to grant one's wishes.

The serpent-dragon legends of the east also share a thematic body of lore. The serpent-dragons benefit humanity. They guard lakes, rivers and bodies of water. They also guard treasures, but dispense them to the worthy. They often protect the spiritual seeker-sage. There are themes of death and rebirth and immortality associated with them. They are considered semi-divine and give spiritual knowledge and wisdom to those they come in contact with. The serpent-dragon's body falling to earth creates jewels of rubies, emeralds, and sapphires for humanity.

These mythic traits of the western and eastern serpent-dragons are remarkably similar to the symbolic qualities astrologers ascribe to the Moon's Nodes; the Dragon's Head and Tail.

Mythic Measurements

The mythology of the heavens—the stars, the Sun, the Moon, and the planets—comprise a great body of astrological information. As astrologers, we utilize this information as mythic measurements in our profession. The rich symbolism allows us to comprehend a cosmos, that is *beyond our logical understanding* as we search for our place within that cosmos. The mythological lore of the serpent-dragons are one such body of information.

The Moon's Nodes are actual points on the ecliptic where the Sun and the Moon were "swallowed up" regularly in ancient times and still continue to be so today in the phenomenon we know as eclipses. The myths of antiquity depicted this as a battle between the forces of light and darkness. In this process the Sun and Moon are reborn, and so is the Earth and all her inhabitants.

This process of birth, death, and rebirth is symbolically represented in the Greek symbol of the "tail-biter; the "Uroboros." This symbol of a serpent-dragon holding its tail in its mouth is a symbol of the corner-stone of our profession; the circular horoscope; that has no beginning and no end. The Uroboros more powerfully invokes the image, as in the ancient creation myths, of a serpent-dragon encircling the earth in its embrace. *This serpent-dragon's embrace represents the Nodal Axis.* Its head and tail are respectively, the North and South Nodes of the Moon. It is here at these points that rebirth takes place. It is here where the divine, as represented by the Sun, crosses the path of the personal, as represented by the Moon. It is here where there is treasure or wisdom, depending on your vantage point, following the words of the Persian poet, Rumi, "Where your heart is, your treasure will be there also."

In Zecharia Sitchin's book, *The 12th Planet*, he describes the Sumerian goddess, Ninhursag, who brings forth the first man. She was known by her popular name, "Mammu," from which our word, "mamma" is derived. Her symbol was the "cutter," the tool for cutting the umbilical cord at birth. This tool of the genesis goddess is in every way *identical to the symbol astrologers use for the*

Moon's North Node. The cutting of the umbilical cord severs the Uroboros, the serpent biting its tail. The circle is broken, eternity is lost, and the child ushers forth into the world of creation. The umbilical cord is a symbol of the serpent-dragon whose slaying, or severing, cuts the connection to the divine, as represented by the womb, and the child comes forth into the linear world of time and space, represented by the snake, the severed umbilical cord; the Uroboros lost.

As we have uncovered so many times in these myths, the symbol of the Moon's Nodes speaks of birth, death, and rebirth. They are symbols of the transmigration of the soul from one reality to another; from one life to another. To explain the difference between the western and eastern serpent-dragons' meanings in summary, we can point to western culture as generally materialistic and aggressive, so the myths of the serpent-dragons tell of conquest, treasure, and magical powers. As eastern culture is generally conceded to be spiritually based and more subtle in action, its myths tell of protection, knowledge, and enlightenment. The differences can best be summed up in the symbol of the Chinese dragon clutching a pearl. The West sees the pearl as a symbol of wealth; the East sees the same pearl as a symbol of wisdom. Based on this symbolism, we can measure the Dragon's Head and the Dragon's Tail meaningfully.

The Moon's North Node: The Dragon's Head

Western astrologers impart to the Dragon's Head an overall beneficial profile, not unlike the constellation Draco, where the placement of Draco's head grants wishes. Some advantage is said to be gained where the North Node is place by sign and house. It is said to be a place where we draw energy into our lives. Correct social behavior is associated with this Node. It is also said that where the North Node is placed is where we are evolving in this life. Some astrologers say it is where we have been unselfish in past lives. The theme of reincarnation, as we have previously seen, is linked strongly with the Nodes.

In eastern Hindu astrology, the Moon's North Node is called Rahu, the serpent's head. In Sanskrit it means; "to engulf," "hide," or "conceal." It is an energy of worldly desire, and can be the greatest "maraka," or evil-causing energy, in the chart. It is associated with worldly accomplishment and wealth. It is also associated with the power of the mind; from the myth of Rahu's separation into a head and body by the God Vishnu. The mind, without the senses, creates illusion, and Rahu is the indicator of worldly illusion.

This contrast between western and eastern astrological meanings of the Moon's North Node closely parallels the difference between the western and eastern serpent-dragons legends. Because the west is a material-minded culture it sees things that reinforce that as being positive, whereas, the east being spiritual, sees materialism as illusion. When the newborn child enters this world it enters head first. The Dragon's head is associated with this world .

The Dragon's head is associated with material manifestation. We associate it with the process called "involution," the descent of spirit into matter. It has an all-engrossing effect by planet, sign, and house. The Dragon's Head of the Nodal Axis is where we are manifesting our worldly desire, or, in other words, where the one becomes the many in the process of differentiation. It represents how and where *our desires turn to deeds*. The Sanskrit word for desire is "kama," and the Sanskrit word for deed is "karma." Your kama determines your karma. We can have the illusion in linear time that we are free from the effects of our deeds, but when the serpent becomes the Uroborus again, the effects await us on the wheel of life, death, and rebirth.

The placement of the Moon's North Node involves us in the desires of this life. It creates an awareness of those desires and an awareness of a world waiting to fulfill them. This awareness is an intoxication, one of the magical properties of the serpent-dragons breath and bite. In the right dosage, its venom can lead to worldly accomplishments; in the wrong dosage, this venom can lead to the madness of insatiable desires .

The Moon's South Node: The Dragon's Tail

Western astrologers generally see the Dragon's tail as an overall adverse influence. It represents a place of loss, where we lose energy. It is connected with anti-social behavior. It is said to represent past lives, thus the connection again to the serpent-dragon's myths of reincarnation. Some say it is where we have been selfish in the past.

In Hindu astrology, the Moon's South Node is called Ketu. The Hindus sages describe Ketu in Sanskrit terms meaning: "a sign" or an "arrow." In Hindu astrology Ketu is known as Gnana Karaka and Moksha karaka. These names mean "the indicator of knowledge," and "the indicator of enlightenment," respectively. Ketu has the potential to be the most spiritual energy in the horoscope. Ketu is associated with perception and spiritual insight. Rahu's body, Ketu, falling to earth, creates the jewel kingdom and jewels of wisdom as well. It is the power of the senses, as separate from the power of the mind, that speak to us, and, when turned inward, reclaim our lost divinity. Ketu represents perception.

This contrast again parallels the difference between western and eastern serpent-dragon myths. Again, the west being generally a material culture, things that are associated with spirituality, such as asceticism, poverty, chastity, and material loss, are not popular themes and do not go over well with western people in general. When the newborn child enters the world, the broken end of the umbilical cord trailing from the mother is a sign that points back to the womb, the eternal, and is associated with the heavenly world lost. The Dragon's tail is not of this world.

The Dragon's tail is associated with otherworldly perception, with the process of evolution, in which what is gross becomes fine. It has a quickening effect by planet, sign, and house. With the Moon's South Node, we are moving away from the grossness of desire, as represented by the North Node, to the subtlety of perception. With perception we have the ability to see through our desires and free ourselves from their entangling effects. The Dragon's Tail represents where we can free ourselves from this world. It is where the many return to the one, the process of evolution that leads to Enlightenment. We become free of the illusion of a separate existence that the mind perpetuates. Further, we become free from the illusion of linear time and the limitation of space; as the serpent becomes the Uroboros we perceive the cycle of life, death, and rebirth. This is why the Dragon's Tail is linked to mystical experience in the Hindu system, for we do not possess words to describe such a realization.

The placement of the Moon's South Node represents a momentum of latent tendencies from past experience, what are known as "samskaras" in Sanskrit. It is where we are bringing a momentum of perceptual energy whose direction is away from this world, away from this life. It represents the process of how we unclothe that which our desires have adorned us with; how we untangle ourselves from the Karma of past experiences. This is accomplished by burning our worldly desires in the sacrificial fires of a greater perceptual, albeit spiritual, experience. The unclothing process can lead us to an awareness that this world is but an illusion. This awareness is an intoxication caused by the serpent's bite. In the right dosage, its venom can bring the holy intoxication of the dervish, sage, or knowledge seeker. In the wrong dosages, it will create intoxicating perceptual problems not of this world, insanity and all kinds of madness; spiritual, sexual, unworldly, and the like.

The Moon's Nodes in Chart Interpretation

It is beyond the scope of this chapter to delineate all possibilities of the Moon's Nodal Axis sign, house, and by planetary aspects, but we can concentrate our examination on planets that conjoin the Moon's Nodes, within an orb of 5 to 6 degrees. Let's study how the planetary energy is highlighted by the planet falling on the Dragon's Head or falling on the Dragon's Tail, in tune with the ideas we have been discussing. Remember, the Moon's Nodes are the points on the ecliptic where the serpent-dragons of antiquity swallowed the Sun and Moon; where the divine touches the personal.

☊ ☋ ☌ ☉ When the Dragon's Head conjoins the Sun, there is an intensification of ego. The Sun, being an energy of recognition and achievement, can benefit on an egoistic level from its association with the Dragon's Head. The combination can correspond to fame and material success due to its materially engrossing nature.

Actress Brooke Shields has the Dragon's Head conjoined the Sun in Gemini, in the 9th House. By age eleven, she was already a professional model. Within two years, she was a millionaire and on the road to fame. Manfred Von Richthofen, the World War I German flying ace, has this conjunction in Taurus, in the 5th House. He was born into a prosperous military family. His desire for recognition was so strong that, in only two years of aerial combat with the flying service, he recorded over eighty Allied kills. By his early death, at age twenty-six, he had achieved lasting fame as "The Red Baron." Lastly, Richard Alpert, known as "Ram Das," has this close conjunction in Aries, in the 10th House. He was a well-known Harvard psychology professor and associate of Timothy Leary, who embraced eastern philosophy and became famous as a western Guru with such books as *Be Here Now, Grist for the Mill,* and *The Only Dance There is.*

Personal clients also exhibit intensification of ego with this Sun-North Lunar Node combination. A woman with a close conjunction in Cancer in the 7th House had found no lasting satisfaction in relationships. She had been married four times, yet was not about to give up. The desire for marital bliss was always "just around the corner" in the next relationship. Another woman with this conjunction in Aquarius in the 11th House is deeply involved in a spiritual quest in this life. She had been a member of several spiritual groups, but ultimately grew disillusioned and left. But, her desire for spiritual communion was so strong that she ultimately began the all-engrossing search again in a new form. A man with a close conjunction in Taurus in the 12th House has unsuccessfully tried to market a "new age" product to the business community. He continually failed to the point of personal bankruptcy, but he was not dissuaded. His desire for recognition based on his ideas is so strong not even bankruptcy will deter him. We will probably be reading about him in a "rags to riches" story in coming years, because the ego-emphatic need is so intense he does not know the meaning of the word "quit."

The Dragon's Head with the Sun gives an intense need to fulfill ego drives in the world of materiality. There is an intense need for recognition. Fame and fortune often follow these individuals, but the drive for more is always there. This can lead to spirituality, as in Alpert's case, but only after there is dissatisfaction with the material life one has *already* acquired. This combination can also lead to destruction, as in the case of Von Richthoffen. Here the ego drive is never satisfied, always demanding more, until balance is lost and the self is destroyed.

℧ ☌ ☉ When the Dragon's Tail conjoins the Sun, the ego is often removed from this world. The person identifies with what is unusual, different, or otherworldly. The ego needs for achievement are still there but they are directed through unusual or spiritual channels, ultimately seeking to transcend the self usually motivated by some perceived personal loss.

The enigmatic German General, Erwin Rommel, had the Dragon's Tail closely conjoined the Sun in Scorpio in the 10th House. He acquired fame as the "Desert Fox" through his unusual desert war strategies, and ultimately sacrificed himself for an even greater ego need: his suicide insured his family safety and fame for himself. The famed film actor, Paul Newman, has this conjunction in Aquarius in the 1st House. Interestingly, his first film, "The Silver Chalice," portrayed him in a spiritual light. Many of his other films, such as "Cool Hand Luke," "Hombre," "The Mackintosh Man," and others portray him as a loner and iconoclast. Sadly, he lost his son, Alan Scott Newman, through drug overdose. Alan Scott also had this conjunction within two degrees. Lastly, famed film director, Roman Polanski, has this closely aligned conjunction in the 8th House. Although professionally very successful, personal tragedies have plagued his life: the loss of his mother at Auschwitz, the murder of his wife, Sharon Tate, allegations of sexual impropriety destroyed his reputation in Hollywood, ostracism and isolation in Europe.

Personal clients and associates have also experienced *a loss of worldly identification*. A client with the Dragon's Tail in Pisces closely conjoined the Sun in the 6th House experienced personal abuse and ego loss at the hands of her father. She latter pursued a life of personal service to others as a social worker. Another client has this conjunction in the 12th House: her intense psychic visualizations, combined with out-of-body experiences, at first played havoc with her sanity. But, once she realized and accepted that there was a reality greater than this world, she threaded this energy into her life and became a healer, channeling energies from the greater reality. Lastly, three well-known astrologers have the Dragon's Tail closely conjoined their Suns. The first in Sagittarius in the 1st House; the second in Scorpio in the 6th House; the last in Virgo in the 12th House. They are all of a private, retiring nature. They all have experienced personal loss, and this loss has transformed their worldly identification. They are most helpful to clients in crises and trauma because they have been there and directly experienced it themselves

When the Dragon's Tail conjoins the Sun there is a relinquishing of what the ego has identified with and accomplished, as in the cases of Rommel, Newman, and Polanski. This usually happens through some personal loss. This combination often directs the ego-aware self back to the divine, or some other reality, in an attempt to comprehend what is beyond the ego's ability to control or change. In this way, the self is redeemed from the world of materialism and ultimately can become spiritual. The serpent's bite with the Sun tears the individual away from the accomplishments of this world, and yet the children of sorrow are the bringers of joy.

☊ ☌ ☽ The Moon is a planet of consciousness. It is identified with the senses, the awareness created by our senses. It is from this awareness that our feelings are formed. When the Dragon's Head conjoins the Moon, it intensifies the awareness of the senses and the mind. There is an intensification of sensory experience and a restlessness of the mind as it yearns for greater satisfaction. This combination increases perception to extraordinary levels, often resulting in genius. The German philosopher Friedrich Nietzsche had the Moon closely conjoined the Dragon's Head in Sagittarius close to the Ascendant. His perceptual skills were immense and (complicated by syphillis) ultimately led to his death by insanity. Cult murderer Charles Manson has this closely aligned conjunction in Aquarius in the 10th House. His powers of perception were so persuasive that he enthralled "The Manson Family" to act upon his mad genius. The cult minister, Jim Jones, also had this conjunction, closely aligned in Aries in the 3rd House. His insatiable drive for spiritual awareness led to the founding of a spiritual organization called The People's Temple. Like Manson, he founded a family in true lunar fashion, but when his perceptions turned paranoid he persuaded almost a thousand of his followers to commit mass suicide in Guyana in 1978. Lastly, on a positive note, we have Karl Marx, philosopher, social theorist, writer, and political activist. He has the Dragon's Head closely conjoined the Moon in Taurus in the 2nd House. His perception of social class, as presented in *The Communist Manifesto* and *Das Kapital*, persuaded a generation to embrace his ideology in the grand social experiment, Communism. Another man of insight and genius was Emanuel Swedenborg. His conjunction is in Taurus in the 3rd House. This brilliant mystic received a revelation in 1745 that led him to teach that Heaven and Hell are not places of existence, but rather states of consciousness right here on earth.

The Dragon's Head with the Moon gives an intense awareness and an ability to influence the masses. Its insatiable drive, when combined with the Moon, can produce the intoxication of great genius, like Marx and Swedonborg, or mad genius, as in the cases of Manson and Jones.

Personal clients who have this conjunction have also exhibited great perceptual and persuasive powers. One woman, with this conjunction in Scorpio in the 8th House, is a multi-level marketing genius and has achieved great affluence through her marketing strategies. Another man, who has this conjunction in Gemini in the 11th House, is a gifted teacher of several disciplines involving massage, homeopathy, and kinesiology. He is immensely popular. Lastly, a new age lecturer, who has this conjunction in Aries in the 2nd House, travels internationally, enthralling audiences around the globe with her profound insights. In this case, her mother has been diagnosed as insane, creating an unusual, early-family background of perceptual intensity. This conjunction has created immense awareness that has translated into security and success, in the worldly sense, for these business people, teachers, and healers.

☊ ☌ ☽ When the Dragon's Tail conjoins the Moon, it roots the senses and mind in unworldly realms. It intensifies the awareness of other planes of consciousness. The person is aware of a greater reality. This can greatly spiritualize the awareness, or lead to dementia. The person senses and perceives an order of reality that other people are just not aware of. This perception floods the mind and loosens its grip on material reality. One of India's greatest saints, Sri Ranmana Maharshi, has the Dragon's Tail conjoined the Moon in Cancer in the 9th House. Having been born just after a lunar eclipse, this great sage's philosophy was simply "Be as you are." He often communicated his immense awareness of the nature of life in the language of silence, as an experiential flow to those seeking Enlightenment. The great

German composer Richard Wagner had this conjunction in Aquarius in the 9th House as well. Instead of the universal language of silence, this genius drew on the universal language of music as his medium. His perception soared to other worldly realms, the realm of myth, in his cycle of operas, *Der Ring des Niebelungen*. His themes depicted the eternal conflict between the forces of light and darkness. We find the serial killer Theodore Bundy with the Dragon's Tail conjoined the Moon in Sagittarius in the 4th House. Here we have a sensorial awareness drenched in madness, only aware of its obsessive, otherworldly compulsions.. His manner was so persuasive and charming that he lured over a hundred women to their death.

Personal clients with the Dragon's Tail conjoined the Moon have experienced similarly intensified awareness. One woman with the Dragon's Tail closely conjoined the Moon in the 12th House uses her extra-sensory awareness to help her close real estate sales. Another woman with this conjunction in Pisces in the 4th House comes from a very religious family. Her mother directed her attention to the divine at an early age and allowed her to appreciate other people's spiritual beliefs. Another has a close conjunction in Sagittarius: her otherworldly perceptions created confusion. Psycho-pharmaceuticals were prescribed and resulted in a further deterioration of her grip on reality. Sadly, she committed suicide in a moment of despair. Lastly, a woman client has this conjunction in Gemini in the 12th House. This woman is very spiritually aware. She had been married to a Minister. There are still other realities that come into her awareness that require on-going psychological therapy.

The Dragon's Tail with the Moon intensifies the awareness of the individual. This intensification heightens the perception of other realms of consciousness and can create deep spiritual or idealistic awareness, as in the cases of SriRamana Marharshi and Wagner. It can also create extreme dementia and otherworldly obsession, as in Bundy's case.

☊☋☌☿ When the Dragon's Head conjoins Mercury, the intellectual abilities of the mind become heightened. There is a strong desire to comprehend and name all the phenomena the mind experiences. This often leads to a mastery of the phenomenal world, increasing the commercial and worldly function of the intellect. The brilliant financier J. P. Morgan had the Dragon's Head conjoined Mercury in the 2nd House. Here we have a mind dedicated to the enormous accumulation of worldly wealth. In this vein we also find Nelson Rockerfeller with this conjunction in Cancer in the 9th House. Having inherited close to a half-billion dollars from his father, he utilized these immense resources to achieve personal and political power. The great French novelist and prolific playwright, Honore De Balzac, has the Dragon's Head closely conjoined Mercury in Taurus on the Midheaven. He was known as a tireless writer, with over two thousand characters filling his novels and his mind. On the dark side, we have Anton Lavey, who had this conjunction in Taurus in the 2nd House. He is the author of *The Satanic Bible*, and founded The First Church of Satan, in San Francisco in 1966. Grigori Rasputin had this conjunction in Gemini in the 4th House. The mad monk was well-known to have exerted an immense manipulative influence on Alexandra, wife of Czar Nicholas, and the royal family .

Personal clients with the Dragon's Head conjoining Mercury exhibit varying degrees of intellectual acuity. One man with the Dragon's head closely conjoining Mercury in Taurus in the 4th house is a brilliant marketing manager for a large computer software company. Another man with this conjunction in the 12th House staffs a technical support line for computer-related problems. Each one of these people is intensely aware of their special area of knowledge.

The Dragon's Head conjoined with Mercury intensifies the activities of the mind. It becomes voracious for more knowledge as it measures, quantifies, and places worldly value on information. This combination can create great commercialism, as in the cases of Morgan and Rockefeller, or powerful persuasive intellects such as Balzac, Levy, and Rasputin.

☋☌☿ When the Dragon's Tail conjoins Mercury, it directs the intellect to explore and measure otherworldly realms of perception. There can be an interest in spiritualism or the occult. The mind is often drawn away from the everyday world into another reality that is visionary or fantasy-oriented. Psychic Uri Geller has the Dragon's Tail closely conjoined Mercury in Sagittarius in the 2nd House. His telekinetic abilities have been tested and verified by the Stanford Research institute. Johann Eckart, dubbed "Hitler's Spiritual Grandfather," had this conjunction in Pisces in the 1st House. Eckart was known as a poet and dramatist, and partly received his visionary perceptions from his addictive use of alcohol and morphine. The late comic, Freddie Prinze, had this conjunction in Cancer in the 9th House. This standup comedian skyrocketed to fame with his quick quick-witted style of humor. He sadly took his life in a futile moment of depression. Lastly, the heir to the Baskin Robbins ice cream fortune, John Robbins, has a close conjunction in Scorpio in the 3rd House. Here we have a writer, lecturer, and visionary spreading the message of full world food production in our time; all the more credible, for having turned his back on the family fortune.

In the everyday world, people having the Dragon's Tail conjoined Mercury are also interested in alternative realities and exhibit unusual mental abilities. One woman with this conjunction in Aquarius in the 3rd House is a sales representative for an international health food product. Another woman, who has this conjunction in Gemini in the 12th, has traveled the world in search of spiritual teachers and information. A third with this conjunction in Scorpio in the 4th House complains of weird dreams and depressive turns of mind beyond her mental control. In summary each one of these individuals exhibits a mental intoxication or fascination with some mental pursuit.

With the Dragon's Tail conjoining Mercury there is some unusual mental ability, as in the cases of Geller and Eckhart. The mind is drawn into other realms from the visionary as with Robbins, to the disturbed, as with Prinze. The serpent's bite intoxicates and quickens the intellect's ability to grasp otherworldly phenomena.

☊ ☋ ☌ ♀ When the Dragon's Head conjoins Venus, there is an intensification of Venusian traits, such as artistry, music, beauty, and a heightened sense of fated relationship. This position can lead to fame in the arts as it envelopes the person in all manner of personal attention. They are often drawn to Karmic relationships with others.

Connie Francis, the popular singing sensation of the sixties, had the Dragon's Head closely conjoined Venus in Sagittarius in the 12th House. Her four marriages ended in divorce and in 1974, after being beaten and raped, she lost her beautiful voice and went into several years of seclusion. Jean Anouilh, one of the leading post-war playwrights, had a close conjunction in Taurus in the 1st House. His heroes rejected relationships with others in favor of being alone. He is best known for "The Waltz of the Toreadors." Sigmund Freud had a close conjunction in Aries in the 6th House. Founder of psychoanalysis, his work involved ongoing close personal contact with his patients. Lastly, astrology teacher Jonelle Arien had a close conjunction in Cancer in the 11th House. She met and married her husband within ten days of his attending one of her classes. Six years later, he murdered her, then turned the gun on himself.

Personal clients have exhibited similar obsessive relationship traits. One man, who has a close conjunction in Aquarius in the 9th, is a spiritual minister to a large congregation. He is known for his special sensitivities; he claims a past-life connection to the group. Another man, with this conjunction in Cancer in the 12th House was consistently victimized by his wife over several years. When he lost his job, she left him. Lastly, a woman with this conjunction in the 10th was repeatedly abused and humiliated by her mother as a child. She continues this dynamic by becoming involved with very specific individuals who repeat this family pattern. The aforesaid individuals exhibit powerful, personal obsessive relationship patterns that draw them into karmic relationships with others.

☋ ☌ ♀ When the Dragon's Tail conjoins Venus it heightens and can spiritualize, or idealize, Venusian qualities. There is a powerful need to experience relationship on a greater level. This creates a heightened otherworldly orientation to life and others. This orientation can be spiritually, idealistically, or fantasy based.

Christopher Isherwood had the Dragon's Tail closely conjoined Venus in Virgo in the 4th House. His writings were principally concerned with Vedanta philosophy, pacifism, and a search for the meaning of life. Michelangelo had this conjunction in Aries conjoined the I.C. Noted for his frescoes, sculptures, and his painting of the Sistine Chapel in Rome, he projected the humanity and drama of religiousness as never before. Dean Martin, actor and singer, also has this conjunction, almost exact, in Cancer in the 4th House. He had a Fated relationship with Jerry Lewis and with his son Dino, who tragically died in a military plane crash. On the dark side, we have William Bonin, known as the California Freeway Killer. Bonin has this conjunction in Sagittarius in the 2nd House. This serial killer murdered over twenty boys, enlisting the aid of other youths to help commit the crimes.

In the charts of personal clients, an obsessive relationship pattern has also emerged. One woman has a close conjunction in Gemini in the 8th House. She has been sexually obsessed with a certain man for most of her life, and compares all others to him. Another woman has this conjunction in Cancer in the 9th House. She is drawn exclusively to people of oriental extraction.

With the Dragon's Tail conjoined Venus we have literary and artistic inclinations, as with Isherwood and Michalangelo. But most importantly, there is strong yearning for personal relationship that transcends this world. It can lead to spiritual heights of awareness, and close personal relationship with one's artistry or one's god, or an obsessive relationship madness, as with William Bonin.

☊ ☋ ♂ When the Dragon's Head conjoins Mars there is an intensification of desire. This can lead to great ambition, inspiration, passion, and accomplishment. This person can be a powerful proponent of personal conviction. There is often worldly recognition from Mars being linked with the materialization process. But, when blocked in fulfilling worldly desires, these individuals can easily experience anger and express violence.

Hugo Black, famed Associate Justice of the U.S. Supreme Court, had the Dragon's Head closely conjoined Mars in Virgo in the 10th House. He was described as a "militant humanist" in his legal endeavors. Sir Richard Burton, the famed British Orientalist, had this same close conjunction in Pisces in the 4th House. This adventurer traveled through Arabia, Ethiopia, and Africa, recording all he saw. Lastly, the actor, Sal Mineo, had this conjunction in Scorpio in the 10th House. He started on Broadway at age eleven with unbounded enthusiasm. Tragically, his intensity was partly responsible for his violent death in 1976. Here we see individuals with great drive and passion for what they do. It is often their sheer drive that propels them to the tops of their fields. The Dragon's Head with Mars is continually restless, looking for the next accomplishment.

In the charts of personal clients, this conjunction is no less powerful. One woman has a close conjunction in Gemini in the 1st House. She was the president of a corporation appropriately named "Competitive Intelligence." She later left this to run a shelter for battered women. Another woman, who has a very close conjunction in Aquarius in the 10th House, has been instrumental in founding several businesses and is currently founding a nonprofit foundation. Both these woman are very successful natural leaders. By their sheer will they achieved recognition and acclaim in their chosen fields. They are both restless and certainly will achieve and accomplish still more.

With the Dragon's Head conjoining Mars, the serpent's bite intoxicates the desire nature. These individuals passionately pursue what they desire, and it can lead them to positions of power and prestige, as in the cases of Black and Burton. However, there is often a growing dissatisfaction and restlessness with what has been accomplished, spurring the person to start the cycle all over again.

☊ ♂ ♂ When the Dragon's Tail conjoins Mars the desire nature is driven in a similar way as with the Dragon's head. However, its source of inspiration is unworldly. The need to achieve is often powerfully idealistic and can be spiritualy inspired at times. If the intense desire nature is blocked in any way these individuals can become frustrated, angry and when provoked, violent.

Mark Spitz, the famed Olympic Swimmer, has the Dragon's Tail closely conjoined Mars in the 2nd House. He began swimming at an early age, and his intense desire nature led him become known as "The World's Best Swimmer" at age 17, by breaking five world records and receiving seven gold medals in the 1972 Olympics! Presidential candidate Edmund Gerry Brown, has this conjunction in Taurus in the 10th House. Elected Governor of California in 1974, Gerry was known to friends and campaign workers alike to be a workaholic. Here we have the driving energy of Mars being harnessed to an idealistic political cause, a man who never quits, and will be heard from again and again because of the tireless combination of Mars with the serpent. Lastly, King Rama Mongkut IV had this conjunction, almost exact, in

Leo in the 11th House. He was made famous and glamorized in the book and movie "Anna and the King of Siam," and on Broadway in "The King and I." He was known to have fathered over sixty children, all the more remarkable because he lived celibate for twenty-seven years before assuming the throne. Here, the powerful Mars desire is transcended, due to an idealistic, spiritual drive to remain chaste in the eyes of the divine.

Personal clients exhibit similarly defined Martian traits. One man has the Dragon's Tail closely conjoined Mars in Libra on the Ascendant. He is a charismatic massage therapist and adored by his students. Another man has the same conjunction in Libra in the 5th House and achieved distinction in the martial arts. Here we have again the transcending of the strong Martian nature, due to some greater idealistic, otherworldly reality. Lastly, a woman with this conjunction in Capricorn in the 2nd House has been victimized by sexually violent relationships. Her husband killed himself with a gunshot to his head.

With the Dragon's Tail, the desire nature of Mars is intensified and intoxicated by the serpent's bite, inspiring the individual to idealistic accomplishments, like Spitz and Brown. The desire nature, being intensified, seeks to express itself passionately in a reality that is not of this world. This reality can be idealistic, or spiritual, like King Mongrut IV, but it can also be otherworldly and obsessive.

☊☌♃ When the Dragon's Head conjoins Jupiter, it creates a powerful combination of forces for great worldly accomplishments. The person can have an exaggerated sense of purpose, or importance. Often there is great knowledge and ability to teach others, in one's chosen area of accomplishment. There can be grand plans with strong humanitarian and social themes. The intoxication of the serpent of worldly desire with the planet of growth will almost always play itself out in some grand way.

Jean Claude Killy, famed Olympic skier, has the Dragon's Head closely conjoined Jupiter in Leo on the Ascendant. He is one of only two people in the world to win the Triple Crown in the Winter Olympics. Here we have great ability, ambition, and achievement and recognition. Dr. Louis Berman, famed endocrinologist, had the same close conjunction in Aries in the 4th

House. Though a shy and retiring man, Berman's knowledge helped map the endocrine system of the human body. He was the first to isolate the parathyroid hormone. Lastly, the genius, Nikola Tesla, had this conjunction in Aries in the 12th House. A scientist, grand theorist, and prolific inventor, his dream was always to help humanity in some way

This theme of importance pervades the everyday person as well. One man has the Dragon's Head conjoined Jupiter in Scorpio in the 3rd House. He is a salesman and declares he can sell anything. He sells art and oriental rugs from all over the world. He realized at eighteen, while selling shoes, that he could just as well sell something much grander with the same effort. He is very successful and wealthy, and lets everyone know it. Another woman has this conjunction in Libra in the 5th House. She is a massage therapist and has a sincere desire to help all who come to her. She continues to grow in her knowledge by including other therapies within her profession.

With the Dragon's Head conjoined Jupiter, greatness can be achieved in the public domain, as in the cases of Killy and Berman. The individuals are often very knowledgeable and philosophical, with an immense grasp of their subject matter. Teslar comes to mind as a representative here. The goal is to make a personal mark on the world.

☊☌♃ When the Dragon's Tail conjoins Jupiter, there is often a deeply humanitarian, philosophical, or spiritual bent to the person. They seem capable of grasping large themes that are well beyond the scope of ordinary people. They long for an understanding of idealistic or divine principles in their lives. Their head is in this world, but not of it. They are often grand philosophers or social theorists.

The great reformationist, Martin Luther, had the Dragon's Tail almost exactly conjoined Jupiter in Libra in the 3rd House. He was a popular professor of theology when he broke with the Catholic church and began the Reformed church in 1525. This man's vision of spirituality still influences us today. The grand astrologer, Alan Leo, had this conjunction in Leo in the 12th House. He was one of the founders of the Theosophical lodge in England. He almost single-handedly helped popularize astrology in his day through his prolific writings. Here we have a Jupiterian philosopher who helped astrology reclaim its western spiritual roots. The grand statesman, Sir Winston Churchill, had a close conjunction in Libra in the 1st House. Twice Prime Minister of Great Britain and Nobel Prize recipient in literature, this man's breadth of vision helped Britain play a grand role in world politics, when in fact she was in world decline. Other notable individuals are Lord Alfred Tennyson, Victorian poet, with an almost exact conjunction in Aries in the 11th, and William F Buckley, pompous political pontificator, with the same conjunction in Capricorn in the 9th House.

Personal clients have exhibited similar traits but on a less than grand level. One client, with the Dragon's Tail closely conjoined Jupiter in Scorpio on the Midheaven, publishes a successful foreign magazine, appropriately called *The Planet*, which deals with philosophical and spiritual issues. Another woman, with the same conjunction in Scorpio in the 5th House, is a practicing physician who travels third-world countries, spreading knowledge and healing. Lastly, a client has a close conjunction in Cancer in the 12th. He is a spiritual devotee and spends much of his time in spiritual seclusion.

When the Dragon's head conjoins Jupiter, it lifts the individual into idealistic, visionary, and prophetic realms of experience. Their worlds can uplift humanity, as the in cases of Martin Luther, Alan Leo, and Winston Churchill. There is also an otherworldliness that can serve as a place of refuge, or escape. The serpent's bite with Jupiter has an overall idealistic temperament, reaching into the realms of humanitarianism and spirituality.

☊ ☌ ♄ The Dragon's Head conjoining Saturn is a powerful combination for worldly mastery. The serpent with Saturn is a benchmark of wisdom, for wisdom is knowledge experienced. This wisdom is intensely directed toward worldly affairs. There can be an insatiable need for greater and greater mastery of one's personal, fated metier. There will also be a strong sense of isolation, going it alone through life.

The famous French artist, lithographer, and painter, Honore Daumier, had the Dragon's Head closely conjoined with Saturn in Scorpio in the 4th House. His mastery and drive were so great that he produced about 4,000 lithographs and some 200 paintings.

He became famous, in true Saturn fashion, shortly after his death. Augustus Caesar, Emperor of Rome, had this same conjunction in Taurus in the 8th House. Under this cold, calculating politician, Rome reached its zenith. He ushered in a great, golden age of literature and architecture. Here, we have two examples of the powerful personal mastery of this combination. Benvenuto Cellini, renowned renaissance artist and goldsmith, had a close out-of-sign conjunction between Taurus and Gemini in the 11th House. It is generally conceded that he was the greatest designer of metal of the medieval period. Lastly, we have Heinz Guderian, famed German Panzer General. He mastered the art of tank warfare on both the western and eastern fronts, known as much for his defensive skill in the later part of the war as he was for his "Blitzkrieg" attacks in the early days. Once again, we have a great artist and strategist excelling in their fated forms of expression. Each one's skill was copied and admired by friend and foe alike.

One woman client has the Dragon's head closely conjoined Saturn in the 8th House: she is a powerful executive secretary for a large corporation. Another woman has an almost exact conjunction in Taurus in the 2nd House: she comes from a wealthy family, where the father runs the family corporation. She has chosen to shun the family, father, and money for now, and go it alone with the goal of becoming self-sufficient.

With the Dragon's Head conjoined Saturn, the individual's great abilities propel him or her to places of power and recognition, as in the cases of Daumier, Caesar, Cellini, and Guderian. They often feel "alone at the top" of their profession. Their great mastery and wisdom are often admired and, at times, are sought out by apprentices, who wish one day to have similar abilities. Here the serpent's bite makes them masters of self-containment and self-sufficiency in their quest to master this world.

☊ ☌ ♄ When the Dragon's Tail conjoins Saturn it is the mark of the ascetic, the master of spiritual realms of existence. This person has a compelling need to retreat from the everyday world of humanity. The serpent's bite here can give an austere aloneness or a great dignity; a calling to leave this world and enter another. There can be great depression or spirituality. Theirs is the spiritual mastery found in retreat, in monasteries and places of seclusion; the spirituality of being alone with the divine.

Jean Paul Sartre, famed French philosopher, novelist, and playwright, had this conjunction within minutes of being exact, in Pisces in the 2nd House. Leader of the French Intelligencia after 1939, his philosophy of existentialism propounded that this world holds no meaning for the individual, that it is up to each of us, alone, to choose our destiny. Here the serpent's bite leaves no desire for this world, creating self-sufficiency and self-responsibility for each and every lot. Again, famed astrologer Elbert Benjamine, known as C. C. Zain, had the Dragon's Tail closely conjoined Saturn within minutes in Taurus in the 6th House. He studied to be a naturalist until 1900, when he had a mystical experience. He founded the Church of Light in Los Angeles and wrote a series of spiritual and astrological books. Another architect of spirituality was the astrologer Max Heindel, who had this conjunction, within a degree, in Libra in the 4th House. Heindel founded the Rosicrucian Fellowship of the United States at the turn of the century. Here we see the calling to enter the other realms and to found a permanent form, an institution, so that others may be able to follow into this spiritual reality for themselves. Lastly, the great poet, philosopher, and artist, Kahlil Gibran, had this conjunction within minutes of being exact, in Taurus in the 9th House. His solitary figure in *The Prophet* speaks eloquently of this man's otherworldly mastery and insight. Claude Bragdon said of him, "His power came from some great reservoir of spiritual life else it could not have been so universal and potent."

In the everyday world, we find a similar dignity and asceticism. One client who had this conjunction in the 1st House was very wealthy, but was absolutely unchanged by it all. He had a measured dignity about him and was concerned chiefly with his purpose in life. A woman had this conjunction in Aquarius, within minutes of being exact in the 10th House. She has followed a spiritual path for most of her adult life. There is a complete honesty about her. She suffers from a feeling of isolation and depression and is determined to conquer this through spiritual mastery alone. Lastly, a woman client has this conjunction in Aries in her 5th House. She has suffered much sorrow and financial reversals from speculation, but now heads a spiritual consortium that helps publish "new age" books.

With the Dragon's Tail conjoined Saturn, there is other worldly mastery, as in the cases of Rapheal, Zain, Heindel, and Gibran.

The emphasis here with Saturn, the most realistic of the planetary energies, is to embrace a reality greater than this world. Each person must find this reality, measure it, and master this reality in experiencing it for themselves. It is not important if other realms exist; it is only important if they exist for them. The serpent's bite removes these individuals from this world by asceticism, retreat and, at times, by loneliness in preparation for the world to come. The serpent's bite here leaves the mark of the spiritual architect.

The Dragons Conjoined Uranus, Neptune, and Pluto

The outer planets, from Uranus on out, move so slowly that they conjoin the Dragon's for extended periods of time, and for that reason these conjunctions are quite common. Close conjunctions on or close to an Angle however are not at all common.

When the Dragon's Head conjoins Uranus, on an Angle, there is an intensification of the individuality, that results in some special genius driving to make its mark on the world. The heightened individuation leads to strong feelings of uniqueness and being different. This results in feeling misunderstood, and at worst, being separate and alienated from others.

The infamous Nazi Martin Bormann had the Dragon's Head closely conjoined Uranus in Sagittarius near the Midheaven. He was known as "Hitler's evil genius" and became second only to Hitler in command of the Third Reich. He was one of the most powerful, yet enigmatic and least understood of the Nazis. Here the serpent's bite creates a worldly, warped genius, trying to mold reality into the image and likeness of his unique, disturbed, Sagittarius vision.

When the Dragon's Tail conjoins Uranus on an Angle, there is an intensification of the individuality that results in some other worldly or spiritual genius carried over from past lives. The heightened individuation leads to strong feelings of uniqueness and being different that often leave the person feeling they are not of this world. This results at times in feelings of being separate and alienated from others.

Mozart had the Dragon's Tail closely conjoined in Pisces on the Descendant. Here we have a powerful, otherworldly genius. Mozart learned to play several instruments at age three, in concert at age five, drawing on a special wealth of musical ability from past lives. He is recognized as perhaps the greatest musical genius of all time. Here the serpent's bite bestows an otherworldly genius expressed through the universal language of music in purist Piscean fashion.

When the Dragon's Head conjoins Neptune on an Angle, there is an intensified yearning for an idealized or glamorized worldly existence. The person feels an ongoing need to surrender to an image and experience of self that continually change to reflect current circumstances. As the Dragon's Head represents the process of involution, there is an ongoing need to manifest the dream of self in the worldly plane of existence. This can lead to experiences of spiritual surrender, resulting in a greater sense of self. It also can lead to deception and dementia, resulting in experiences of worldly fantasy, deceit, and delusion. This is dependent on the evolution of the individual.

The famed stage and film actor, Rex Harrison, had the Dragon's Head conjoined Neptune, within a few minutes of arc, in Cancer close to the Descendant. He portrayed a variety of roles from his Oscar-winning performance in "My Fair Lady" to "Cleopatra," and "Doctor Dolittle." Here we have the consummate actor. The Dragon's Head with Neptune here allows the individual to surrender and transcend the singular self and play out several roles in the world. The serpent's bite here intensifies worldly vision. It also intensifies the need to lead a glamorized material existence.

When the Dragon's Tail conjoins Neptune, on an Angle, there is a intense longing for an idealized, spiritual, or otherworldly existence. The person feels an ongoing need to surrender to an image and experience of self that comes from another reality, a result of past lives. As the Dragon's Tail represents the process of evolution, there is an ongoing need to express the dream image of self in spiritual or otherworldly planes of existence. This can lead to spirituality or enlightenment experiences, or can result in out-of-body experiences and madness.

The German naturalist, physician, and mountain climber, Karl Herrligkoffer, had the Dragon's Tail closely conjoined Neptune, within a few degrees of his Leo Ascendant. Here is the longing for other worldly experience, in conquering the mountains of the Himalayas. There is an experience of belonging to something more vast than this worldly realm. The serpent's bite here intensifies spiritual and other worldly vision.

When the Dragon's Head conjoins Pluto, on an Angle, there is a fanaticism of worldly purpose. The person is obsessively drawn to charismatic, transformational, self-annihilating, worldly experiences, in which the self lives, dies, and is reborn. There will be power and control struggles. This person continually experiences the cutting edge of being in control; of not being in control. When the fear of not being in control is conquered (ultimately the fear of death), this soul becomes liberated on this plane of existence.

Famed evangelist, Marjoe Gortner, has the Dragon's Head closely conjoined Pluto in Leo within a few degrees of the Ascendant. From childhood on he preached the word of God in this world through his touring ministry for fifteen years. This was his calling from God. Later he left the church to become a film actor. Here the serpent's bite creates a powerful sense of purpose early on in the life. This purpose, however, must die and perhaps be reborn in the epic struggle between divine and personal purpose.

When the Dragon's Tail conjoins Pluto, on an Angle, the person is drawn to charismatic, transformational, self-annihilating, spiritual, or otherworldly experiences, in which the self lives, dies, and is reborn. This person also continually experiences the cutting edge of being in control; being not in control. When the fear of not being in control is conquered, and ultimately the fear of death, this person becomes liberated on spiritual or otherworldly levels of existence.

Famed model and mistress of Alfred Bloomingdale, Vicki Morgan, had the Dragon's Tail closely conjoined Pluto in Leo within a few degrees of the Ascendant. Here the transformational, self-annihilating experiences are of the other worldly variety as Vicki was engaged in a predominantly sadomasochistic relationship with Bloomingdale. The tendencies to self-annihilation moved from the sexual world with Bloomingdale to the real world when her companion and lover beat her to death with a baseball bat during an argument. Here the serpent's bite calls to the otherworldly realms. The cutting edge of being in control; not being in control, was played out in the world of sexual fantasy. This obsessive need for transformational otherworldly experience eventually led her into the other fantasy realms of drugs and alcohol abuse. In true

Dragon's Tail with Pluto fashion she lost herself, and then she lost her life. Here the serpent's bite plays out one of the greatest divine mysteries of life; when to be in control and when not to be in control. That is the ultimate Pluto question. By being in control we are often not in touch with what is really happening in our life. But paradoxically, by being in touch with what is really happening in our life, we are mysteriously most in control. One experience is divine, the other insane. To know the difference between the two is wisdom, and for that we need the bite of the serpent.

Conclusion

Following this chapter's thesis, you can see for yourself that the Dragon's Head and Dragon's Tail are not only powerful points on the ecliptic where eclipses happen, but powerful points for chart interpretation as well. The creation myths and serpent-dragon lore of both east and west have help us to understand and assess these powerful points on the ecliptic. Use them in close conjunction with the planets and your chart interpretations will have an added dimension of meaning. They are powerful tools of measurement. With them you can measure where the divine touches the personal.

Bibliography

Behari, Bepin. *Myths and Symbols of Vedic Atrology.* Utah: Morson Publishing, 1990.

Braha, James. *Ancient Hindu Astrology for the Modern Western Astrologer.* Miami: Hermetician Press, 1986.

Hamilton, Edith. *Mythology.* Boston: Little Brown and Company, 1942.

Hillebrandt, Alfred. *Vedic Mythology.* 2 Vol. Delhi: Motilal Banarsidass Publishers, 1990.

Hogarth, Peter J. *Dragons.* Toronto: Viking Press. 1979.

Keith, Arthur B. *The Religion and Philosophy of the Veda and Upanishads.* 2 vols. Delhi: Motilal Banarsidass Publishers, 1989.

King James Version. *Holy Bible.* World Bible Publishers, Inc.

Sitchin, Zecharia. *The 12th Planet.* New York: Avon, 1976.

Tom Bridges

Tom Bridges is an astrologer who lives in Big Rapids, Michigan, and works at Matrix Software, developer of astrological software for personal computers (and provider of astrological charts in this article). His main interests in astrology are Uranian and horary. When he isn't consulting the heavens for lost cats or whether he needs catastrophic automobile insurance over the next six months, he tends a garden with his wife Randee.

Tom went to Dartmouth College and the University of Minnesota, and out of a variety of majors somehow landed in restaurants, where he trained for several years as a chef. Tom has also been active in the astrological field as a freelance editor of extraordinary skill and acumen for several popular astrology books.

As an introduction to his chapter, focused subtly on measurement of relationship factors, Tom wishes to dedicate his thoughts to his wife, with the words of Sir Thomas Browne in *Religio Medici* (1643):

> *So When thy absent beames begin t' impart*
> *Again a solstice on my frozen heart,*
> *My winter's ov'r.*

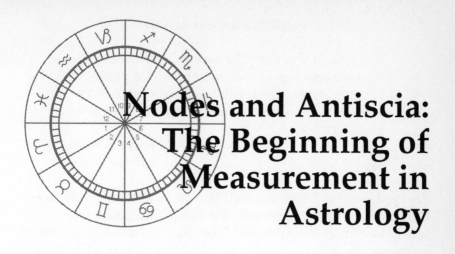

Nodes and Antiscia: The Beginning of Measurement in Astrology

Tom Bridges

"You arrive even in the solsticie
And the highest point of sun-shine happinesse."
1602, John Marston
The History of Antonio and Media; part two:
Antonio's Revenge

"The floure [flower] twists Æquinoctionally, from
the left hand to the right, according to the daily
revolution."
1658, Sir Thomas Browne
Hydriotaphia, or *Urne Buriall*

"When all the air is serene in the sultry solstice of
summer."
1847, Henry Wadsworth Longfellow
Evangeline

"There is in every constitution a certain solstice."
1860, Ralph Waldo Emerson
The Conduct of Live

Nodes and Connection

The structure of our solar system is defined by the
interrelationship of the various orbital planes of
which it is composed. This interrelationship is con-
veniently expressed by the complete system of
planetary nodes.

Michael Erlewine
Interface Nodes

The nodes of the Moon are well known in astrology; less so are
the planetary nodes, especially the Earth/Sun nodes more commonly known as the Aries and Libra points. Nodes, or the inter-
secting orbits in our solar system; they are astrology's flagbearers
of personal interactive potential, symbolizing our various and
complicated connections to our fellow beings.

Nodes are taking on greater significance as interpretive sign-
posts in present-day astrology. It is not that they were ever
neglected, but now seems to be a time when *relationships* rattle at
the root of many global issues. Geographic borders are changing;
the "mundane" is now dramatic as people are at each other's
throats in search of new modes and, indeed, loving.

Antiscia and the Four Corners of the Year

The clarion call of the seasons wakes astrologers and nonas-
trologers alike. Who can ignore the changing of the guard, from
winter to spring, spring to summer, summer to fall, and fall to
winter again? It is literally clockwork. These four seasonal transi-
tions are all "zero points" of the soul, where we descend to
ground zero, finish something old, and begin something new.

Astrologers call these turning points of orbital interaction *antiscia*; also called solstice points, mirror points, or, in the German-
speaking countries where they are widely employed by astrologers,
Spiegelpunkte. (The point opposite an antiscion (singular form of
antiscia) is generally called a contra-antiscion. But if antiscia are
"solstice points," I prefer to call contra-antiscia "equinox points.")

These four seasonal points, the solstices of summer and winter and the equinoxes of spring and fall, are the crosshairs of our

bead on life on this Earth, the interpretive potential of which remains in the womb of astrological thinking. Uranian and horary astrology have made some hay with these axes in different ways, but many other techniques in astrology have not. At a time when people may opt for relationships with cars or horses, when many are stifling a primal, fundamental whine for human interconnectedness, these symbols of the social interaction of beings demand our attention and enrich our astrological awareness.

Antiscia—Another Kind of Aspect

One horoscope is different than another because of where the planets are in the course of time. If you've read Ptolemy's *Tetrabiblos*, you've gotten an earful about sign familiarity ("oikeiosis"; another translation might be "affinity"). It's a root concept of the way we practice astrology. The different mutual relationships of the planets are called aspects, which in Ptolemy's time meant quite literally the mutual glare of planets across the ecliptic, casting their aspects (from a Latin word meaning "to look at") or glances at one another. Two planets in aspect are, figuratively speaking, looking at each other across the ecliptic. When the way in which the planets look at each other is especially strong—like when you turn to look at someone because you know that person is looking at you—the planets have a strong connection, influence each other, or have a mutual bearing on the chart. The great seventeenth-century English poet John Milton knew his heavens, his cosmology, and his astrology. Look at his elaborate explanation of "the reason for the seasons":

> . . . The Sun
> Had first his precept so to move, so shine,
> As might affect the Earth with cold and heat
> Scarce tolerable, and from the North to call
> Decrepit Winter, from the South to bring
> Solstitial summer's heat. To the blanc Moon
> Her office they prescrib'd, to th' other five
> Thir planetary motions and aspects
> In *Sextile*, *Square*, and *Trine*, and *Opposite*,
> Of noxious efficacy, and when to join

In Synod unbenign, and taught the fixt
Thir influence malignant when to show'r,
Which of them rising with the Sun, or falling,
Should prove tempestuous: To the Winds they set
Thir corners, when with bluster to confound
Sea, Air, and Shore, the Thunder when to roll
With terror through the dark Aereal Hall.
Some say he bid his Angels turn askance
The Poles of Earth twice ten degrees and more
From the Sun's Axle; they with labor push'd
Oblique the Centric Globe: Some say the Sun
Was bid turn Reins from th' Equinoctial Road
Like distant breadth to *Taurus* with the Sev'n
Atlantic Sisters, and the *Spartan* Twins
Up to the *Tropic* Crab; thence down amain
By *Leo* and the *Virgin* and the *Scales*,
As deep as *Capricorn,* to bring in change
Of Seasons to each Clime; else had the Spring
Perpetual smil'd on Earth with vernant Flow'rs,
Equal in Days and Nights, except to those
Beyond the Polar Circles; to them Day
Had unbenighted shone, while the low Sun
To recompense his distance, in thir sight
Had rounded still th' *Horizon,* and not known
Or East or West, which had borbid the Snow . . .

Ptolemy describes several ways in which signs—and by association planets—are "familiar" with one another, or have something in common:

- **Aspects:** the well-known formations of sextile, square, trine, opposition, and (it goes without saying, conjunction), here with reference to signs;

- **The Commanding and Obeying Signs:** pairs of signs equally disposed from the equinoctial signs Aries and Libra: Taurus-Pisces, Gemini-Aquarius, Cancer-Capricorn, Leo-Sagittarius, and Virgo-Scorpio;

- **The Beholding Signs:** Pairs of signs equally disposed from the solstitial signs Cancer and Capricorn: Gemini-Leo,

Taurus-Virgo, Aries-Libra, Pisces-Scorpio, and Aquarius-Sagittarius;

- **Disjunct ("Asyndeta") Sign:** A sign complying to none of the above three: adjacent to or five signs removed from another sign.

The second and third categories above are the ancestors of antiscia, commanding and obeying pairs corresponding to equinox points and beholding pairs corresponding to solstice points. The great scholar of astrology, A. Bouché-Leclerq, notes that one of the great turning points in astrology occurred when astrologers eschewed the anathema of "disjunct" signs and embraced the full symmetrical potential of the 360° zodiac. The change made "commanding and obeying" signs contra-antiscia (or equinox) degrees equally located from the equinoctal degrees 0° Aries and 0° Libra, and made "beholding signs" antiscia degrees, equally located from the solstitial degrees, 0° Cancer and 0° Capricorn:

> The association of two contiguous signs, one necessarily feminine and the other masculine, was an astrological heresy. If one looks at the exact symmetry, this problem is also apparent in the pairing of degrees. The odd-numbered degrees—that is to say masculine, after the doctrine of Pythagoras—are associated with the parallels of even-numbered degrees on the opposite side. . . . Dorotheus of Sidon rectified this establishing, within each sign, an "empty" degree—the 30th—such that a sign's first degree reflects a sign's 29th degree across the equinox, the second degree reflects the 28th, and so on, the rule that requires the likeness of sign gender being observed.
>
> (A. Bouché-Leclerq, pp 161-162)

The association of contiguous signs paved the way for antiscia and represents the break from ancient to modern astrology. The standard aspects (conjunction, sextile, square, trine, and opposition) all indicate various distances from one planet to another around the ecliptic, from zero (conjunction) to diametrically opposite (opposition). These are all measurements along the ecliptic. But what about distances *above or below* the ecliptic, when two planets or points are the same distance from the celestial equator? *That's where solstice points come in*, and they can really be eye-openers, whether in your own chart or in a comparison of your chart with other.

Solstice points measure planets' vertical orientation to the equator. When one planet is as far from the equator as another, *each stands at the solstice point of the other*. When the orb (distance from exact) is close, solstice points are strong aspects in a chart; and the closer the orb, the stronger the aspect. For solstice points, I have found that only a relatively small orb is admissible. Where for a conjunction you might allow eight degrees of orb, for solstice points the limit is less, just a degree or so, a couple degrees max.

Horary astrologer Gilbert Navarro describes the special quality of antiscia through the ancient idea of the familiarity of signs. Gilbert describes antiscia degrees (as well as their cousins, parallels) as a kind of "way out" when two planets evince no basic familiarity by sign, aspect, or nature. For example, Venus and Saturn don't normally get along (this is horary-speak). But when they are parallel or at each other's antiscia degrees, they do work together; "Love" and "Delay" can find a common ground. Isn't that like life? I think this common ground idea is why antiscia show up so significantly when looking at relationships.

Antiscia Are Nothing New

> A Christian hath no solstice . . . where he may
> stand still, and go no further.
>
> 1631, John Donne
> *Selections from the Works of John Donne*

Some of the greatest astrologers who have ever lived included antiscia in their reticule of techniques. Ivy Goldstein-Jacobson, for example, used antiscia:

> Antiscia mark a turning point in some way when aspected. The solstice point is the Sun's turning point in 0° Cancer and 0° Capricorn as he goes back

to the celestial equator from his greatest distance away . . . Progress the solstice point at the Sun's rate . . . and note any aspects it forms to the natal planets and angles, observing particularly any action of the ascendant-ruler's solstice point . . . We can use [solstice points] in rectifying the time of birth, insofar as progressed aspects between them and the midheaven or ascendant are exact or not.

And who can resist William Lilly, the Shakespeare of renaissance English astrology and great horary master, whose dulcet phrasings now seem like a foreign language. Lilly was well versed in antiscia:

The Antiscion Signes are those, which are of the same vertue and are equally distant from the first degree of the two Tropick Signes Cancer and Capricorn, and in which degrees whilest the Sun is, the dayes and nightes are of equall length; by example it will be plaine; when the Sun is in the tenth degree of Taurus, he is as farre distant from the first degree of Cancer as when in the twentieth degree of Leo; therefore when the sun is in the tenth of Taurus, he hath his Antiscion to the twentieth of Leo; that is, he giveth vertue or influence to any Star or planet that at the time either is in the same degree by Conjunction, or castesth any Aspect unto it . . . As there are Antiscions, which of the good Planets we think are equall to a sextile or trine; so are there Contrantiscions, which we find to be of the nature of a square or opposition.

Uranian astrology, in the first decades of this century, latched onto antiscia in a big way [for more on the Uranian system, see Arlene Kramer's chapter in this volume—Ed.]. Antiscia and their symmetrical likenesses, midpoint axes, are fundamental in the current-analysis techniques of Uranian astrology. In the words of Udo Rudolph, son of early Uranian pioneer Ludwig Rudolph and present-day director of Germany's Hamburg School of astrology:

The antiscia known to the classical school of
astrologers are reflection points over a given axis
(Cancer-Capricorn). Witte noted that around every
axis these reflecting points exist. In other words, he
admits that every degree of the zodiac can be the
centre of an axis . . . A sensitive point is for Witte
the reflecting point that is not occupied by a planet or other factor in the radical chart. He points out
that a planetary picture becomes effective when a
sensitive point is made active by a progressed,
directed, or transiting factor moving over the
reflecting point concerned, and thereby completing the formula.

This fantastic idea of "completing the formula"—where you
can ask the natal chart a question and get an answer—also has use
in synastry. Other people, relationships in general, "complete" us.
We are born as equations with nothing on the right side of the
equals sign. *One way you complete those equations is when planets
from your chart reside at antiscia degrees in my chart.* Antiscia reach
across the personal barriers and defenses we routinely erect.

Continuity—Something, Someone, on the Other Side of the Fence

The temples were oriented solstitially or equinoc-
tally.
        1894, *The Athenæum: Journal of Literature,
        Science, and the Fine Arts*

There is a dramatic mundane symbol of the continuity of seasons
and the personal interpretive potential of antiscia in the Arc de
Triumph in Paris. Given clear sky conditions, you can see the sun
rising through the arch on or around November 6. If you stand
facing east, there it is: golden Phoebus' chariot conquering the
night. You can see the identical phenomenon exactly on the other
side of the winter solstice on or around February 6 every year.
What do these dates have in common? The zodiac positions of
the Sun on these days are antiscia degrees, in this case *equidistant*

from the winter solstice point 0° Capricorn on December 21 (each Sun date, 15 Scorpio and 15 Aquarius, respectively, is 45 degrees away from the reference point at 0° Capricorn). Great and sacred objects throughout the world often have such a celestial orientation.

Who rises through your Arch de Triumph? Who in your life is the other side of the solstice and equinox axes? Later in this article we will see specifically how to find the antiscia degrees of planets in your chart. When planets in other people's charts occupy these degrees, there is, on some level, a great and sacred match.

Day Equals Year

You've heard of grand cross aspect patterns in the birth chart. Well, the equinox and solstice axes mark the grand cross of the heavens, common to (and active in) *all* astrological charts. The astrological significance of the equinox and solstice axes is that they represent the common ground between the Earth's two motions: the Earth's daily spin-motion on the axis of its north and south poles, accounting for the rising and setting of the Sun, and its annual orbit-motion around the Sun, accounting for the four seasons. The interplay of these terrestrial go-rounds also accounts for astrology's major tenet—"a day is like a year," the superficially nonsensical notion that "a day in the timetables of the heavens is as a year in a person's life."

Grant Lewi, one of the great astrologers of this century, nonetheless generally dismissed the idea of "day for a year" as having little basis in reality. It's easy to see why, for it seems to be an indissoluble riddle, how a day is like a year. It begs the question, what do the annual and daily motions of the Earth have to do with each other? In what way are they connected? Any time we have two motions or orbits, we have two nodes, two points of orbit intersection. As mentioned, 0° Aries and 0° Libra are the nodes of the Earth's motions in the Tropical zodiac and are extremely important points of reference.

Certainly on the surface, the idea that a day in the ephemeris is as a year in life seems to defy logic. Actually, the logic is tight, concrete, and compelling. And the key is antiscia—also called solstice points. Let's begin by calling antiscia and contra-antiscia astrology's vertical counterpart to the traditional horizontal (longitudinal) aspect sequences of conjunction, sextile, square, trine, opposition, and other harmonic divisions of the 360° circle. They exist vestigially today in mainstream astrology as parallels and contraparallels. There are parallels of latitude (relative to the ecliptic) and parallels of declination (relative to the celestial equator). Both show the planets' "mirror point" relative to the ecliptic, in the case of parallels of latitude, and relative to the celestial equator, in the case of parallels of declination.

Two celestial bodies are in parallel by declination when they have the same elevation off the celestial equator (contraparallel when one is above the celestial equator and the other is below). The measurement is made along a circle known as an "hour circle," which is a circle on the celestial sphere perpendicular to the celestial equator, passing through the planet in question, and, by necessity, passing through the north and south pole of the celestial equator.

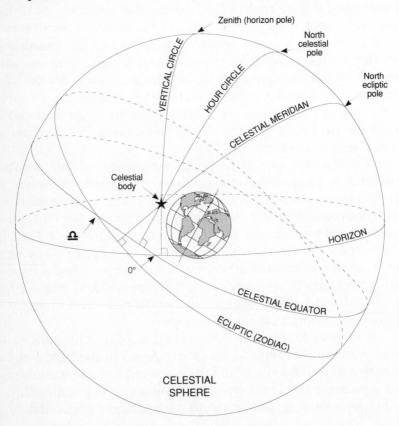

Note that the measurements determining whether planets are in parallel by declination bear no direct relation to the ecliptic. It just so happens that the ecliptic is always fairly close by. *This is where parallels differ from antiscia, for in the case of antiscia, the ecliptic is everything.*

With antiscia, here we are dealing only with points on the ecliptic, not with planets themselves, unless they happen to be exactly on the ecliptic. Planets spend a lot more time off the ecliptic than on it—always pretty close, but not often actually on it. So how are planets measured on the ecliptic? They are "brought there" via a circle perpendicular to the ecliptic and passing through the planet and the poles of the ecliptic. This is called "projection by perpendicular," the traditional means of establishing a standard astronomical measurement. *To make any sense out of the location of planets in the sky, we have to "bring them" to a place where they all have something in common. This is the ecliptic.*

Antiscia are an abstraction of the equator in terms of the ecliptic. They are pairs of points on the ecliptic the *same distance from the celestial equator.* To say that the ecliptic position of two planets bear the same relationship to the celestial equator is to say that they are equidistant from the 0° Cancer-0° Capricorn solstice axis or the 0° Aries-0° Libra equinox axis.

Any planet has its antiscion as many degrees away from the 0° Cancer-0° Capricorn axis as the planet itself is, *but on the other side of the axis.* It is the reflection or reflex point across this significant axis defining the tropical solstices. An equinox point (contra-antiscia) is the point opposite the antiscion), is the reflection or reflex point across the 0° Aries-0° Libra equinoctal axis. Remember the word "reflection" when interpreting solstice and equinox points in your chart.

Celestial Orbits

> The diurnal revolution is from the motion of the
> earth, by which the equinoctial circle is described
> upon it.
>
> 1656, Thomas Hobbes
> *Elements of Philosophy*

An individual's most basic orientation to the cosmos is determined at the moment of birth by where the various orbits of the
cosmos cross or intersect. "Star-crossed" indeed! Crossing, inter-
secting—these orbits have to do with relationships, particularly
the intersections of the two motions of the Earth, our fated orientation to the Sun and to the Suns of others.

Scientists are just getting around to articulating why physical life is possible on the Earth and not on other planets. For
astrologers, the "why" happens to be something so clear: our resonance and sympathy with cosmic events, chiefly, our solar system's Sun. As the key determinant in the possibility of physical
life on Earth, the scientists point to the angle at which the Earth is
inclined to its orbit about the Sun, which, for all intents and purposes, is a constant 23.5°. This angle is known as the "obliquity of
the ecliptic." Welcome to the club!

The fact that this inclination, the obliquity of the ecliptic,
varies only minutely over the centuries and millennia means that
the Earth's seasonal orientation to the Sun changes imperceptibly
in the course of a human lifetime. It is a life and death matter to
rely on spring, summer, fall, and winter (equinox, solstice,
equinox, solstice) to occur when they do. It is dyed in the fabric of
our being. Like a dog following the window-Sun around the
house throughout the day, our sympathy with the seasons is literally our very nature. In the winter, many people notice a tendency to want to sleep more, at least until the Sun gets up. In the
summer, we tend to get up earlier and work later, while the Sun
still shines. And why do we "save" Daylight time?

If the seasonal cycle of our existence changed from year to
year, if the Earth, from year to year as it orbited the Sun, rocked
back and forth on its polar axis, then there would be wild variations of temperature, peaks and valleys completely inhospitable
to physical life as we know it on this planet. We'd be blazing-close

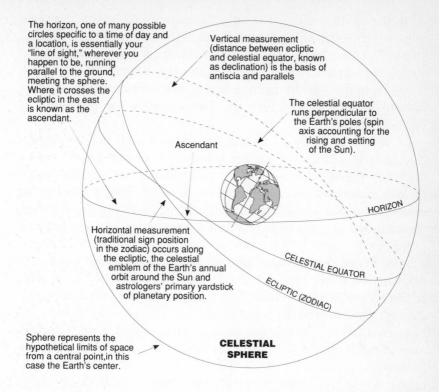

The horizon, one of many possible circles specific to a time of day and a location, is essentially your "line of sight," wherever you happen to be, running parallel to the ground, meeting the sphere. Where it crosses the ecliptic in the east is known as the ascendant.

Vertical measurement (distance between ecliptic and celestial equator, known as declination) is the basis of antiscia and parallels

The celestial equator runs perpendicular to the Earth's poles (spin axis accounting for the rising and setting of the Sun).

Ascendant

Horizontal measurement (traditional sign position in the zodiac) occurs along the ecliptic, the celestial emblem of the Earth's annual orbit around the Sun and astrologers' primary yardstick of planetary position.

HORIZON

CELESTIAL EQUATOR

ECLIPTIC (ZODIAC)

Sphere represents the hypothetical limits of space from a central point, in this case the Earth's center.

CELESTIAL SPHERE

to the Sun one season, and in an ice-cold, blue distance the opposite season. It would depend on how much shifting was going on in the orientation of a planet's polar and equatorial axes; the greater the shifts, the wilder the changes in climate, and the less likely the planet would be to support life. But the constancy of the relationship between the Earth's two motions is the mortal pipeline in the body of all growing things, establishing and balancing the energies of life.

Zero Aries—The Beginning of Measurement

Due to the obliquity of the ecliptic, the celestial equator (the projected sky-emblem of the Earth's daily spinning motion on its polar axis) crosses the ecliptic (the projected sky-emblem of the Earth's orbit around the Sun) at two points diametrically opposed to each other. Astronomers and astrologers call these the Aries and Libra points. Zero Aries determines the beginning of measurement—the zero point—in "right ascension" (the counting system along the celestial equator). On the previous page is a diagram showing the Earth at the center of the "celestial sphere." The celestial sphere is an imaginary geometrical construct of no known limit, whose center is the center of the Earth. It has been devised by human beings who want some means of measuring and comparing the two-dimensional positions of celestial bodies.

Now, back to the Nodes: as we know, a node is the intersection of two orbits, or more accurately, two orbital planes (great dishes in the sky aligned with a planet's orbit around the Sun). From a geocentric or earth-centered point of view, a node is the intersection of a planet's orbit with the ecliptic; the lunar nodes are included in this category. From a heliocentric or Sun-centered point of view, a node is the intersection of any two *planets'* orbital planes. When one of those planets happens to be the Earth, the node lies on the ecliptic; otherwise the node has to be "projected" to the ecliptic (along a circle that is perpendicular to it and passes through the poles of the ecliptic).

Two orbits always intersect at two nodes. One is called ascending: that which a planet crosses as it passes from negative (below) to positive (above) latitude—from below the ecliptic to above it relative, to the observer. The other node is descending: that which a planet crosses as it passes from above the ecliptic to below it. The ascending node is sometimes called north, and the descending node south, though a north node to an observer in the northern hemisphere is a south node to an observer in the southern hemisphere, and vice versa.

Up is Down, Down is Up

Antiscii—those who live on the same meridian, but on the opposite side of the equator, so that their shadows at noon fall in opposite directions.

1658, Edward Phillips, 1706 (ed. J. Kersey)
The New World of English Words:
or a General Dictionary

[At Jerusalem], . . . a spere [spear] that is pight [put] in to the erthe [earth], vpon the hour of mydday whan it is Equenoxium . . . sheweth no shadwe [shadow].

c. 1400, Sir John Maundeville
The Buke of John Maundeuill, Being the Travels of
Sir J. Mandeville Knight

Let's pause for a moment and consider the confusion of beings living on opposite sides of the Earth's equator. It breeds an insoluble dyslexia of spirit. In New York, you look south to watch the Sun arc from one horizon to the other. In Christchurch, New Zealand, you look north. If you're a gardener in the northern hemisphere, in whom the ideal southern exposure is ingrained, you'd be thrown for a loop if you moved to the southern hemisphere and started looking for a farm with an ideal northern orientation to the life-giving Sun.

Antiscion is a Greek word—"ante" + "skion"—meaning "opposite shadow." It appears in Ptolemy's Almagest in its original reference as a description of people who live along the same meridian of longitude but on opposite sides of the equator. What's true for people who happen to live in this orientation with each other is that objects, at the same time of day, *cast the same shadow, but in opposite directions*, hence the name, "opposite shadow." Such people are "equal under the Sun" but opposite in their orientation. You and I are equals, but opposite in our views, separate candles connected by a common taper. We have to cut the taper to fire the energy of spirit that makes life real. It is as if "Antiscia"—these "counterpartners" of the earth—facing the equator to look at each other, look at themselves in a mirror, where right appears on the left and left on the right. Therefore antiscia are also called shadow points or mirror points *(Spiegelpunkte).*

The concepts can begin to get difficult, detailed, and fussy. I personally feel that the core concerns of intersection, reflection, balance, and rapport between these pairs of motions and points are all the same. All the north-south, conjunction-opposition considerations are important for background understanding, but they must not cloud the issue at hand, *the overall pairing and complementation among these measurements and references.*

Ptolemy himself professes mixed opinion regarding the virtue of one Earth angle over another as the starting point of the year. Since we're dealing with a circle, he says, it could just as well be one as another. Ptolemy mentions this in his discussion of what is the "New Moon of the Year":

> To be sure, one could not conceive what starting-point to assume in a circle, as a general proposition; but with the circle through the middle of the zodiac one would properly take as the only beginnings the points determined by the equator and the tropics, that is, the two equinoxes and the two solstices. Even then, however, one would still be at a loss which of the four to prefer.
>
> (*Tetrabiblos*, II.10, pp. 195-197)

Astrologers *over*-treat the solstice and equinox axes like angles, sensitive to aspects from natal planets and therefore paradoxically personal in nature. *It is a fact that planets in strong aspect to 0° Aries and 0° Libra are significantly more influential, in terms of our personal orientation to the world, than planets having no aspect with these points.* And as we shall see, there are more "aspects" than immediately meet the eye.

Equally significant in terms of your personal orientation to the world are the two points square (90° away from) 0° Aries, namely, 0° Cancer and 0° Capricorn. These points mark the two seasonal solstices and mark changes in the Sun's north-south or vertical direction. At 0° Cancer, the Sun has reached its most northern point; at 0° Capricorn, its most southern. All four of these points—0° of Aries, Cancer, Libra, and Capricorn—have to do with the Sun's orientation to the celestial equator. In the diagram (page 189), look how the Sun (which is always on the ecliptic) is right on the celestial equator at 0° Aries and 0° Libra, and as far from the celestial equator as it ever gets when it gets to 0° Cancer and 0° Capricorn. These pairs of points are, respectively, the Sun's minima and maxima in its annual nodal cycle.

Getting the "Bends" for Astrology

Ptolemy called the maxima points in a planet's orbit the "bendings" (Greek, "kampe," bend) and implied, in the following passage from *Tetrabiblos* III.12, that no distinction interpretation was to be made between the minima and maxima points. III.12 is about injuries and diseases ("sinon kai pathon somatikon"). Ptolemy tells us everything we don't want to think that astrology can tell us: that fateful, fearful stuff about being deformed, or about genital dysfunction due to such-and-such a configuration of planets, life's bilgewater.

> If the luminaries, together or in opposition, move toward the maleficent planets upon the angles, or if the maleficent planets move toward the luminaries, particular when the Moon is at the nodes or her bendings, or in the injurious signs such as Aries, Taurus, Cancer, Scorpio, or Capricorn, there come about deformations of the body such as hunchback, crookedness ["bendings"], lameness, or paralysis.
>
> (Ptolemy, *Tetrabiblos* III.12, pp 325-327)

The point is that Ptolemy, the person who has had the greatest effect on the way Western astrologers ply their trade, seemed inclined to make little, if any, distinction among conjunctions, squares, and oppositions in terms of interpretation. In the following passage, Ptolemy also goes on to imply that conjunctions, oppositions, and squares of the Moon's nodes act similarly. Twentiethth-century astrologers have gotten a lot of mileage out of this idea, especially Uranian astrologers and cosmobiologists, and, as well it is central to Solar Arc measurement and theory.

Antiscia Table

	VII	V	III	I					
Cardinal	270	180	90	00	90	180	270	360	
	271	181	91	01	89	179	269	359	Mutable
	272	182	92	02	88	178	268	358	
	273	183	93	03	87	177	267	357	
	274	184	94	04	86	176	266	356	
	275	185	95	05	85	175	265	355	
	276	186	96	06	84	174	264	354	
	277	187	97	07	83	173	263	353	
	278	188	98	08	82	172	262	352	
	279	189	99	09	81	171	261	351	
	280	190	100	10	80	170	260	350	
	281	191	101	11	79	169	259	349	
	282	192	102	12	78	168	258	348	
	283	193	103	13	77	167	257	347	
	284	194	104	14	76	166	256	346	
	285	195	105	15	75	165	255	345	
	286	196	106	16	74	164	254	344	
	287	197	107	17	73	163	253	343	
	288	198	108	18	72	162	252	342	
	289	199	109	19	71	161	251	341	
	290	200	110	20	70	160	250	340	
	291	201	111	21	69	159	249	339	
	292	202	112	22	68	158	248	338	
	293	203	113	23	67	157	247	337	
	294	204	114	24	66	156	246	336	
	295	205	115	25	65	155	245	335	
	296	206	116	26	64	154	244	334	
	297	207	117	27	63	153	243	333	
	298	208	118	28	62	152	242	332	
	299	209	119	29	61	151	241	331	
Fixed	300	210	120	30	60	150	240	330	Mutable
	301	211	121	31	59	149	239	329	
	302	212	122	32	58	148	238	328	
	303	213	123	33	57	147	237	327	
	304	214	124	34	56	146	236	326	
	305	215	125	35	55	145	235	325	
	306	216	126	36	54	144	234	324	
	307	217	127	37	53	143	233	323	
	308	218	128	38	52	142	232	322	
	309	219	129	39	51	141	231	321	
	310	220	130	40	50	140	230	320	
	311	221	131	41	49	139	229	319	
	312	222	132	42	48	138	228	318	
	313	223	133	43	47	137	227	317	
	314	224	134	44	46	136	226	316	
	315	225	135	45	45	135	225	315	
					II	IV	VI	VIII	

Back to Antiscia (Solstice Points/Equinox Points)

Let's review our formal definition: two zodiac degrees are each other's antiscia when they are the same distance from the equator—and traditionally on the same side of the equator. This occurs *when the ecliptic degrees are equidistant from either 0° Cancer or 0° Capricorn, the two solstice points.* For example, 27° Gemini has its antiscion (singular form of antiscia) at 3° Cancer; both are 3° from 0° Cancer. Likewise, 12° Sagittarius, which is 18° from 0° Capricorn, has its antiscion at 18° Capricorn, the same distance from 0° Capricorn, but on the other side of the axis. It is important to say "zodiac degrees" rather than "two planets" since planets have orbits that, with respect to the Earth's, undulate above and below the ecliptic.

The table on page 194 will let you find antiscia in your charts.

Doing This by Hand (If You Don't Have a Computer Yet)

You can use the table on page 194, but first you may want to convert the position of a planet from its normal notation to what's called 360° notation. The easiest method is to determine what number the sign of the planet is in the standard zodiacal sequence:

Aries	1	Libra	7
Taurus	2	Scorpio	8
Gemini	3	Sagittarius	9
Cancer	4	Capricorn	10
Leo	5	Aquarius	11
Virgo	6	Pisces	12

Now take the number of the sign occupied by the planet or point, and *subtract 1*; for example, if the sign is Capricorn, your number is 9. Multiply this number by 30; for Capricorn, the answer is 270 (9 x 30). Then, add the number of degrees the planet has in the sign; if it's 15° Capricorn, the result is 285 (270 + 15). Now go to the table and look for 285.

There's a trick to finding the numbers in the table, which may at first glance appear to be out of sequence. Use the roman numerals at the top and bottom of the columns to find your way. Roman numeral I starts the counting, down to 45°, column II goes bottom-up from 45° to 90°, followed by column III from top to bottom, and so on. 285° is a third of the way down column VII (the first column listed). The next step is the key one. Take all the numbers in the same row with 285°:

285 195 105 15 75 165 255 345 —

These numbers are *all* the antiscia points (both solstice and equinox varieties) of 15° Capricorn. Now convert the positions back to regular sign notation (with enough practice, you'll start doing this in your head). It's easy: divide each of the numbers by 30 and *add 1 to get the number of the sign*. For example, from the list above, 30 goes into 195 six times, with 15 as a remainder. "Seven" is therefore the number of the sign (Libra.) The remainder becomes the number of degrees in Libra. 15° Libra is the answer. (Note that when the number is less than 30, the sign is automatically Aries.) The other points in this set of solstice and equinox points, in sequence are 15° Cancer, 15° Aries, 15° Gemini, 15° Virgo, 15° Sagittarius, and 15° Pisces.

Each row of the table has eight numbers corresponding to degrees of the ecliptic. Cardinal degrees—the first 30 degrees in the first four columns—are always matched with Mutable degrees—the first 30 degrees in the last four columns. Fixed degrees are always matched with themselves—the first 15 degrees of Fixed signs with the last 15 degrees of Fixed signs. You've probably already noticed one of the neater astrological tricks of symmetry, that the axis of 0° of Cardinal signs, which for convenience we are labeling 0° Aries, has 15° of Fixed signs at the other end, meaning that when you use the 90° dial, degrees that are equidistant from 15° of Fixed signs, but on opposite sides, are also antiscia degrees. So for all intents and purposes, you can treat 15° of Fixed signs just like 0° of Cardinal signs. This gives eight antiscia fulcrums in the 360° circle.

Get a Computer

You can only do so much of this by hand before you start thinking "there must be a better way." And there is. The best means of finding antiscia quickly is with the use of *midpoint trees* and *midpoint sorts*, two special computer printouts.

Midpoint Trees

Midpoint trees are a practical graphic representation of the importance of a midpoint axis in a chart. A midpoint axis is simply a line connecting a midpoint with its opposite point; the two planets or points involved straddle this line. There are as many midpoint axes in a chart as you have possible pairs of planets, *but to find antiscia you look at only the zero-cardinal axis;* and to find both solstice and equinox points, you look at a midpoint tree in 90° format, in which all grand cross degree quadruplets in the zodiac are melded

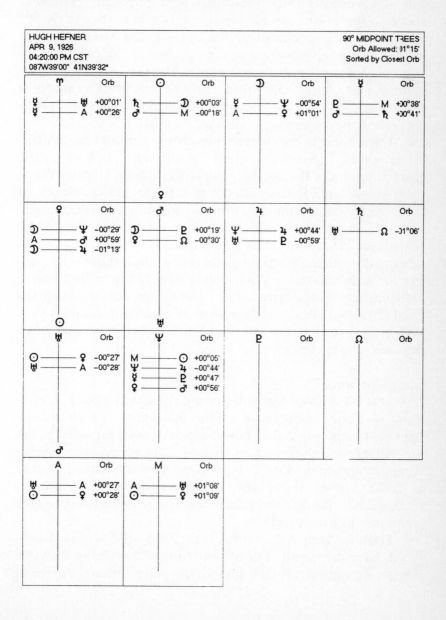

into a single degree, the result of which is that a contact to one degree manifests conjunction, square, or opposition aspects, all at once. (See midpoint tree, page 197.) This is an "Aries tree" in 90° format, what you need to find both solstice and equinox points.

The midpoint tree on the previous page shows a planet within or at the stem-root of one of the pairs that follow; this is the axis—the vertical "truck" line off which midpoint "branches" shoot. To find solstice and equinox points, cast the tree in the 90° format and look specifically at the tree with the Aries symbol at the top, as above. (Note that you can generate a midpoint tree for any axis, not just the zero-cardinal axis. This is where the Uranian system of astrology really shines. See Arlene Kramer's chapter in this volume, and see the reference section at the end of my chapter to see how you can generate a printout like this yourself).

The antiscia in the chart are simply the pairs of branch planets or points. The tree also gives the orb, which is how far the exact midpoint of the two branch planets is from 0° Aries. When the tree is ordered from smallest orb (at the top) to widest orb (at the bottom), and inasmuch as orb is a good indication of strength, you have an instant list of the antiscia in the chart from strongest to weakest. What a useful tool! And this is only natal; there's a lot you can do with midpoint trees and prediction, but this is the subject for another article. What you'll soon notice is that you're matching up equal degrees of *all Cardinal signs,* or equal degrees of *all Fixed signs,* or equal degrees of *all Mutable signs.* It's a slick system and, once you've got your Cardinal-Fixed-Mutable bearings, it's easy to remember.

Midpoint Sorts

This is the second way of finding antiscia in a chart. A midpoint sort is a collection of all the midpoints in a chart—the halfway points between all possible planet/planet, planet/point, and point/point combinations you are using, sorted or ordered in some convenient manner. To find antiscia, the convenient manner is "zodiac," or starting at zero and progressing upward in numerical sequence. This is a real pain in the neck to do by hand, but the computer does it instantly.

Look for zero Aries on the sort (000°)—the very first item listed. Now decide on your orb—for antiscia, no more than one degree, I recommend—and find all the pairs within a degree of zero. Don't neglect the pairs at the end of the sort, also within a degree of 000°, for the zodiac is not some abruptly ending thing, but a continuum. The end is the beginning.

JESSE HELMS   OCT 18, 1921

Zodiacal Sort

Midpoints: 90° Dial				
☽/♆ 000°21'	♃/☊ 011°30'	♅/A 027°53'	♄/♇ 050°41'	♆/☊ 076°55'
☉/♅ 000°23'	☊/M 012°22'	♆/♇ 027°53'	☉/A 052°14'	♂ 078°15'
☿/♆ 000°57'	☉/♄ 013°01'	☽/☊ 031°34'	♃/♇ 052°27'	♄/♅ 078°40'
♀/♃ 001°09'	☉/♃ 014°48'	☿/☊ 032°10'	♇/M 053°19'	A 079°45'
♄ 001°19'	☉/M 015°40'	♂/A 034°00'	♅/♆ 055°52'	☉/♆ 080°13'
♀/M 002°01'	☽/♂ 016°37'	☽/☉ 034°52'	♇/☊ 059°06'	♃/♅ 080°27'
♃/♄ 003°05'	☿/♂ 017°13'	☉/☿ 035°28'	♂/♆ 061°59'	♅/M 088°18'
♂/☊ 003°12'	♆/A 017°43'	♅/♇ 038°03'	☽/A 062°22'	♀/♂ 082°51'
♄/M 003°57'	☊ 018°08'	♀/A 038°36'	☉/♇ 062°24'	♂/♄ 084°47'
♃ 004°51'	☽/♀ 021°13'	♄/A 040°32'	☿/A 062°58'	♂/♃ 086°33'
♃/M 005°43'	☉/☊ 021°26'	♃/A 042°18'	♅ 066°02'	♅/☊ 087°05'
☉/♂ 006°30'	☿/♀ 021°49'	M/A 043°10'	♀/♆ 066°35'	♂/M 087°25'
M 006°35'	☽/♄ 023°09'	♂/♇ 044°09'	♄/♆ 068°30'	♀ 087°27'
♀/☊ 007°48'	☿/♄ 023°45'	☽ 045°00'	♃/♆ 070°17'	♀/♄ 089°23'
♄/☊ 009°43'	☉ 024°44'	☽/☿ 045°35'	♆/M 071°09'	♇/A 089°54'
♇ 010°03'	☽/♃ 024°55'	♆ 045°42'	♂/♅ 072°09'	
☽/♅ 010°31'	☿/♃ 025°31'	☿ 046°11'	☽/♇ 072°31'	
☉/♀ 011°06'	☽/M 025°47'	♀/♇ 048°45'	☿/♇ 073°07'	
☿/♅ 011°07'	☿/M 026°23'	☊/A 048°56'	♀/♅ 076°45'	

Standard Sort

Midpoints: 90° Dial				
☽ 045°00'	☽/♅ 010°31'	☿/♃ 025°31'	♂/♅ 072°09'	♅/♆ 055°52'
☉ 024°44'	☽/♆ 000°21'	☿/♄ 023°45'	♂/♆ 061°59'	♅/♇ 038°03'
☿ 046°11'	☽/♇ 072°31'	☿/♅ 011°07'	♂/♇ 044°09'	♅/☊ 087°05'
♀ 087°27'	☽/☊ 031°34'	☿/♆ 000°57'	♂/☊ 003°12'	♅/M 088°18'
♂ 078°15'	☽/M 025°47'	☿/♇ 073°07'	♂/M 087°25'	♅/A 027°53'
♃ 004°51'	☽/A 062°22'	☿/☊ 032°10'	♂/A 034°00'	♆/♇ 027°53'
♄ 001°19'	☉/☿ 035°28'	☿/M 026°23'	♃/♄ 003°05'	♆/☊ 076°55'
♅ 066°02'	☉/♀ 011°06'	☿/A 062°58'	♃/♅ 080°27'	♆/M 071°09'
♆ 045°42'	☉/♂ 006°30'	♀/♂ 082°51'	♃/♆ 070°17'	♆/A 017°43'
♇ 010°03'	☉/♃ 014°48'	♀/♃ 001°09'	♃/♇ 052°27'	♇/☊ 059°06'
☊ 018°08'	☉/♄ 013°01'	♀/♄ 089°23'	♃/☊ 011°30'	♇/M 053°19'
M 006°35'	☉/♅ 000°23'	♀/♅ 076°45'	♃/M 005°43'	♇/A 089°54'
A 079°45'	☉/♆ 080°13'	♀/♆ 066°35'	♃/A 042°18'	☊/M 012°22'
☽/☉ 034°52'	☉/♇ 062°24'	♀/♇ 048°45'	♄/♅ 078°40'	☊/A 048°56'
☽/☿ 045°35'	☉/☊ 021°26'	♀/☊ 007°48'	♄/♆ 068°30'	M/A 043°10'
☽/♀ 021°13'	☉/M 015°40'	♀/M 002°01'	♄/♇ 050°41'	
☽/♂ 016°37'	☉/A 052°14'	♀/A 038°36'	♄/☊ 009°43'	
☽/♃ 024°55'	☿/♀ 021°49'	♂/♃ 086°33'	♄/M 003°57'	
☽/♄ 023°09'	☿/♂ 017°13'	♂/♄ 084°47'	♄/A 040°32'	

Notice something strange about this sort? It ends at 90 degrees. This is because it has been cast in the 90° format. Realize that 360, while not exactly arbitrary (it roughly corresponds to the number of sunrises in a year) could just as well be another number. This is where it gets interesting, and where you can trim a great deal of labor from your astrological investigations. Going with the idea that conjunctions, oppositions, and squares are essentially the same thing, let's take a point in the zodiac, say 13° Cancer, and find what points are opposite or square to it—13° Capricorn, 13° Aries, and 13° Libra—or 13° of Cardinal signs. Now let's call these *the same point*. That's the essence of the 90° format, which saves you from tallying conjunctions, oppositions, and squares as separate phenomena and lets you get at the nut of the chart.

Interpreting Antiscia—"We Are the World"

The Earth's annual and daily motions result in the two apparent motions of the Sun: its daily trek from east to west across the sky, and its annual pace through the constellations surrounding the ecliptic. The Sun exhibits beautiful, predictable symmetries relative to the Earth. Solstice points are the interpretive extension of these symmetries.

Solstice points embody the symbolism of the Sun—one's very being, essence, or body. A planet's solstice point is its reflection, a complementary point with which it shares the unique attribute of being the same distance from the equator. It's as if a solstice point (or equinox point) is a planet's other half; hence its significance in synastry. We look for complementary people to spend our time with—people the same distance from the ground we are, but on the opposite side.

I think of antiscia as the "we are the world" aspect in astrology, especially in relationships. They represent a back door out of the "solitary confinement" that seems to characterize existential reality. Antiscia are your connection to the world, your links, your outlet to "what's happening out there." They have the flavor of fate or destiny, as any personal interface with the interpersonal world seems to have, but more than that, they harpoon our hearts to each other. *When a degree of a planet in my chart is the antiscion of a degree of a planet in yours, it may or may not be love, but it feels like you've got Moby Dick on the other end of the line, according to the planets involved*: It's a wild ride. How could it not be, for we suddenly find ourselves connected to the world through another person!

Antiscia also represent an insight through the miasma of self-doubt, through the "I can't believe this is happening to me" syndrome. With antiscia, there's more than just "me"; there's you, and you probably have a different outlook than I do. When antiscia are involved, no person is an island.

Depending on the planets involved and your predisposition to change (your stubbornness quotient), antiscia aspects belong to the astrological college of hard knocks, or learning the hard way. Just as antiscia aspects aren't the first thing you notice in a chart, their manifestations can be a little slow in arriving to your consciousness. It's not immediately apparent what's going on when you hook up with another person. We all know what it's like to wake up one morning and feel you're with a different person than you went to bed with. Antiscia tend to get under your skin until you can't deal with it anymore. When looking at antiscia in your chart, you should ask yourself how much of your motivation to change tends to come from the outside, from other people, from forces beyond your control, from fate and destiny. Antiscia also leave an indelible impression. They stick in your craw till you do something about them. *When antiscia involve the angles of the chart, they are of course changed in a relocated chart.*

Any Mystery Degrees in Your Chart?

I first become interested in antiscia when I kept noticing "hits"—pairings of events in my life to my chart—to a degree of the zodiac *that seemed to have no aspect relationship to any of the points in my chart.* I was beginning to doubt that I was working with the right birthtime; I thought the Ascendant or Midheaven must be in exact aspect to this point. Then as I was studying horary astrology and learning about antiscia, I realized that the "degree that wouldn't go away" (especially with personal relationships) was the *antiscion* of my Moon degree. That's when I got the antiscia bug. I would recommend, if you have any "mystery degrees" in your chart, that you find out what the antiscia of those degrees are, and whether *those* points are in aspect to anything in your chart. For me, doing this was what astrologer Michael Erlewine calls an "ah-ha experience."

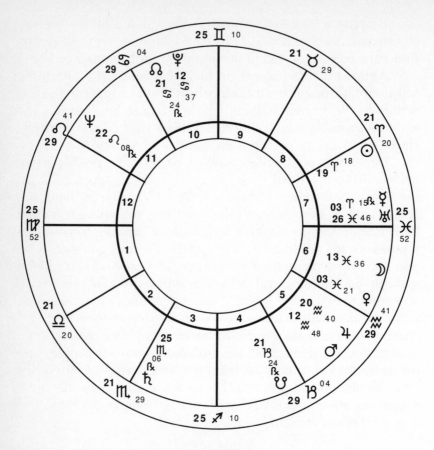

Hugh Hefner
April 9, 1926, Chicago, IL
4:20 P.M. CST
87W39 41N39
Placidus Houses

Example – Hugh Hefner and Jesse Helms

It'll be a cold day in hell when these two people, Hefner and Helms, share a table, but let's look at one way this is revealed in their charts. We have two world figures who represent what seem to be diametrically opposed philosophies: "Hef," is publisher of *Playboy* magazine and is a radical entrepreneur; Helms is a moralizing politician and our modern-day St. Augustine (without the sense of humor).

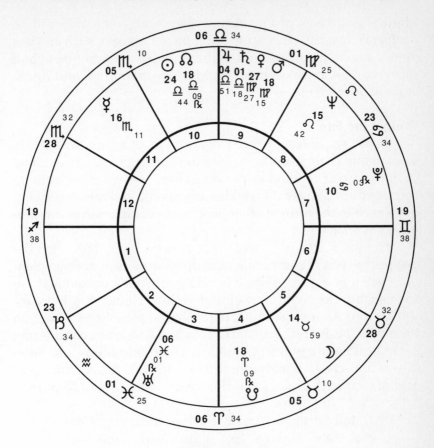

Jesse Helms
October 18, 1921, Monroe, NC
11:00 A.M. EST
80W33 34N48
Placidus Houses

Helms' Mars is at 18° Virgo (12 degrees away from 0° Libra, an equinoctal point). The question is, does Hugh Hefner have anything at 12° of a Cardinal sign—the reflection or antiscia point of 18° of a Mutable sign? He has Pluto at 12° Cancer. So Helms and Hefner are "roped to the world" via Mars and Pluto. That seems very fitting: the two rulers of Scorpio and (oversimplifying here) the two "sex planets." Hefner is Pluto in this drama, the greater transformer, while Helms, with his Mars in

Virgo, is something of a prude (no offense, all you Mars-in-Virgo people; Helms has other stuff going on in his chart, such as Mars tightly square his Ascendant, representing his environment and surroundings, and closely sextile Mercury in Scorpio, putting his brain in overdrive).

Double the Fun

If you really want to see a connection, compare the antiscia pairs in one chart to antiscia pairs in another chart; i.e., see how an antiscia pair in another person's chart "answers" an antiscia pair in yours. We are all walking questions, and answers many times exist in the form of other people, the completion of our personal equation.

Not all charts, of course, have antiscia pairs, but when the two people you're comparing both do have pairs of antiscia planets, there's going to be some bonding, one way or another. We have such a case with Hefner and Helms. Hefner has Mercury and Uranus as antiscia in his natal chart—see midpoint tree on page 197. This is "revolutionary thought," which fits, considering the radical nature of his publication. Helms has Moon and Neptune as antiscia—see midpoint sort on page 199. Alfred Witte, pioneer of Uranian astrology, has this to say about Moon/Neptune:

> To fall asleep. To dream. State of dreaming. Cerebral state of sleep. Not quite clearly conscious. Dazed. Receptive brains. Delicacy, tact. *To have a scent for something* [my emphasis].

The revolutionary thinker meets the hound dog of morality and tact. Is the quality of their mutual connection to the world any surprise? Antiscia are one means of comparing world figures who seemingly have nothing to do with each other—personally. From a world perspective, Hugh Hefner and Jesse Helms do have a lot to do with each other: Hefner is the playboy and Helms is the accusing moralizer. Their interplay, not necessarily personal but mundane, is evidenced through antiscia. Remember that, in Ptolemy's day, "antiscia" referred to people living along the same meridian of longitude on opposite sides of the equator!

Appendix

Advanced Study: Woody Allen and Mia Farrow

A comparison of Woody Allen and Mia Farrow reveals the strength of antiscia in chart interpretation. First of all, there's no shortage of traditional synastry ties in their charts, making it no surprise that these two established a personal and professional alliance. Nonetheless, the antiscia contacts between their charts provide additional and useful information. Their horoscopes follow:

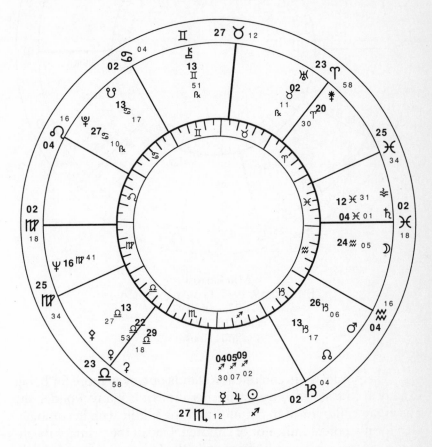

Woody Allen
December 1, 1935, Bronx, NY
10:55 P.M. EST
73W54 40N39
Placidus Houses

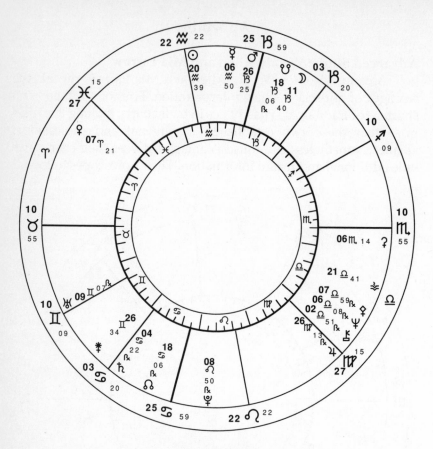

Mia Farrow
February 9, 1945, Los Angeles, CA
111:27 A.M. PWT
118W15   33N52
Placidus Houses

Their exact Mars conjunction stands out, even more for being exactly at Mia's Midheaven, trine her Jupiter. Is it any wonder she has many children? Mars, Jupiter, and the Midheaven in combination form a potent indicator of children. One of the primary meanings of Mars/Jupiter combinations in the Uranian system is birth, and therefore children. Midheaven/Jupiter combinations signify children themselves. Even more interesting is that Woody's Mars stands exactly between Mia's Mars and Midheaven. Woody is definitely connected to Mia's predisposition to children.

But does the fact figure in that many of these children are adopted? We can look to the asteroid Ceres, significator of adoption (bereft children; children and mother separated) Consider the Greek story of Demeter and her daughter Ceres, who is kidnapped by Hades, god of the underworld. Demeter scours the Earth looking for her daughter and is the symbol of grievous separation. Ceres is the lost child. Mia's Ceres forms the second closest solstice/equinox point in this synastry dynamic, with Woody's Moon (the public, the process of adoption), only 21' from exact. But we're getting ahead of ourselves; first let's finish the brief look at the traditional synastry indicators in Mia's and Woody's charts. Here is a table of their many close aspects, listed in order of exactness:

Mia	Woody	Aspect	Orb	Mia	Woody	Aspect	Orb
MC	MAR	CJN	0 07	VES	JUP	SSQ	1 35
JUP	MAR	TRI	0 07	CHI	MER	SXT	1 39
SUN	PAL	SXT	0 10	VEN	SUN	TRI	1 42
MAR	MAR	CJN	0 20	ASC	VES	SXT	1 42
PAL	MAR	QNX	0 28	VEN	MOO	SSQ	1 45
CHI	URA	QNX	0 41	MOO	JUN	SQU	1 47
MAR	MC	TRI	0 46	VES	MER	TRI	2 14
MOO	VES	SXT	0 51	SUN	VEN	TRI	2 14
JUP	MC	TRI	0 59	VEN	JUP	TRI	2 14
JUN	SUN	SXT	1 03	VES	SUN	SSQ	2 21
MAR	VES	SSQ	1 05	ASC	NOD	TRI	2 24
JUN	MOO	SQQ	1 07	PAL	MOO	TRI	2 29
CHI	SAT	QNX	1 09	JUN	CER	TRI	2 44
VES	PAL	OPP	1 12	VES	MOO	TRI	2 44
VES	VEN	CNJ	1 12	SUN	MOO	CJN	3 26
MOO	NOD	CJN	1 32	MAR	VEN	SQU	3 32
MC	VES	SSQ	1 32				

This is an impressive list, with enough tight, traditional synastry contacts, even without the asteroids, to keep an astrologer busy for some time. One might also note Woody's vertex conjunct both his and Mia's Mars. The vertex is a chart "angle" (like a cusp) indicating fate or destiny, especially in relationships. "Fate" here is not some outside power, but a certain sense the two people have—"it must be destined"—about being together. The relationship seems larger than life and perhaps a matter of compulsion in addition to choice. Don't overlook the vertex when you're examining synastry, but remember that, as with the Ascendant and Midheaven, vertex contacts in synastry depend on a chart with an accurate birthtime ("around noon" won't do).

Mia's vertex makes a strong contact to the midpoint between Woody's Venus and Juno, indicators of love and marriage. There is a lot going on in this synastry, more than you'll probably find in most couples. In fact, there's so much to note, you may have forgotten that the subject of this article is solstice and equinox points. But with all these other aspects, why even mention them? For one reason, the solstice and equinox point contacts provide not only more information, but *different* information: they shed new light on the relationship.

Have you ever been dealing with two charts and not seen what you expected to see? Perhaps it's a salient feature of the relationship that doesn't immediately present itself in the horoscopes. It's not unusual, and astrologers are fairly notorious for finding additional factors in the horoscopes to account for the reality of the situation. It's easy to understand the claim often leveled against astrology and astrologers that, with enough factors in play, you can explain anything that comes your way. So there has to be some integrity in how the astrologer interprets this plethora of factors. Two such assurances of integrity are tight orbs and sticking to a relatively small set of cogent keywords for the different factors with which you are working.

Here is a list of the solstice and equinox point-contacts in the synastry of Woody Allen and Mia Farrow, starting with the smallest orb, up to a maximum of about 1.5 degrees. These contacts are revealed by comparing Woody Allen's and Mia Farrow's midpoint trees and midpoint sorts.

Mia	Woody	Orb	Mia	Woody	Orb
MC	SAT	0 00	MER	MOO	0 56
CER	MOO	0 21	MAR	MER	0 57
URA	PAL	0 23	MAR	ASC	1 19
MAR	SAT	0 27	NOD	CHI	1 20
MC	MER	0 30	MAR	JUP	1 33
NOD	VES	0 37	MOO	NEP	1 38
VES	SUN	0 45			

This is quite a few contacts to work with. We can not cull the list by ridding it of pairs that already exist in the list of traditional aspects since there aren't any, and this brings up an interesting point: it's no accident that there aren't any, for, due to the symmetry of the zodiac, repetition is possible *only in the event that the contact occurs around 0° of Cardinal and 15° of Fixed signs* (8th-harmonic aspects) *and 15° of Cardinal, 0° of Fixed, and 15° of Mutable signs* (12th-harmonic aspects).

Let's limit the list in another way: by throwing out the pairs whose orb is great than one degree. You could also throw out the asteroid contacts, if you don't work with these bodies. Limiting the orb to one degree gives a list of nine contacts, plenty to give a synastry reading! We'll look at the salient features, with a little from Uranian astrology and an asteroid thrown in for good measure.

Look first at the solstice/equinox point contact with no orb whatsoever. This is Mia's Midheaven and Woody's Saturn. (If Mia's birthtime is really a minute or two one side or the other of what we are given, this aspect would lose its zero-orb status, but in any event the aspect is very tight.) As mentioned with regard to Mars and Jupiter, Mia's Midheaven is already a strong factor in the synastry dynamic, but Woody's Saturn adds a new dimension.

What does this Midheaven/Saturn contact mean? There are lots of possibilities for this combination, but let's keep it simple. I subscribe to the Uranian notion of Midheaven as soul or "very self" and of Saturn as restrictions and hindrances (we'd tell our friends and loved ones that Saturn means something like maturity and perseverance, but we know it isn't always such a rosy picture). I find this Midheaven/Saturn contact in Mia's and Woody's synastry very interesting for it suggests some struggle where the traditional indicators don't: the traditional comparison is loaded with favorable aspects. This gives us something to chew on in the light of the well-publicized Allen/Farrow fidelity scandal. Woody's Saturn—restriction and hindrance—makes a direct hit with Mia's midheaven—down to her very core. Mia can find Woody an extremely limiting influence.

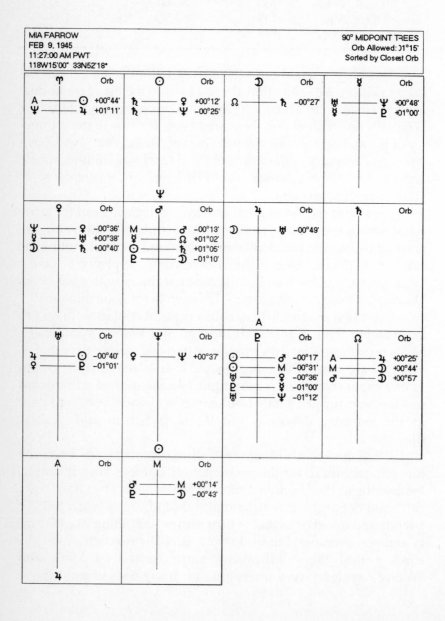

You might have wondered what the trouble could be with all those sextiles and trines in the traditional synastry aspects—it looks so hitch-free! Yes, this is itself a clue that as a couple these two may lack some resources when it comes to surmounting a crisis, yet the Midheaven/Saturn contact gives me something more solid: *these two people do indeed have a seed of dissent in their natal makeup.*

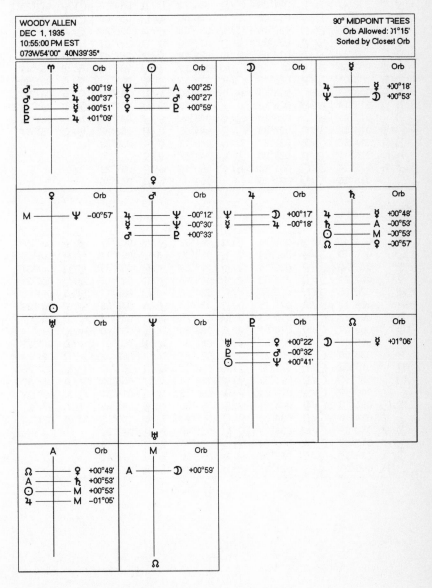

WOODY ALLEN
DEC 1, 1935
10:55:00 PM EST
073W54'00" 40N39'35"

90° MIDPOINT TREES
Orb Allowed:)1°15'
Sorted by Closest Orb

MIA FARROW FEB 9, 1945

Zodiacal Sort

Midpoints: 90° Dial									
☉/A	000°44'	♃/A	018°31'	☿/♂	031°38'	♀/♄	050°52'	♀/♇	068°06'
♃/♆	001°11'	☽/M	018°50'	♇/M	032°25'	♃/☊	052°10'	☉/♃	068°27'
♀/♃	001°47'	☽/♂	019°03'	♂/♇	032°38'	☽/♆	053°54'	♅	069°07'
♅/M	002°33'	☿/♄	020°36'	♃/♅	032°40'	☽/♀	054°31'	☽/A	071°15'
♂/♅	002°47'	♄/♇	021°36'	☉/☊	034°23'	♅/A	054°58'	☉/♆	073°24'
♄	004°22'	☊/M	022°02'	☿	036°50'	♃/M	056°06'	☉/♀	074°00'
♆	006°08'	♂/☊	022°16'	♅/♆	037°38'	♂/♃	056°20'	☊/A	074°27'
♀/♆	006°45'	♆/A	023°29'	☿/♇	037°50'	♆/☊	057°07'	M/A	078°24'
♀	007°21'	♀/A	024°05'	♀/♅	038°14'	♀/☊	057°43'	♂/A	078°38'
☿/♅	007°59'	☽/☿	024°16'	☉/M	038°19'	♆/M	061°04'	♄/♅	081°45'
☽/♄	008°01'	☽/♇	025°16'	☉/♂	038°33'	♂/♆	061°17'	☿/A	083°50'
♅/♇	008°59'	M	025°59'	♇	038°50'	☿/♃	061°32'	♇/A	084°50'
♄/☊	011°14'	♂/M	026°13'	A	040°49'	♀/M	061°40'	☽/♅	085°24'
☽	011°41'	♂	026°26'	☉/☿	043°45'	♀/♂	061°54'	♃	086°13'
☉/♅	014°53'	☿/☊	027°28'	☉/♇	044°45'	♃/♇	062°32'	♅/☊	088°37'
☽/☊	014°53'	☉/♄	027°31'	♃/♄	045°18'	☿/♆	066°29'		
♄/M	015°11'	♇/☊	028°28'	☽/♃	048°57'	☿/♀	067°06'		
♂/♄	015°24'	☽/☉	031°10'	♄/♆	050°15'	♆/♇	067°29'		
☊	018°06'	☿/M	031°25'	☉	050°40'	♄/A	067°36'		

Standard Sort

Midpoints: 90° Dial									
☽	011°41'	☽/♅	085°24'	☿/♃	061°32'	♂/♅	002°47'	♅/♆	037°38'
☉	050°40'	☽/♆	053°54'	☿/♄	020°36'	♂/♆	061°17'	♅/♇	008°59'
☿	036°50'	☽/♇	025°16'	☿/♅	007°59'	♂/♇	032°38'	♅/☊	088°37'
♀	007°21'	☽/☊	014°53'	☿/♆	066°29'	♂/☊	022°16'	♅/M	002°33'
♂	026°26'	☽/M	018°50'	☿/♇	037°50'	♂/M	026°13'	♅/A	054°58'
♃	086°13'	☽/A	071°15'	☿/☊	027°28'	♂/A	078°38'	♆/♇	067°29'
♄	004°22'	☉/☿	043°45'	☿/M	031°25'	♃/♄	045°18'	♆/☊	057°07'
♅	069°07'	☉/♀	074°00'	☿/A	083°50'	♃/♅	032°40'	♆/M	061°04'
♆	006°08'	☉/♂	038°33'	♀/♂	061°54'	♃/♆	001°11'	♆/A	023°29'
♇	038°50'	☉/♃	068°27'	♀/♃	001°47'	♃/♇	062°32'	♇/☊	028°28'
☊	018°06'	☉/♄	027°31'	♀/♄	050°52'	♃/☊	052°10'	♇/M	032°25'
M	025°59'	☉/♅	014°53'	♀/♅	038°14'	♃/M	056°06'	♇/A	084°50'
A	040°49'	☉/♆	073°24'	♀/♆	006°45'	♃/A	018°31'	☊/M	022°02'
☽/☉	031°10'	☉/♇	044°45'	♀/♇	068°06'	♄/♅	081°45'	☊/A	074°27'
☽/☿	024°16'	☉/☊	034°23'	♀/☊	057°43'	♄/♆	050°15'	M/A	078°24'
☽/♀	054°31'	☉/M	038°19'	♀/M	061°40'	♄/♇	021°36'		
☽/♂	019°03'	☉/A	000°44'	♀/A	024°05'	♄/☊	011°14'		
☽/♃	048°57'	☿/♀	067°06'	♂/♃	056°20'	♄/M	015°11'		
☽/♄	008°01'	☿/♂	031°38'	♂/♄	015°24'	♄/A	067°36'		

WOODY ALLEN DEC 1, 1935

Zodiacal Sort

Midpoints: 90° Dial

☿/♂	000°19'	☿/♄	019°16'	♀/M	040°03'	☽/A	058°11'	♀/♇	070°02'
♂/♃	000°37'	♃/♄	019°34'	☽/♂	040°06'	☽/♄	059°04'	♄/♆	070°21'
☿/♇	000°51'	♂/☊	019°40'	☽/♇	040°38'	☿/M	060°52'	♂/♅	074°09'
♃/♇	001°09'	♇/☊	020°12'	☿/♀	043°42'	♃/M	061°10'	♅/♇	074°41'
♅/A	002°13'	☉/A	020°39'	♀/♃	044°01'	A	062°15'	♆	076°41'
☉/♂	002°35'	☉/♄	021°32'	♂/A	044°11'	♀/☊	063°04'	☊/M	080°13'
♄/♅	003°06'	♆/M	021°57'	♅/M	044°42'	♄/A	063°08'	☽/♀	083°30'
☉/♇	003°07'	♀	022°54'	♇/A	044°43'	☉/M	063°08'	☿/☊	083°52'
♀/♆	004°48'	☿/♆	025°36'	♆/☊	044°57'	♄	064°01'	♃/☊	084°10'
♅/♆	009°26'	♃/♆	025°54'	♂/♄	045°04'	☿	064°31'	☉/☊	086°08'
☽/M	010°39'	♂	026°06'	♄/♇	045°36'	☿/♃	064°49'	♂/M	086°39'
☊	013°13'	♂/♇	026°39'	☉/♀	045°58'	♃	065°07'	♇/M	087°12'
☽/☿	014°19'	♇	027°11'	☿/♅	048°21'	☽/♆	065°24'	♀/A	087°35'
☽/♃	014°37'	♀/♅	027°33'	♃/♅	048°39'	☉/☿	066°47'	☽/♅	088°09'
M/A	014°44'	☉/♆	027°52'	☉/♅	050°37'	☉/♃	067°05'	♀/♄	088°28'
♄/M	015°37'	♅	032°11'	♂/♆	051°24'	♅/☊	067°42'		
☽/☉	016°34'	☽/☊	033°40'	♆/♇	051°56'	☉	069°03'		
☿/A	018°23'	☊/A	037°44'	☽	054°06'	♆/A	069°28'		
♃/A	018°41'	♄/☊	038°37'	M	057°12'	♀/♂	069°30'		

Standard Sort

Midpoints: 90° Dial

☽	054°06'	☽/♅	088°09'	☿/♃	064°49'	♂/♅	074°09'	♅/♆	009°26'
☉	069°03'	☽/♆	065°24'	☿/♄	019°16'	♂/♆	051°24'	♅/♇	074°41'
☿	064°31'	☽/♇	040°38'	☿/♅	048°21'	♂/♇	026°39'	♅/☊	067°42'
♀	022°54'	☽/☊	033°40'	☿/♆	025°36'	♂/☊	019°40'	♅/M	044°42'
♂	026°06'	☽/M	010°39'	☿/♇	000°51'	♂/M	086°39'	♅/A	002°13'
♃	065°07'	☽/A	058°11'	☿/☊	083°52'	♂/A	044°11'	♆/♇	051°56'
♄	064°01'	☉/☿	066°47'	☿/M	060°52'	♃/♄	019°34'	♆/☊	044°57'
♅	032°11'	☉/♀	045°58'	☿/A	018°23'	♃/♅	048°39'	♆/M	021°57'
♆	076°41'	☉/♂	002°35'	♀/♂	069°30'	♃/♆	025°54'	♆/A	069°28'
♇	027°11'	☉/♃	067°05'	♀/♃	044°01'	♃/♇	001°09'	♇/☊	020°12'
☊	013°13'	☉/♄	021°32'	♀/♄	088°28'	♃/☊	084°10'	♇/M	087°12'
M	057°12'	☉/♅	050°37'	♀/♅	027°33'	♃/M	061°10'	♇/A	044°43'
A	062°15'	☉/♆	027°52'	♀/♆	004°48'	♃/A	018°41'	☊/M	080°13'
☽/☉	016°34'	☉/♇	003°07'	♀/♇	070°02'	♄/♅	003°06'	☊/A	037°44'
☽/☿	014°19'	☉/☊	086°08'	♀/☊	063°04'	♄/♆	070°21'	M/A	014°44'
☽/♀	083°30'	☉/M	063°08'	♀/M	040°03'	♄/♇	045°36'		
☽/♂	040°06'	☉/A	020°39'	♀/A	087°35'	♄/☊	038°37'		
☽/♃	014°37'	☿/♀	043°42'	♂/♃	000°37'	♄/M	015°37'		
☽/♄	059°04'	☿/♂	000°19'	♂/♄	045°04'	♄/A	063°08'		

Next let's look at Ceres/Moon—mentioned previously with regard to adoption. This is a provocative combination. The Moon, besides its general affiliation with changeability and mood, also refers to the public and general populace. There is Demeter, looking the world over for her kidnapped daughter Ceres; there are "missing" placards posted on every tree and everybody—the public—knows about it. And what astrologer could resist wondering whether Woody's role as Hades or Pluto, "kidnapping" Mia's daughter, figures into this dynamic? Of course! The tightest solstice/equinox point contact in Woody's natal chart is Neptune/Hades, within 14 minutes of orb. The kernel meanings of this pair are deception, damage through mistakes, and opaque thinking. When these planets are solstice or equinox points, and so involving the 0° Aries, the meaning extends to self-deception about one's relationship with the general world and the public's lack of certainty about how it feels about this person. The 60 Minutes interview of Woody Allen while the scandal was going down made both apparent. Woody wasn't coming quite clean with us, yet there was the sense that he has ignited some inscrutable, relentless, and divine fury in Mia, such that we weren't quite sure what the retribution should be. But Woody had kidnapped her daughter; she had a right to go berserk, and where is this passionate sense of justice borne out in Mia's own solstice/equinox point dynamic? Her closest antiscia is ascendant/Zeus, which means unstoppable forces in the immediate environment. Anyone having the ascendant and Zeus as antiscia is likely to feel a little pressured or impinged upon by others. When you combine this with intense feelings about children and Woody's stealthy affair with her daughter, you get the picture: Mia wanted her pound of flesh. Note also that the second closest antiscia in Mia's own chart is Sun/ascendant, a combination signifying personal relationships, a charged issue for her.

How to Read Mutual Antiscia Pairs in Synastry

Mutual antiscia pairs are the chart-comparison version of the planetary pictures used in Uranian astrology. An invaluable resource exists for interpreting the pictures. Once you have a basic understanding of planetary symbolism, I recommend the Witte-Lefelt *Rules for Planetary Pictures* to get your interpretive juices flowing.

Planetary pictures are combinations of planets usually in the form of A + B – C = D. For a single chart, the left side of the equation is the "question" and the right side—a directed or transiting point—is the "answer." [See Arlene Kramer's article in this volume for more information on planetary pictures.—Ed.]

The formula $A + B - C = D$ can also be written as $A + B = C + D$. Now we can assign the left side of the equation to one person and the right side to a second person—as long as we have a common reference point for both people. In the case of antiscia, we want to use 0° of Cardinal signs, or Aries at the root of a midpoint tree in the 90° format, but we could use any reference point, as long as it is common to both people.

When we compare the Aries-90° Midpoint Trees for Woody Allen and Mia Farrow, we get the following results (see Midpoint Trees on pp. 210–211). For the sake of simplicity, I have excluded Uranian points and asteroids, but the Witte book gives interpretation for all Uranian combinations:

SU + AS = ME + MA	ME + MA = JU - NE
SU + AS = ME + PL	ME + PL = JU - NE
SU + AS = MA + JU	MA + JU = JU - NE (MA = NE)
SU + AS = JU + PL	JU + NE = JU + PL (NE = PL)

These are the mutual planetary pictures for Woody Allen and Mia Farrow. There are two ways to read each formula. For example, the first one is SU + AS – ME = MA, or SU + AS – MA = ME. The Rules book provides interpretation for both combinations on the left side of the equations. You complete the interpretation yourself: there are already thousands of three-planet combination; adding a fourth point, the "answer," pushes the total into the tens of thousands, almost beyond comprehension. That's why you have to be solid in your understanding of the symbolism of the planets. Witte himself said this is the only way.

Witte provides interpretation for pairs as well as pictures. Here are the pairs that make up the picture synastry for Woody and Mia. This gets you thinking about how these two might interact.

SU + AS — Personal relationships. Physical relation to other people.

JU + NE — Material success. Sudden luck; or misfortune if Jupiter is posited in a poor picture.

JU + PL — Fortunate development, change, or transformation.

ME + MA — Energetic thought. Hasty and energetic action. Malice. Quarrelsome thoughts. Quarrels and debates. Critics.

ME + PL — The function of the nerves. External and internal motion. The development of thinking. From thinking to understanding.

MA + JU — Joyous happenings. Betrothal. Fortunate deed. To create something. To produce. Propagation. Pregnancy. Generation. Children. Fruits. Births.

Now let's put the combinations together. The text is for the first three planets. We have to supply the "answer."

SU + AS - ME (= MA) — Fellow students, schoolmates, or teachers. Relationship to young or younger students; to similar thinking or equal people.

Pick the interpretations that seem most fitting for Woody and Mia. Who, in the light of Woody Allen's affair scandal, can resist "relationship to young or younger students"? The answer here is Mars, adding action, resolve, doing, drive, and ambition to the meanings above.

SU + AS - MA (= ME) (= JU) (= PL) — Co-workers. Social relations with male persons, co-workers, or soldiers. Rights, brawls, and quarrels. Persons in the environment who are not master of their emotions. Not under self control.

Here there are three answers. Mercury makes the brawls and quarrels mental. Jupiter means successful co-workers (acting together—not everything is bad!). Pluto turns "not master of emotion" into emotional upheaval on a large scale.

Here are the remaining combinations in the mutual planetary pictures synastry of Mia Farrow and Woody Allen. Using your knowledge of Mia and Woody and your understanding of basic planetary symbolism, you can pick the appropriate text from Witte and complete the picture with the planet or planets after the equals sign. Keep in mind that throughout this process you're getting a great deal of information about Mia and Woody and you haven't even touched a traditional aspect. Good luck!

SU + AS - JU = (MA) (= PL) — Lucky acquaintances. Advantages through connections.

SU + AS - PL = (ME) (= JU) — No steady relation. Always new relations. Change of relation. Change of social intercourse during meals.

ME + MA - ,JU (= NE) — Successful thinking. Merry conversation. Laughing. Valuable debates. Cheerfully proceeding to action.

ME + MA - NE = (JU) — To speak badly. To lisp. Defect of speech. Strong imagination. To commit blunders. To get excited over nothing. Will to destroy.

ME + PL - JU = (NE) — Fortunate development of the trend of thoughts. To come to recognizing happy changes of conditions.

ME + PL - NE = (JU) — Uncertainly regarding the near future. Sneaky, uncertain conditions.

MA + JU - NE = (JU) (MA = NE) — Denials of betrothals. Dissolution of promises or understandings. Hopeless relationship. Not executed intentions. End of a happy activity. Happy activity, but without success. Impotence. Miscarriages.

JU + NE - PL (= JU) (NE = PL) — Beginning of a hidden fortunate development. Increase of possessions not noticed on the surface of things.

Sources

The horoscopes, midpoints trees, and midpoint sorts used in this article are provided courtesy of Matrix Software, which holds the copyright. The diagrams in this article, done by the author, are provided courtesy of Matrix Software, who holds the copyright to their use. If you are interested in using any of them in books or articles, please contact Matrix Software in Big Rapids, Michigan. The data for the personalities used as examples in this article is from Matrix Software's *Richard Nolle Compact Data Library*.

Arlene Kramer

Arlene Kramer was born and raised in New York City. She earned her BA and MA degrees from Hunter College. Her skills as a teacher and lecturer were developed as she taught school in the New York City Public School System.

During the late 1950s, the 60s, and 70s, Arlene lived in Connecticut. A chance encounter with astrology led to full absorption in the subject and a new career. She became a professional astrologer in 1969. Continuing study led her to an interest in cosmobiology and then in Uranian astrology. She became a student of Hans Niggemann, who was at the time the master of Uranian astrology in the United States. Arlene now incorporates Uranian astrology with traditional astrology in her professional practice.

Arlene is a well-known lecturer and teacher, in both traditional and Uranian astrology, and is the creator of the 90° Star Dial System. Her expertise as a Uranian has established for her an international reputation. Since 1982, Arlene has lived in Woodland Hills, California.

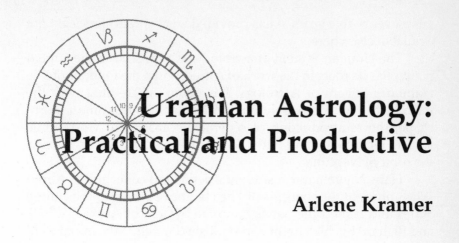

Uranian Astrology: Practical and Productive

Arlene Kramer

F or at least three millennia, astrology has been evolving. The body of knowledge grew out of pragmatic experience. The last three centuries brought accelerated growth because the telescope allowed man to discover Uranus, then Neptune, then Pluto. Each time a new planet was seen, astrologers had to learn what the new body represented in a person's horoscope and what it represented in the mundane affairs of mankind. The last thirty years has brought an explosion of information concerning asteroids and comets. Astrologers have learned about these newly discovered celestial bodies by studying horoscopes: natal, progressed, directed, and mundane. Some astrologers, satisfied with what they already knew, refused to accept or to learn about new celestial influences or new techniques.

Through the centuries, styles have changed. Techniques such as Arabic Parts, Primary Directions, Eclipse Saros Cycles, and Planetary Hours, along with many different house systems, have seen their days of popularity and their days of disfavor and disuse. Improper teaching and the consequent faulty use of techniques or the burden of difficult calculations has sometimes been the cause of disfavor and disuse. The advent of economical modern computing equipment may do away with this last burden.

Astrology must continue to evolve. The world is changing and traditional astrology does *not* provide all the answers. The Uranian System of astrology is practical and productive. For the past seventy-five years, it has provided answers and precision not available elsewhere.

The Uranian System of astrology, as practiced in the United States, has its roots in the work of Alfred Witte, the founder of The Hamburg School of Astrology. His genius is credited with the introduction of a movable dial with which to examine a horoscope, the reintroduction of several discarded but worthwhile ancient techniques, and with the postulation of "planets" beyond the orbit of Neptune.

Hans Niggemann, a student, friend, and colleague of Alfred Witte, brought the concepts of The Hamburg School to the United States and coined the name "Uranian System of Astrology." He and Richard Svehla taught and published much of the initial techniques of this exciting Uranian astrology. I am proud to have been a student and friend of Hans Niggemann.

The Uranian System is distinguished from other systems by the use of all of the following general characteristics:

- The use of the movable dial
- The Meridian House System
- Planetary Pictures
- Solar Arc Directions
- Incorporation of the TransNeptunian "Planets" into the horoscope.

The competent Uranian astrologer is also a competent traditional astrologer, and uses the techniques of each system to supplement the other.

This chapter will give an overview of the features unique to the Uranian System and a description of techniques particular to the Uranian System. (In Europe, this system is still referred to as the system of the Hamburg School.) Some of the features and techniques to be described are:

- The Movable Dial
  The 90° Dial
  The 22°30′ Aspect
- Planetary Pictures
  Equations
  Occupied Midpoints

Unoccupied Midpoints
Arc Openings
- Sensitive Points
- Personal Points
The Aries Point
Antiscia
- Solar Arc Directions
- Meridian House System
Equatorial Ascendant
- The TransNeptunian "Planets"

The 90° Dial (and its associated chart), in its basic concept, divides a circle into three equal arc-segments with all Cardinal signs superimposed in one segment, all Fixed signs superimposed in another segment, and all Mutable signs superimposed in the remaining segment. See figure 1. Each segment is divided into thirty major parts, representing the 30 degrees that each sign holds.

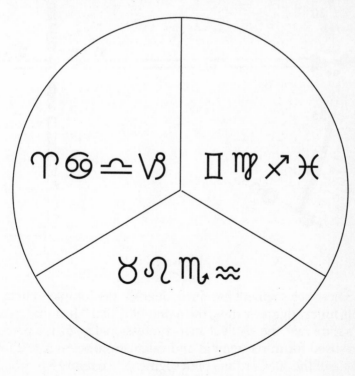

Figure 1

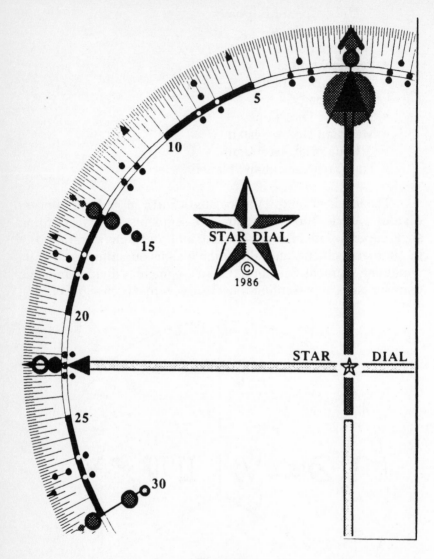

Figure 2

Since each segment has thirty degrees, the complete circle represents ninety degrees; thus, the name "90° Dial." Just like an engineer's slide rule, the 90° Dial, in its professional form, is a precision
device used for measurement and calculation. See figure 2 for an
example of the 30° Cardinal Sign segment. See figure 3 for the precision the 90° Dial provides for measurement and calculation.

What one finds using the 90° Dial is that all conjunctions, squares, and oppositions *appear to be in the same place.* For example, 3° Aries and 7° Cancer would appear close to each other on the 90° Dial in the Cardinal segment, while 17° Gemini and 18° Virgo would ap-pear close to each other in the Mutable segment at 77° and 78° respectively. In like manner, 3° Aries and 3°

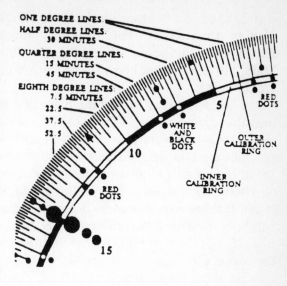

Figure 3

Cancer and 3° Libra are at 3° of the Cardinal section. Across the dial, at 18° of the Fixed segment, their semisquare and sesquiquadrate are easily visible.

The 90° Dial is sometimes used as an aspectarian for a traditional look at a horoscope that has been drawn in the 90° format. Once the arrow of the dial is pointing at a planet, any planet that appears at the dial's 30° mark is easily seen to be at either a sextile, semi-sextile, trine, or inconjunct aspect to the planet at the arrow. By referring to the traditional horoscope, the astrologer determines which aspect is there.

Unique to the Uranian System is the 22° 30′ aspect (one-half of a semi-square; one-sixteenth of the circle). Just as the 90° Dial instantly shows all aspects of a circle cut into eight parts, it also shows the points cutting the octile in half, giving the 22° 30′, 67° 30′, 112° 30′, and 157° 30′ relationships. With the circle cut into sixteen parts, the powerful sixteenth harmonic is revealed very easily.

The concept of midpoints is well understood. Through years of experience, the significance and meanings of midpoint combinations have been characterized and described by various authors. Astrologers have discovered that there is a combined strength at the point between two horoscope planets and that the significance of this strength depends on the function of the two planets themselves. For example, the significance of the Sun/Venus midpoint differs from the significance of the Mars/Pluto midpoint because the natures of the planets involved are different.

The easiest way to find the place of a midpoint is by using a movable dial. The 360° Dial shows the *actual* place; the 90° Dial shows its actual place *plus all the hard aspects to it.*

Let me take you through the concept of equations, as they are at the core of Uranian measurement systems. By definition, two planets involved in a midpoint are equidistant from the midpoint. If there happens to be a planet *at that midpoint,* the shorthand notation for this combination is A/B = C, where A/B is the midpoint of the two planets that, in this example, is occupied by the planet C.

So, if the notation is   A/B = C

this really means that $\dfrac{A+B}{2} = C$

Remember your algebra? In all equations, one can do anything one wants to one side of the equal sign, as long as one does the same (equal) to the other side of the equal sign. In order to do away with the fraction, we can multiply each side of the equation by two, resulting in

A+B = 2C, or

A+B = C+C

Again, using the same rule, we can subtract C from each side, resulting in

A+B-C = C

What if the midpoint of A + B were not occupied by C? Unique to the Uranian System is the investigation of this midpoint axis *when there is no occupant of the midpoint.* Here is born the concept of "planetary pictures." A planetary picture is a combination of three or more zodiacal elements *around a common axis.* The meanings of each of these many possible combinations are well known to the Uranian astrologer. These combinations were first published in the United States by Hans Niggemann and reflect the technology, views, and interests of the World War I era. I have modernized many of these definitions to reflect the current technologies and interests of the world, and they are presented later in this chapter.

As an example of equation-manipulation using the dial, let's suppose that in a given horoscope, the midpoint of A + B *is the same as the midpoint of C + D.* This could come about on the 90° Dial when two planets ten degrees apart share the same midpoint with two planets twenty degrees apart. As an illustration see figure 4: the Sun is at 20° Aries and the Moon is at 10° Cancer (both Cardinal signs, of course, read in the same third of the dial). The actual midpoint is at 0° Gemini, but appears to be at 15° of the Cardinal segment on the 90° Dial, diametrically across the dial from 0° of the Mutables.

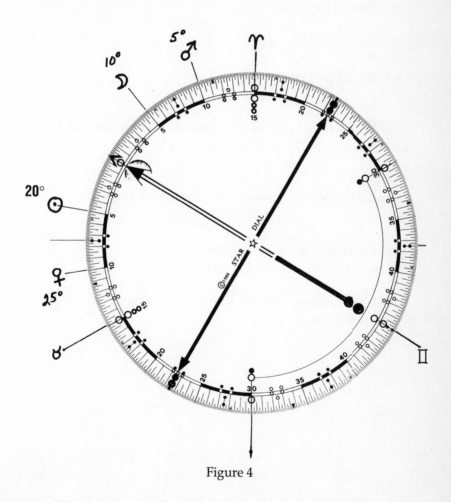

Figure 4

Let us further suppose that Venus is at 25° Aries and Mars is at 5° Capricorn. The actual midpoint of Venus and Mars is at 0° Virgo, but appears to be at 15° of the Cardinal segment on the 90° Dial.

Both sets of midpoints share a common axis, and this presents a specific planetary picture for the hypothetical horoscope. Note also that the resultant 5° arc opening between the Sun and Venus is the same as the arc opening between the Moon and Mars, on the 90° Dial.

In shorthand notation, the preceding example can be expressed as

$$Su/Mo = Ve/Ma$$

which really means

$$\frac{Su+Mo}{2} = \frac{Ve+Ma}{2}$$

which can also be expressed as

$$Su + Mo = Ve + Ma$$

Returning to the rule of an equation, we can subtract Venus from both sides, resulting in the Planetary Picture

$$Su + Mo - Ve = Ma$$

Similarly, we can subtract Mars from both sides of

$$Su + Mo = Ve + Ma$$

to obtain the Planetary Picture

$$Su + Mo - Ma = Ve$$

To the Uranian astrologer, these two planetary pictures have different meanings.

Plotting Potential

Two important uses of Planetary Pictures are to find the natal promise in a person's horoscope, and to find the timing of specific events.

When the Uranian astrologer is faced with any question, he knows that one of the planetary pictures of interest is A + B - C, where A, B, and C are specific planets or personal points that apply to the question. When the person's horoscope has been placed in 90° notation and the movable dial is centered on the thumbtack around which it rotates, the Uranian astrologer asks the horoscope the question by finding the midpoint of A + B and locating C. He then establishes the position of D by marking it on the chart at a distance from the arrow *equal to the distance between the arrow and* C. The equation is now A + B - C = D. This means that there is an axis where A + B = C + D, or in shorthand notation, A/B = C/D.

If a planet occupies the D position, known as a *Sensitive Point,* the definition of the planet *describes the answer to the question as a promise of the natal chart.* Once this Sensitive Point is determined, the astrologer looks across the dial to the semisquare and sesquiquadrate position and to each of the 22°30′ positions to get further definition.

Should nothing occupy any of these equivalents of the Sensitive Point, the astrologer determines, by true Solar Arc Direction, when a planet will occupy this point.

In order to rectify or validate a birth time, the astrologer uses this Solar Arc technique with known dates of past events in the person's life *and planetary pictures that correspond to these events.* Of course, the Uranian astrologer makes use of the TransNeptunian "planets" and thus has many Planetary Pictures to work with in his search for corrections to the Midheaven and Ascendant.

As an example of the first use, consider the question, "Can I be an Author? Is it in my chart?" To answer this question, the astrologer knows there are at least three planetary pictures to consider.

They are: Me + Ne - Su Author
Su + Ju - Me Success through writings
Su + Ze - Me To be leading in writing
["Ze" is "Zeus"; please see page 242.—Ed.]

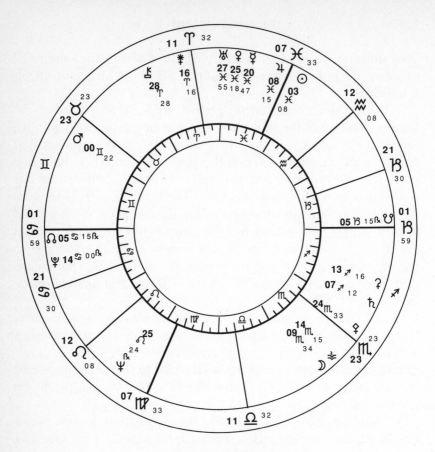

Figure 5
Possible Author
February 22, 1927, Lakeview, IL
12:21 P.M. CST
87W39 41N46
Placidus Houses

The first two planetary pictures will be discussed below. The third planetary picture involves Zeus, a TransNeptunian "planet." These "planets" will be discussed later.

Figure 5 shows the horoscope of the person who asked the question; figure 5a, the same horoscope in 90° notation. Note that the horoscope has glyphs and locations for the traditional planets, the Personal Points, and the TransNeptunian "planets." The Personal Points include the Midheaven, the Ascendant, the Vertex,

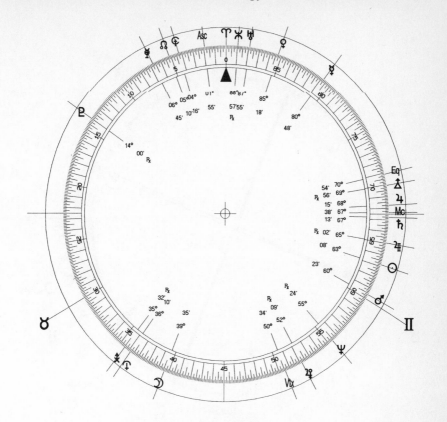

Figure 5a
Possible Author
February 22, 1927, Lakeview, IL
12:21 P.M. CST
87W39   41N46
Placidus Houses

the Equatorial Ascendant, the Sun, the Moon, the North Node, and the Aries Point.

The first planetary picture (see figure 6) is created when the 90° Dial is superimposed on this horoscope. On the dial, the distance between Mercury and Neptune is 25° 24'. The midpoint (half-sum) of these two is seen in figure 6 to be at 68° 06' and Mercury + Neptune - Sun is at 73° 04'. This is exactly 22° 30' from the Vertex, a very personal point meaning that authorship is "fated" for this person. Authorship, of course, can range from writing advertising copy to writing a best seller.

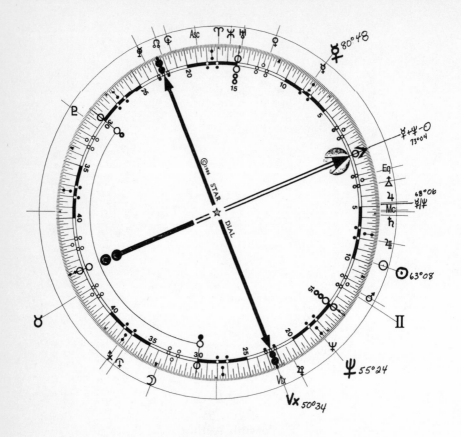

Figure 6
Possible Author
February 22, 1927, Lakeview, IL
12:21 P.M. CST
87W39 41N46
Stardial

The second planetary picture is shown in figure 7 (same horoscope with the pointer of the dial redirected). The midpoint of Sun and Jupiter is indicated at 65° 41′ and Sun + Jupiter - Mercury equals 50° 34′. This is again exactly the Vertex, and is another indication of an affirmative answer to the question.

A total review of the horoscope, in both the classical and 90° format, and examination of additional planetary pictures is required before a definite answer to any question is given.

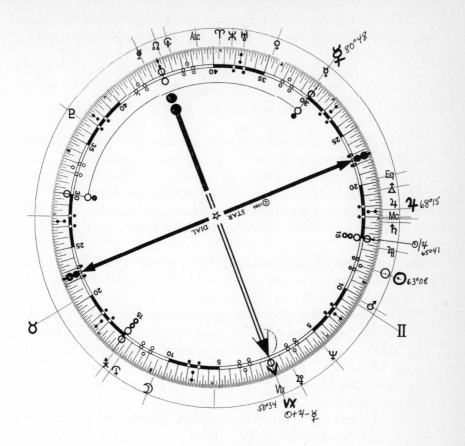

Figure 7
Possible Author
February 22, 1927, Lakeview, IL
12:21 P.M. CST
87W39 41N46
Stardial

Timing Events

The second use of Planetary Pictures is for timing of events. For questions of timing, the Uranian astrologer makes use of Solar Arc Directions, a very precise technique. The Solar Arc is defined as the amount of zodiacal distance (number of degrees, minutes, and seconds) between the Natal Sun and the Secondary Progressed Sun. For timing purposes, the Uranian astrologer calculates a range of this measurement to establish *a range* of dates for a possible event.

Let us consider the question, "When will I move?" The astrologer knows there are at least three planetary pictures to consider. They are:

> Me + Sa - Asc To move. To take leave.
> Me + Sa - Pl   To move off.
> Asc + Pl - Sa   Moving. Change of location.

The 90° notation horoscope of the woman who asked this question is shown in figure 8. This woman, with a birthday in April, will always have a Solar Arc smaller than her age. Indeed, on her fifty-sixth birthday, her Solar Arc was only 53° 59' 39", i.e., her Progressed Sun, moving slowly, had accumulated only 53° 59' 30" of arc in fifty-six years of life. Figure 9 shows her horoscope with the arrow pointing at Me + Sa - Asc at 51° 11'. This figure provides a clear example of a planetary picture A + B - C where there is nothing at the sensitive point D. The sensitive point will be activated by a Solar Arc direction.

The Uranian astrologer employs several different Planetary Pictures, and measures when they are due. By compiling a list of "due dates," the astrologer looks for a cluster of times. He then knows when the event *will* occur. Only when there are many Solar Arc Directions due on the same date can the astrologer make a firm prediction.

For this example, this formula was chosen first because in simplified Uranian analogy, Mercury is "to say," Saturn is "goodbye," and the Ascendant is "the environment." Me + Sa - Asc means "To say goodbye to the environment." Therefore, this is another way of saying "to move."

The next step in determining whether a move is imminent (within the next year or two) is to establish the range of Solar Arc to be studied. In this case, the range of 54° to 55° is selected as the range of interest because this woman was concerned with her immediate future.

With the arrow of the 90° Dial pointing at 51° 11', *the sensitive point,* the procedure is to look on the dial to see whether any planet or personal point of the horoscope can be located *displaced from the arrow by the Solar Arc range of 54° to 55°.*

The sensitive point in question will "come" to the Ascendant at Solar Arc 54° 09' which occurs on June 18, 1987. It will "come" to Uranus at Solar Arc 54° 55' which occurs on April 7, 1988.

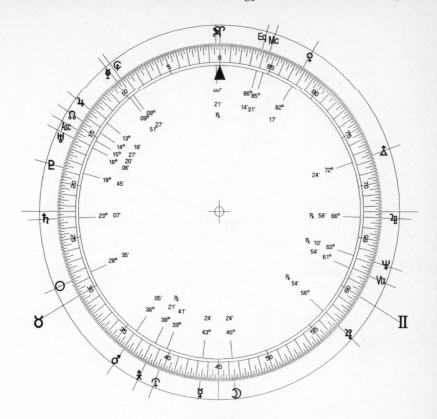

Figure 8
Possible Mover
April 19, 1931, Brooklyn, NY
9:52 A.M. EST
73W56 40N26
Stardial

Meanwhile, the Equatorial Ascendant will "come" to the sensitive point at Solar Arc 54° 57', due on April 19, 1988.

Figure 10 shows the 90° Dial turned by 22° 30', pointing the arrow at 73° 41', a point synonymous with Me + Sa - Asc. Pluto will arrive at this point at Solar Arc 54° 56', which will occur on April 13, 1988. The Sensitive Point will reach Zeus at Solar Arc 54° 40' which occurs on January 1, 1988.

The formula Mercury plus Saturn minus Pluto calculates to 47° 46' on the 90° Dial, The arrow in figure 11 is pointed at 70° 16' because the dial has been rotated 22° 30'. This is the equivalent of

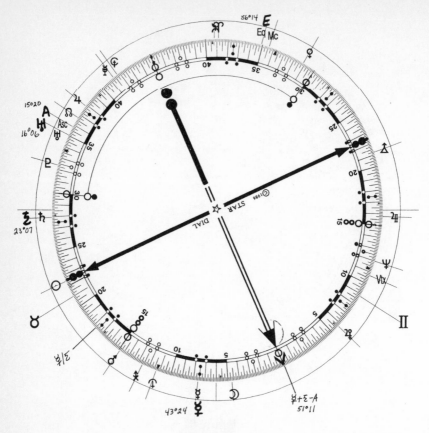

Figure 9
Possible Mover
April 19, 1931, Brooklyn, NY
9:52 A.M. EST
73W56   40N26
Stardial

47° 46'. The Ascendant will "come" to this point at Solar Arc 54° 56' which will occur on April 13, 1988.

The formula Ascendant plus Pluto minus Saturn means "Change in the environment because of separation. Separation from the environment." The astrologer must be aware that when a client asks, "Will I move?" she may really be asking, "Will I sell my house?" or "Will I get married?" or "Will I leave my husband?" or "Will that man in San Diego ask me to join him?" Figure 12 shows the arrow pointing at 78° 28', which is 22° 30' away

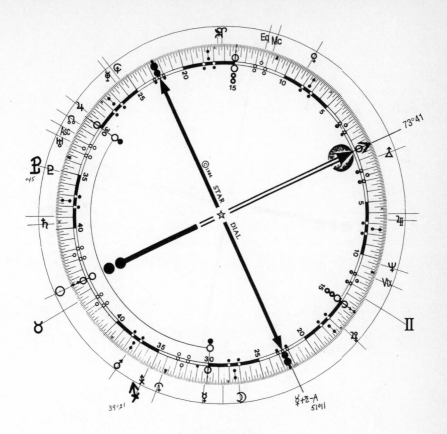

Figure 10
Possible Mover
April 19, 1931, Brooklyn, NY
9:52 A.M. EST
73W56   40N26
Stardial

from 10°58′, where Ascendant plus Pluto minus Saturn falls. This Sensitive Point will contact Mercury at Solar Arc 54°56′ which will occur on April 13, 1988.

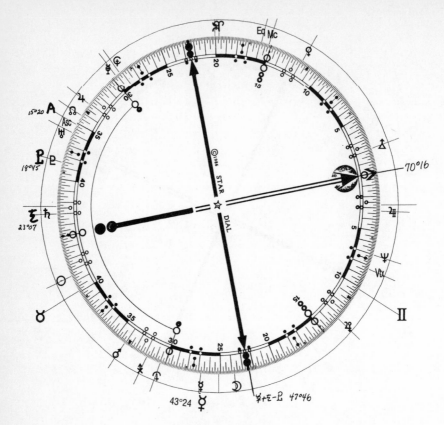

Figure 11
Possible Mover
April 19, 1931, Brooklyn, NY
9:52 A.M. EST
73W56   40N26
Stardial

A tabulation of Solar Arc "due dates" reveals:

Solar Arc		
54° 09'	due on	June 18, 1987
54° 40'		Jan 01, 1988
54° 55'		Apr 07, 1988
54° 56'		Apr 13, 1988
54° 56'		Apr 13, 1988
54° 56'		Apr 13, 1988
54° 57'		Apr 19, 1988

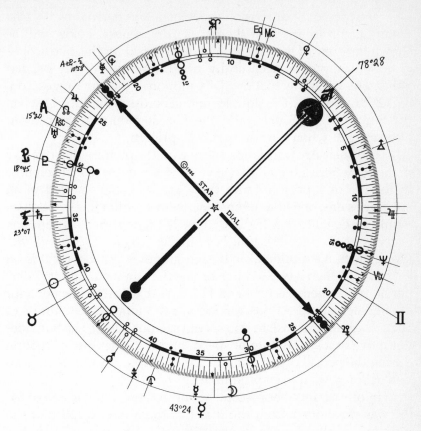

Figure 12
Possible Mover
April 19, 1931, Brooklyn, NY
9:52 A.M. EST
73W56   40N26
Stardial

It is apparent from this tabulation that there is a cluster of
dates around April 13, 1988. Since a Solar Arc moves approximately one minute every six days, one or two dates may fall six
days before or after the actual event, because of the round-off of
thirty seconds in calculating planets. Experience has shown that
the Solar Arc technique does provide a timing precision of six
days on either side of the center of the cluster.

The preceding discussion used Solar Arcs derived by 90° Dial manipulation to arrive at the list of "due dates." Below will be shown how one of these dates was determined for this horoscope.

Getting precise, technically: an examination of any printed ephemeris will show that the daily motion of the Sun ranges from 57' 12" to 1°01' 10". The slowest motion occurs about June 21 when the Sun is at 0° Cancer, and the fastest motion occurs about December 21 when the Sun is at 0° Capricorn.

The Solar Arc translation starts with the premise that one day in the ephemeris is equal to one year (365.25 days) of elapsed time in the life of a person. Since there are 24 hours implied in an ephemeris day, one hour of ephemeris time within this symbolism would be equal to 365.25 divided by 24 (giving 15.22). Therefore, every hour of ephemeris time is equivalent to *15.2 days in real time.* [Were the Sun's motion exactly sixty minutes per day (as it is on October 30), then it would be clear that the Sun would move 2' 30" per hour of ephemeris time and 15.2 days of elapsed time per hour of ephemeris time. At this specific rate of motion, each minute of Solar Arc would translate into six days of one's life.] The Sun does not move at a steady rate of speed, and the exact rate of motion during the period of interest must be used for an accurate translation of Solar Arc into elapsed time.

In our example horoscope about moving, a Solar Arc of 54° 09' was developed from the dial manipulation. Recall that the birthdate of the client was April 19, 1931. By adding 54° to her natal Sun, it is seen in the ephemeris that the progressed time of interest is between June 14 and June 15, 1931. The Sun's rate of motion on that ephemeris date is 57' 19".

June 14 in the ephemeris is 56 days after birth, and equivalent to the client's fifty-sixth birthday, April 19, 1987. On this date, her Solar Arc is 53° 59' 39" when calculated from a noon ephemeris. The noon (GMT) ephemeris was chosen because the client's natal GMT was 14:52:20. This Solar Arc of 53°59' 39" was arrived at by subtracting the position of the Sun in the ephemeris on the date of birth from the position of the Sun in the ephemeris on June 14, (fifty-six days after birth.) A similar technique, using high-speed computers with modern astrological software for the exact birthtime will yield a slightly different result.

On the client's fifty-sixth birthday, her Solar Arc is 53°59' 39", and the Sun is moving at the June 14 rate of 57' 19". In order to reach *the first calculated Solar Arc of 54° 09'* (recall our due date table on page 237) how many additional days must elapse? The difference in Solar Arc is 9' 21". At a rate of 57' 19" it will take three hours and fifty-five minutes of ephemeris time to traverse 9' 21".

Here's how that works: since each hour is equivalent to 15.2 days of elapsed time, the Solar Arc of 54° 09' will be completed on June 18, 1987, *sixty days after her birthday.* The arithmetic to support these last few steps is easily done on a hand calculator as follows: three hours and fifty-five minutes equates to 3.9166 hours multiplied by 15.2 days to arrive at the number of days (sixty) *to add to the birthday.* (Some of the above calculations can be expedited by using Diurnal Motion of the Sun tables such as those used to erect a horoscope.)

It should be noted here that if the astrologer has the person's birth data and the date of an event in the person's life, the astrologer can calculate the Solar Arc for the date of the event by taking the above steps in reverse. A list of such Solar Arcs is needed to rectify or validate the person's birth time. It just takes practice and familiarity to make all of this second nature!

The Cardinal Points

Another feature of the Uranian System is the incorporation of the Cardinal Points in every horoscope. The modern mundane astrologer casts a horoscope for the moment the Sun enters 0° of each of the Cardinal signs in order to make a forecast for the coming three months. This is an ancient technique of known value. The use of a 90° Dial allows the Uranian astrologer to modify the technique for use in personal horoscopes. *Since all Cardinal signs lie together on the 90° chart, only one point is used to represent 0° of all the Cardinals, and this is 0° Aries.* 0° Aries is known as the Aries Point. This is the point at which the astrologer sees the individual's connection to the world in general. World-famous people have the Aries Point active in the planetary pictures of their horoscopes. The Aries point is looked upon as a Personal Point and is handled as such in the interpretations of planetary pictures.

The use of Antiscia is another ancient technique adapted for the Uranian System. A line is drawn from 0° Cancer to 0° Capricorn to provide an axis for Antiscia. Each planet has its Antiscion at the point across and equidistant from this axis, making 0° Cancer or 0° Capricorn *the midpoint between the planet and its Antiscion.* The Antiscion of a planet or Personal Point is in itself another Sensitive Point. When the Antiscion is activated by Natal, Directed, or Transiting planets, the Uranian astrologer has an additional insight into the horoscope. The 360° and 90° Dials clearly show Antiscia. [See Tom Bridges' chapter on antiscia in this volume for a full presentation.—Ed.]

The Meridian House System is the house system used by all Uranian astrologers. Unlike all other traditional house systems, where the cusp of the 1st House is always the Ascendant, the Meridian House System's 1st House cusp is *not* the Ascendant. The cusp of the 1st House in the Meridian House System is known as the *Equatorial Ascendant,* because it would indeed be the Ascendant if the person were born at the Equator. The traditional Ascendant, arrived at by the consideration of latitude, is still the Ascendant of the chart. Notice that in all horoscopes shown in this chapter, there is an Ascendant (marked A) as well as an Equatorial Ascendant (marked Eq).

All astrologers can improve their productivity and their accuracy of delineation and forecasting by using a movable dial, Planetary Pictures, the Equatorial Ascendant, and Solar Arc Directions.

The Additional "Planets"

The Uranian astrologer uses all these techniques plus eight additional "planets" in each horoscope. Have these "planets" been sighted? Is it claimed that these "planets" exist as physical bodies? The answer to both questions is no. But this is unimportant. The better questions that should be asked are, "Does the use of these 'planets' work in the horoscope?" Are astrological insights gained by the use of these "planets"? Here the answer is a resounding yes! The "planets" have been studied and used advantageously for more than *seven decades.* Please note that this is much longer than Pluto has been studied and used. Several of these "planets" were first postulated during World War I, predating the sighting of Pluto by fifteen years.

To avoid using quotation marks around the word "planet" and to avoid using the word "hypothetical" before it, some astrologers refer to the TransNeptunian "planets" as the TNPs. Ephemerides now exist for the TransNeptunian "planets" in published form and electronically in every major software program.

It is said that Alfred Witte wanted all planets, planetary pairs, and Planetary Pictures defined and described in short, precise, and keyword fashion. This tradition continues to this day. I've prepared the brief descriptions of the "planets" below for the modern astrologer. They adhere to the staccato nature of the Witte concept and expand upon and modernize the descriptions published by Hans Niggemann.

The "planets" are listed in order of their presumed distance from the Sun. Each planet is named, its modern American pronunciation is shown, and some key words are given. For some of the "planets," an explanation of the glyph is presented. As with "real" planets orbiting the Sun, the Geocentric view of each "planet" shows forward and apparent retrograde motions each year. A brief summary of the orbital motions follows each description.

The Eight TransNeptunian Planets
of the Uranian System

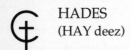 CUPIDO
(coo PEE doe)

Getting together. All groups: family, marriage, society, partnerships, organizations, corporations, collections. Art . . . Cupido is a Super-Venus. The glyph is a combination of Venus and Jupiter, so where Venus means beauty, Cupido means art. Where Venus means love, Cupido means marriage. This is the planet of Togetherness. Cupido is the fastest of the TransNeptunian "planets" and advances 1° 23' per year. Cupido's orbit around the Sun takes 262 years.

 HADES
(HAY deez)

All that is unpleasant, useless, antique, or deeply buried. The occult . . . Hades is misunderstood, because many think only of the negative meanings: dirt, garbage, sewage, sickness, poverty, mistakes, and all things ugly and sinister. There is a positive side that deals with antiquity, depth, and past lives. Hades advances 1° 01' per year, so its orbit around the Sun takes a little over 360 years.

ZEUS
(zoos)

Controlled, directed energy. Machines; creativity; leadership. All things military. Combustion engines. Compulsion. Drive . . . Zeus is like a loaded gun that is aimed. Even the glyph looks like a rocket. It signifies well-planned efforts. Zeus advances 0° 48.2' per year. Its orbit around the Sun takes 455 years.

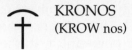 **KRONOS**
(KROW nos)

Superiority: the highest quality attainable; the ultimate in authority; standard of excellence; undisputed expert . . . Zeus and Kronos traveled in very close square from 1900 to about 1970. All natal horoscopes from 1900 to 1950 have these two planets together on the dial. These two together speak of energetic, creative activity of the highest quality. Unfortunately, they also speak of warfare, armament, and military commanders. The world experienced both sides of this combination. Kronos advances 0° 48.1' per year, just six seconds less than Zeus. The square between them is widening, with Kronos falling behind. Kronos takes 521 years to orbit the Sun.

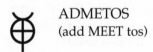 **APOLLON**
(AP pull on)

The multiplier: expansion and spreading; growth and increase. Science, commerce, trade, industry, peaceful efforts . . . The glyph is a combination of Jupiter and Gemini, and Apollon is truly a Super-Duper-Jupiter. Apollon advances 0° 37' per year, so it takes 576 years to go around the Sun.

ADMETOS
(add MEET tos)

The brick wall: steadfast, stable, immovable. Shrinking. Narrowing down to a sharp focus. Specialization. Endurance . . . The glyph for Admetos shows an affinity for the sign Taurus and must be drawn with a base line to show the Admetos capacity to be steadfast, stable, and immovable. Admetos describes inertia, slow motion, and things that go around in a circle like phonograph records and ceiling fans. Admetos advances 0° 35' per year, and takes 617 years to go around the Sun.

VULCANUS
(vul CAN is)

All that is mighty and powerful. Strength. Intensity . . . If a sentence has the word mighty or powerful in it, the Planetary signature will have Vulcanus in it. If the Sun and Vulcanus are together, the vitality, strength, and muscular power describe outstanding good health. Vulcanus advances 0° 32′ per year. The orbit of Vulcanus around the Sun takes 663 years.

POSEIDON
(po SIDE in)

Spirituality, truth, ideation, enlightenment, illumination. Wisdom and culture . . . Poseidon has an affinity for Pisces and its glyph looks like a sideways version of Pisces. Be careful drawing the glyph, so it is not mistaken for Neptune. Poseidon is Super Neptune without a negative side. Poseidon advances only 0° 29′ per year and takes 720 years to circle the Sun.

The preceding discussion gives a brief description of the basic natures of the TransNeptunian "planets." The practical applications and usefulness of these "planets" are found in their *combinations with Personal Points and other planets*, both traditional and TransNeptunian. A discussion of all possible combinations would be quite extensive and beyond the scope of this chapter. However, a few examples are provided to whet your appetite.

The examples below show how the fundamental nature of Cupido is modified when combined with other planets.

SUN + CUPIDO

Since Sun classically refers to a person, this can mean the artist, the married man, the member of a society or family. The Uranian astrologer also interprets the Sun as the physical body, so this will mean a body able to express an art (pianist, ballet dancer). Other meanings are art object, club member, fraternity brother, corporate man.

MOON + CUPIDO

Since Moon is female, the combination of Moon and Cupido means the wife or the bride. It can also mean Ladies' Association, or a social gathering. The Uranian astrologer recognizes the Moon as also meaning the time interval HOUR, so Moon Cupido means hours of art or sociability. The Moon also refers to the public, so look for public manifestations of one of the attributes of Cupido.

MERCURY + CUPIDO

Mercury is generally considered to be the planet of communication: thought, speech, writing. It is also the planet of youth. When combined with Cupido, the following key phrases are developed: Thinking about marriage; talking about marriage. Thoughts or opinions about marriage. Thoughts or opinions about art. To think of the family. To call home. To phone some relatives. Social conversations. Speech, music, song. Intellectual associations. Youth groups: Boy Scouts, Girl Scouts. The staff of a newspaper or magazine. The Telephone Company; AT&T. ITT. Sprint. MCI. Dear Abby column.

VENUS + CUPIDO

Because the glyph for Cupido has Venus and Jupiter, this combination has Venus twice. The combination leads to the following key phrases: Marital happiness. Love Marriage. Social pleasantries. Pleasant company. Beautiful art creations. Group of Fashion Designers. Group of Beauticians. Collection of *objets d'art*.

MARS + CUPIDO

Mars is the planet of action. Mars combined with Cupido describes someone active in art or art activities, someone who is an active member of a club or community. Key phrases include: Marriage. Marriage partnership. Work partnership. Working with others. Group activity. Stress in the family. A fight in the family. A gun collection. Gun Club. National Rifle Association.

JUPITER + CUPIDO

Cupido has elements of Venus and Jupiter along with other characteristics, so the combination of Jupiter with Cupido leads to the following key phrases: Happy marriage. Successful artist, who makes money through his art. Fortunate or successful partnerships. Family happiness. Sociability. Money through marriage. Money through the arts. Happy group of artists. Travel group.

SATURN + CUPIDO

Classically, Saturn represents limitation and restrictions. The Uranian astrologer defines Saturn also as separation. The combination of Saturn and Cupido leads to the following key phrases: Separation from associations. Separation in the family. Separation of marriage. Separation from partnerships. Divorce. Losses in art. Nursing home. Attending a wake. To leave a corporation or a company.

URANUS + CUPIDO

Uranus is the planet of the unusual, the innovative, the astrological, and the electrifying. The combination of Uranus and Cupido leads to the following key phrases: Sudden marriage. Sudden wedding. Elopement. Sudden event in the family. Astrological Society. Unusual group. Innovation in art. The Electricians' Union. Airplane Pilots. Computer organization. IBM.

NEPTUNE + CUPIDO

Neptune, in its negative sense, is the planet of illusion, delusion, dissolution, deception, and fraud. In its positive sense, it implies dreams, inspiration, the medium of film, and the theater. The combination of Neptune and Cupido leads to the following key phrases: Spiritual association or community. A nunnery. A seance. Dissolving a marriage or partnership. Photography Club. Film Company (Kodak). Actors' Group. Swimming Team. Drinking group. Alcoholics Anonymous. Artistic inspiration. The Gas Company. Violin section. Dance Troupe. Anesthesiologists.

PLUTO + CUPIDO

Traditionally, Pluto is considered to be the planet of gangsters, the underworld, the underground, street gangs, the mysterious, the forbidden, and sex. To the Uranian astrologer, Pluto also represents subtle change, growth, development, transformation, and metamorphosis. The combination of Pluto and Cupido leads to the following key phrases: Changes in the family. Changes in a partnership. Changes in the human society. Social transformation. Development of art. Growth of a company.

Planets in Combination

☉	⚷	The Diseased Body. The Keeper of Secrets.
A	⚷	Disagreeable Things in the Environment. Doctor's Office.
☽	⚷	The Woman Who Cares. The Nurse.
♂	⚷	Activity in the Occult.
♃	⚷	Fortune out of Misfortune.
♇	⚷	Psychiatry. Psychology. Archeology. Anthropology.
♃	⚷	Collection of Antiques. Museum. Historical Society. Medical Society. Ancient Art. Therapy Group. Astrology Class. AFA Convention.
⚷	♈	Big Criminal. Crime Police. Medical Doctor. Astrologer.
♅	♃	Revolutionary Knowledge. New Science, Mathematics. Astrology.
♆	♃	Chemistry. Science of the Future. Occult Science.
⚷	♃	Garbage and Junk Dealers. Science of the Past. Secret Science.
♂	⊕	Special Work. The Specialist.
♅	♓	Light. TV. Cinema. Clarity of Insight. Illumination. Enlightenment.
♆	♓	Metaphysics. Psychology.
⚷	♓	Secret Science. The Spirit of Antiquity.
♃	♓	Metaphysics. Spiritual Science. Spreading of Ideas.

The European pioneers of Uranian astrology, fresh from their World War I experiences and witnessing the postwar devastation, formed negative interpretations of many of the planetary combinations. The early publications of the Hamburg School are replete with such interpretations. I've adjusted to a more optimistic view of the world, as seen in the presentation beginning on page 245, the modern keywords for some planetary combinations.

Uranian astrology is not yet in its final form. There is a brilliant body of work that already exists, but modern technological advances and changes in the global environment and global concerns require added interpretations for some of the planetary pictures. Where are the formulae for Astronauts, Magnetic Resonance Imaging, Angioplasty, Cellular Telephones, Ozone Layer Depletion, and Space Stations? These can only be developed from the experiences of today and tomorrow, and from the talents of skilled astrologers working on astrology's most dynamic frontier.

Bibliography

Ephemerides

Michelsen, Neil F. *Uranian TransNeptune Ephemeris 1950–2050.* Franksville, WI: Uranian Publications, Inc., 1989.

Note to computer users: all major software programs provide accurate ephemrides of the TransNeptunian Planets.

Tools

Kramer, Arlene and Pincus, Steve. Star Dial System.

Texts

Ebertin, Reinhold. *The Combination of Stellar Influences.* Wurttemberg, Germany: Ebertin-Verlag, 1960. (While this is not a Uranian text, it has an excellent treatment of occupied midpoints.)

Niggemann, Hans. *Rules for Planetary Pictures (Uranian System).* Published by the Author, 1959.

_____. *The Key to Uranian Astrology.* Published by the Author, 1969.

_____. *The Principles of the Uranian System.* Published by the Author, 1961.

_____. *Uranian Astrology.* Published by the Author, 1969.

Witte-Lefeldt. *Rules for Planetary Pictures.* Translated by Curt Knupfer. Hamburg, Germany: Witte-Verlag, 1973. (This is an English translation of a German text, and is similar to the Hans Niggemann "Rule" book.)

Jacobson, Roger A. *The Language of Uranian Astrology.* Franksville, WI: Uranian Publications, Inc., 1975.

Michael Munkasey

Michael Munkasey has been an astrological researcher for over 23 years. He holds professional astrologer certifications from both the AFA (PMAFA) and The Astrologer's Guild. Michael has written hundreds of articles and letters on astrology, and maintains a busy and far-reaching lecture schedule. His books include *The Astrological Thesaurus, Book 1, House Keywords* (Llewellyn Publications, 1992), *Midpoints: Unleashing the Power of the Planets,* and *The Concept Dictionary* (both released in June, 1991).

Michael has served on the Board of Directors of NCGR since 1976, is currently the Clerk, and was instrumental in writing their by-laws and organizational structure. He was NCGR's Director of Research from 1982 to 1985. He writes book reviews for NCGR and for *Dell Horoscope* magazine. Michael received the Professional Astrologer's, Inc. award for "The Outstanding Astrological Lecture of 1991," and the 1991 Matrix "Pioneer of Astrology" award.

Michael has degrees in engineering and management, is president of his own business, and has been an information processing consultant to the public transit industry since 1965. His public transit information systems are being used in such cities as Washington, New York, Chicago, and San Diego. He resides in Issaquah, WA, part of the greater Seattle metropolitan area.

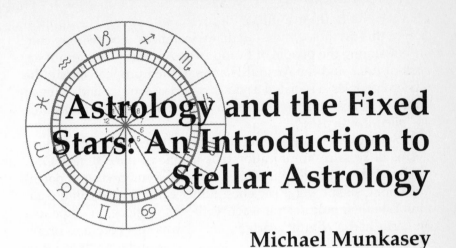

Astrology and the Fixed Stars: An Introduction to Stellar Astrology

Michael Munkasey

The sky! Look at the sky! Its depth, its color, its expanse! Why does the sky so capture our attention? There are different ideas on how mankind's fascination with the sky began.

Let's explore three of these ideas: a popular version, an unusual version, and a spiritual version. In the popular version, cave-dwelling peoples or hunter-gatherer clans carefully observed the night sky and its panorama of stars. They found these heavenly patterns seasonal and those in the clans who had awakened imagination began to place familiar animal patterns among the stars. While the more obvious patterns and cycles of the Sun and Moon matched the march of the seasons, the sky-picture-animal concept evolved to help perpetuate and time religious or ceremonial rites. Mythological tales about the animal patterns in the sky were passed from generation to generation to help people remember the various areas of the sky. After many generations, these patterns and tales became such an integral part of local culture that many persist in some form even to this day.

Early in mankind's history the sky along the Sun's path was divided into twelve "bands" by astute observers, and the overall sky itself was further divided into forty-eight animal, hero, beast or mythical figures. These figures mirrored the patterns among stars in the night sky. Most cultures, anywhere on earth, had their own version of these animals, figures, and objects. The application of this mythology was, in many instances, surprisingly consistent among the people of Europe, the Americas, western Asia, eastern Asia, and the Austral-Islands. If the European or Middle Eastern peoples associated a star or a part of the sky with danger, terror, or beheading, the Chinese might refer to this same sky area as "piled up corpses."

Such consistency among ancient cultures with no obvious means of cross communication tells us one of three things. One, modern historians are unaware of the early communication potential among such diverse societies. Either early people could communicate their cultural ideas across the entire globe, or all people on earth had a common origin, and it was this common origin group which invented the "star tales." Two, different cultures in different parts of the world each evolved shrewd shaman-type observers of the heavens who were able to correlate society's events with heavenly passages. These shamans, or priests, were the people who communicated, within the society, the cultural ideas which were passed down over many centuries. Different shamans in different cultures evolved the same ideas. Three, "visitors" from outside our Solar System taught many ancient, culturally diverse people the same information. Which of these three stories you believe depends on your orientation. Maybe parts of all three are correct. Maybe only one is correct. What is consistent is that all cultures shared a fascination with the sky, whether it was because of their need for accurate calendars or to support a religion.

In a second, more unusual version of how mankind's fascination with the sky began, a less "scientifically" promoted version if you will, an interesting story arises. An African tribe, the Dogon, claim that "men" flew in from the skies and imparted knowledge to them about certain parts of the sky. If you believe that such had indeed happened, then it would be folly for you to think that the Dogon were the only such people on earth given such celestial knowledge. I doubt that an advanced civilization would travel forty-plus light-years to a remote outpost in a distant galaxy, peopled with diverse cultures, and only contact one of those cultures.

Lastly, there is the view I prefer of how mankind's fascination with the sky began. This is a spiritual view which I have combined from many sources like Edgar Cayce, Zecharia Sitchin,

William Bramley, John Michell, Bruce Cathie, early mythological tales, tales from native American cultures, etc. The view starts with the premise that man began as a purely spiritual being, without physical form, that both the spirit world and the physical world are intertwined with subtle cosmic forces. There is a fundamental, primal part of mankind's inner orientation that forces us, through our genes, to view "the sky" as the place of our personal spiritual origin. Mankind, the sky, and the Earth are linked through unrecognized, all-pervasive forces.

Mankind started not as physical beings, but as pure spiritual beings without bodies, without substance, without form. Over many, many, many millennia, some of the early spiritual forms of proto-man became more and more physical in their outward form. The spiritual beings created their physical bodies from matter in and of the earth. This happened because these spiritual beings became fascinated with the diverse possibilities which the physical form allowed. There probably were splits in thinking among these early spiritual beings; some becoming intent on pursuing a more perfect body (physical) vehicle for exploring earthly manifestation, and some preferring to remain closer to their original spiritual forms. Yet, over eons, these beings remained in communication with each other until those in the physical form became so matter-evolved (involved) that they began to lose their direct communication links with the spiritual beings. These beliefs mirror the ideas that angels and humans existed together in times past.

Despite this loss of communication, the tie between the beings in physical form and their "sky origins" or spiritual ties remained a part of their inner heritage. This "memory" gradually switched from an ethereal subjective energy to gene-encoded chemical messages. Physical man's need to maintain a connection to what or who the source is, and what or who the sky represents, remained. This remained as the inner urge which mankind expresses with his or her fascination toward the sky. The more that modern man explores possibilities in the sky, the more that modern man strives for planetary and interplanetary travel, then the more mankind will have to define and resolve its possible early spiritual ties to sky origins. The more science constructs machines that travel to the Moon, to Mars, or wherever, the more religious ideas will be pressed to expand and define our spiritual heritage.

Most modern religions, having evolved over the last two thousand years, are inadequate for explaining man's early spiritual ties to the sky. Thus, as global society becomes more sophisticated about the heavens, the religions based on Christianity, Islam, Judaism, etc., are under increasing pressure to evolve into new forms suitable for explaining an emerging new-age consciousness. The concepts based on religious ideas within the Bible gave adequate religious solace for many centuries. But, people are questioning these tales in light of what science is discovering about mankind's origins and patterns of evolution. I can foresee new religions eventually arising to replace the older religions. This won't be done in one day or in one year, but slowly, over time, new ideas about the spiritual parts of our being should arise to replace religious ideas of the last two thousand years which are increasingly losing popular favor.

Historically, *it is to the stars that mankind looks for answers.* This is an innate part of our beingness. The more people suppress or ridicule this urge to find mankind's spiritual roots among the stars, the more this urge shouts from our inner selves for a rational explanation. If, in fact, mankind had its origins "in the sky," then it is mankind's destiny to return to the sky to find and rediscover those stellar origins. Why does mankind universally look to the sky? Why do our calendars match the movement of heavenly bodies? Why is "God" associated with "up," or "the sky?" Why? Why? Why?

Astrology and the Fixed Stars

When you look into the sky on a clear night, you can see what appear to be dots of light. Five of these dots can be the visible planets of our Solar System, but astrologers commonly refer to those other points of light as "the fixed stars." Stars are stellar bodies, much like our Sun is also a stellar body in space. Some are larger than our Sun, and some are smaller. Because the stars are so far away when compared to our Sun, they appear to our eyes as points of light. Some of the dots of light you see are actually two or more bodies so close together that you can not visually distinguish their separateness. Some of the bright bodies have a darker companion, or maybe even two or more, which rotates around them, and thus their brightness varies with the period of their darker companion. The bodies have different "temperatures," and thus exhibit different colors. Some are red, others green, others bluish-white, some yellow, etc. Their spectacular colors can be quite pure and contrasting.

The common name given to these bodies "the fixed stars," is quite misleading. The bodies are *not* fixed in space. They move. But over a human lifetime, the amount of movement is so small that it is difficult to distinguish any changes in this heavenly background. Each of the bodies has two different and distinct sets of motion. The background of stars moves according to the Earth's precessional rate, and each star also has its own individual (proper) rate of motion. Over ten or twenty or even fifty years, their overall rate of motion is less than one degree, i.e., 1/360° of a circle. That is a very small amount to move in fifty, seventy, or eighty years. No wonder they are commonly referred to as "fixed." For most stars, the Earth's precessional motion is the major part of their movement as seen from Earth.

The Earth spins like a child's conical top would spin in a slow moving circle, round and round. A spinning top has at least two sets of motion: one is the top's rate of spin, which is usually quite fast; the other is that the central axis of the top, as it spins, describes a small circle in the air. This latter motion is done much more slowly than the spin of the top. The Earth acts just like a top. It spins on its axis, once a day against the Sun. This gives us our sensation of day and night. The Earth also rotates around the Sun, and this movement gives us our sensation of the year. In addition to these movements, the Earth has a precessional motion, a wobble, if you will. This precessional movement takes about 25,700 years to complete its circle. Because of this precessional movement, all stars appear to move slowly with time. Polaris, which is currently our "North Star," will eventually be replaced. About 3,000 years ago the star "Thuban" appeared as the "North Star" in our heavens. Some 22,000 years from now Thuban will be back in that position. The continuous motion of space, time, tide, and ideas is relentless.

Ancient people looked into the skies and saw these points of light, these stars. They grouped these stars into related clusters or constellations which they named after local animals or mythic figures. European cultures, primarily Greek (Phonecian) and Roman, provided the names for the groups of stars we use today. Some of these names are Orion, Andromeda, Cepheus, and

Aquarius. We call these groups constellations. Some of the constellations share the same names as signs of the zodiac, but *signs and constellations are quite different*. Signs refer to a band of the sky in which the Sun travels, while constellations cover a section of the sky and are not associated with the travels of our Sun.

The Greeks and Romans probably got their ideas for the constellational groups directly from the Sumerians, with certain embellishments provided by the Egyptians, who got their ideas for the constellational groups from the Babylonians. The Babylonians got their ideas from the Assyrians, who copied ideas from the Sumerians. Now we are back to about 3000 B.C. and earlier. History doesn't clearly record how the Sumerians got their constellational ideas.

The sky you see today is not the same sky that the Sumerians examined. Because of each star's rate of proper motion, and also because of the Earth's precessional motion, the overall outline and feature of the sky has changed considerably. In the 5,000 years between the Sumerian sky catalog and a present day 2000 A.D. sky catalog, an average star may have wandered between sixty and ninety degrees. That is, each star is moving in its own direction. The average rate of motion would be about seventy-two degrees over the 5,000 years of this period. Imagine looking at the sky one night and noting the relations among the fixed stars, and then not looking up again until 5,000 years later. Each star would have moved an average of seventy-two degrees! The second sky would look totally different to you. All of the original constellational boundaries would be lost. Time would have marched by both so slowly and so fast that your mind could not comprehend those two motions together. That is why the stars appear fixed. It is all due to a mechanism, a playful trick if you will, of our temporal minds.

Mankind's systematic and precise study of heavenly body motion in the skies is at least 25,000 years old. Deer antlers (and other such bones) from that period have been found with notched notations which record the passage of lunar phases and other heavenly body motion. Celestial awareness was clearly important.

Mankind began to cultivate cereal grains around 8000 B.C. in the Middle East. But there is also solid evidence that people had built a very good working system of agricultural watering and drainage ditches in Indonesia about 20,000 B.C. The living memory of the Australian Aboriginal people goes back at least 40,000 years, as does their knowledge of the movement of bodies in the heavens. So, when did civilization begin? Western civilization as we know it probably originated with the cultivation of grains about 8000 B.C. in what today is the area around Iraq, Iran, and the Ukraine.

Grain farming and cultivation require accurate calendars for the annual planting and harvesting cycles. If mankind has an inherent understanding of the celestial cycles from their spiritual origins, then the formulation of calendars based on these cycles would have been due more to knowledge than chance and repeated observation. But, who knows the truth about this subject? Calendars evolved. Calendars were used by farmer peoples. Calendars are based on natural Sun, Moon, and other Earth-related cycles. Each culture throughout the world has its form of calendar. The Sumerian people, in Mesopotamia, were the first people in the western civilized world to record divisions of the sky into constellations. The Sumerians were careful recorders of the stellar body positions and movements over many years. The Sumerians were the first to pass to us their divisions of the sky into forty-eight constellational areas. The Assyrians conquered the Sumerians and picked up pieces of their ideas. The Assyrians passed this on to other people. Eventually this knowledge reached the Egyptians, who passed it to the Greeks, who passed it to the Romans, who passed it to the Arabs, who passed it back to the Europeans, who passed their ideas on to North American settlers, who gave it to you and me in the United States. What exactly was it that we have received?

If thirty reasonably intelligent people stand side by side in a large room, and a stranger whispers a long message to the first person at one end of the line, and asks that person to pass the message on, then it has been shown that the message becomes quickly garbled. By the time the thirtieth person has heard that repeated message it will sound nothing like the original message. *Information becomes altered with its passage.* This is part of human nature.

Now, imagine a message repeated not just thirty times, but passed from generation to generation, in different languages, over some 5,000 years! What will the receiver understand about the original message? Did the Sumerians work with the fixed stars? Yes. Did the Sumerians invent the present-day concept of constellations? Probably, but we don't know if this was original work by them, or if they had knowledge passed to them. Did the Sumerians work with a circle of the zodiac? Yes, but it really wasn't until about 400 B.C. that the Greeks invented the concept of the modern zodiac as western astrologers use it today. Did the Sumerians work with both Solar and Lunar cycles? Yes. This history, and this passage of information, has colored our perception of the basis for astrology and how astrology works. Let us examine (with some humor, please), the passage of astrological information from today, *back* through various stages of history! This will dramatize our premise that, while there is research, development, expansion, and, indeed, progress through the line of centuries, fundamentals can be lost. Astrologers have indeed lost sight of the stars!

Astrological Practice through the Ages

Imagine that our journey begins in present day East Coast U.S.A. at the shop of a group of reknowned astrologers. A client has requested a natal reading, and is listening to how one famous twentieth-century astrologer has prepared the chart and how the astrologer will proceed with the reading. The astrologer explains that a computer was used to cast the chart for the date, time and place of birth, and that certain asteroids, Chiron, the Vertex, etc., were added to the chart. Twenty different sets of house cusps were also computed, as were fifty or so Arabic Parts. In addition, if the person wanted a Uranian astrologer's interpretation using the eight hypothetical planets, that was available, too. Using the latest psychologically based astrological theories developed in the late 1970s and early 1980s, the astrologer intends to interpret the chart for the client. The client can also choose from several ritual based interpretation techniques, and astro-drama. In addition, the latest computer chart interpretation programs are available to produce thirty-plus pages of written material to supplement the spoken interpretation of the natal chart. And life goes on . . .

Thirty years earlier, in a midwestern American city, a client has called an astrologer for the interpretation of a natal horoscope. The astrologer explains that it will take several hours of work to cast the chart using logarithms, and manual double interpolation techniques using the latest math tables and ephemeris. It took many astrologers ten to fifteen years to learn this arduous chart-casting technique. The table of houses being used dates from the 1890s. The theories of interpretation to be used are based on ideas generated in the 1930s and refined in the 1940s and 1950s. Time zones and world-wide latitude and longitude books are newly available. The astrologer would use the ten known planets, the mean Node of the Moon, the Ascendant and MC, and tropical Placidian techniques. This is the latest hot stuff! And life goes on . . .

In Germany some forty years earlier a client calls upon members of the Hamburg school and requests a natal chart interpretation. The client asks how this will be done. They explain their latest theories about the use of the 90° dial, Solar Arc, the use of midpoints and planetary pictures, the use of four hypothetical planets, etc. All known planets through Neptune would be used. About the same time, in England, the same type of event occurs. A client calls a prominent astrological house and asks about their interpretation and chart-casting techniques. They will use an 1890 table of Placidian houses, an ephemeris produced by German astronomers, etc. Hand calculation of the horoscope using manual arithmetic dominates. Their theories of interpretation are based upon the very latest work by Alan Leo and his group, who has copied and then modernized the best of what the seventeenth century astrologers from England, Italy, and Germany had to offer. They will be using the newly invented and standardized time zones, etc. And life goes on . . .

One hundred years earlier, in England, a client visits an astrologer and asks about astrological procedures and methods of interpretation. The client is told that it will take about two days to cast the chart, using logarithms, quill, and ink. The chart will be hand drawn, and the same tables developed in the seventeenth century by Placidus de Tito will be used for the houses. Primary to this interpretation will be the rulers of the signs and decanates, the faces and terms, etc. Yes, they are assured, the newly discovered planet, Uranus, can be included in this reading, but astrologers in general are still unaware of its affect. The zodiac to be used will be tropical, and some dramatic fixed stars and their ecliptic positions will be added. The use of Moon Mansions and the constellations will have a role in the astrological chart interpretation. Standardized time keeping will begin in about eighty years. Turn up the light from the oil lamp! And life goes on . . .

Around the year 1690, a client visits a famous London astrological house and requests that a horary question be answered. The client inquires about the technique. The procedures to be used, the astrologer explains, are quite similar to the procedures described in ancient Arabic and early medieval texts. The seven known planets are studied, and their rulerships, terms and faces are to be noted. Also noted will be the Arabic parts, some fixed stars in their ecliptic positions, the planets, the signs and their planetary rulers, etc. There are no watches generally available. Clocks are large and heavy, and not very accurate. World maps are a rare novelty. Time zones are 200 years in the future. It has only been in the last one hundred years since a more modern theory of planetary motion has been developed to replace the Earth-centered systems used for thousands of years before that. Candles and daylight help with just being able to see the chart. Clear glass windows are a luxury for the rich. And life goes on . . .

Around the year 1000 A.D., a client visits an astrologer's home near Baghdad and inquires about astrological technique. The astrologer explains how the Arabic people have preserved the methods of the ancients. The astrologer will use an astrolabe to measure the angles between each of the planets and as they rise or set over the horizon. These will be matched against the diurnal movement of the fixed stars to note if there are any paran occurrences. (A paran is a simultaneous rising and/or setting of at least two bodies. For example, Jupiter rising and the Moon on the Meridian simultaneously, would be one form of paran. Parans can occur between fixed stars, planets, etc.) The latest in a growing list of Arabic parts can be included for an extra fee. At this point there are no clocks, no time zones, the ephemeris of the seven known planets is only accurate to plus or minus fifteen minutes of arc (if in fact you can find a copy at all), books are hand copied, and the mathematics of space has not yet been invented (and won't be for another 600 years). And life goes on . . .

It is the year 12 A.D., and the astrologer Phillipi has just set up his shop in the bazaar in downtown Jerusalem. His client, a young man of about 18, is requesting an astrological reading to help him focus on how to begin his life's occupation. He claims that he was born of Joseph and Mary in the village of Bethlehem during the reign of the Emperor Caesar Augustus and of Herod the Great, etc. The astrologer gets out his astrolabe and measures the angles between the heavenly bodies, notes the rise and set time of the constellations, and the time when they pass over the local meridian, etc. The astrologer explains that use of the newly developed concept of the ecliptic zodiac as formulated by the Greeks a short time ago should help in the interpretation of the horoscope. Time of day is measured between sunrise and sunset, which demark the day hours from the night hours. There are twelve daylight and twelve night-time hours. These hours also divide the sky into segments. Later this concept of "hours" will be expanded into various house theories. There are no clocks, no concept of time zones, no easily accessible pens, pencils, paper, etc. Books of any kind on this subject are generally available only in large cities, like Alexandria, some one month's travel on foot from this place. The astrologer's fee is negotiated before any work is begun. And life goes on . . .

About 2500 B.C., on a wind swept plain in southeastern England, a Druid priest is using the latest astronomical tool for the determination of eclipses, phases of the moon, etc. The priest explains how this "henge" of large, carefully placed stones is used. If you look through the alignment of stones and note the angles of rising stellar bodies, you can create a calendar. Time is measured by the passage of the Lunar month, and the year is noted by the passage of the seasons. There is no concept of the use of the zodiac in astrology as astrologers understand it today. The observation of stellar bodies is used for religious and agricultural purposes. There is an innate understanding of man's role in and with the Cosmos. There is an innate understanding of the subtle Earth forces. All of these natural cycles have their role in daily life. And life goes on . . .

About 3500 B.C., in the hot dry desert area of Mesopotamia, a group of young scribes is being instructed in the art of accurately copying planetary phenomena onto their clay tablets. The priests have made the observations with their instruments, and it is up to the scribes to copy them neatly for preservation and future usage. The theories of the forty-eight constellations are explained, and their boundaries are noted with surprising precision. All of the visible stars are assigned to specific constellations. Quite accurate tables for the positions of the planets are calculated and preserved. Here great attention is paid to the paran-crossing of paired planets and stars. The fixed stars, their constellations, the Lunar Mansions, etc., play heavily into the art of astrological technique. Many of the more scholarly priest astrologers understand that there are probably three additional "invisible" planets in our Solar System. They understand that the Earth is round, and that the Sun is the center of our Solar System. Then the Assyrian peoples invade, and much knowledge is lost. The culture of the sky was understood very well. A little more than 5,000 years will pass before it is understood as well again by European-based mankind. And life went on from there.

The Use of the Fixed Stars

The single thread which ties the practice of astrology today with the practice of astrology ages ago is the use of the sky. The stellar bodies, the constellations, paired body configurations at rising, meridian passage (across the MC), setting, etc., have been continually important, but modern astrologers have lost sight of the important role which observational astronomy played in the techniques of their craft. Computers are a great boon for the astrologer, but one's ability to operate an astrological computer program does not an astrologer make. An astrologer historically relies on the patterns shown among the celestial bodies. The skill of an astrologer lies in the coherent interpretation of these patterns. The skill of an astrologer lies in the understanding that there is a dual role in nature, a yin and a yang, a positive and a negative, a male and a female. Duality. It is there. It exists. Astrologers have used that idea over the ages because it is meaningful. Keyboarding ten or forty computer commands and printing a chart on a printer does not alter the fact that astrology involves the interpretation of real astronomical events. *Astronomical phenomena* are the common thread that ties astrologers of all ages together. Central within these astrological ties must be the use of the constellations and their fixed stars. We must recover the important knowledge from the line of history before us.

Ptolemy listed forty-eight constellations in *The Almagest*, which was published in the second century A.D. Their names, listed alphabetically in their Roman form, are as follows:

Andromeda	Coma Berenices	Lupus
Aquarius	Corona Australis	Lyra
Aquila	Corona Borealis	Ophiuchus
Ara	Corvus	Orion
Argo Navis	Crater	Pegasus
Aries	Crux	Perseus
Auriga	Cygnus	Pisces
Bootes	Delphinus	Piscis Austrinis
Cancer	Draco	Sagitta
Canis Major	Eridanus	Sagittarius
Canis Minor	Gemini	Scorpius
Capricornus	Hercules	Taurus
Cassiopeia	Hydra	Triangulum
Centaurus	Leo	Ursa Major
Cephus	Lepus	Ursa Minor
Cetus	Libra	Virgo

To these names scientists have added many more constellations since the seventeenth century, rearranging the boundaries in the older constellational figures. For instance, Argo Navis was cut up into at least four "modern" constellations (Argo, Carina, Puppis, and Vela). Today's map of the sky now holds about eighty-eight constellations, depending on which authority you use as your standard. Many of the modern constellations have object names, such as the Pendulum Clock, the Telescope, the Sextant, etc. Obviously, words for these objects did not exist in more ancient cultures.

In 1603, Johann Bayer, a lawyer living in Augsberg, published his *Uranometria* atlas. In addition to the forty-eight Ptolemaic constellations, he added the twelve new constellations of the southern hemisphere as defined by the Dutch navigator Pieter Dirkszoon Keyser. Bayer was the first to use Greek letters for star designations. Ian Ridpath's *Star Tales* gives an interesting account of how modern star catalogs evolved.

In the appendix to this chapter, extracts from Ptolemy and Copernicus's works summarize some of their thinking on the role and use of fixed stars. I've observed their style of wording as closely as possible in these sections. Please persevere with those few pages; it's important to our tie with the past.

The Most Important Point

Before telescopes and automated tabular records of celestial movement, Ptolemy and Copernicus and so many other brilliant astrologers throughout the centuries relied on the line-of-sight positions of the fixed stars as they rise and/or set with the Sun, Moon, and planets. *It is not the ecliptic position of the star, but its line-of-sight position which they held as crucially important.* Let us take the fixed star Algol as an example.

Algol's ecliptic longitude position for the year 1950 is at 25 Tau 28, and its zodiacal latitude position is 22 N 25. The latitude tells us that Algol is a little over 22 degrees off of the ecliptic, or the path of the Sun. This means that when the Sun is on the horizon (as at sunrise or sunset), then Algol is *still some twenty-two degrees away.* Since we measure distances in space along curved circles, we can *not* simply add or subtract twenty-two degrees to determine when Algol rises or sets, or what equivalent rising or setting degree of the ecliptic should be associated with Algol. But, with the help of a few trigonometric equations (on your computer program), one can determine the mundane rising or setting ecliptic degrees for Algol for a particular place on Earth. Doing this for the year 1950, for a latitude of 40 degrees North, close to New York City, we find that Algol is conjunct the horizon when 29 Psc 49 is on the Ascendant; Algol is on the MC when 18 Tau 41 shows there; and Algol is line of sight on the Descendant when 13 Gem 40 is there. Wow! Reread this paragraph, please. Look at those discrepancies!

Here's what this means in practical terms: A client comes for a reading, and the astrologer has determined that for this birth near New York City in the year 1950 the Ascendant is 25 Tau 30. Oh, the astrologer states, you have Algol conjunct your Ascendant. *WRONG!* The client has Algol's *ecliptic degree* conjunct the ascendant. If the client had 29 Psc 49 rising then Algol would be exactly conjunct the Ascendant line of sight. *Line-of-sight!* This means that if, in the year 1950, you had looked to the East when 29 Psc 49 was on the Ascendant and you were at 40 degrees North, then you would have seen Algol conjunct the Ascendant. Not 25 Tau, but 29 Psc! 25 Tau is the closest point on the ecliptic to the sky position of Algol and is used at the *cataloging* position of Algol.

For Ptolemy and Copernicus line-of-sight awareness is all important.

If you have 13 Sag rising and were born around the year 1950 in the vicinity of New York City, then you have Algol line-of-sight on your Descendant. If your natal Sun is about 0 Cap and you were born around 1950 close to New York City with your Sun exactly on the MC, then you have 29 Psc rising, and Algol is line-of-sight conjunct your Ascendant. Star movement in general, such as Algol, is about eight minutes of arc every ten years. Thus Algol's 1940 Ascendant equivalent is at that latitude about 29 Psc 41, etc.

How did I determine my star positions? Did I use exotic formulae? Do I have some secret methods? Yes, and no! I used a common table of houses. I used some ingenuity. I purchased a planetarium program for my computer and looked at the rising and setting degrees for the dates and times I wanted to investigate. I used the planetarium program to put the Sun on the horizon and then I looked and saw which stars were rising or setting. No, you don't have to be a mathematical genius to determine these positions. All I used were some available tools and a little common sense. Yes, I could mathematically compute all of these positions. No, the equations for doing this aren't all that difficult to find or use. Any hand-held calculator with trigonometric functions would suffice as the calculating device. Knowing what to do, and how to do it, and having some persistence to trace it all through is what is noteworthy!

To get a better feeling for how stars move over many years, note this overview ephemeris: in the year 1950, Algol's ecliptic position was at 25 Tau 28. In 1900 it was 24 Tau 46, and in the year 2000 it will be at 26 Tau 10. Thus, in one hundred years Algol's ecliptic position moves one degree and twenty-four minutes. In the year 0 A.D. Algol's ecliptic position was at 28 Ari 36. So, in 2,000 years, Algol's ecliptic position moves 27 degrees and 34 minutes. Contrasting this movement with another star, Sirius, we get one degree and twenty-three minutes of movement along the ecliptic for the twentieth century, and 27 degrees and 29 minutes of movement in 2,000 years. The movement of each of these stars has to be measured individually. Each has its own rate of motion, and each is in a different place relative to the pole of the celestial equator. Thus precessional motion will affect them differently.

Ptolemy and Copernicus's material presents the traditional way of using the body of material on the fixed stars. We have been coddled by contemporary books which copy each other's material and *equate the ecliptic position of the fixed stars as the positions which should be used in our astrological practices*. Do the ecliptic positions of the fixed stars work? Maybe. Sometimes. But if astrologers want to harness the fundamental, eternal power of the fixed stars, then they should be looking for paran positions of the stars with the Sun, Moon, and other planets. In addition, they should be looking at the mundane positions of the fixed stars to see what is rising, setting, or culminating *with the various planets at birth*.

John F. Kennedy

John F. Kennedy, who became the 35th President of the United States in January, 1961, was born at 2:52 P.M. EST on May 29, 1917, in Brookline, Massachusetts (source: Lois Rodden's "Astro-Data" book material, as updated). JFK was quite sickly and weak as a child. He fought as a PT boat commander in the South Pacific in World War II, and was decorated as a war hero. A graduate of Harvard University, he also wrote books and even won a Pulitzer Prize. His father's relentless pressure led him to run for Congress, to which he was elected at age twenty-nine. Later he was elected to the Senate. In 1960, JFK beat Richard Nixon by the narrowest of margins to become President of the United States. His administration had to face up to the Cuban missile crisis. That was perhaps the closest the United States and Russia had ever come to using nuclear weapons against each other. He was shot and killed in Dallas, Texas, on November 22, 1963. He voiced many good ideas, but was embroiled in political battles with Congress which stymied his national programs. He was known for his family image and promotion of a sports and fitness image, yet rumors persisted of his many extra-marital affairs. While a congressional blue-ribbon commission investigating his assassination concluded that a lone gunman had acted, many questions about how and why he was killed persisted, even to this day.

On the day JFK was born, the Sun rose at 4:11 A.M. EST at Brookline, Massachusetts, crossed the meridian at 11:41 A.M., and set at 7:11 P.M. EST. At that location, on that day, the following fixed stars were rising, culminating or setting with the Sun (times are accurate only to within three or four minutes, for technical reasons. The stars noted below are all brighter than magnitude 4.0, visible with normal vision and clear dark skies.):

Constellation Name	Popular Name	Time of rising or setting
Lamda Scorpii	Shaula	4:04 A.M., star rising with Sun
Beta 1 Scorpii	Graffias	4:11 A.M., star rising with Sun
Alpha Grus	Al Nair	4:19 A.M., star rising with Sun
Alpha Indii	The Persian	stayed conj. horizon most of day
Epsilon Cygni	Gienah	4:06 A.M., star on MC at sunrise
Alpha Scorpii	Antares	4:05 A.M., star setting at sunrise
Alpha Canis Major	Sirius	7:11 P.M., star set with the Sun
Gamma Orionis	Bellatrix	7:01 P.M., star set with the Sun
Gamma Andromedae	Alamaak	7:12 P.M., star set with the Sun

On that day and at JFK's time of birth, the following stars were on the horizon or the meridian (orbs of about or under 1-1/2 degrees are generally used; altitude is the distance, in degrees, by which the star body is off the horizon, with minus numbers indicating that it is below the horizon, plus numbers above the horizon):

Alpha Cygni	Deneb	altitude at 2:52 P.M. was -1° 08'
Gamma Velorum	Suhail al Borealis	altitude at 2:52 P.M. was 0° 01'
Alpha Coronae Borealis	Alphekka	altitude at 2:52 P.M. was -1° 36'
Delta Corvi	Algorab	altitude at 2:52 P.M. was 0° 20'
Epsilon Corvi	Minkar	altitude at 2:52 P.M. was -0° 46'
Zeta Virginis	Heze	altitude at 2:52 P.M. was -0° 26'
Alpha Gemini	Castor	conj. MC at 2:52 P.M.
Beta Gemini	Pollux	conj. MC at 3:02 P.M.
Alpha Canis Minoris	Procyon	conj. MC at 2:56 P.M.
Beta Canis Minoris	Gomeisa	conj. MC at 2:45 P.M.

On that day and at that time, the following constellations were on the meridian at the time of JFK's birth:

Capricornii	Equus	Microscopium (one of the modern constellations)

The constellation Scorpio was setting, right across the middle part of the Scorpion's tail.

On that day, at 7:52 P.M. EST, setting along with Venus, the ruler of JFK's Ascendant, was the malefic fixed star Algol. Algol has been associated with "losing one's head." JFK was killed by a bullet which literally ripped the top of his head off.

JFK was born under a Moon and Venus paran, for Moon rise occurred at 12:14 P.M., and Venus transited the MC at 12:19 P.M. Moon and Venus combinations such as this would account much for his immense popular appeal. At this same time, the following stars were also contributing to this paran:

Epsilon Aurigae	Al Anz	conj. the MC at 12:19 P.M.
Iota Aurigae	Hassaleh	conj. the MC at 12:14 P.M.
Beta Leonis	Denebola	conj. the MC at 12:09 P.M.

The Moon set at 12:13 AM on this day. Accompanying the Moon at that time and helping to define its influence for that day were the following stars:

Alpha Leonis	Regulus	star set at 12:15 A.M.
Epsilon Centaurus	(unnamed)	star set at 12:20 A.M.
Alpha Aurigae	Capella	altitude at 12:13 A.M. was -1° 30'
Beta Aurigae	Menkalinan	altitude at 12:13 A.M. was -1° 28'
Beta Lupi	Ke Kwan	altitude at 12:13 A.M. was 0° 45'
Beta Corvi	Tso Hea	altitude at 12:13 A.M. was -1° 18'
Alpha Telescopii	(unnamed)	altitude at 12:13 A.M. was -0° 44'
Delta Capricornii	Deneb Algiedi	altitude at 12:13 A.M. was 0° 51'

On that day and in that location Venus rose at 4:48 A.M. It was accompanied by the following stars in critical angular positions:

Beta Taurus	Alnath	star rose at 4:43 A.M.
Theta 2 Taurus	(unnamed)	star rose at 4:44 A.M.
Alpha Bootis	Arcturus	star set at 4:52 A.M.
Alpha Grus	Al Nair	altitude at 4:48 A.M. was 0° 17'
Beta Grus	Al Dhanab	altitude at 4:48 A.M. was -0° 42'
Psi Ursae Majoris	Tien Tsan	altitude at 4:48 A.M. was -0°

As you can see from JFK's natal chart, he has four planets and the Sun in the 8th House, classically ruled by Mars. As Mars rose at 3:14 A.M., Saturn was transiting the IC of the birth location. This Mars and Saturn paran also has the following fixed stars associated with it on that day and in that place as it was rising or setting:

Beta Ceti	Diphda	star rose at 3:09 A.M.
Theta Scorpio	Sargas	star rose at 3:11 A.M.
Alpha Aquilae	Altair	star was on the MC at 3:10 A.M.
Beta Gemini	Pollux	conj. IC at 3:03 A.M.

Saturn set at 10:40 PM that day in that location. The following stars were assisting in delineating Saturn's properties on that day.

Theta Scorpio	Sargas	altitude at 10:40 P.M. was -0° 27'
Alpha Lupus	Men	altitude at 10:40 P.M. was -0° 13'
Alpha Aurigae	Capella	altitude at 10:40 P.M. was 1° 50'
Delta Persei	(unnamed)	altitude at 10:40 P.M. was 0° 13'
Alpha Persei	Mirphak	conj. the MC at this time
Gamma Tri. Australis	(unnamed)	conj. the IC at this time

What does all of this mean? This listing of stars is simply dazzling, but *the interpretation of their astrological influence on the planets is quite another thing.*

Only a few of the implications in this list can be covered in the short space of this chapter. Let us start with some of the more obvious "hits" in the above list. The Moon sets with Regulus (the star of Kingship), and the man became President of the United States. Castor and Pollux (the paired primary stars of the constellation of Gemini, associated with communication) straddled his horizon at birth, and the man won a Pulitzer prize for his writing and was celerated as a speaker. As noted earlier, Venus, the ruler of his Ascendant, and Algol set simultaneously, and the man was killed when a bullet tore off the top of his head. Venus was rising as Arcturus was setting, and the man was a philanderer. Antares, the star historically associated with war, was setting as the Sun was rising, and he presided over the Cuban missile crisis which brought the world to the brink of nuclear crisis. JFK was born with a Mars-Saturn paran, along with Diphda, which is traditionally associated with physical and psychological restrictions. He was so sickly as a child few thought he would survive. He was locked in a losing battle with Congress as President. Mars and Saturn did bring him many frustrations.

Saturn is paired with the star Capella. V. Robson in his book on the Fixed Stars (see bibliography later) writes this of Saturn with Capella: "Shrewd, tidy, fond of luxury, many detrimental habits, makes much money but does not keep it, trouble from the opposite sex and domestic disharmony, bad health at the end of life (JFK injured his back in World War II and this bothered him all of his life) and afflicted in arms, legs or eyes restricting movement." Many of these statements fit JFK quite well: shrewd, tidy, domestic disharmony, trouble from the opposite sex, trouble with back and legs, etc., were all prominent problems which he suffered life long. R. Ebertin in his book (see bibliography) on the fixed stars notes that Capella gives people a "persistent, annoying and inquisitive quality." JFK with his Gemini Sun was well known for asking difficult questions.

Graffias helped to color the Sun on that day. One unnamed reference on this star notes: "Sun to: Riches and preferment, attended by danger, violence, troubles and illness." Bellatrix also contributes to the Sun's interpretation. Of this Robson writes "Vacillating, changeable, indecisive in business, mechanical ability, riches and honor but final ruin, . . . , violent death." This description fits JFK quite well.

Now have I used just the *ecliptic* positions of the fixed stars? No. I didn't use that approach at all. I used the same method which Ptolemy and Copernicus used and described in their works. How did I do the math for this? I didn't. I cheated. I used a planetarium program on my PC, and set the planetarium sky to the date and time of JFK's birth, added in the meridian and horizon lines, and copied the star information out by hand. This exercise took me all of about one-half to two hours for each chart examined, depending on the depth of the stellar interactions which I copied. Did I pick JFK years ago and study his chart for months and months? No, I picked it at random for this article and spent less than two days pulling all of this material together. These techniques really work! You don't have to search or stretch for answers when using them. For centuries, astrologers worked with Fixed Stars in the Ptolemaic tradition more than they did with planets!

Kareem Abdul-Jabbar

Another example of the powerful effects these ancient techniques bring to astrological interpretation shows that on the day and in the place where Kareem Abdul-Jabbar was born (April 16, 1947, 6:30 P.M. EST, New York City), a Sun and Pluto paran occurred, with the Sun on the MC and Pluto rising at that location simultaneously. Kareem Abdul-Jabbar, the star basketball player of the Milwaukee Bucks and Los Angeles Lakers for many years in the late 1960s, 70s, and 80s, stands 7 feet 2 inches tall and possesses some twenty NBA performance records. According to traditional astrology, the Sun rules the body and Pluto indicates extremes. Wouldn't that apply to all people born that day in New York City? The Sun is on the local MC at 11:55 A.M. Stellar bodies helping with this paran are:

Pluto		altitude of 0° 35′ at 11:55 A.M.
Alpha Canis Majoris	Sirius	altitude of -1° 46′ at 11:55 A.M.
Beta Canis Majoris	Murzim	altitude of 1° 19′ at 11:55 A.M.
Eta Canis Majoris	Alkaid	altitude of 0° 07′ at 11:55 A.M.

Conjunct the chart angles at time of birth (6:30 PM EST) we find:

Omicron Ceti	Mira	setting at 6:30 P.M.
Alpha Andromedae	Alpheratz	setting at 6:26 P.M.
Alpha Virginis	Spica	rising at 6:20 P.M.
Beta Corvi	Kraz	setting at 6:18 P.M.
Alpha Velorum	Suhail al Muhlif	on the MC at 6:28 P.M.
Zeta Puppis	Naos	on the MC at 6:23 P.M.
Saturn		on the MC at 6:36 P.M.

Kareem was born almost at sunset, with the Sun-Pluto paran earlier in the day, and a Sun-Saturn paran occurring at the time of birth. The two brightest stars in Canis Major (i.e., "Top Dog") are defining the local MC at his birth location for the day. The brightest star in the heavens, Sirius, illuminates his

MC. These planetary and stellar configurations look just like what one of the greatest basketball players of his era would seek, if he were deliberately choosing his time and place of birth before the event.

Indeed, everyone born that day in New York City would have the Sun-Pluto paran, but only at Kareem's birthtime would it be personalized and empowered, if you will, by the culmination of Sirius. The great astronomer/astrologer Tycho Brahe (who catalogued 777 fixed stars by line of sight!), in his analysis of King Christian IVs horoscope in 1577, noted Sirius on the Midheaven, promising grand Jupiterian benefits, luck, honor, and recognition to the fullest extent.

In Conclusion

I reach this point with some sadness because I have only covered a very tiny portion of the overall material I had wished to cover on this enormous and very important subject. My regret is that I can not cover more people or event examples due to the lack of space. While two examples may give you some idea of the power which lies behind the fixed stars, they do not do justice to this subject.

I suggest that there are about 500 fixed stars with which astrologers should work. This number comes from adding all stars visible to the naked eye (that is, all stars brighter than magnitude 3.8, which is about all one can see in the night sky with house and street lights nearby, cars passing by, etc.), all stars to about magnitude 8.0 (much fainter than one can see with the unaided eye) but which lie in the zodiac and can be occulted by the planets, and about thirty or forty globular clusters, nebulae, assumed black holes, etc. This latter group includes those stellar types also mentioned in astrological books on the fixed stars. Adding the bodies in these three categories together gives about 500 bodies—the so called "fixed stars." Actually, this list of 500 stellar bodies isn't too far off the number that the hypothetical astrologer Phillipi would have used for his work in Jerusalem in 12 A.D., or the Druid-Priests at Stonehenge, etc.

The fixed star "Polaris," our "North Star," lies along the meridian of every person's horoscope born in either hemisphere for the last one thousand years. Thus Polaris *is in daily paran with all of the planets and everyone's MC (or IC)*. The implication of this observation is that Polaris exerts tremendous influence on each of us, in MC and IC ways. I can only guess, at this time, at the importance of this statement, and the impact of Polaris on humanity for a thousand years and more. This is startling.

There are some problems with the general astrological references on fixed stars listed in the appendix to this chapter. Some of their stellar positions are wrong. Not by much, but enough to be annoying when you compare what the astrologers give and what the astronomers give. Some of the astrologers' star names are wrong. The same errors have been copied from astrological author to astrological author. An emphasis is placed in all of the modern astrological works on the use of the ecliptic position for the fixed stars, and *not their line of sight positions*.

Here is an example of the name problem: according to astronomical sources, "Propus" should be listed as Eta Gemini. J. Rigor, V. Robson, D. Rosenberg, and my unknown source, all astrologers, call Eta Gemini "Tejat." Allen, Robinson, and Hamilton, all astronomical sources, call Eta Gemini "Propus." The astrologers list Iota Gemini as "Propus," whereas the astronomers list it as unnamed. How confusing! The astrologers list Mu Gemini as either "Nuhaiti" or "Dirah," while the astronomers list it as "Tejat." Before astrology can gain acceptance as a viable profession, astrologers must agree on the definition for their basic terms, especially when these basic tools are borrowed from other sciences.

Now, at this closing, it is time for my plea: astrology needs *you* to start using and studying the fixed stars, constellations, Moon Mansions, etc. These are a vital part of our astrological heritage. These are important techniques in our work. The Earth goes around the Sun in 365 days. The Moon goes around the Earth in twenty-nine-plus days. If we take the Moon cycle length and apply it to the 360 degree circle which represents the Sun's cycle, we get the divisions of the Moon's Mansions. If we note the constellations rising and setting at birth, and apply good mythology to that symbolism, we stand to enrich astrology. If you quickly want to improve your astrological acumen, then study and use the astrological lore of our heritage. That is my plea. Let's check the stellar messages that have come down the line to us from times past. Let's revive our use of them.

Appendix

PTOLEMY

THE ALMAGEST, BOOK VIII
"Great Books of the Western World"
Encyclopedia Brittanica, Inc., Vol. 16, p. 263
(A condensation of Ptolemy's original material is presented,
emphasis added)

Of the constellational fixed star configurations there are those
which are considered with respect only to:

- the planets and sun and moon or parts of the ecliptic
- the earth
- the earth, and at the same time to the planets, sun and
  moon or parts of the ecliptic

Those configurations of the fixed stars which are with
respect only to the planets and parts of the ecliptic, are gotten in
general whenever the fixed stars and the planets are on one and
the same great circle drawn through the ecliptic's poles, or on a
different one *but forming triangular or tetragonal or hexagonal distances*—that is, forming an angle which is either right or greater or
less than the third of a right angle. And they are gotten in particular in the case of those fixed stars over which some one of the
planets can pass (and these are those arranged in the band of the
zodiac containing the latitudinal passages of the planets): with
respect to the five planets, at their apparent appulses or occulta-
tions, and with respect to the sun and moon, at the heliacal or
lunar settings, conjunctions, and heliacal or lunar risings. We call
heliacal or lunar setting any star begins to disappear in the rays of
the luminaries; conjunction whenever the star is in a straight line
with the center; and heliacal or lunar rising whenever it begins to
appear from the rays.

There are four configurations of the fixed stars with respect
to the earth alone:

- rising   (Conjunct the Ascendant)
- upper culmination   (Conjunct the MC)
- setting   (Conjunct the Descendant)
- lower culmination   (Conjunct the IC)

The configurations of the fixed stars with respect to the earth or planets or parts of the ecliptic together are gotten in general from the simultaneous risings, culminations or settings either with one of the planets or with some part of the ecliptic, and are considered with respect to the sun in nine ways.

1. **Early morning east wind** is when the star at rising is with the sun. There is a kind called *invisible morning after-rising* when the star, beginning its heliacal setting, rises immediately after the sun; a kind called *true morning co-rising* when the star rises together with and at the same time as the sun on the horizon; and a kind called *visible morning fore-rising* when the star, beginning its heliacal rising, rises before the sun.

2. **Early morning culmination** is when the star, with the sun rising at the horizon, is culminating either above or below the earth. And again of this there is a kind called *invisible morning after-culmination* when the star culminates immediately after sunrise. There is also a *true morning co-culmination* when the star culminates as the sun rises, and a morning fore-culmination when the sun rises immediately after the star's culmination.

3. **Early morning west wind** is when the star is on the western horizon while the sun is on the eastern. There is a kind called *invisible morning after-setting* when the star sets immediately after the sun rises; a kind called *true morning co-setting* when the star sets at the same time the sun rises; and there is a kind called *visible morning fore-setting* when the sun rises immediately after the star sets.

4. **Noontide east wind** is when the star is on the eastern horizon while the sun is on the meridian. *Invisible day time* is when the star rises as the sun culminates above the earth, and *visible night time* when the star rises as the sun culminates below the earth.

5. **Noontide culmination** is when the sun and star are on the meridian together. There are two invisible day time kinds when, with the sun culminating above the earth, the star either culminates with it above the earth or culminates diametrically opposite below the earth. There are two night time kinds with the sun cul-

minating below the earth. Of these there is the *invisible* when the star culminates with the sun below the earth, and the *visible* when the star culminates diametrically opposite above the earth.

6. **Noontide west wind** is when the star is on the western horizon while the sun is on the meridian. And again of this there is the invisible daytime kind when the star sets as the sun culminates above the earth, and there is the visible night-time kind when the star sets as the sun culminates below the earth.

7. **Late east wind** is when the star is on the eastern horizon while the sun is on the western. There is the kind called *visible evening after-rising* when the star rises immediately after sunset; there is the kind called *true evening co-rising* when the star rises exactly as the sun sets; and there is the kind called *invisible evening fore-rising* when the sun sets immediately after the star rises.

8. **Late culmination** is when, with the sun on the western horizon, the star is on the meridian either above or below the earth. There is the kind called *visible evening after-culmination* when the star culminates immediately after sunset; there is the kind called *true evening co-culmination* when the star culminates exactly as the sun sets; and there is the kind called *invisible evening fore-culmination* when the sun sets immediately after the star culminates.

9. **Late west wind** is when the star is on the western horizon together with the sun. There is the kind called *visible evening fore-setting* when the star, beginning its heliacal setting, sets immediately after the sun; there is the kind called *true evening co-setting* when the star sets exactly with the sun; and there is the kind called *invisible evening fore-setting* when the star, beginning its heliacal rising, sets before the sun.

COPERNICUS

ON THE REVOLUTIONS OF THE HEAVENLY SPHERES, Book 2
(op. cit., p. 584, emphasis added, starting at his Chapter 13)

13. ON THE RISING AND SETTING OF THE STARS

The rising and setting of the stars also seems to depend upon the daily revolution, not only the simple risings and settings of which we have just spoken, but also those which occur in the morning or evening; because although their occurrence is affected by the course of the annual revolution, it will be better to speak of them here.

The ancient mathematicians distinguish the true risings and settings (of the fixed stars) *from the apparent.* The morning rising of the star is true when the star rises at the same time as the sun; and the morning setting is true, when the star sets at sunrise; for morning is said to occur at the midpoint of this time. But the evening rising is true when the star rises at sunset; and the evening setting is true when the star sets at the same time as the sun; for evening is said to occur at the midpoint of this time, namely the time between the time which is beginning and the time which ceases with night.

But the morning rising of a star is apparent when it rises first in the twilight before sunrise and begins to be apparent; and the morning setting is apparent when the star is seen to set very early before the sun rises. The evening rising is apparent when the star is seen to rise first in the evening; and the evening setting is apparent, when the star ceases to be apparent some time after sunset, and the star is occulted by the approach of the sun, until they come forth in their previous order at the morning rising.

This is true of the fixed stars and of the planets Saturn, Jupiter, and Mars. But Venus and Mercury rise and set in a different fashion. For they are not occulted by the approach of the sun, as the higher planets are; and they are not uncovered again by its departure. . . .

Now it can be understood how (the risings and settings] may be discerned, and together with what degree of the ecliptic the star rises or sets and at what position, or degree opposite—if the sun has become apparent by that time—the star has its true morning or evening rising or setting. The apparent risings and settings differ from the true according to the clarity and magnitude of the star, so that the stars which give a more powerful light are less dimmed by the rays of the sun than those which are less luminous. . . . *Therefore when we have teamed with what degree of the ecliptic **the star rises or sets** and what the angle of section of the ecliptic with the horizon* at that point is . . . we shall pronounce that the first emergence or occultation of the star has taken place . . .

14. ON INVESTIGATING THE POSITIONS OF THE STARS AND THE CATALOGUE OF THE FIXED STARS

After the daily revolution of the terrestrial globe and its consequences have been expounded by us, the demonstrations relating to the annual circuit ought to follow now. *But since some of the ancient mathematicians thought the phenomena of the fixed stars **ought to come first** as being the first beginnings of this art,* accordingly we decided to act in accordance with this opinion, as among our principles and hypotheses we had assumed that the sphere of the fixed stars, to which the wanderings of all the planets are equally referred, is wholly immobile. . . . *We are even admonished by the wasted attempt of those who thought that the magnitude of the solar year could be defined simply by the equinoxes or solstices **without the fixed stars**.* . . . The knowledge of (the positions of the Sun and the Moon) will afford us some facilities for investigating the other stars, and thus we shall be able to set forth before your eyes the sphere of the fixed stars and an image of it embroidered with constellations.

. . . (a long discussion follows of how to use an astrolabe instrument to measure such stellar angles) . . .

(Find) the position of the moon as seen in longitude. For without the moon there is no way of discovering the positions of the stars, as the moon alone among all is a partaker of both day and night. Then after nightfall, when the star whose position we are seeking is visible, we shall adjust the outer circle (of the astrolabe) to the position of the moon; and thus, as we did in the case of the sun, we shall bring the position of the astrolabe into relation with the moon. Then also we shall turn the inner circle towards the star, until the star seems to be in contact with the plane surfaces of the circle and is viewed through the eyepieces which are on the little circle contained [by the inner circle]. For in this way we shall have discovered the longitude and latitude of the star.

When this is being done, the degree of the ecliptic which is in the middle of the heavens will be before the eyes; and accordingly it will be obvious at what hour the thing itself was done.

For example, in the 2nd year of the Emperor Antoninus Pius, on the 9th day of Pharmuthi, the 8th month by the Egyptian calendar, Ptolemy, who was then at Alexandria and wished to observe at the time of sunset the position of the star which is in the breast of Leo and is called Basiliscus or Regulus, adjusted his astrolabe to the setting sun at 5 equatorial hours after midday. At this time the sun was at 3-1/24° of Pisces, and by moving the inner circle he found that the moon was 92-1/8° east of the sun: hence it was seen that the position of the moon was then at 5-1/16° of Gemini. After half an hour—which made six hours since noon—when the star had already begun to be apparent and 4° of Gemini was in the middle of the heavens, . . . The addition of 57-1/10° to this locates the position of the star at 2° 30' of Leo at a distance of about 32-1/2° from the summer solstice of the sun and with a northern latitude of 1/6°. This was the position of Basiliscus; and consequently the way was laid open to the other fixed stars. This observation of Ptolemy's was made in the year of Our Lord 139 by the Roman calendar, on the 24th day of February, in the 1st year of the 229th Olympiad.

That most outstanding of mathematicians took note of what position at that time each of the stars had in relation to the spring equinox, and catalogued the constellations of the celestial animals. *Thus he helps us not a little in this our enterprise and relieves us of some difficult enough labour, so that we, who think that the positions of the stars should not be referred to the equinoxes which change with time but that the equinoxes should be referred to the sphere of the fixed stars, can easily draw up a description of the stars from any other unchanging starting-point.* We decided to begin this description with the Ram as being the first sign, and with its first star, which is in its head—so that in this way a configuration which is absolute and always the same will be possessed by those stars which shine together as if fixed and clinging perpetually and at the same time to the throne which they have seized. But by the marvelous care and industry of the ancients the stars were distributed into forty-eight constellations with the exception of those which the circle of the always hidden stars removed from the fourth climate, which passes approximately through Rhodes; and in this way the unconstellated stars remained unknown to them. *According to the opinion of Theo the Younger in the* Aratean Treatise *the stars were not arranged in the form of images for any other reason except that their great multitude might be divided into parts and that they might be designated separately by certain names in accordance with an ancient enough custom,* since even in Hesiod and Homer we read the names of the Pleiades, Hyas, Arcturus, and Orion. Accordingly in the description of the stars according to longitude we shall not employ the "twelve divisions," or dodekatemoria, which are measured from the equinoxes or solstices, but the simple and conventional number of degrees. We shall follow Ptolemy as to the rest with the exception of a few cases, where we have either found some corruption or a different state of affairs. We shall however teach you in the following book how to find out what their distances are from those cardinal points [i.e., the equinoxes].

Suggested Supplementary Reading
(listed in my order of importance)

Allen, Richard Hinckley. *Star Names, Their Lore and Meaning.* New York: Dover Publications, 1963, originally published in 1899. Paperback, 563 pages. ISBN 0-486-21079-0. The original and still *the* reference book on this overall subject. Allen doesn't interpret the meanings of the bodies as an astrologer, but he does give exhaustive information on the meanings of the constellations, what the star names mean, star names from alternate cultures (Indian, Greek, Chinese, Persian, African, etc.). If you are really interested in this overall subject then you shouldn't proceed without studying this book.

Ebertin, R. and Hoffmann. *Fixed Stars and their Interpretation.* Tempe, AZ: American Federation of Astrologers, 1971, paperback, 98 pages. No ISBN. Much original work and research seems to be included here, although many of the people references are obscure for an American audience. I found some errors in the names and positions of the stars used. Therefore normal caution is advised when using this book.

Motz, Lloyd and Carol Nathanson. *The Constellations.* New York: Doubleday, 1988, hardback, 411 pages, ISBN 0-385-17600-7. Not quite as complete, uses more of a breezy approach to tales of the sky, and thus suffers in comparison with the above references.

Ridpath, Ian. *Star Tales.* New York: Universe Books, 1988, hardback, 163 pages. ISBN 0-7188-2695-7. Recommended. An excellent overall view of what the title promises, tales about stars, the constellations, star lore from around the world, etc.

Rigor, Joseph E. *The Power of the Fixed Stars*. Chicago, IL: A & S Publishers, 1979, paperback, 471 pages. Years ago when I met the author I asked him if this work was really new and original, and he assured me it was. Nevertheless some sections share identical sentence wording with other books, including the same mistakes in star names, positions, etc.

Robson, Vivian. *The Fixed Stars and Constellations in Astrology*. York Beach, ME: Samuel Weiser, Inc., first published 1923, hardback, 264 pages, ISBN 87728-033-9. A classic, still one of the better books available on this subject. This is the basic book from which most all of the other authors copy.

Sesti, Giuseppe Maria. *The Glorious Constellations*. New York: Harry N. Abrams, Inc., 1991, 493 pages, hardback, ISBN 0-8109-3355-1. Highly recommended, especially the opening ten chapters which have one of the better overall discussions of how astronomy and astrology have evolved over the millennia.

Staal, Julius D. W. *The New Patterns in the Sky*. Blacksburg, VA: The McDonald and Woodward Publishing Company, 1988, paperback, 300 pages. ISBN 0-939923-04-1. A very good update of a very popular book originally written in 1961. Recommended.

Tucker, W. J. *Your Horoscope and the Fixed Stars*. Wellingborough, Northamptonshire, England: Aquarian Press, paperback, 283 pages, ISBN 0-85030-200-5. Not as useful or complete as the others, but worth investigating.

Laurence Ely

Laurence Ely began studying chemistry on his own, later entering Princeton University with advanced standing in chemistry and graduating cum laude in physical chemistry with a minor in art history. He subsequently found in "astrologia" a blend of scientific and artistic interests. As a spiritual scientist, he derives research data from history. His work on true progressions resulted in his writing for *Matrix Magazine* in July 1982.

Laurence's wife directs a college library. They have two sons and live in western Massachusetts, where he runs a rectification service for astrologers themselves, for their clients, and for students of astrology. He is currently writing a book on the location of Sidereal Aries, whose location he regards as the primary theoretical problem in astrologia which needs to be solved.

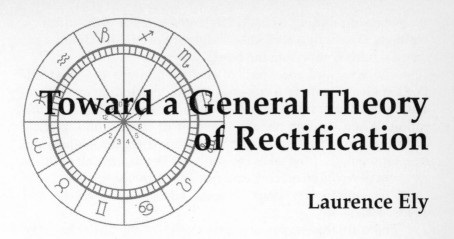

Toward a General Theory of Rectification

Laurence Ely

P lease, don't be afraid of the title of this chapter. Rectification is a subject that is vital to a sound grasp of astrology, the determination of the true chart starting with an approximate chart. It has not received attention in any way commensurate with its importance. It is not a specialized subject to be regarded as the province of only a few, nor is it an advanced subject to be postponed until later in one's astrological training. Rather, *it is fundamental.* It should be learned by all who would call themselves astrologers; it should be studied early in one's training, at the same time one learns progressions, for example. Certain historical forces in astrology have perpetuated erroneous attitudes about rectification—especially that it is difficult, if not impossible—and it is high time that these attitudes are dispelled.

A Path to a Revitalized Astrologia

There are four facets to this discussion of rectification: the "why" of rectification (its importance and integral place in a modern astrological approach), the spirit of rectification, the scope of rectification, and the "how" of rectification. The why of rectification is the basic philosophical motivator and needs to be understood at the start. The spirit, attitude, or frame of mind of one who does the rectifying undergirds and facilitates the use of rectification methods. The scope and knowledge of specific techniques are integral parts comprising the how.

The why and the spirit of rectification are the most important ideas I want to focus on, since understanding and appreciating them are critical to being able actually to perform rectification. When you appreciate the spirit of rectification, placing astrology strongly alongside other scientific disciplines in western development, the how takes care of itself. Permeating all of this is *the scope of rectification*, consisting of five dimensions: *the type of chart, time-uncertainty, chart elements, relationship extension,* and *accuracy level.*

There are three types of charts to rectify: the birth chart, the conception chart, and the death chart. These may be human or corporate (event-oriented or mundane). The conception chart must refer to a different dimension or level of life than the birth chart. No one has yet done any correct and extensive work in this area, to my knowledge. Ptolemy, in the beginning of book III of the *Tetrabiblos*, addressed the conception chart in relation to the birth chart, but his treatment struck me as trivial and confused. He alludes to a similarity of chart configuration between the moment of conception and birth, and most likely this is the tradition coming from Nechepso and Petosiris apparently in Egypt from somewhere between the 7th and 2nd centuries B.C.[1] The idea was expressed by another Ptolemy in classical times, pseudo-Ptolemy, in his *Centiloquy 52.*[2]

The idea of such a relationship between the two charts has come down to us in a tradition, which in our era has been referred to as *The Truitine of Hermes.* It purports to find the conception date and approximate time starting from the birth chart by an interchange between the Moon and Ascendant using these rules: 1) The position of the conception Moon must be that of the birth Ascendant or Descendant, and 2) The position of the conception Ascendant or Descendant must be that of the birth

---

1 Cf. *Sternglaube und Sterndeutung,* Boll-Bezold-Gundel, B. G. Turner, Leipzig, 1926, p. 154; *L' Astrologie Grecque,* Bouche'-Leclercq, pp. 376, 379; *A History of Western Astrology,* Jim Tester, The Boydell Press, PO Box 9, Woodbridge, Suffolk IP12 3DF, England, 1987, pp. 20, 21, 23, 78–79.
2 Cf. *Astrological Pioneers of America,* James H. Holden and Robert A. Hughes, AFA, 1988, p. 172.

Moon. (This need not be mathematically exact; the usual orbs are allowed.)

British astrologer E. H. Bailey (1876-1959), working in conjunction with Sepharial, popularized this ancient theory, calling it *The Prenatal Epoch,* in his book by the same name. But after ardently propounding it, he subsequently disavowed its efficacy.[3] The aspect of Bailey's and Sepharial's work that strikes me as odd is that, rather than taking an interest in interpreting and studying the conception chart derived from the birth chart using this theory, they instead employed the theory as a method of rectification, the idea being that, once the prenatal epoch was found, *the location of the prenatal epoch Moon fixed the position of the birth Ascendant or Descendant.*

My research with the Prenatal Epoch Theory for finding the conception chart has shown the theory to be bogus. I have also found that the use of the prenatal epoch for rectifying one's birth chart to be bogus. Geoffrey Dean quoted Zipporah Dobyns as having stated that it has "proved unreliable in my experience."[4] I do not know whether Dobyns found both components of the theory as bogus as I did, or just one. Martin Freeman finds an objection to use of the prenatal epoch in rectification of the natal chart by observing that "identical twins, presumably, have the same pre-natal epoch, but are nevertheless born at different times," which is an interesting observation indeed.[5]

However, the *conception* chart most assuredly is valid (not devined by prenatal epoch), but its level of meaning is something not yet clear to me. I think there is spiritual wisdom in the study of the conception chart, and in this connection it is my suspicion that the traditions that have come down to us regarding this idea are basterdized by oral embellishment since occult matters such as these were rarely written about. The conception chart must be found by general rectification, as will be explained next in the discussion on time uncertainty.

The death chart is the birth chart for the entity's existence *in the spiritual world.* It remains to be found out whether its chart

---

3 Holden and Hughes, Op. Cit., p. 172–173.
4 *Recent Advances in Natal Astrology*, Geoffrey Dean, Astrological Association, England, 1977, p. 475 citing: *Progressions, Directions and Rectification,* Zipporah Dobyns, TIA, Los Angeles, 1975, p. 17.
5 *Forecasting by Astrology*, Martin Freeman, The Aquarian Press, Wellingborough, Northamptonshire, England, 1982, p. 117.

movements have any connection with entities still living: for example, if this chart's Midheaven is transited, would a living person be thinking about the person now in the spiritual world? One might debate whether such a thing as a conception chart or death chart exists for a corporate being. One last aspect of scope relating to chart type is that one could also include the heliocentric chart along with the geocentric chart for each of these three types. If the geocentric chart is rectified, *so is the heliocentric*, of course. If one rectified the heliocentric chart, one would have the rectified geocentric chart, provided one knew the place on the earth where the chart came into being.

As our discussion builds, we must remember two important points about rectification: first, there is only one way to rectify, namely, fitting the chart to the entity in terms of both attributes and events. By "attributes," I mean the qualities of the person both physically and in soul qualities such as gesture and psychological and spiritual qualities. For a human entity, physical appearance and handwriting would be appropriate attributes to consider in connection with rectifying the birth chart, but are probably *not* appropriate in reference to the conception chart and certainly not to the death chart. By "events," I mean both inner and outer events. Inner events are those not necessarily discernible to other people, such as a realization or a thought.[6] Outer events are events like marriage or a public recognition, in which other people or entities are involved.

The second point is that rectification is possible because each point in time does have a unique chart, which gives both a unique set of attributes (interpretation) and a unique pattern of events in terms of quality of event and its date of life occurrence. There is only *one* birth chart for an entity, only *one* conception chart, and only *one* physical death chart. These are the major hallmarks in life, but in truth, charts are being created continuously. There is a chart for the moment when I finished the last letter in the previous sentence . . . and this sentence. In the practical sense, obviously, one can not keep up with time in trying to cast charts for every moment. Key ones must tell the story.

The second of the five dimensions of the scope of rectification I enumerated was *time-uncertainty*. This refers to the level of

---

6 I thank Al H. Morrison for bringing this important distinction to my attention.

accuracy of the supplied time for the coming into being of a chart. One may conceive time-accuracy as being the minute, the hour, the day, the month(s), or the year(s). These could be described in terms of their respective sources: birth certificate or some other recorded time (BC), the memory of the family (MEM), knowledge of just the date (DAY), knowledge of a range of months (MONTHS), and knowledge of a range of years (YEARS). We astrologers know full well the huge problems posed by various ambiguities or deficiencies in birth times or dates. Here are some typical example-situations that relate to the above-named categories: having angles that do not work with transits or progressions in a correctly calculated chart based on a recorded birth time, crude birth times from family members' memory, "she was born some time in the afternoon," ambiguity of the time zone in the case of a recorded birth, ambiguity of whether standard time was used or daylight time, lack of a birth time—no recorded time and no family memory, and ambiguity of whether an historical personality or event has already been converted to Gregorian (New Style) from Julian (Old Style) or not, and other calender problems.

The common understanding of rectification of birth charts is that it applies to only the MEM and DAY types of time-uncertainty. However, as will be explained later, the BC type must *always* be rectified as well. The MONTHS and YEARS type are uncommon to come across and are, of course, more difficult. (A human conception chart is a MONTHS type, since there is no known date provided.) In the MONTHS type of uncertainty, one determines the day by inspecting sign ingresses of progressed planets in connection with the entity's life events. This then reduces to the hour type. A typical example of the MONTHS type is the case of birth charts of the corporate type, in which the historical information only specifies the month, not the day when certain nations, say, came into being. For example, the first university was formed in November 1158, and England was declared independent from the Roman Empire in the autumn of 410 AD. In the YEARS type, one necessarily focuses one's attention on what signs Jupiter, Saturn, and Uranus, for example, are in, and works on in from there. This problem is then reducible to a MONTHS type of concern.

As to chart elements, the Midheaven and the Ascendant are the elements that must *always* be found (rectified). This includes, of course, the Equatorial Ascendant (the Ascendant if the chart had come into being at the Earth's Equator—EA) and the Vertex (VX), the point on the ecliptic that is exactly West. Please note that other chart data may need to be found (rectified): it is possible for someone to have a time and date of (birth, conception, or death) but not the location, thus the latitude and longitude must be found. Once the time of day is rectified by reference to planet-planet interactions whether by transit, progression, or transit in a (birth, conception, or death) chart, then the MC may be rectified. This will determine the longitude. Then when the AS is rectified, this will determine the latitude.

However, there are other chart elements (planets, nodes, perihelia longitudes, stars, etc.) which may need to be rectified in the case of historical charts sufficiently far back in time. For example, in the case of the Moon and the outer planets, astronomy has relatively less knowledge of their orbits as you start going back before the eighteenth century, and the accuracy degenerates the more you go back in time. The Moon might be off by 30' to 60' in the fourth century B.C. Uranus might be off some 10', Neptune some 60', and Pluto some 5 degrees back then. Other astronomical quantities bearing on the chart that may be rectified are the obliquity of the ecliptic, delta-T, and the precessional rate. We must remember that to have a rectified chart means that *all* of the chart's elements are rectified. When dealing with charts from the eighteenth century on, only the angles need to be rectified, and when they *are* rectified, the chart itself is rectified.

When we view rectification in its broader positional scope in terms of rectifying *all* the chart elements and not just the MC to get the time, we enter into the field of astronomical astrology. Here, we can actually do what astronomy cannot do by itself: we can obtain evidence from the past about astronomical positions without any recorded positional observations. We can do this provided we have historical evidence (written history), provided we know our astrology, and provided we can rectify. But more importantly, we can reunite the two fields of astrology and astronomy, and heal the artificial division we have lived under since the early centuries B.C., which is a point I will come back to.

The fourth dimension of the scope of rectification is "relationship extension." This is the point of view that, given a particular type of chart (let us say a birth chart), one not only rectifies by consideration of the birth chart itself (attributes and events) but also by consideration of its internal and external relationships. By internal relationships I refer to two disparate classes of relationship: harmonics and House values. In the case of harmonics, this birth chart is to be regarded as the first harmonic. Residing inside this birth chart are any number of harmonic charts of two kinds: integer and element-pair. By virtue of the particular harmonic number in the case of the integer harmonic, and by virtue of the particular element-pair (elements are angles, planets, nodes, cusps, stars, etc.) in the case of the element-pair harmonic, the harmonic chart will refer to a certain level of experience which can be traced in rectification by attributes and events. An element-pair's harmonic number is created by subtracting the smaller longitude from the larger longitude and dividing this into 360. This decimal number when multiplied by all the first harmonic (original chart) elements produces a harmonic chart in which the original pair is now brought to conjunction. I will provide the details later.

In the case of House values, the idea is that every non-cusp element in the chart may be given a 0 to 30 degree value by House. If a planet is exactly on the AS its House value is 0 AR 00. If on the 2nd House cusp its value is 0 TA 00. If half way between the 2nd House cusp and the 3rd House cusp, its house value is 15 TA 00. Of course, in getting the house value chart, the astronomical method wherein the house cusps were created must be used. For each valid house system, a natal chart possesses a set of house values for the chart elements. These house values may be traced in rectification by attributes and events.

The usual situation in rectification, and indeed the level or scope that is usually sufficient to complete the rectification, is that one works with just the birth chart. This is the first harmonic chart when seen more generally. At this level, one works with attributes to get the approximate time (MC and AS) and with transits and progressions, for example, to study the more refined position of the angles.

Relationship extension also applies to external relationships. This is the realm of synastry and composite charts (of all types: space, time, and harmonic) between the chart being rectified and one or more other charts. When significant relationships are known involving other entities and when events have happened between the entity whose chart is being rectified and other entities, then these may be traced in external relationship extension in both attributes and events.

The fifth and final dimension to the scope of rectification is to define to what level of accuracy we would like to rectify the MC and AS (or other chart elements). What should be our goal or ideal here? Over time, astrologers have disagreed about what level can actually be achieved, with some astrologers only striving to determine the MC to the nearest degree (even in recent times) while most strive to attain 5′–10′ arc. A school of thought coming from Uranian or Cosmobiology speaks of "zero orb" astrology, which in practice has meant more like 2′ arc. Charles Emerson and Charles Jayne spoke of this level of accuracy. These astrologers would have liked to have been more accurate, but errors in calculating Secondary Progressions and Solar Arc Directions based on them have not allowed them and others to break this barrier. Later in this discussion, in the "how" part, I address how this barrier is broken. It is my point of view that 1′ (plus or minus 30 seconds of arc) is possible and should be the goal, i.e., no greater error than 1′ should be tolerated. With the leveraging effect afforded by the use of harmonic charts, this level is easily transcended, and, in fact, it is quite possible to reach the 1″ level! Let us say that one is in error by 1′ in the MC of the first harmonic (the natal chart), then one will be off by 10′ in the 10th harmonic chart, for example. If the 10th harmonic chart's MC were to be rectified to 1′, then the natal chart's MC would be known to 0.1′ or 6″ arc.

The reason that 1′ is chosen as a minimum accuracy to strive for is that 1′ is the common accuracy to which the planets are tabulated, including the Sun and the Moon. Of course, those who do Solar Returns know that we must use the full astronomical accuracy of 1″ for the Sun. In any event, given that the MC and AS are equally as important as the Sun and the Moon, if not more so, since 1′ is used for the Sun and the Moon customarily, at least the same accuracy should be used for the MC and AS.

A direct consequence of this goal of 1′ accuracy for the MC is that rectification is required even for a hospital birth (BC time). Because hospital births are only expressed to the nearest minute of accuracy on the BC (2:14 A.M., say), this implies (assuming for the moment that this expressed time were the true time of birth rounded to the nearest minute) that the time of birth was between

2:13:30 and 2:14:30. Thus one has a potential error of 30 seconds in the time, which translates to plus or minus 8' error in the MC since every some 240 seconds of time the MC moves 60' arc.

But it is not reasonable to think that the BC recorded time actually records the true time of birth within 30 seconds. While being aware of our scientific western culture's penchant for measurement and accuracy, a reasonable person nonetheless appreciates the fact that when it comes to births in hospitals, doctors do not place any scientific value in the exact recording of birth times. It is a bureaucratic, legal value in their eyes, not a scientific value. Unlike the astrologer, the doctor obviously does not appreciate the value in accurately and scientifically recording the birth of a baby. The doctor records to the nearest minute only because clocks are graduated to the nearest minute. The doctor is not particularly concerned about the accuracy of the clock in the strict sense of whether it is set to some accurate standard clock. And the doctor does not profess even to know what actual physical event constitutes birth. What physical event (if any) constitutes birth is a spiritual-scientific fact that has not yet been determined. Astrologers in collaboration with doctors might be able to shed light on this some day. For these reasons, a reasonable person would not expect recorded birth times to be accurate to the nearest minute even though birth times are recorded to the nearest minute.

To drive home the point about the unrealistic accuracy afforded by a recorded birth expressed to the nearest minute, let me list some more issues. First off, the hospital clock may not be accurate. In recording at the hospital, it is possible for one to confuse AM and PM. It is also possible to misread the clock, writing down say 3:36 when it was 3:41 (incorrectly reading the minute hand). It is possible to transpose numerals and write 3:14 when 3:41 was intended, for example.

Besides recording errors at the hospital, there are possible transcribing errors in making the BC from the hospital record. It is possible to confuse AM and PM, to misread the hospital record, or to transpose numerals.

Besides these, there are the possible misinterpretations of the BC time by the astrologer by using the wrong time zone, daylight vs. standard time, or both. This misinterpretation problem is quite common in several American states where time zones run or used to run through the state, and where individual cities and towns were given local authority to choose which zone to be in or whether and when to go on and off daylight time.

The experience of rectifiers demonstrates that one may expect perhaps plus or minus 16 minutes of error in a BC time (plus or minus 4 degrees on the MC). Something like this amount is what you would expect in 95 cases out of 100, say. It is more likely that the BC time is within 4 minutes of exactness than it is within 8 minutes of exactness, more likely that it is within 8 minutes than 12 minutes, etc. But for the particular BC recorded time one has on one's desk at a given moment, one has no idea how accurate it is until one rectifies: you do not know if you have an instance of the 0-4 minutes error on your hands, an instance of 4-8 minutes error, etc.

To summarize the discussion of BC births, being prepared to expect a some 4-degree error in the initial MC based on the BC time is a reasonable approach to take. Sixteen minutes of time roughly comports with how long the delivery and clean up period is in the hospital. It is reasonable to assume that some doctors may record the clock time after cleaning up, while others may try to estimate how much time they thought had elapsed since birth occurred and correct the clock time backwards accordingly. I want to make it clear that it is my point of view that *every* chart needs to be and should be rectified no matter what type of chart (birth, conception, death) or what time uncertainty (BC, MEM, DAY, MONTHS, YEARS).

The Why of Rectification

Astrology has a lot to offer the confused and spiritually hungry world in which we currently live. Astrology has been held in contempt by the ruling scientific, materialistic world view largely because its view does not recognize any forces through which astrological influences could manifest under scientific methodological circumstances. Astrology is also derided because of its lack of refinement. This consists of the lack of general education on the part of its practitioners and the concomitant irrationality inherent in its mode of practice. This irrationality lies in the fact that astrologers must have a birth time, but do not check if the birth time is right before making predictions which are dependent on knowing the birth time. From an outsider's point of view, this is all quite independent of whether astrology works or not: from the outsider's point of view, astrologers are not using the ideas that they themselves say do work!

Astrology can not change science but it can change itself: it can become more rational, more enfused with a knowledge of the world, more conscious. Doing so will render science more open to seeing its evidence. And engaging in rectification is one big way in which astrology can become more rational. If astrology is to become creative and if it is to carry on research, rectification is an indispensable avenue or tool for such research. With a rectified chart, many ideas in astrology may be amply tested in a direct and intuitive way, not in an indirect and flawed way as has been done in the past using statistics. Astrology was not born of statistics and it will not grow with statistics. Statistics is a hands-off, non-spiritual practice. *Astrology is a hands-on, spiritual practice.*

The spirit of rectification is to be found in the word "astrologia." You may well be asking what constitutes astrologia and how it differs from astrology, and what the connection is between rectification and the revitalizing of astrologia. Understanding all this requires some understanding of the history of astrology, which I will bring to our attention soon, but for the moment, think of astrologia as the combination of astronomy and astrology. The practitioner of astrologia, the astrologian, understands the basics of astronomy such as measuring angles in spherical astronomy— what the great circles are around the earth—and has some grounding in basic mathematical reasoning. The astrologian on the astrology side is interested in developing his intuition beyond the level employed in astrology, by having an attitude of attempting to work actively with intuition and trusting that it will work. Thus astrologia stretches out more broadly than astrology in both the quantitative-mathematical side and in the qualitative-intuitive side. But above all, the astrologian understands and values that this can and should be done all within the same person rather than having these capacities exist in separate, specialist people.

I am convinced that being able to rectify requires, first and foremost, coming at rectification in the right spirit, in the spirit of astrologia. To be able to rectify requires a knowledge of actual techniques, of course, but astrologers already have the techniques—oddly they do not realize that they do, or do not or cannot utilize them. This observation leads me to know that, when it comes to rectification and certain other technical areas, astrologers have a philosophical blockage, a mentality, an institutional mindset or culture formed of historical precedents. I want to bring all of this into the open as this discussion proceeds.

I would like to approach the distinction between astrology and astrologia by examining the "logia" or "logy" part of these words. These come from the ancient Greek *Logos,* which makes reference to the nature of creation. Divine inspiration guided the creators and leaders of the Greek culture from which the concept of Logos came, and the Greeks and other so-called heathens or pagans were part and parcel of the divine plan for the continual unfolding of the one human race in relation to its one God.

We know from Genesis that "In the beginning God created the heavens and the earth." The word "heavens" refers to the spiritual world, and the word "earth" refers to the material world. The same statement about the nature of creation is expressed in Hinduism which speaks of purusa (spirit) and prakrti (matter). In Hinduism, there are recurring dissolutions (prayala) and re-creations (pratisarga) of world conditions over vast lengths of time, and on the level of the individual soul these are paralleled by recurring excarnations into the spiritual world and incarnations into the material world. Esoteric Judeo-Christian tradition has the very same conception. Other traditions speak the same. It is the truth.

The fundamental character of creation as being composed of a spiritual world (macrocosm) and a physical world (microcosm) is the very basic starting point of astrology. I think it is fair to say, however, that astrology today has lost its feeling for this. Astrology is so caught up in the trees that it has lost sight of the forest. It has become psychological rather than spiritual, and the psychological level is only the trivial, surface level. To work in the psychological is like seeing a red Ferrari automobile and summing up its essence by saying it is red and fast and makes noise. The ancient astrologers were brought up in a *complete* understanding and were instructed, say, that Mars was the physical body wherein a host of spiritual beings of a certain character had certain functions to perform in relation to other planetary beings and to man. They knew that Mars and other planetary beings were capable of being changed. For example, it is related by the highest spiritual authority I know of that Mars beings were made less hostile starting in 1604 A.D. by the Buddha individuality while in the spiritual world.[7] Because astrology has been cut off from spiritual training as a context into which to put its technical, geometrical calculations, it has lost the teleological understanding of the human being and of human society that it once had: in looking at a spiral where the center is going somewhere, it sees only the rotation of the periphery.

As to the nature of the Godhead, we have the same statements coming from the esoteric Judeo-Christian tradition, the esoteric Hindu-Buddhist tradition, and the Taoist tradition. "In the beginning was the Word, and the Word was with God, and the Word was God" said John, the initiated disciple of the Christ. In the Hindu-Buddhist tradition, the positive affirmation in the chant of the Sanskrit word, Om ("yes; I acknowledge"), speaks to the resonance from the same lofty reaches of the spiritual world. In the Taoist tradition, the Tao is the "Way" having its head at the source, from which one gets one's guidance and to which one continues to fix one's attention. And the very same conceptualization of creation as the above is referenced by the ancient Greeks with their conception of Logos, which is the main idea in their word "astrologia." The idea of Logos comes first, and the astre (star) prefix or modifier comes next in importance.

For the Greeks, Logos meant the word or form which expresses a thought, specifically a thought communicated throughout the community of beings in creation. There is implied an ordering principle and a rational structure and timeless truth that can be comprehended by the human soul because it is of like nature. There is also implied an intellectual, spiritual challenge in discerning this ordering pattern that is recognized to be partly hidden, partly recognizable in the flux of the material world. This was the motivation for consulting an oracle, who was a being versed in perceiving the Logos out of direct intuitive, clairvoyant ability.

But the Greeks, and also the later Babylonians and Chaldeans, were in the situation of being cut off from this direct intuitive, clairvoyant ability that their ancestors in previous ages possessed. The ancient Greeks had to invent the concept of the Logos, "a form which expresses a thought," because of this situa-

---

7 *From Buddha to Christ*, Lecture V "The Mission of Gautama Buddha on Mars", Rudolf Steiner, Anthroposophic Press, Hudson, NY, 1978.

tion of being cut off from clairvoyant ability. In terms of the development of human consciousness through history, they were given the heroic task of being left alone, of being abandoned, of having the realization that direct guidance by beings higher than human had been severed, so that they would develop certain human faculties referred to as the intellectual soul. At the level of the intellectual soul, one is concerned with the internal consistency of one's mental construct or system—one is captivated by it, you might say—and there is no consciousness of comparing it with the outside world to see if it works or not. This was the task of humanity in the Arian Age which lasted from circa 2200 B.C. until Christ.[8]

Peoples in previous ages were guided by beings higher than human via a spiritual leader as an intermediary, usually in the name of a priest-king. The people had to be taught to take hold of the earth, to be at home in it, and they were instructed in these matters by the priest-kings. The specific task of humanity in the age immediately preceding the Greeks was to develop the sentient soul, to develop feelings of solidarity for the group and for the social structure supportive of the civilization. (The picture of the positive aspects of the community of Catholics is an apt comparison.) The task of this age was to feel that all is well dwelling on the earth.

In past ages, the earth felt foreign to humanity since then human beings identified more with the spiritual world than with the material world. The natural tendency of the people was to live in their clairvoyant, dream-like consciousness in which they had direct experience and communication with the higher beings of the spiritual world, such as the beings of the planets or of the zodiac, as a matter of course in their daily lives. They had no need for words or abstract concepts to refer to these spiritual experiences, for they had them directly. This was the picture of affairs in

---

8   I have gotten my understanding of the evolution of consciousness as seen in epochs of history from the philosopher-scientist-artist Rudolf Steiner (1861-1925), a true, conscious clairvoyant and initiate. He is generally regarded by those who have read him thoroughly as the same individuality who previously was Aristotle of ancient Greece. Aristotle was responsible for setting up the foundations of western physical science. Steiner has set out a basis for spiritual science in parallel with this. The dates however, are mine. Cf. *The Evolution of Mankind*, Guenther Wachsmuth, Philosophic-Anthroposophic Press, Dornach, Switzerland, 1961. Wachsmuth was a scientist and biographer of Rudolf Steiner.

the Taurean Age. But for the Greeks, out of cosmic memory of this previous state of being, it was necessary for them to develop words and concepts to hold onto this earlier knowledge and experience of prior peoples.

Humanity began working at developing the basic understanding of the working of the heavens in earthly affairs during this Taurean Age circa 4400–2200 B.C. These developments had their principal center in ancient Babylonia. At this time, the whole economic state was being ordered and measured around astronomical principles reflective of the cosmos. But it remained for the Greeks to individualize and synthesize these considerations: to invent the birth chart starting in the fourth century B.C. Astrologia may be said to have had its inception (in so far as it applies to individual humans' destiny) in the eighth century B.C., at which time we see Hesiod in his *Works and Days* expounding on lucky and unlucky days, and with the later Babylonians beginning to tabulate planetary correspondences and developing the Zodiac.

To do the individualizing and synthesizing that the Greeks did required their mathematical and esthetic turn of mind to look for patterns and principles, to be theoretical and rational. They said if there are signs, we can replicate the pattern and make houses. They said if Aries is the rising of the Sun in the spring, then the horoscopus, what we now call the AS, is the point of rising of the Tropical Zodiac (created by the Sun) and by analogy this is the beginning of the 1st House. And out of the same analogy came the day for a year progressions (a sunrise each day is like the beginning of spring each year) which we know today.

So, for the Greeks, the development of astrologos (astrologia) was the working out of patterns wherein the Logos could be measured and understood. The beings of the planets and stars (astre) and the beings of the Zodiac all involved the communication of meaning: the configuration of the Macrocosm (the spiritual) would be resounded in the Microcosm (the material world).

Astrologia contained both a mathematical-quantitative-astronomical side, and a qualitative-inferential side. Due to the details of ensuing historical developments there was created a separation into two subjects of study of what was once a unified study: astrologia broke into astronomy and astrology. Astronomy was left thinking that the stars and planets had only a physical body, and they set out to measure their positions and movements and eventually their physical constitutions. Astrology was left thinking that these physical bodies had psychological and physical effects on man and earth, but astrology no longer regarded the stars and planets as being living spiritual beings and therefore had no conception of what man's relationship was to these beings. Somewhere between the beginnings of the development of astrologia in the eightth century B.C. and the increasing sense of a distinction between astronomy and astrology in the fourth to seventh centuries A.D., we can point to certain historical forces at work in the name of the Age of Pisces, a sign of duality.

The task of our Piscean Age is to broaden consciousness. This is the developing of the "consciousness soul" in Rudolf Steiner's language: the human ego is being developed to evaluate phenomena outside itself and refer to the memory of personal experiences to aid in learning. Also involved is the ability to stand apart from phenomena and sensations, and, rather than identify with them, be a spectator and evaluator of them. This approach to the world, emphasizing experience and experiment (letting phenomena of the world do the educating, which is called empiricism) has allowed the development of science as we now know it. This give and take between the world and oneself, is of course, one and the same as what astrology calls mutability, since Pisces is a mutable sign.

To the Christian understanding principally, but to philosophical schools at the time as well, a reliance on astrologia was anathema to the development of the independence of the ego that was required to master the earth physically. This was not a consciously understood attitude, rather it was the working of spirit in the Piscean Age. The influence of the heavens on man had to be forgotten for the time being so that science could be developed. (There was much to be learned from the give and take with the earth, before the give and take between the earth and the heavens could be properly addressed.) In the Aquarian Age to come, the influence of the stars can then be reintroduced and we will have astrologia again, we will have "spiritual science," to use Steiner's terminology.

The Piscean Age is a mental age. Among other things, the incarnation of Christ may be seen as a mystery for man to ponder, thus as a motivating picture to send man off into a mental, puzzle-solving frame of mind. With the separation of astrologia into astronomy and astrology, the thinking and new discoveries, the social resources went into astronomy. There has not been much new done in astrology. (My comments apply to the bulk of the age. Currently one could reasonably argue that astrology is in a renaissance, and I would agree. But this has to do with our currently being in the transition between two ages.) But as knowledge of it had to be maintained so that it could flourish again one day, astrologers of course were contributing to evolutionary developments in humanity. Astrology began a decline only to be resurrected in part in the Renaissance in the fourteenth to sixteenth centuries. It began another decline with the rise of science in the seventeenth century from which it has only slightly recovered. All the while astronomy has progressed, but all the while astrologia has been near dead.

As a transitional figure near the inception of the Piscean Age, the great Ptolemy (fl. second century A.D.) played what might be argued to be an important part in astrology's mentality remaining intellectual. Ptolemy worked as an astronomer and geographer in second century A.D. Alexandria, then in the Roman Empire. He is regarded by historians, whether accepting astrology or not, as playing an important if not crucial role in systemizing and codifying the knowledge he received from the ancients and transmitting it to the new age. Since astrology was coming under increasing fire from Christian thinkers in the first several centuries of the Christian age, astrology was in need of a repository of information from which it could get a new start at a later time. To my knowledge, it is a never-challenged commonplace to refer to Ptolemy's *Tetrabiblos* as the bible of astrology, if astrology may be said to have a bible. His *Syntaxis*, in which he laid out the astronomical calculations for the planets, held sway for an incredible one and a half millennia, until Kepler introduced knowledge of eliptical orbits in the early seventeenth century.

In his *Tetrabiblos*, Ptolemy addressed rectification (the first writer I am aware of who did so), outlining a method of rectifying recorded birth times, but, as we shall see subsequently in a working example, his method makes no sense in reality: it is based on considerations from inside looking outside, rather than looking down on both at the same time, as is done in the consciousness soul. From inside the all-encompassing intellectual world mentality, he reasons (out of reasoning totally within his system of astrology's rules of interactions) that there is a sympathetic connection between the configuration of the chart for the full or new Moon immediately preceding birth and the eventual, true birth chart. But he is blind to factors from outside, such as the appearance of the person or his life events in connection with his birth chart as confirming or denying the determined angles (birth time). He knows that rectification is important, but *he lacks the proper consciousness* to see how one would actually do it. It is in this sense that Ptolemy can be seen as partly in the intellectual soul of the preceding Arian Age and partly in the consciousness soul of our Piscean Age. Ironically, because he was such a great authority and because his rectification method *does not work*, his effort to render astrology empirical and scientific most likely had just the opposite effect: it most likely discouraged the attempt at rectification and thereby retarded astrology's development along empirical, consciousness soul lines.

Another writer that needs to be mentioned in connection with this transitional period in the development of the new consciousness, and who by contrast with Ptolemy will help to illustrate the incipient consciousness soul we see in Ptolemy, is Firmicus Maternus (fl. fourth century A.D.). His *Mathesis*[9] also served to preserve astrological traditions. But while Firmicus Maternus appreciated the importance of knowing the AS accurately (to the nearest degree) he made no explicit reference to the concept of rectification as such. By way of comparison, his work is a huge, encyclopedic cookbook containing all kinds of detailed descriptions of astrological combinations, whereas Ptolemy's work is a philosophical, scientific treatise of what astrology is, its problems, its scope, and its principles.

Maternus' regard for having the correct degree for the AS is amply demonstrated by his theory called myriogenesis,[10] in which every degree from the first to the thirtieth of every sign is given a specific description and fate when it is the rising degree. Maternus said ". . . the entire measurement of the chart must be located so that the true degree, discovered with the accustomed

---

9 *Ancient Astrology Theory and Practice* (Matheseos Libri VIII, Eight Books of the Mathesis), Julius Firmicus Maternus, trans. Jean Rhys Bram, Noyes Press, Park Ridge, NJ, 1975.

10 *Op. Cit.*, p. 281 ff.

computation, will make the forecast trustworthy. If the measurement is not correct the promised forecast will be shadowed with vicious lies." You and I can see that he could have used his theory to rectify by fitting the observations of character and life events of an adult whose chart he was reading to the appropriate description in the myriogenesis. This would have involved either keeping the degree rising as it was or changing it. In either case, *this would have been rectifying.* He may have done this, but we have no explicit statement by Maternus that he did so.

Currently in astrology, the typical astrologer has committed musical scores to memory, but he can not play music. He has inherited a vast edifice of meanings and correspondences, but he can not add to it or criticize it. He does not actively hear the logos. He tells his clients what his heritage (gleaned from the ancients) had heard from the logos. But, as I am developing as seriously as I can, I maintain and repeat that, if you want to rectify, *you must actively hear the logos yourself.* If you start listening for the logos, beings will help you hear it. Put another way: you will be inspired in your thinking.

In order to do rectification, one must be engaged empirically with the materials at one's disposal—the characteristics and biographical facts of the entity on the one hand, and the chart on the other. But beyond that, one must approach the matter with an open, interested curiosity in the frame of mind of a puzzle-solver who likes to solve puzzles. One must make active hypotheses or guesses and not fear being wrong. (You are doing a crossword puzzle using a number one pencil which you can easily erase if you are wrong.) It is this open, active attitude which one must have, must endeavor to inculcate in oneself. If you are wrong initially in your choice of angles, this will be brought to your attention when you examine other events. This provides you with more information that then leads you to a new hypothesis or guess and so on until you infer the whole pattern. When you are right, you will know it because *everything will work like clockwork.*

One must approach each chart one rectifies from a fresh perspective and look at it in its own terms. The chart will offer you its own hypotheses right away: "I wonder what happened when progressed Jupiter squared her Sun? I see that it would have been February 1 if this chart is right. Oh, she had a policy argument in her advertising agency March 15. Could her Sun be 1' arc greater?"; "I wonder if transiting Uranus two years ago will confirm this position of the Sun? I think I will look up which days those would have been"; "Eureka! These were the days she got interested in astrology. So now what about the AS? If I am right to about 1' arc on the Sun, I'll be right, let me see, to 360' on the AS, which is 6 degrees. Oh, but it is late Aries so it'll be an advancement of 11 degrees. OK, so that makes her AS 28 Aries, so now I'll check that out and the associated MC." And so it goes.

You *never* approach rectification from hard and fast rules that specify that particular configurations (aspects, midpoints) among particular planets must be involved with a particular kind of event. You only have to use your knowledge of the meanings of the elements of astrology to evaluate the mapping between configurations and the events or changes in the entity for the corresponding time.

I have sketched for you the basic change in point of view that needs to be made in one's approach to astrology as it regards rectification. I have gone ahead of myself a bit, because I needed to flesh out the conception of what rectification is when viewed from the modern consciousness of Piscean Age empiricism. We can now compare this view with the view we are given by Ptolemy.

Given that the correct time of birth is an obvious and central concern in astrology to anyone with more than an initial introduction to the subject, it should not surprise us that Ptolemy addressed rectification in a separate chapter in his *Tetrabiblos* ("four books"), the oldest complete extant book on astrology we have. Let us now hear what Ptolemy had to say about it. Of the two translations available in the American astrological distributions, I use the Robbins translation, but I refer to the Ashmand translation whenever there is uncertainty in meaning[11]:

> Difficulty often arises with regard to the first and most important fact, that is, the fraction of the hour of the birth; for in general only observation by means of horo-

---

11 *Tetrabiblos*, Claudius Ptolemaeus (c. A.D. 100-178), III.2 "Of the Degree of the Horoscopic Point," ed. and trans. F. E. Robbins, Harvard Univ. Press, Cambridge, 1940. *Tetrabiblos*, Claudius Ptolemaeus (c. A.D. 100-178), III.3 "The Degree Ascending," trans. J. M. Ashmand, Symbols and Signs, North Hollywood, CA, 1976.

scopic astrolabes[12] at the time of birth can for scientific observers give the minute of the hour, while practically all other horoscopic instruments on which the majority of the more careful practitioners rely are frequently capable of error, the solar instruments by the occasional shifting of their positions or of their gnomons,[13] and the water clocks by stoppages and irregularities in the flow of the water from different causes and by mere chance. It would therefore be necessary that an account first be given how one might, by natural and consistent reasoning, discover the degree of the zodiac which should be rising, given the degree of the known hour nearest the event, which is discovered by the method of ascensions.[14]

Ptolemy then described his method for discovering "the degree of the zodiac which should be rising." In citing the following text, there are many small occasions to footnote for the modern reader. I have interjected words in parentheses rather than footnote so that the flow of reading is not unduly interrupted:

"We must, then, take the syzygy (conjunction or opposition) most recently preceding the birth, whether it be a new moon or a full moon; and, likewise having ascertained the degree accurately, of both the luminaries if it is a new moon, and if it is a full moon that of the one of them that is above the earth (horizon), we must see what stars (planets) rule it (this degree of the syzygy) at the time of the (syzygy).[15] In general the mode of dom-

---

12 Robbins: "An instrument consisting of a graduated circle with a movable arm by which angles above the horizon could be taken."

13 Robbins: "The 'solar instruments' are sun-dials, the gnomons of which cast shadows, the position and length of which are significant. Clepsydrae, or water-clocks, operated on the principle of the hour-glass, except that water was used instead of sand."

14 Calculation of AS from a supplied time. This supplied time is to be rectified. The event referred to is birth. Ashmand helps make this clear.

15 Robbins had "birth"; I substituted "syzygy" so the reader would not get the wrong picture. The time of the birth is not known yet; the procedure for determining the time of birth (degree rising) is what Ptolemy is enunciating. Ashmand makes it clear the time of syzygy, not birth, is intended.

ination (rulership) is considered as falling under these five forms:[16] when it is trine (triplicity relationship, thus in the same element), house (traditional sign rulership), exaltation (as we still understand it), term,[17] and phase or aspect (the traditional idea of aspect); that is, whenever the (degree)[18] in question is related in one or several or all of these ways to the star that is to be the ruler. If, then, we discover that one star is familiar with the degree in all or most of these respects, whatever degree this star by accurate reckoning occupies in the sign through which it is passing, we shall judge that the corresponding degree is rising at the time of the nativity in the sign which is found to be closest by the method of ascensions (calculating the AS). But if we discover two or more corulers, we shall use the number of degrees shown by whichever of them is, at the time of birth, passing through the degree that is closer to that which is rising according to the ascensions (according to the calculated chart). But if two or more are close in the number of degrees, we shall follow the one which is most nearly related to the centres (the other angles: mid-heaven, descendant, and IC) and the sect.[19] if, however, the distance of the

---

16 These five forms of domination are his standard rulership system. He never spells them out clearly or gives examples. We are left to infer certain ideas from what we know. He refers to these again in determining the "prorogation," which is the calculation of the length of life (III.10).

17 Divisions of a sign into five irregularly-sized, whole-degree sectors ranging from 2 to 8 degrees, and totaling 30 degrees per sign. Each term is ruled by a planet (Me, Ve, Ma, Ju, or Sa). There are contradictory systems, and Ptolemy used an Egyptian one over a Chaldean one. Cf. I.20-21.

18 Robbins had "place," but this is confusing because it has a technical meaning referring to a 2 1/2 degree part of a sign. Ptolemy rejects "places" (I.22 "Of Places and Degrees"): "Some have made even finer divisions of rulership than these, using the terms 'places' and 'degrees.' Defining "place" as the twelfth part of a sign, or 2 1/2 degrees, they [begin with the sign in which the star is and] assign the domination over them to the signs in order. Others follow other illogical orders; . . ." Ashmand used the word "degree", which is correct.
    The Hindus use a twelfth part, the dwadasama. The earliest record of twelfth parts is the Babylonian ammat, as seen in Babylonian observations 568–105 BC (*Ancient Planetary Observations and the Validity of Ephemeris Time*, Robert Newton, Johns Hopkins Univ. Press, 1976, p. 351.)

19 There are two sects (planet groups), the sect of the Sun and the Moon. In the former are Su, Ju, Sa, and Me when it rises before the Sun. The latter contains Mo, Ve, Ma, and Me when it sets after the Sun. Cf. I.7.

degree occupied by the ruler from that of the general horoscope (calculated rising degree)[20] is greater than its distance from that of the corresponding mid-heaven (the MC in the calculated chart), we shall use this same number to constitute the mid-heaven and thereby establish the other angles."

To understand Ptolemy's methodology here we need to understand his terminology from some earlier chapters. He said there are five forms or ways in which one is to judge how the degree that holds the syzygy Moon or Sun is dominated (ruled) by a planet: "trine, house, exaltation, term, and phase or aspect."

By "trine" he refers to the four triplicities. He says that the Sun assumes first governance of the fire triplicity by day and Jupiter by night (I.18). Presumably governance means the same thing as rulership. By "house" he refers to the classical planetary rulership, with Saturn ruling Capricorn and Aquarius, Jupiter ruling Sagittarius and Pisces, etc. His use of the word "exhaltation" is just as we use it. The word "term" refers to a division of each sign into five segments of varying width, with each segment having a planetary ruler. All the planets except the Sun and the Moon are rulers of terms. He cites a Chaldean scheme and two Egyptian schemes, one of which he accepts because it was published along with "a natural and consistent explanation of their order and number . . ." For the sign Leo, for example, he gives these terms: 0 to 6 degrees—Jupiter; 6 to 13 degrees—Mercury; 13 to 19 degrees—Saturn; 19 to 25 degrees—Venus; and 25 to 30 degrees - Mars. The word "aspect" means what we understand, except he takes only 0, 60, 90, 120, and 180. But the 120 has already been considered under the "trine" form and the 0 or 180 to the Sun or Moon must not be counted because that is always there by virtue of having chosen the syzygy.

---

20 Robbins comments that "general" means "presumable" in this case. Ashmand gives the same meaning, using the word "ordinary."

Here is the synopsis of his text as I understand it:

1. Find the degree of the syzygy planet (Sun or Moon). If Full Moon, take luminary above the horizon.

2. Find what planet most rules this degree by reference to "trine," "house," "exaltation," "term," and "aspect."

3. If we have two or more rulers we take the one having a degree by sign closest to the degree by sign of the calculated rising degree based on the provided birth time.

4. If two or more rulers are close (what constitutes close is not specified) in the number of degrees to the calculated rising degree, we use the one most nearly related to the other syzygy chart angles (MC, DESC, IC), presumably by rulership or aspect, and the sect, whether Lunar or Solar.

5. The number of degrees the ruler is in its own sign, without reference to the sign, will be the number of degrees of one's true (rectified) AS or MC. The signs of the AS and MC and the degrees of those signs have already been calculated by using the approximate time. But now, either the previously calculated degree of the ASC, or the previously calculated degree of the MC needs to be changed to be exactly the degree of the ruler. To determine whether it is the calculated AS or the calculated MC which is to be so changed, the following rule is applied: If the distance between the calculated AS and the ruler is greater than the distance between the calculated MC and the ruler, we shall take the degree of the ruler to be the degree of the rectified MC, otherwise it is the degree of the ASC.

Let us take my own birth chart as a Ptolemaic example. I was born February 3, 1945, and my birth certificate gave 7 A.M. War Time in New York (41 North, 74 West) as my birth time. The birth planets are: Sun 14-1/4 Aquarius, Moon 23 Libra, Mercury 27 Capricorn, Venus 1-1/4 Aries, Mars 21-1/2 Capricorn, Jupiter 26-3/4Rx Virgo, and Saturn 4-3/4Rx Cancer. The calculated birth angles are: MC = 16-3/4 Scorpio and AS = 22-1/4 Capricorn.[21] My syzygy is 8 Aquarius-Leo which occurred previously on January 28, 1945 at 6:41 G.M.T. The syzygy planets are: Mercury 18 Capricorn, Venus 24-3/4 Pisces, Mars 17 Capricorn, Jupiter 27Rx Virgo, and Saturn 5Rx Cancer. The syzygy angles are: MC = 1-1/2 Virgo and AS = 19-3/4 Scorpio.

In this Full Moon case, the Moon is the luminary that is above the horizon. By the "trine" consideration, there are no other fire planets. However by night Jupiter rules the fire triplicity, and Jupiter is 27 Virgo. By "house," the Sun rules Leo, the sign which the Moon is in. The Sun is 8 Aquarius. By "exhaltation" no planet has Leo as its sign of exhaltation. By "term" (see above) 6 to 13 Leo is ruled by Mercury, which is in 18 Capricorn. By the "aspect"consideration, there are no aspects.

Thus we have these candidates for rulership degree: 8, 18, and 27. By step 3 we see that since the calculated rising degree is 22-1/4 degrees, we see that 18 degrees is 4-1/4 degrees shy of it, while 27 degrees is 4-3/4 more than it. Since 18 is closer to 22-1/4 than is 27, 18 degrees is thus the ruler's degree.

However, if we regard the difference between 4-1/4 and 4-3/4 as close, then we would be required to follow step 4 to find the rising degree. By step 4 we see that in the syzygy chart Mercury at 18 Capricorn has by far the closer relationship to the centres (the angles of the syzygy chart) than does Jupiter at 27 Virgo, for the syzygy angles are AS = 19-3/4 Scorpio and MC = 1-1/2 Virgo. Mercury makes a close sextile to AS. Mercury is thus more related by the principles of centres. As to the consideration of sects, both Mercury and Jupiter are of the Solar sect, so this is not a factor in this case. Mercury is in the Solar sect because it is a morning star since it rises before the Sun. Thus we find 18 degrees to be the ruler's degree here in step 4, just what we got in step 3.

Finally, step 5 says that if the separation between the ruler and the calculated AS is greater than the separation between the ruler and the calculated MC, then the number of degrees of the ruler, namely 18 degrees, will be the rectified MC degree, not the rectified AS degree in the birth chart. Because the separation between the MC and the ruler is 61-1/4 degrees (18 Capricorn

---

21 All positions are rounded to nearest 15'. This is the accuracy Ptolemy would have had, had he been measuring with his astrolabe. Cf. *Ancient Planetary Observations and the Validity of Ephemeris Time*, Robert Newton, Johns Hopkins Univ. Press, Baltimore, 1976, p. 534.

minus 16-3/4 Scorpio), and the separation between the AS and the ruler is 4-1/4 degrees (22-1/4 Capricorn minus 18 Capricorn), we see that the separation between the AS and the ruler is the smaller. Thus 18 Capricorn is the rectified AS.

But supposing my recorded time of birth had been 7:15 A.M. instead of 7:00 A.M. The calculated AS would then be 27 Capricorn and the calculated MC would be 20 1.2 Scorpio. By step 3 if we have two or more rulers, we take the one having a degree by sign closest to the degree by sign of the calculated rising degree based on the provided birth time. Thus of the three candidates for ruler found earlier, in this instance it would be Jupiter at 27 Virgo that would be the ruler. Then by step 5, since Jupiter is closer to the calculated MC than it is to the calculated AS, the rectified MC is found to be 27 Scorpio and the rectified AS based on this MC is found to be 5 Aquarius.

Ptolemy's procedure for rectification gives me an AS of 18 Capricorn if my recorded time had been 7:00, while it gives me an AS of 5 Aquarius if my recorded time had been 7:15. Clearly, *changing the recorded time cannot change the time I was actually born* (whatever it was), so his procedure does not work.

In summary, I think it is instructive to experience this example of a scheme created by the intellectual soul. From the point of view of the intellectual soul, one is concerned with the internal logic and consistency of one's system with *no regard for anything external to it*. The only regard for something external to the system of astrological elements in Ptolemy's conception of rectification is the recognition that the birth time may be somewhat inaccurate, and that this inaccuracy will have a direct impact on the rising degree. Ptolemy's rectification procedure is reasoned all within the system of charts and astrological elements with the assumption that a certain sympathy must exist between the syzygy chart and the birth chart. There is no interaction between his internal scheme and the reality of the entity's life as seen from other measures outside of strictly internal astrological measures. Ptolemy offers a cut-and-dried formula that puts into rules to be mechanically followed in all instances something that can not be mechanical and predictable . . . the mystery of the human incarnation. By contrast, the consciousness soul, where our consciousness must be centered when doing rectification, must contend with its internal astrological set of factors as well as the environment external to it in a give and take process. It is the mentality of empiricism, of modeling reality from the evidence and facts that reality offers.

I have spoken of the correct spirit required to accomplish rectification: that of active, interested puzzle-solving in which one needs to make guesses and see what things look like when one does. This first guess then leads to other guesses, etc. We now have to put some flesh on this spirit of rectification by addressing the conception of rectification in the working sense. Because astrology's very material is an orchestra or kaleidoscope of continuously changing qualitative factors in a mathematical-quantitative rhythmic carousel, an astrologer has to be both an artist-musician to be fluent in the qualitative factors and a mathematician-scientist to be fluent in the quantitative side. The material to which I refer may be seen and experienced directly by looking up and out at the sky. This seeing and experiencing has its qualitative, esthetic side and its mathematical-scientific side in terms of point of view and appreciation.

Like a doctor, architect, or engineer, the astrologer is a technical artist of a sort. Astrologers of course vary in where they fit between being almost all qualitative on the one side, and almost all quantitative on the other side: the interpreter-counselor-artist vs. the researcher-theorist-scientist. The rectifier has to be somewhere near the middle, or be able to move into the middle at will. To help fit yourself for rectification or to improve on your proficiency at it, you need to cultivate or fortify the soul qualities you are weak in. If you are more to the quantitative side, you need to learn about handwriting, for example, and how that correlates with signs and planets. You need to study pictures of representative faces for the twelve signs to see the imprint of the heavens on human physiognomy. If you are more to the qualitative side, you need to learn more about astronomy and math. You need to become quicker in mental arithmetic. You need to become more abstract in your thinking.[22] Since the art of astrology is a composite art fusing the qualitative and the quantitative, it is especially important for one's progress that one be well versed and quick in basic arithmetic.

---

22 The coffee table books on astrology, such as Julia Parker's *The Compleat Astrologer* are very helpful for learning the physiognomy of the signs. As to handwriting, I would recommend *Astrographology*, Lucia D. McKenzie, La Casa Della Madonna, P.O. Box 633, Scottsdale, AZ, 1971.

To do rectification, the astrologer needs to get in synchronization the lightning quick intuitions coming from the qualitative side synchronized with calculational corroboration from the quantitative side. If you get on top of the math, if you regard it as a creative endeavor rather than as a chore and a bother, then the synchronization is improved. You can then work at a higher level, and this working at a higher level is especially crucial in doing rectification.

Studying the many positions coming from transits and progressions across several events, one develops the ability to have a good memory for these various positions as one seeks out a pattern in what often starts out as just a maze of information. The significance or importance of some new bit of information might escape one's notice if the memory of the previous positions is not at ready recall. I believe that having a developed mathematical sense goes hand in hand with the ability to recall from memory the mathematical positions, thus the importance of having the math well mastered. Another component to the math, of course, is having a good knowledge of the daily speeds of the planets for evaluating transits and for calculating and visualizing how the tentative chart would be changed in positioning by a change in time. This would also involve a basic sense of the speeds of the cusps, for example that an Aries AS moves 2' for each 1' movement of the MC. The knowledge of speeds must also extend to the speeds of progressing planets.

If we picture a chart before us, we know that it represents or is a picture of the constantly changing view of the heavens from the place for which the chart was drawn. To use a photographic analogy, if one could see all the planets and the differentiated zodiacal signs, the chart is a snapshot of the heavens as seen from our vantage point at a particular place on the earth. The MC and the other eleven house cusps measure the daily east to west rotation of the heavens around this place relative to Zero Aries. In the constantly-rotating heavens, there are the planets (Sun, Moon, Mercury, etc.), the planetary structures (nodes, perihelia, interfaces,[23] etc.), the planetary gestures (stations, midstations or max-

---

23 These are the intersections of the planets' elliptical orbital planes as seen either from the Earth or the Sun. Cf. *Interface: Planetary Nodes*, Michael Erlewine, Margaret Erlewine, David H. Wilson, Heart Center, Matrix Software, Big Rapids, MI 49307, 1976.

imum speeds,[24] etc.), and the stellar points (Galactic Center, Super Galactic Center, Stars, etc.). Each of these chart elements, from all these four classes of astrological voice, is representable in position as a function of time. In the vernacular, each is expressible as an equation giving position when you plug in the time. By appreciating the continuously changing qualitative factors in the orchestra of heavenly motions, and by understanding the basic descriptive astronomy of the planets, the planetary structures, the planetary gestures, and the stellar points and how these all move in the zodiac, one then has a proper conception of the material of astrology, and this then makes possible the proper conception of rectification: *a conception created by an amalgam or composite of the apparently disparate soul dimensions, the qualitative vs. the quantitative.*

For the purposes of the immediate discussion, let us regard the meaning of time as being time in the astronomer's or physicist's sense, which is conceived as being a uniformly flowing stream of time going on forever and measured in so many days and fractions thereof from some starting date. This is to be distinguished from the common sense of the meaning of the word time, in which it is used to refer to the hour of the day. What rectification is all about (in terms of the definition of the problem) is to find at what point in the stream of time a chart came into being. How many days and fraction of a day, for example, were you born from January 1, 1900 midnight? If you knew the day and hour from a BC, you could calculate it for me directly, and you would be accurate within the error inherent in the time of day as given in the BC. Suppose you only knew the day of your birth: January 3, 1900. Then if I were to ask you how many days and a fraction of a day were you born from January 1, 1900, you would have an uncertainty of 24 hours (one day) in your knowledge of your birth time in the stream of time. You would tell me between 2.0 and 3.0 days. If you only knew that you were born in January 1900 you would have an uncertainty of 31 days in your knowledge of your birth time in the stream of time.

Toward the beginning of the discussion when presenting the time-uncertainty dimension of the scope of rectification, I listed the following named categories of time uncertainty: the minute

---

24 An idea expressed in private conversation by Norman Davidson, March 1991. Davidson is a teacher at the Waldorf Institute, 160 Hungry Hollow Road, Spring Valley, NY 10977.

(BC), the hour (MEM), the date (DAY), the month (MONTHS), and the year (YEARS). From the immediate discussion about the stream of time, we now see that such distinctions or compartmentalizations in the stream of time are arbitrary and insignificant from the point of view of the problem of rectification, which, to state again is: to find at what point in the stream of time a chart came into being. To define rectification in this way is to define it generally, most broadly. By defining it generally, its essential nature is thereby demystified and made evident. I am trying to drive home the point that the constantly changing movements of the planets in the zodiac are a reflection of the continual stream of time and also that the positions of the planets are a measure of the stream of time, or simply time in the astronomical sense. If the positions of the planets in the zodiac are a measure of the time, then by finding the positions of one's planets one finds one's time and thereby one's chart, as we shall now see.

We can now approach the essential idea of rectification by looking at the following example. Let us say we are told that someone was born sometime within a five-day span in some month in some year. This person wants to find the time more precisely, specifically the day and then the hour and minute. We calculate the planets for the beginning of this time interval and for the end of the interval. We only calculate the planets, not the full charts. Between the boundary dates we note: the Moon moves 60 degrees, the Sun moves 5 degrees, Mercury 10 degrees, Venus 6 degrees, Mars 3 degrees, Jupiter 1 degree, Saturn 30', Uranus 20', Neptune 7', and Pluto 5'. Without any reference to where these planets are by sign, we can now study transits to these various intervals of degree-space and look for appropriate events. For example we could look at transiting Mars to the Mars interval. Or we could take transiting Jupiter to the Jupiter interval. In these instances we would probably want to look at the 0, 90, 180, and 270 aspects.

We would likely find a pattern here: we might find that from the timings we found in connection with the kinds of events or states of being to expect, both Mars and Jupiter look to be about 1.3 of the way between the earliest boundary position and the latest boundary position. One might think that Saturn and the outer planets have too small a difference in position to study in the same fashion, yet one might try look at Saturn and Uranus, for example, in the same vein. One might get confirmation or one might not find any specific enough information here. (One has to expect some latitude of individual reaction to the planets.) To be surer of one's results from Mars and Jupiter, one could now take the outer planets (Uranus on out) in transit to the inner planets (again using the 90-degree family of aspects): Sun, Mercury, and Venus. Of course, one would calculate where these would be at 1.3 the interval from the earliest boundary position.

More than likely, one will get corroboration, provided the Mars and Jupiter data were not serendipitous. Due to the many combinations in a chart coming from midpoints, planetary pictures, etc., there can be many places around the 360 degrees of the chart which have similar qualities. Therefore, the hypothesis that Mars's position in this person's chart is 1.3 across this interval could be wrong. One might have been getting the Mars/Moon midpoint, for example. But as one gets more and more confirmation from the study of the other planets, such as the outer planets to the inners just mentioned, the realization grows that one is on the right track. One might then try out the Moon position, which would allow the time to be pinpointed more accurately. From the outer planets transiting the inner planets, one might expect an accuracy of something like 1' arc, which would represent something like 10–30 minutes of time, say. The Moon would then be expected to have a space range of 5–15 minutes of arc. At some point in this process, one would feel confident to set up the chart for the determined time. And then it is on to inspecting the angles.

To generalize upon this example a bit, let us realize that we could have been given a much broader time interval in which to start our rectification. Suppose you wanted to find your conception date. You would subtract 280 days (the average human gestation period) from your birth date. Then you would allow perhaps a month on either side of this, making a sixty-day interval in which to rectify. With a broader interval, you would likely not use Mars, but use Jupiter on out for your planetary return cycle study. Jupiter might have an 8 degree interval, Saturn 6 degrees, etc.

Now to elaborate on these examples, one could also attempt to reflect on the placements by sign of the planets. It might have been the situation in the five-day case that some of the inner planets changed sign. Some of the outer planets may have changed sign too, but the farther out the planet, the less easily its sign can be perceived. (In the sixty-day conception case, of course, more sign changes are possible.) Beyond placement by sign, one can reflect on the aspects and judge by these the more probable time range inside the initial time range. Additionally, one could consider synastry between the planets in these time ranges and planets in charts of entities with which the entity has strong connections. And lastly, one could study ingresses by sign of progressed planets. These are quite strong, fruitful kinds of configurations to explore. For example, I remember vividly the shift in my life in my sixteenth year when in my birth chart my progressed Sun moved from Aquarius to Pisces. It was then that I began to have a strong interest in writing poetry. Since the progressed Sun moves 5' each month, if we can pinpoint to the nearest month when the sign ingress of the progressed Sun occurred, we thereby have determined the Sun to 5' and the time to two hours. If we can pinpoint the ingress to the nearest 1', then we determine the time to 24 minutes.

If we look at corporate charts that have a long history, then we can see many instances of sign ingresses. Especially noticeable are the sign ingresses of the progressed Sun, which are about thirty years apart once the first is established. To illustrate this particular rhythm, let's inspect the sequence of thirty-year passages for a corporate entity. If we take the example of the United States, we can see that we have the "era of good feelings" and the Monroe Doctrine (asserting to Europe that they should have no territorial intentions in the Americas) occurring in the thirty-year Leo passage, President Jackson and the rise of the common man in the Virgo passage, the Civil War in the Libra passage, the robber barons in the Scorpio Passage, the roaring twenties in the Sagittarius passage, the Cold War in the Capricorn passage, and the end of the Vietnam War and the Cold War in the Aquarian Passage. One can actually see turning point dates at the exact ingresses, and you may be interested to pursue these lines.

An unresolved case still is for the birth date of the independence of England from the Roman Empire, which was sometime in the autumn of 410 A.D.[25] Perhaps you would like to inspect the rhythms in English history and look for the pattern here.

---

25 *Mundane Astrology*, Michael Baigent, Nicholas Campion, and Charles Harvey, The Aquarian Press, Wellingborough, Northamptonshire, England, 1984, p. 430.

The above examples to do with transits require that the person have a good recall of life events and their dates, which is assuredly not always the case, especially when questions have been put to the person requiring knowledge of the date down to the nearest day. So to some degree these examples, especially the transit examples, are a bit hypothetical. But my point is twofold: to ease into the practical details of rectification, and, especially, to convey the idea of the stream of time, that rectification is not limited to DAY type, nor to only studying movements of the angles and inspecting house placements in attempting to rectify the DAY type. This appreciation of the stream of time is an important part of the conception of rectification.

Another important conception of rectification is that there is only one method of rectification, but within this one method there are facets or emphases. A facet or emphasis would be favoring transits over progressions, for example. I have gotten the distinct impression that many people feel that there are many methods of rectification, and I think this has tended to keep some people away from trying to rectify. *There is only one.*

Rectification method is the study of inner and outer events in connection with dynamic factors (transits, progressions, and directions) interacting with trial natal elements (angles, planets, etc.) in which, for each event, a comparison is made between the expected or probable outcome or range of outcomes as deduced from the interaction and the actual reported event. If the comparison is not apt, then the trial natal element is judged to be nonexistent (not where it was hypothesized to be). Different positions of the trial natal element are then evaluated, using the same comparison procedure, until an apt comparison is made. This trial natal element by its position then determines the time, and then, using this time, the other chart elements are recalculated and some of them may be studied for aptness of comparison in the same fashion. If the MC were the trial natal element just found to be apt, then one would want to calculate the associated AS and EA, for example, and test them for aptness. Because astrology is assumed to be valid at the level at which it is used and because of the assumption that there is only one unique time for the coming into being of a particular type of chart, rectification in this fashion is expected to be ultimately successful in finding the true time for the coming into being of the chart.

It is important to interject a practical procedural matter at this juncture, which also bears on how one conceives of the rectification process with event fitting. When a trial MC has been found, it is a bore and unnecessary to have to recalculate it manually from the new Sidereal Time, what the corresponding GMT or UT is so that the planets can be recalculated. The computer program should be set up to allow MC input as well as time input. Also, when one is working at rectification, one does not want to be distracted from the astrological thinking one is engaged in by having to perform a menial calculation. Additionally, once the chart is rectified, it is inappropriate to have to memorize the birth time or to have to record it somewhere in order to be able to calculate the chart and perhaps study it with transits or progressions. What one does want to memorize is the MC for the chart. This is the level at which one wants to develop one's astrological memory. The same arguments of course also apply to the AS, which according to your astrological-political leaning, you may prefer to memorize over the MC. I have the ability to input MC, AS, EA, or VX, depending on the political affiliation of the friend who may happen to pop in.

Interwoven and inseparable from this dynamic study of events, we can say "event fitting," is the other side of the coin: which is "*chart* fitting." The chart must fit the entity in character, appearance, and measures of personal characteristics, such as handwriting. Due to the complexities of the many combinations of element interactions in a chart, such as midpoints and planetary pictures, house rulerships, etc., one might get an event-fit or several event-fits involving one or more chart elements serendipitously. It is possible to make a mistake, in doing the chart fitting. As an example, because of the similarity of the qualities of the planets and the signs that they rule, one might confuse Capricorn rising with having Saturn on the AS. Depending on the location of Saturn, this might not involve much of a change in the time, and not much of a change in positions of the Moon and inner planets; the aspect-level of a chart-fit would not be of any help. Quality and quantity are so inseparable in astrology that, in the conception of rectification, it makes no sense to conceive of event fitting and chart fitting as being separate methods that can stand alone exclusive of the other and be relied on for correct rectification just by themselves.

Another issue in the event-fitting process that needs to be considered is the distinction between provided events and pure events. Provided events are what the entity provides to you as being most important out of his or her memory or personal record of events that he or she wants to be known. Provided events, such as a marriage, are generally strong due to there being more than the usual number of dynamic factors operating at the same time. Pure events, on the other hand, are events that come about by an isolated but important factor coming to exactness. An example would be the progressed MC coming to 0 Aquarius or when Uranus conjoins the Sun. The pure event comes in the form of the rectifier posing the question by calculating the date when the astrological factor would be exact, and asking the person what happened at this date. Pure events are thereby considered as confirmation or authentication of the tentatively rectified chart. Sometimes, when there are not many provided events, the rectifier must glean some "provided events" by asking for pure events.

To finish the discussion on the method of rectification, I am aware of a few instances where a name has been given to a "method of rectification." We already mentioned the Prenatal Epoch, which I have stated is bogus. Another method is the Nadi method, apparently of Hindu origin, which asserts that births can only occur at fixed, prescribed uniform intervals of time. I have found this method to be bogus, too. Another named method is the Kundig method, which I am not totally familiar with, but I understand that it is a system implementing solar arcs. [A German system, very popular in Denmark.—Ed.] From my perspective, I would call this a facet of event fitting. It is confusing in this field to give names to purported methods of rectification, for it makes it appear that there is some magic formula or set of rules which will release one from the necessary work. Let us not forget the instance of Ptolemy's proscription for how to rectify recorded births to make them more accurate. Just think how his erroneous method retarded the work of subsequent generations of astrologers attempting rectification.

The essence of rectification is *pattern recognition*. Out of the composite mentality of the astrologian, versed in both the quantitative-mathematical and the qualitative-intuitive, come judgments and evaluations of the importance of astrological configurations in connection with past events in the person's life. After tabulating the transits and progressions for several important events, one invariably starts to notice that *certain degrees or certain degrees and minutes keep recurring*. When this occurs, one is getting close to getting the chart rectified. It remains to see to which angle this "hot" degree measurement belongs by astrological sign.

A good portion of the reason for the view that rectification is difficult is that people have brought invalid astrological concepts and tools to bear on the problem. One might be wrong in using these when doing interpretations or readings for a client. If so, there is so much redundancy in astrology, that one can get away with it: the deficiency is not brought to one's attention. However, when doing rectification, which is an objective feedback exercise, one is made aware of deficiencies quite rapidly. The proof of the pudding is that one is unable to resolve the question of the time of birth (or conception or death). After disposing of astrological theory, I shall turn to the principles of rectification and the techniques of rectification. The principles are sort of guidelines and the techniques are sort of helpful tricks or practical details.

Specific Principles and Techniques

The elements of astrology (points that move relative to the signs) as I have spoken about already are the angles (MC, ASC, EP, VX) and intermediate cusps, the planets, the planetary structures (nodes, perihelia, interfaces), the planetary expressions (stations, midstations or maximum speeds), and the stellar points (Galactic Center, Super Galactic Center, Stars, etc., which move by precession and proper motion). In the planet category, we can also include the asteroids and the Uranian bodies. One must choose what elements to use—nobody uses all of them—and some of them such as perihelia are experimental. For the remainder of this discussion, by elements I refer to the angles and the intermediate cusps, the planets Sun, Moon, Mercury, etc. and the lunar node. I will refer to all twelve house cusps as Cusps.

These elements occupy signs. By signs I refer to the Tropical Zodiac, as I do not think it is correct to employ the Sidereal Zodiac when doing geocentric astrology. It would take us too far afield to discuss this right now, but my statement is based on both observation and theoretical understandings. (I would interject that when doing heliocentric astrology, just the opposite obtains: it is not correct to refer to the Tropical Zodiac in this domain. The Sun does not know that the Earth is tilted, and it is this tilt which creates the Tropical Zodiac.) Aside from the signs, it is important to include the 0 Aries point, referred to simply as Aries in Uranian Astrology. It is thought of as a planet, but of course it never moves from where it is relative to the signs. It refers to the general environment, to the impersonal outside world.

The next area of concepts is that of interactions. By these I mean how the elements interact with each other to form "compounds," to use an analogy from chemistry. Astrology recognizes three interactions: aspects, midpoints, and planetary pictures. As to aspects, it is useful in rectification to use all multiples of 30 degrees (because they are readily seen), but as well it is useful to use the 45-degree family. I strongly urge you to become facile in seeing these in a chart: they are calculated by adding 15 degrees to an element and then jumping ahead one sign. Then, you inspect the 90-degree cross from this position in order to see the whole 45 family for that element. The 22.5-degree aspect is important too, but seeing and using this aspect involves the use of the 90-degree dial [and see Kramer chapter in this volume.—Ed.].

The next interaction is midpoints. So-called traditional astrologers have eschewed this measurement spectrum, but midpoints are very important for understanding astrology well. To those traditionalists, I would like to inform you that midpoints are also "traditional": they were spoken of in classical times.[26] Sextus Empiricus noted that "and they say that the stars are 'guarded' when they are in the middle of other stars and in continuity with the Signs; thus if in the same Sign one star occupies the first portions and another the last and another the midmost, then the star in the middle is said to be 'guarded' by those occupying the extreme portions." Guido Bonatti, the famous astrologer from the thirteenth century that I previously referenced in connection with rectification, also employed midpoints, and closer to our time, Alan Leo apparently used them.[27]

A midpoint is the exact halfway point between any two elements, regardless of how far apart they are and whether or not

26 Sextus Empiricus, *Op. Cit.*, p. 339.
27 Reinhold Ebertin, *Op. Cit.*, intro. p. 21.

they are in aspect. If x and y are two elements and x is 2 degrees and y is 9 degrees, then their midpoint, written x/y, is 5.5 degrees (5 degrees 30 minutes). If there is no element located on the midpoint, the midpoint will be activated when a dynamic factor (transit, progressed, or directed element) comes to it. All three elements will then interact. If there is an element on the midpoint in the chart, then when a dynamic factor comes to it, one has a four-fold elemental interaction. Orbs to midpoints are only 1 degree, with 0.5 degrees being a better value. Of course people vary on the size of the orbs they use for aspects, and it is no different for midpoints. Finally, two midpoints may be conjoined (share the same axis, as it is called). In the example given, if f and g are two other elements situated at 1 degree and 10 degrees, they also form a midpoint of 5.5 degrees, thus sharing the midpoint axis of x/y. We would write this as x/y = f/g. If an element a is on the b/c midpoint, this is written a = b/c.

The third interaction recognized by astrology is called the planetary picture. It is a configuration created by three elements, let us call them p, q, and r. As in the spirit of midpoints, these can be any place in the 360 degrees of the zodiac. Let us regard the order p, q, r as being that of increasing degrees in the zodiac. Element q then has a certain angular separation from element p, which is q - p. There exists another point in the zodiac, call it s, such that it is as much separated from r as q is from p. In other words, s - r = q - p. Thus, s = q - p + r. You should draw this out on a piece of paper so you see the idea physically. When a dynamic factor reaches point s (where there is no element) then the factor enters into a 4-way elemental interaction. These are quite powerful and exact in their timings, and very small orbs are used: like a *minute* or two of arc. They are very useful for predictions and therefore rectifications. (To be able to discern these at a glance, requires working with a dial, to which I will return soon.

Instead of finding a point s equally as far ahead of r as q is ahead of p, we could have found a point t, equally as far back from r as q is ahead of p. In other words: r - t = q - p, which becomes t = r + p - q. You should also draw this out to see it physically (draw it on the same diagram as the other).

Of course, just as with midpoints, it is possible to have point s occupied by a planet in the chart (not temporarily occupied by a dynamic factor). In this instance, you have four elements in interaction as part of the interpretation for the entity. Charts are full of hundreds of these planetary pictures, and on the interpretational level, they are very useful.

The basic theory or principle behind planetary pictures is that the angular separation between any two elements, p and q say, in the zodiac sets up a vibrational frequency between them whose value is found by: 360 / (q - p). We are speaking of the harmony of the spheres here, referred to by the ancients. Note that for this calculation you would have to convert q and p to decimals, make the subtraction (the smaller from the larger), and then divide into 360 to get a decimal number. This decimal number could be written as y/z in which y and z are some integers (whole numbers). Then z would refer to the significance by number symbolism of this harmonic number y/z. For example if q is 74 degrees and p is 2 degrees, then 360 / (q - p) becomes 360/72 = 5/1 or 5. The symbolism for the number 5 would then qualify p and q's relationship—but back to the harmony of the spheres: if r and s are equally separated from each other as are p and q, then r and s have the same "frequency" as p and q. They are thus in tune, or we could say, they are in sympathetic vibration, or simply in sympathy. You should realize that this applies to comparing the separations of two elements in the sky (transiting) with two elements in the chart. Or two elements in the progressed chart to the chart. Any combination of levels (chart, transiting, progressed) mutually or across levels may be used because they all reside in the same 360 degree zodiac.

Beyond what astrology currently understands, there is a fourth interaction, which I have just recently discovered. I call this interaction: *the balance point*. It applies to any number of elements. The idea is that the elements participate in a relationship in the chart in the same way that a group of people of equal total weight participate if distributed on both sides of a see-saw. If you picture a see-saw in balance, with several people of equal total weight on one side of the balance point and several people of the same equal total weight on the other side, you can see that we can do the same thing with the zodiac by cutting it at the 0 Aries point and opening it up into a straight line. Then, considering as many elements (planets, say) as you want, you would find at what place in the zodiac the balance point is. The formula is quite easy, you just add up the individual longitudes of the planets (each first expressed as a decimal in 0 - 360 format) and divide by the number of planets.

The importance of this interaction is first, that it adds to our knowledge of the theory of astrology. Second, it raises some interesting areas for research. For example, you could take all 12 cusps and see where this balance point is. Or you could do the same for all the planets. Or just the outer, trans-Saturnian planets. A third reason that balance points (think of averages) are important is a very practical one, I think for the future of astrology.

Recognition of the existence of the balance point affords the ability to do composite charts (both space and time) for any number of people. John Townley and then Rob Hand wrote about space composites and gave examples of two, three, and four people. But their work was by no means definitive; they were rather exploratory gestures. The question their work raised that continued to hound me was whether a composite chart existed for three or more people (for the principle of the interaction of three did not exist in the tradition of astrology). The idea of a composite between two people was astro-logical enough, since midpoints exist between elements in one person's chart, and from general synastry theory, one can overlay charts between two people as if they occupied the same zodiac. Additionally, I recognized that interactions between levels is possible in the sense of chart elements, transit elements, and progressed elements all occupying the same zodiac, as I just touched on above in discussing planetary pictures. I then realized, by combining my previous background with midpoints, that four people could be composed into two composite charts of two couples, and these two couples could be composed by midpoints into just one composite chart. But the problem remained about how to handle an odd number of people, how to compose them, if it were at all possible.

It turns out that even numbers are not able to be explained entirely by repeated midpoint taking, as I had mentioned for the case of four people. For the number 6 is even, yet if you view this number as three duos, then after composing each duo using midpoints, you are left with three duos, which cannot be composed without the existence of the principle of the balance point. I come from a family of six individuals, and I found very sound astrological factors explaining events in my family by forming my family's chart by the balance point both in terms of space and in terms of time. (The time composite was introduced by Ronald Davison, who termed it the Relationship Chart, to give it an astrological commodity.)

The next astrological concept to address is the question of houses. This has been a pet peeve of mine and, as well, a fascination. Since I have a book on houses welling up inside me, I must be careful that I do not get carried away in this discussion about rectification. But after all, the reason one rectifies is to find the correct AS and MC, which is equivalent to saying that one rectifies to find out which houses the elements (planets) are in. So we are back full circle, as in so much of astrology. Having done considerable research in houses from the point of view of tabulating whether the intermediate cusps of many house systems produce the appropriate events, changes, or feelings in an entity when stimulated by transits, progressions, and directions, I can offer some sound advice about this area, which I would now like to do in some broad strokes.

The principle of houses is that there is an analogous circle to the ecliptic and this comes about by making the analogy of a day being like a year, just as in progressions. What is being addressed by houses is the impregnation by the spiritual forces in the heavens working out on the Earth. The Greeks developed the ideas of houses and progressions, which are intimately related, but we, now in the Piscean Age of empiricism, and taking up the challenge of coming to know the Earth through experience and consciousness, are involved with exploring the mysteries of houses. It is astrology's task for the Piscean Age.

First of all, we could postulate that there are three levels of house, each making reference to a different spiritual orientation of the human being or the entity. In recognition of the day-for-a-year analogy, the highest point of the Sun in the year is at 0 Cancer, and this is what the MC pictures on the daily level. By a strange inversion, which would take too long to develop now, we actually associate the MC with 0 Capricorn. (We have some huge mysteries here, and this relates as well to the problem of the southern hemisphere having Christmas when it is 90 degrees outside!)

The MC as the beginning of the 10th House (by analogy to Capricorn being the tenth sign), forms an association physically and spiritually with a horizontal member, and this can be one of three axes: the Ascendant, the Equatorial Ascendant, or the Vertex. Thus we can postulate three levels of chart. The Ascendant chart feels to me to relate to the astral level (humans and animals share an astral body, which gives mobility and passions). The Vertex feels to me like the etheric body (passive, life body which not only humans and animals have, but plants as well). And the Equatorial Ascendant feels like the ego or consciousness soul to me, making a reference as it does to a global, impersonal stance to the world (the spectator taking in experience). This meaning comports with the physical fact that the EA is the Ascendant not locally and personally, but it is the Ascendant as if the entity had come into existence at the Equator of the Earth. Thus the tie-in with the global and impersonal level. Another idea bearing on this is that the EA, unlike the AS, does not have a bearing on the physical appearance or the personality, as the more personal AS does.

We have been incorporating the EA and the VX into our Ascendant charts, in which the Ascendant is the beginning of the 1st House, drawing the EA and VX as axes and treating them as independent elements combinable with the AS via aspects, midpoints, and planetary pictures. But I think we should now consider these three different horizontal axes as forming the 1st-7th House axes, in which the MC is the 10th House in each of the three levels of chart. This is not to say that one can not form, for example, the AS/EA midpoint and use it for interpretation, prediction, or rectification. In fact, this idea works, but I am just trying to introduce an exploration of how these angle elements are related to the spiritual makeup of the human being.

So where do the so-called house systems come in? The house systems, such as Placidean or Koch, are theories or methods for performing a trisection between the vertical axis, the MC, and the horizontal axis. In the past, of course, the horizontal axis has always been the AS. But now we can realize that we can apply any trisection theory (Placidean, Koch, etc.) to the AS chart as well as to the EA chart, as well as to the VX chart.

When it comes to the trisection methods, I have tested the following: Alcabitius, Campanus, Koch, Morinus, Placidus, Porphyry, Regiomontanus, and Topocentric. Of these I only find the Alcabitius, Campanus, and Koch to work. Because the others do not work (in the sense of giving appropriate events), it is my view that they do not exist. Thus only Alcabitius, Campanus, and Koch may be applied to the three different levels of chart.

Intermediate cusps are valuable to inspect in rectification, since they afford more information relative to the evaluating of a hypothesized MC (time). Often one can go back to just the recent past and investigate outer planet transits to the intermediate cusps for a quick look at the initial chart when one is rectifying a BC type chart. Another observation is that very often in the case of marriages, you will find the MC coming by progression to the 11th House cusp.

Another idea on houses is a principle I discovered back in 1974. It turns out that there is a symbolic economy involved with planetary pictures and house cusps. If one forms the planetary picture AS + MC - H(11), where H(11) refers to the 11th House, then the quality of this planetary picture is of the 12th House. I call this idea "House Transforms." Let us refer to the 12th House Transform as T(12). Then T(12) is given by:

$$T(12) = A + M - H(11).$$

Conversely, T(11) is given by:

$$T(11) = A + M - H(12).$$

When we wrote: A + M - 11 = 12, earlier, we can see that this can be interpreted as coming about by the following formula: 13 + 10 - 11 = 12, in which we substitute the number of the sign corresponding to houses, with the MC being the 10th house, and the AS being the 1st house. Because we go around again, we can call 1 and 13 the same value, thus 13 was substituted for 1 above for the AS.

The equivalence or near equivalence of 1 and 13 is interesting in two lights. First we know of the expression "E Pluribus Unum," out of many one, which refers to America's original 13 colonies. Also interesting is that Rob Hand has noticed that the significance of the number 13 is similar to 1 in his study of the 13th harmonic chart, in which every chart element is multiplied by 13 (and then reduced to 0-360 if 360 is exceeded by subtracting 360 repeatedly).[28] And finally, one may place exactly twelve

---

28 *Essays On Astrology*, "Dodekatemoria: An Ancient Technique Reexamined," Rob Hand, Para Research, Rockport, MA, 1982, p. 115.

spheres around a central sphere such that the contacts among all 13 are perfect: it is mathematically exact in the solid geometry sense. This is illustrative of Christ and the 12 disciples.

What the equation A + M - 11 = 12 might suggest is that, on the planetary rulership level, we could make the following equations of planetary transform: Ma + Sa - Ur = Ne or Pl + Sa - Ur = Ne or Ma + Sa - Sa = Ju.

A concept in astrology that is crucial for rectification is obviously the whole area of dynamic factors: transits, progressions, and directions. These may be calculated both forward and backward in time, and when backward they are referred to as converse transits or progressions. I have not spent much time at all investigating the backwards direction, but I have seen powerful evidences of the backwards transits working, so the backwards progressions must work as well, because progressions are based on transits. It remains to be distinguished what the difference is between forward and backward directions in terms of level or meaning.

As I have already mentioned in different contexts in the discussion, transits, progressions, and directions form the backbone of rectification, for in truth, rectification is actually *backwards prediction*, and prediction needs dynamic, changing factors. I have not addressed the details about these, but I wish now to provide you with some useful ideas about these based on work I have done that was published in 1982.[29]

I have shown that directions are actually a subset of progressions. The idea of progressions derives from the analogy of the day and a year, just like the analogy of houses. If one accepts that houses work, one must be prepared to accept that progressions work, no matter how nonsensical they may appear. There are Secondary Progressions and Tertiary Progressions, and in each of these the year or the month, respectively, may be defined not only relative to 0 Aries, which forms the cycle one naturally thinks of, but also in a synodical sense with the other planets. Thus one has really a whole set of progressions to deal with in Secondary Progressions and in Tertiaries. Then when it comes to

---

29 "True Secondary and Tertiary Progressions," Laurence Ely, *Matrix Magazine*, IX, July 1982, Michael Erlewine, ed., Matrix Software, 315 Marion Ave., Big Rapids, MI 49307 (republished as Matrix Monograph Series #11).

directions, not only may the Sun be directed (by taking Secondary Progressed Sun minus natal Sun), but the Moon, Mercury, etc. may be so directed by subtracting *their* natal positions from their progressed positions. All the same applies to Tertiaries as well. In fact, we have a whole family of directions in Secondary Progressions and in Tertiary Progressions. I do not advise using these in rectification until you are more advanced in your studies. Utilizing these theories render prediction more refined and can help with rectification when you need more information, due to the lack of events.

By improving upon the very underlying implementation of all these progressions (making a day be an apparent day, not a mean solar day, and calculating the year or the month by transiting Sun minus natal Sun divided by 360 or transiting Moon minus natal Moon divided by 360 for the tertiaries), I got progressed positions that produced results consistent with transits. The older implementation of progressions introduces errors of 2′ for Secondaries and more for Tertiaries, rendering "zero orb" astrology impossible. I renamed Secondary Progressions as Solar Progressions and Tertiary Progressions as Lunar Progression because these names make a direct and natural reference to their very idea. I also did this because I found that Primary Directions (another Ptolemaic legacy) do not work or exist: thus if there is no primary, why speak about secondary and tertiary?

This finding about Primary Directions leads me now to the last part of my discussion about concepts in astrology. It is now time to eliminate some deadwood. If you have incorrect theories you will not have any success rectifying. Not only are Primary Directions invalid (the 1 degree of Right Ascension for each year of life[30]) but doing Secondary Progressions in Right Ascension is also invalid. In fact, transits do not work in Right Ascension, so it is inconceivable that progressions could work in this great circle. I also found any uniform direction in the ecliptic to be invalid, such as: Naibod, Simmonite, and One Degree per year. Another concept to drop is progressing the MC by calculating the change in the Sidereal Time. The MC should be progressed by adding the solar arc (Solar Progressed Sun minus natal Sun) to the chart MC.

---

30 These were discussed by Ptolemy, *Op. Cit.*, III.10, pp. 287ff.

Other bogus ideas are the following house systems: Morinus, Placidus, Porphyry, Regiomontanus, and Topocentric. The Topocentric system was created by using Primary Directions, so if Primary Directions can be shown not to work, then there goes that system. The so-called Equal House system is not a house system at all. This is a semantic confusion that has persisted. A house system must divide up another circle other than the ecliptic and somehow project back onto the ecliptic, because the whole idea of houses is to make the literal analogy between the day and the year.

Another incorrect idea is the use of the Sidereal Zodiac when doing geocentric astrology. Since the point 0 Aries Sidereal does not rise in the spring, the Siderealist may not make the very analogy necessary to set up houses. He steals from the tropicalists and then jumps back to his Sidereal positions by subtraction of the ayanamsa. This is on the theory side, but also on the research, empirical side I have not found this system to work. But, as I said earlier, when doing heliocentric astrology, it is the Sidereal Zodiac which must be used, not the Tropical Zodiac, which is currently used. The reason that the Sidereal Zodiac is not being used is that nobody knows where it is located yet with the kind of accuracy necessary for doing transits to close orbs, as is common practice both in geocentric and heliocentric astrology.

Finally, there are three concepts that have been introduced in recent astrological thinking coming from the desire to make astrology more scientific. The first of these is the so-called "true lunar node." The "true lunar node" *does not work* and is not where the Moon's node is: the old lunar node we have been using is the real "true lunar node." The second concept is use of topocentric longitudes in which parallax is taken into account. Parallax is a measure of seeing something at a different angle because of the position of the viewer. If the Moon is overhead in Greenwich, and you see it from St. Louis, which is 90 degrees away (a quarter of the way around the globe), you will report it some 1 degree different in zodiacal longitude than the person in Greenwich will. This is due to viewing the Moon along different sides of a narrow triangle having 4,000 miles (the radius of the Earth) as one leg and 239,000 miles (the distance between the Earth and the Moon) as the other leg (and the hypotenuse slightly over 239,000 miles). The viewer in St. Louis views along the hypotenuse, while the viewer in Greenwich views along the long leg. These converge at the Moon at an angle of some 1 degree. *It turns out that astrology does not work by viewing the planets from the place of birth, but from the center of the Earth:* this is a mystery that needs to be explored, because we calculate the AS from the place of birth.

This leads to another Earth-connected theory, that of using the geocentric latitude of birth, not the geographic latitude of birth to calculate the AS and house cusps. The nominal difference is something like 10′ to 15′ in the AS, for a given MC. I have found from empirical evidence in a very accurately rectified chart (down to the level of 0.5″ arc on the MC) that the geographic latitude, that used by cartographers and what we have used all along is the correct theory. When the geographic latitude is used, one is setting up the spherical astronomy of the situation such that the direction of gravity is straight up (through the spinal column, as it were). This has a highly symbolic, spiritual value in connection to man, who stands erect. With the geocentric latitude, the direction of the vertical is not straight up in the same way, but is deflected several minutes of arc.

Returning now to applying all these principles to rectification, I am reminded of the philosophical joke inherent in the following expression: "the cardinal rule is this, that you must not follow cardinal rules." If we remember that I have been exhorting you to be experimental, flexible, and open—to revitalize astrologia—when you approach rectification, that this is the very soul quality that you need to cultivate to be successful, I do not want to counter that point of view. Nonetheless, I hope you will receive the following practical principles as guidelines and appreciate the spirit in which they are presented.

1. Check All Sources

You do not want to make unnecessary work for yourself, so always check or have your client check all sources for a recorded birth time or for a possible family or relative's memory of the time. It is possible, for example, for a hospital or doctor to have a birth record which somehow never found its way to the governmental bureau of vital statistics of the state or province in which the entity was born.

2. Start Mid-Range

When provided with a time range, for example in the MEM type, always set up the chart using *the middle of the range*. This is the more probable time in a mathematical, scientific sense and is thus the time that should be used as a start.

3. Gather Events

Get as many events as possible that the client thinks are important. These may be outer events such as a marriage or a major job promotion, in which case there is almost always an accurate knowledge of both the date and the time. Always seek to know the times and dates as accurately as possible, and for a date or time range ask to be given a conservative range. Also get inner events. These may be turning points in political or religious view that perhaps extended over weeks, months, or years. You may later find that an outer planet transit or progression accounts for the longer periods of change. It is better to have too much information than too little, because you can subsequently disregard some of it.

It is important to get the best picture (in terms of biography) of the client that you can. Each event you get to be fully fleshed out in terms of its significance for the client, who else was involved (possibly their birth data), the quality of the time, helps. You do not want to have just this: marriage 1-2-34. You would like to *characterize* each event much more fully.

4. Additional Image Measurements

Seek out a handwriting sample and photographs. These are a measure of the AS by sign and its configurations (aspects and midpoints). Refer to my citation of McKenzie's book earlier on handwriting. The AS has to do with the personality in the outward sense, but do not disregard trying to ascertain the MC by sign, for the MC very much marks the character, ego, or inner personality. I use the term inner personality to draw a parallel to the AS's outer personality, but I by no means wish to depreciate the value of focusing on the MC sign.

By focusing on both the AS and the MC by sign, one is usually able to be successful. Due to the spherical trigonometry involved in producing certain portions of a sign as an AS for certain portions of signs on the MC, one is able (having determined what signs are on the angles) to narrow down the degree ranges of each angle. If you are not sure of the MC sign, but have a good feeling about the AS sign, then set up the chart with 15 degrees of that sign and go from there.

5. Aspects to Angles

Part of this natal fitting also is considering aspects to the angles from the planets. At this juncture, having set up a rough chart by the reflection on the signs on the angles, now introduce also the EA and the VX to see if anything clicks with what you know of the person in relation to planetary aspects.

Another route to use instead of, or as well as, this sign meditation to arrive at a rough chart, is to consider some recent transit, progression, or direction from a thumbnail measure that may come to mind when you first look at the placement of planets by sign. Often this sort of intuitive zap can get you right to the heart of the matter. You might consider what planet symbolizes you and whether that planet was active in the client's coming to you.

If you have a DAY type and you are not getting any sense of a possible AS, just set up the chart for noon (again the mid-range adage) and start meditating on the aspects in connection with what you know about the client. Consider the lunation cycle. Dane Rudhyar in his *Lunation Cycle* spoke well about this Sun-Moon cycle in connection to how one orients one's soul life with one's spirit. I would only generalize his model by considering there to be not eight, but twelve phases to this cycle: when the Moon has separated from the new Moon by 30 degrees then the Moon has entered the Taurus stage of the synodic cycle, when it has 30 degrees to go before conjoining the Sun at the upcoming new Moon, it has entered the Pisces stage in the synodic cycle. The theory is that the slower moving body in a synodic pair marks the 0 Aries point. The same theory can be applied to all other synodical cycles in the chart, and these may prove instrumental in helping you infer one's birth time.

6. Transits and Progressions

Next calculate the transits and progressions and directions (or just the Solar Arc from the Solar Progressions). These should be tabulated systematically and in chronological order. The MC should be progressed by the Solar Arc, not by the change in the Sidereal Time! Then the AS, EA, and VX should be calculated based on this progressed MC and for the latitude of birth. Use color coding to write in the transits and progressions around the chart. Buy a 90-degree dial and learn how to use it. I cannot stress this enough. This is a circular sliderule that makes visualizing Solar Arc directions really fast. Solar Arc directions are moving all the elements (planets, Cusps, etc.) by the same angular amount. This angular amount is the progressed Sun minus the natal Sun. Sometimes it is a good idea to cut out one piece of 90-degree dial paper into a smaller inner wheel which can rotate against the outer paper underneath, which has an outer ring measured in the same manner. The elements are copied onto the outer ring, so that initially all respective elements are lined up with each other: Sun to Sun, Moon to Moon, etc. By turning the inner wheel clockwise, the outer wheel thereby represents the positions of the Solar Arc-directed elements. Spend a little time with this, make yourself comfortable with the orientation, and the rewards are many.

In all work, whether transits, progressions, or transits, use small orbs like 1' to 2' to calculate, the smaller the better. Pay particular attention to configurations which are exact. Remember to be actively involved and curious, and not afraid to try a hypothesis, a guess. Sooner or later the information you have been studying will educate you and lead you to make more significant hypotheses for what the angles are. The angles are very powerful, and the idea is that the important events will have a large degree of angle involvement.

7. Watch for Personal Bias and Measurement Confusion

Be conscious of not favoring or hoping a certain AS or MC is right. In other words, do not let your ego, in the negative sense of this word, get the better of your better self. This is a subtle problem that you should try to be aware of. One often tries to avoid telling oneself that he or she made a mistake. One wants to think that one made the right insight initially. So be flexible to allow new evidence to have its say.

Note that the EA is important to include because it is always within 4 degrees of being square to the MC, regardless of the latitude of birth. One can often be getting a conjunction to the EA, while thinking it is a square to the MC. Conversely, one can be getting a square to the EA and think one is getting a conjunction to the MC.

The equinoctial signs near the AS present a difficulty because in this case all the angles become near 0 of the cardinals. In this case, it is especially important to consider the intermediate house cusps: those of Alcabitius, Campanus, and Koch (the Meridian as well). In this case, using a harmonic chart is a good tool, because it will get you off the 0 cardinal confluence which proves difficult to rectify initially when one has as one's goal the arriving at the MC to the 1' level of accuracy. I will discuss the harmonic chart principle momentarily.

Keep in mind that signs ruled by the same planet can be confused with each other when you think one of them is the AS. I refer to the classical ladder of the planets in which the rulership of the signs is symmetrical about the 0 Cancer-Leo axis. Thus for example, Taurus rising could be mixed up with Libra rising due to the Venus rulership, Aries rising with Scorpio rising due to the Mars rulership, etc.

Another planet-sign confusion can come about in appearance and disposition when one thinks a particular sign is rising, but rather the explanation for the energy or quality perceived is that the planet ruling that sign is on or close to the AS or in the 1st House. This works in the reverse, as well, where you might think that a particular planet is on the AS or in the 1st House, but the explanation is that the sign that is ruled by that planet is on the AS.

Harmonic charts are useful because they provide more check points. This is especially helpful when you do not have many events. The 5th harmonic has a Venus quality to do with relationships and art. Theodore Landscheidt, in his *Cosmic Cybernetics*, presented a series of prime numbers that relate to planetary distances. The ratios of these prime numbers corresponds to the ratios of the actual distances of the planets from the Sun. I have found the symbolism inherent in this series apt in terms of the results I have gotten doing harmonic charts with them. His numbers are:

Ve	Ma	Ce	Ju	Sa	Ur	Ne	Pl	Pe
5	11	19	37	67	137	211	283	563

All elements are multiplied by the particular harmonic number and then 360 is repeatedly subtracted to bring the value down to a value between 0 and 360.

I have been working with harmonic charts in which the separation between two elements is divided into 360 and then all the elements of the chart are multiplied by this number. Two elements that were chosen to create the harmonic number will be found to be in conjunction. This is a powerful tool when the MC is chosen as one of the elements. Based upon one's career, you might choose to take Uranus to be conjunct the MC. The harmonic charts of this sort that involve the MC (or the AS) are further checks on the rectification.

A principle not to be forgotten for sound rectification is that one should not rely just on transits and directions. This is because due to the complexities of midpoint placements and planetary pictures, certain areas in the chart can take on certain powerful qualities of certain natures, that can be mistaken for the angles, especially if the angles are involved informing these midpoints and planetary pictures. With directions and with transits to the natal chart, these complexes never change relative to each other. In progressions, both Solar and Lunar, however, one sees the angular relationships are always changing. With Solar progressions, study of the progressed lunations is a particularly straightforward and powerful technique for pinpointing the time.

8. "Other" Charts

Finally, in addressing the principles of rectification one must not exclude synastry and composite charts of the time, space, and harmonic type. The time composite (termed the Relationship Chart by its discoverer Ronald Davison) and the space composite (based on midpoints calculated in the zodiac, thus in space, and discovered by John Townley) are applicable to any number of charts as was discussed earlier in the concepts discussion.

Note: An important detail about the time composite chart is that when one is doing time composites between two charts very removed in time, then the question is raised whether time should be conceived as Ephemeris Time on the one hand, or as Universal Time on the other. This is because the planets' positions in the time composite chart depend on how you define the time. Ephemeris Time is conceived as being a uniform measure of time, while Universal Time, having as its basis the daily rotation of the Earth, is non-uniform relative to it. This is because the Earth is slowing down in its rotational speed as you go forward in time. The difference between Ephemeris Time and Universal Time is termed *Delta-T*. When one rectifies a chart and finds the MC, one thereby has found the Universal Time by working backwards in the Sidereal Time arithmetic step calculation. (The MC is converted to the Local Sidereal Time by multiplying the Right Ascension of the MC by 15.) When one then wants to calculate the planets for that chart, one must calculate the planets based on what the value of Ephemeris Time was for that value of Universal Time. To do this one needs to add Delta-T to Universal Time.

If one regards the time-composite as operating in the stream of Universal Time, then one finds the halfway composite time, UT(C), between the two charts. Then one calculates the Delta-T for this value of UT(C), and adds it to UT(C) to get ET(C). If one regards the time-composite as operating in the stream of Ephemeris Time, then one calculates the halfway composite time directly by adding the two individual Ephemeris times and dividing by 2. Let us denote this alternate calculation as ET'(C). ET'(C) will differ from ET(C) by growing amounts as the birth times between the two charts becomes greater. This is not an important consideration unless you are doing a time-composite between yourself and an historical chart. Note that Delta-T is loosely measured by the following equation, where T stands for centuries from the year 1800: Delta-T in seconds = 32xTxT (32 times T squared). Example: in an important historical chart for 747 B.C., Delta-T is 22,000 seconds, while your own Delta-T is 0 seconds. The Delta-T for the halfway point in time from the mid-twentieth century to 747 B.C. is 4,600 seconds. However, when Ephemeris Time is used, it will be implicitly using a Delta-T of 11,000 seconds (one half of 0 + 22,000). This is a 6,400 second difference, almost 2 hours, which will make your composite Moon off 1 degree and the inner planets off on the order of 5 to 10 minutes of arc.

The harmonic composite is something I came up with around 1979 and it may only be applied to two charts. It is formed by consideration of each pair of like planets between the two charts, as is done in the space composite. Instead of taking the midpoint for each like pair however, you find the difference in longitude (as a decimal) for each like pair and then you divide this into 360 to get that like pair's *harmonic number*. This harmonic number times either planet's longitude will show *where in the zodiac the two planets will be conjunct*. If one person has Sun at 14 Aq 15 and the other at 9 Pi 24, then we calculate the harmonic number for this pair this way: 360 / (339.4 - 314.25) = 14.31411531 . . . You then multiply this by either 339.4 or 314.25 and then divide the result by 360, take the fractional part, and multiply it by 360 to get the harmonic position. Finishing the example, I will multiply 14.314 . . . by 339.4 to get 4858.210736. . . Dividing by 360 produces 13.4950 . . . Then multiplying the fractional part (0.4950 . . . by 360 and converting to sexagesimal notation gives: 28Vi13, which is the harmonic composite Sun. The same is then done for the pair of Moons, Mercurys, etc.

If there are people who are close to the client emotionally, there will be significant synastric contacts to the client's angles whether by aspect, midpoint, planetary picture, or balance point. If the client has many close ties and these ties can be characterized astrologically, the tabulation of the positions in the charts of those having ties to the client is a fruitful avenue to finding a pattern (repetition of degree areas) and this then can lead one to the client's angles.

A helpful principle inherent in the use of composite charts is that whatever the error in the current MC you have arrived at in the rectification for the client, this error will be halved by composing his or her chart with the chart of one with whom he or she has a significant relationship (whether romantic or business partnership, say). This assumes that the other person has a fairly accurate chart. In the case of a married couple, where one has a BC based chart, while the other is faced with a DAY rectification, this composite route would be very helpful. If you had a family of four in which one parent's chart needed to be rectified and the other three had charts rectified from birth certificates, then whatever current error you had in the parent's chart being rectified, in the four-way composite the error in the composite angles, would be one quarter of the error in the currently positioned angles in the parent's chart being rectified.

I have found that births do not show up at all prominently in a mother's or father's chart, but they do show up in the composite charts (space and time). Not only that, but the composite for the just-formed threesome also shows the birth when looked at by progressions and transits. An important bit of research I have done with time composite charts shows that when one does progressions in them, one must measure how old the time composite is from the same date for which it is calculated, even though the oldest member has not been born yet. It sounds strange, but I have spent considerable time on it, and it does not work to conceive the time zero point from which to measure the age of the composite to be the time when the youngest member is born. I had originally thought that the time composite would not come into existence until the youngest member was born, but subsequent empirical research has proven the case for me.

This finishes the discussion of how one actually goes about rectifying, stated in terms of theory, concept, and techniques. It was my thought originally when conceiving of the structure of this discussion, that I would end by giving some actual examples of rectifying a particular chart, of implementing the theories, concepts, and techniques. On reflection and after thinking through some ideas in the writing of this discussion, I realized that my discussion necessitated a slightly different course.

I do feel that there are limits to what can be taught in the printed page. It is not within my power in the context of a written document to actually teach you to rectify. I am a firm believer in the necessity of direct, human contact for true teaching to occur, especially when it comes to teaching the arts, in which category I put rectification. To present working examples of how I rectified a particular chart would unfairly depict and misrepresent for you the actual *experience* of rectification I had.

In general, I remember the thought processes I had when rectifying, and their sequence, such as that I perceived that this person had Sagittarius rising and also Virgo on the Midheaven, and that such and such a progressed position helped confirm the more precise degrees of the angles (time). But these were experiences I had, and I can not have these experiences again for you. The whole idea of how one zooms in on the location of the angles by looking at the event correlations and the chart fitting, the mechanics of rectification, is quite simple and natural, *given the knowledge of the general materials and movements with which astrology works.* These rectification mechanics should be intuitively obvious to the intermediate student of astrology. The ingredients of the mechanics, the correlating of events and the chart fitting, are just plain astrological skills that come with time and work. To present a recapitulation of my thought processes and the steps or stages I went through for a particular rectification risks, I fear, lending support to the view that rectification methods can be mechanically specified, which goes against the whole spirit of my discussion. For the whole idea is to approach each chart individually and let your intuition of how to proceed be your guide. Rectification involves the spiritual engagement of soul forces: an "I think I can" attitude. Without this engagement, rectification cannot be performed; the phenomena only make themselves evident when the proper attitude of soul is brought to bear.

In closing, I would now like to address some specific attitudes I have heard expressed about rectification in the course of some recent conversations with astrologers. One curious attitude toward rectification (specifically about rectifying a recorded time) is that if one attempts to rectify, one might get a chart further from the actual chart than one started with. Thus in this view, one is better off sticking with the recorded time. This is the intellectual soul thinking it might fall off the flat earth. If there is anything to astrology it is reasonable to think that by examining a chart in connection with past events one will be able to see a consistent pattern whereby the AS needs to be increased or decreased by a certain amount. It is more reasonable to think that the chart will be improved upon rather than made worse.

Another attitude is that rectification is not possible, so one should not bother. This attitude ranges from the extreme position which includes all sources of birth time (from a recorded time to only knowing the birth date) to a milder form which regards as impossible only the DAY type. This view would also think impossible, of course, the MONTHS or the YEARS type if they were told of the idea in theory.

Since astrology is not taught in the public culture, this leads those educated in this culture to regard astrology as either bogus or worthless for practical life. The same applies to rectification: since astrological training does not include rectification it is regarded as bogus or worthless for practical life in astrological consulting.

Some who hold that rectification is not possible cite the multiplicity of corporate charts, and the seeming lack of resolution of these problems. These are among the most difficult and most abstract charts, and they require knowledge of history and politics beyond a mere pedestrian level, which generally is the level of event knowledge that astrologers have brought to bear in their rectifications. Other doubting Thomases cite the multiplicity of rectified charts propounded by astrologers for given famous (or infamous) persons such as politicians or movie stars, or other mass-culture icons. It must be responded in cases of this sort that these sorts of people naturally tend to keep their personal lives under wraps for various reasons. When it comes to getting dates, one must contend with rumor and hearsay. This is especially the case when there is not a definitive biography. The other aspect which makes this sort of rectification atypical is that there is not the possibility to question the person about events. The possibility for there to be a two-way street is important in rectification, another hallmark of the consciousness soul to which I have spoken.

Yet it is worth noting that there probably have been lots of poorly done rectifications in the past. But to hold to a dogmatic view that rectification is not possible is simply to deny astrological influence and that there is any rationality in the human mind. A better interpretation of the past track record is to appreciate that the tools and the training have not been adequate to the job. I have already outlined at length the philosophical burden that astrology has lived under going back to the bad precedent set by Ptolemy's flawed method. And closer to our time, we must not forget the bogus Prenatal Epoch theory of rectification. But probably most grievous has been the persistence of Primary Directions, a theory which does not work. Coupled with this has been incorrect manner of progressing the MC in Solar Progressions: by calculating the change in the Sidereal Time instead of moving by the Solar Arc.

Astrology has made a lot of technical progress in this century around areas such as midpoints, planetary pictures, Solar Arcs, and harmonics. With the advent of computers this progress will only be accelerated. But the area where there has not been progress is in the spiritual, philosophical side. In between these sides is the subject of rectification. The spiritual side is the inspirational side and the unifying side to life.

I would like to relate what the spiritual scientist, Rudolf Steiner, had to say about studies of the spiritual world (of which astrology is a branch). To paraphrase him he said that those who have the higher faculties developed will agree on what they see in the spiritual world. My experience has certainly substantiated this view. For example, on the occasions when I have looked at a rectification that Charles Emerson has done, such as for Jung, Hitler, or Nixon, I have agreed with his result. Another instance is that after rectifying Benjamin Franklin's chart to 10 Cp 00 on the MC, I subsequently found that Ralph Kraum had gotten the same result.[31] Others have confirmed rectifications I have done.

The rectifier does not always rectify correctly, but that should not be a yardstick to hold up to astrologers. Doctors and engineers sometimes make a mistake as well. Steiner has said that it is possible to make a mistake when using the higher faculties, just as it is when using the lower faculties of the five senses. But just because it is possible to make a mistake does not mean that one should not try.

---

31 *Astrological Americana*, Ralph Kraum and Ernest A. Grant, AFA, 1949, p. 16.

STAY IN TOUCH

On the following pages you will find some of the books now available on related subjects. Your book dealer stocks most of these and will stock new titles in the Llewellyn series as they become available. We urge your patronage.

To obtain our full catalog, to keep informed about new titles as they are released, and to benefit from informative articles and helpful news, you are invited to write for our bimonthly news magazine/catalog, *Llewellyn's New Worlds of Mind and Spirit*. A sample copy is free, and it will continue coming to you at no cost as long as you are an active mail customer. Or you may subscribe for just $10.00 in the U.S.A. and Canada ($20.00 overseas, first class mail). Many bookstores also have *New Worlds* available to their customers. Ask for it.

Llewellyn's New Worlds of Mind and Spirit
P.O. Box 64383-864, St. Paul, MN 55164-0383, U.S.A.

* * *

TO ORDER BOOKS AND TAPES

If your book dealer does not have the books described, you may order them directly from the publisher by sending the full price in U.S. funds, plus $3.00 for postage and handling for orders *under* $10.00; $4.00 for orders *over* $10.00. There are no postage and handling charges for orders over $50.00. Postage and handling rates are subject to change. We ship UPS whenever possible. Delivery guaranteed. Provide your street address as UPS does not deliver to P.O. boxes. Allow 4-6 weeks for delivery. UPS to Canada requires a $50.00 minimum order. Orders outside the U.S.A. and Canada: Airmail—add retail price of book; add $5.00 for each non-book item (tapes, etc.); add $1.00 per item for surface mail.

FOR GROUP STUDY AND PURCHASE

Because there is a great deal of interest in group discussion and study of the subject matter of this book, we offer a special quantity price to group leaders or agents. Our special quantity price for a minimum order of five copies of *Astrology's Special Measurements* is $36.00 cash-with-order. This price includes postage and handling within the United States. Minnesota residents must add 6.5% sales tax. For additional quantities, please order in multiples of five. For Canadian and foreign orders, add postage and handling charges as above. Credit card (VISA, MasterCard, American Express) orders are accepted. Charge card orders only ($15.00 minimum order) may be phoned in free within the U.S.A. or Canada by dialing 1-800-THE-MOON. For customer service, call 1-612-291-1970. Mail orders to:

LLEWELLYN PUBLICATIONS
P.O. Box 64383-864, St. Paul, MN 55164-0383, U.S.A.

Prices subject to change without notice.

FINANCIAL ASTROLOGY
Edited by Joan McEvers
Money . . . investment . . . finance . . . speculation. The contributors to this popular book in Llewellyn's New World Astrology Series have vast financial and astrological experience and are well-known in the field. Did you know that new tools such as the 360 dial and the graphic ephemeris can help you spot impending market changes? You owe it to yourself to explore this relatively new (and lucrative!) topic. Learn about the various types of analysis and how astrology fine-tunes these methods. Covered cycles include the Lunar Cycle, the Mars/Vesta Cycle, the 4-1/2-year Martian Cycle, the 500-year Civilization Cycle used by Nostradamus, the Kondratieff Wave and the Elliot Wave.

Articles by: Michael Munkasey, Pat Esclavon Hardy, Jeanne Long, Georgia Stathis, Mary B. Downing, Judy Johns, Carol S. Mull, Bill Meridian, Georgia Stathis, and Robert Cole.
0-87542-382-5, 368 pgs., 5 1/4 x 8, illus., softcover   **$14.95**

WEB OF RELATIONSHIPS
Spiritual, Karmic & Psychological Bonds
edited by Joan McEvers
The astrology of intimacy has long been a popular subject among professional astrologers and psychologists. Many have sought the answer to what makes some people have successful relationships with one another, while others struggle. *Web of Relationships* examines this topic not only in intimate affiliations, but also in families and friendships, in this eighth volume of the Llewellyn New World Astrology Series.

Editor Joan McEvers has brought together the wisdom and experience of eight astrology experts. Listen to what one author says about the mythological background of planets as they pertain to relationships. Discover how past life regression is illustrated in the chart. Consider the relationship of astrology and transactional analysis. *Web of Relationships* explores the karmic and mystical connections between child and parent, how friends support and understand each other, the significance of the horoscope as it pertains to connections and much more. Each chapter will bring you closer to your own web of relationships and the astrology of intimacy.
0-87542-388-4, 240 pgs., 6 x 9, softcover   **$14.95**

ASTROLOGICAL COUNSELING
The Path to Self-Actualization
Edited by Joan McEvers
This book explores the challenges for today's counselors and gives guidance to those interested in seeking an astrological counselor to help them win their own personal challenges. Includes articles by 10 well-known astrologers: David Pond, Maritha Pottenger, Bill Herbst, Gray Keen, Ginger Chalford, Ph.D., Donald L. Weston, Ph.D., Susan Dearborn Jackson, Doris A. Hebel, Donna Cunningham, and Eileen Nauman.
0-87542-385-X, 304 pgs., 5 1/4 x 8, charts, softcover   **$14.95**

HOW TO MANAGE THE ASTROLOGY OF CRISIS
edited by Noel Tyl

More often than not, a person will consult an astrologer during those times when life has become difficult, uncertain or distressing. While crisis of any type is really a turning point, not a disaster, the client's crisis of growth becomes the astrologer's challenge. By coming to the astrologer, the client has come to an oracle. At the very best, there is hope for a miracle; at the very least, there is hope for reinforcement through companionship and information. How do you as an astrological counselor balance a sober discussion of the realities with enthusiastic efforts to leave the client feeling empowered and optimistic?

In this, the eleventh title in Llewellyn's New World Astrology Series, eight renowned astrologers provide answers to this question as it applies to a variety of life crises. How to Manage the Astrology of Crisis discusses the birth-crisis, the first major transition crisis in everybody's life . . . significant family crises in childhood and healing the inner child . . . mental crises including head injuries, psychological breakdown, psychic experiences, multiple personalities . . . career turning points and crises of life direction and action . . . astrological triggers of financial crisis and recent advances in financial astrology . . . astrological maxims for relationship crises, mid-life crises, etc.

0-87542-390-6, 224 pgs., 6 x 9, charts, softcover   **$12.00**

HOW TO PERSONALIZE THE OUTER PLANETS
The Astrology of Uranus, Neptune & Pluto
Edited by Noel Tyl

Since their discoveries, the three outer planets have been symbols of the modern era. They also take us as individuals to higher levels of consciousness and new possibilities of experience. Explored individually, each outer planet offers tremendous promise for growth. But when taken as a group, as they are in *Personalizing the Outer Planets*, the potential exists to recognize *accelerated* development.

As never done before, the seven prominent astrologers in *Personalizing the Outer Planets* bring these revolutionary forces down to earth in practical ways. Articles by: Jeff Jawer, Noel Ty, Jeff Green, Jeff Jawer, Jayj Jacobs, Mary E. Shea, Joanne Wickenburg, and Capel N. McCutcheon.

0-87542-389-2, 288 pgs., 6 x 9, illus., softcover   **$12.00**

HOW TO USE VOCATIONAL ASTROLOGY
FOR SUCCESS IN THE WORKPLACE
edited by Noel Tyl

Announcing the most practical examination of Vocational Astrology in five decades! Improve your astrological skills with these revolutionary NEW tools for vocational and business analysis! Now, in *How to Use Vocational Astrology for Success in the Workplace*, edited by Noel Tyl, seven respected astrologers provide their well-seasoned modern views on that great issue of personal life—Work. Their expert advice will prepare you well for those tricky questions clients often ask: "Am I in the right job?" "Will I get promoted?" or "When is the best time to make a career move?" With an introduction by Noel Tyl in which he discusses the startling research of the Gauquelins, this ninth volume in Llewellyn's New World Astrology Series features enlightening counsel from the following experts: Jayj Jacobs, Gina Ceaglio, Donna Cunningham, Anthony Louis, Noel Tyl, Henry Weingarten, and Bob Mulligan. Read *How to Use Vocational Astrology* today, and add "Vocational Counselor" to *your* resume tomorrow! Includes the complete 1942 classic by Charles E. Luntz *Vocational Guidance by Astrology*.

0-87542-387-6, 384 pgs., 6 x 9, illus., softcover   **$14.95**

Prices subject to change without notice.

PLANETS: The Astrological Tools
Edited by Joan McEvers
This is the second in the astrological anthology series edited by respected astrologer Joan McEvers, who provides a brief factual overview of the planets. Then take off through the solar system with 10 professional astrologers as they bring their insights to the symbolism and influences of the planets.

Articles by: Toni Glover Sedgwick, Joanne Wickenburg, Erin Sullivan-Seale, Robert Glasscock, Johanna Mitchell, Don Borkowski, Gina Ceaglio, Bil Tierney, Karma Welch, and Joan Negus.
0-87542-381-7, 384 pgs., 5-1/4 x 8, softcover $12.95

THE ASTROLOGY OF THE MACROCOSM
New Directions in Mundane Astrology
Edited by Joan McEvers
Explains various mundane, transpersonal and worldly events through astrology. The perfect introduction to understanding the fate of nations, weather patterns and other global movements.

Articles by: Jimm Erickson, Judy Johns, Jim Lewis, Richard Nolle, Chris McRae, Nicholas Campion, Nancy Soller, Marc Penfield, Steve Cozzi, Diana K. Rosenberg, and Caroline W. Casey.
0-87542-384-1, 420 pgs., 5 1/4 x 8, charts, softcover $19.95

INTIMATE RELATIONSHIPS
the Astrology of Attraction
edited by Joan McEvers
Explore the deeper meaning of intimate relationships with the knowledge and expertise of eight renowned astrologers. Dare to look into your own chart and confront your own vulnerabilities. Find the true meaning of love and its place in your life. Gain new insights into the astrology of marriage, dating, affairs and more!

In Intimate Relationships, eight astrologers discuss their views on romance and the horoscope. The roles of Venus and the Moon, as well as the asteroids Sappho, Eros and Amor, are explored in our attitudes and actions toward potential mates. The theory of affinities is also presented wherein we are attracted to someone with similar planetary energies.

Is it a love that will last a lifetime, or mere animal lust that will burn itself out in a few months? Read *Intimate Relationships* and discover your *natal* attractions as well as your *fatal* attractions.
0-87542-386-8, 240 pgs., 6 x 9, softcover $14.95

THE HOUSES
Power Places of the Horoscope
Edited by Joan McEvers
The Houses are the departments of experience. The planets energize these areas—giving life meaning. Understand why you attract and are attracted to certain people by your 7th House cusp. Go back in time to your 4th House, the history of your beginning. Joan McEvers has ingeniously arranged the chapters to show the Houses' relationships to each other and the whole. Various house systems are briefly described in Joan McEvers' introduction. Learn about house associations and planetary influences upon each house's activities with the following experts.Peter Damian, Ken Negus, Noel Tyl, Spencer Grendahl, Dona Shaw, Gloria Star, Marwayne Leipzig, Lina Accurso, Sara Corbin Looms, Michael Munkasey, and Joan McEvers.

0-87542-383-3, 400 pgs., 5 1/4 x 8, illus., softcover $12.95

Prices subject to change without notice.

PREDICTION IN ASTROLOGY
A Master Volume of Technique and Practice
by Noel Tyl

No matter how much you know about astrology already, no matter how much experience you've had to date, you'll be fascinated by *Prediction in Astrology*, and you'll grow as an astrologer. Using the Solar Arc theory and methods he describes in this book, the author was able to accurately predict the Gulf War, including the actual date it would begin and the timetable of tactics, two months *before* it began. He also predicted the overturning of Communist rule in the Eastern bloc nations nine months in advance of its actual occurrence.

Tyl teaches through example. You learn by doing astrology, not just thinking about it. Tyl introduces Solar Arc theory in terms of "rapport" measurements, which you begin to do immediately, without paper, pencil, or computer, dials, or wheels. Just with your eyes! You will never look at a horoscope the same way again!

Tyl, in his well-known, very special way, also gets personal. He presents 30 Aphorisms, the keenest of maxims, the most practical of techniques, to create predictions from any horoscope. And as if this were not enough, Tyl then presents 20 Aphorisms for Counseling. Look for Tyl's "Quick-Glance" Transit Table, 1940-2040, to which you can refer more quickly than a computer. The busy astrologer will use this Appendix every day for many years to come.

0-87542-814-2, 360 pgs., 6 x 9, softcover **$14.95**

SPIRITUAL, METAPHYSICAL & NEW TRENDS IN MODERN ASTROLOGY
Edited by Joan McEvers

This is the first book in Llewellyn's New World Astrology Series. Edited by well-known astrologer, lecturer and writer Joan McEvers, this book pulls together the latest thoughts by the best astrologers in the field of Spiritual Astrology.

Articles by: Gray Keen: Perspective: The Ethereal Conclusion; Marion D. March: Some Insights Into Esoteric Astrology; Kimberly McSherry: Feminine Element of Astrology: Reframing the Darkness; Kathleen Burt: Spiritual Rulers and Their Role in the Transformation; Shirley Lyons Meier: Secrets Behind Carl Payne Tobey's Secondary Chart; Jeff Jawer: Astrodrama; Donna Van Toen: Alice Bailey Revisited; Philip Sedgwick: Galactic Studies; Myrna Lofthus: Spiritual Programming Within a Natal Chart; Angel Thompson: Transformational Astrology.

0-87542-380-9, 264 pgs., 5 1/4 x 8, softcover **$9.95**

NAVIGATING BY THE STARS
Astrology and the Art of Decision-Making
by Edith Hathaway

This book is chock full of convenient shortcuts to mapping out one's life. It presents the decision-maker's astrology, with the full range of astrological techniques.

No other one source presents all these cutting edge methods: Uranian astrology, the 90° dial, astro-mapping, Saturn quarters, hard aspects, angular relationships, the Meridian House System, secondary progressions, solar arc directions, eclipses, solstice and equinox charts, transiting lunation cycles, monthly kinetic mundascope graphs, among others.

To illustrate the immediate applications of the techniques, the author examines many charts in depth, focussing on study of character, destiny, timing cycles, and geographical location. She draws form 45 wide-ranging personal stories, including famous figures from history, politics, show business, the annals of crime, even corporations.

0-87542-366-3, 320 pgs., 6 x 9, softcover **$14.95**

Prices subject to change without notice.